Strategic Industrial Sourcing

The Japanese Advantage

Toshihiro Nishiguchi

The Wharton School
University of Pennsylvania

D0206249

New York   *Oxford*
OXFORD UNIVERSITY PRESS
1994

Oxford University Press

Oxford   New York   Toronto
Delhi   Bombay   Calcutta   Madras   Karachi
Kuala Lumpur   Singapore   Hong Kong   Tokyo
Nairobi   Dar es Salaam   Cape Town
Melbourne   Auckland

and associated companies in
Berlin   Ibadan

Library of Congress Cataloging-in-Publication Data
Nishiguchi, Toshihiro.
Strategic industrial sourcing: the Japanese advantage / Toshihiro Nishiguchi.
p. cm.   Includes bibliographical references (p.   ) and index.
ISBN 0-19-507109-3   1. Subcontracting—Japan.
2. Industrial procurement—Japan.
I. Title.
HD2385.J3N57   1994
658.7′2′0952—dc20   92-13254

1 3 5 7 9   8 6 4 2

Printed in the United States of America
on acid-free paper

To my parents

PREFACE

Because Japan is becoming one of the world's leading economic powers, its industrial structures and mechanisms are being studied enthusiastically. Formal mechanisms ranging from industrial policy to employment practice to enterprise unionism are topics of much research. Informal social artifacts, including after-hours drinking or weekend employee social gatherings, are emphasized as distinctive "lubricating oil" for the Japanese business system. But there is a curious lack of understanding of how manufacturing activity, which has raised the Japanese economy to its current status, is organized among firms. This book attempts to shed new light on industrial sourcing as a facet of managing and understanding interfirm contractual relations.

The traditional perception that Japanese industry is sustained by unequal subcontracting relations within the framework of dualism is questioned in this book. Based on historical and contemporary evidence, we reexamine the issue of large firms' unilateral exploitation of small subcontractors. Part I shows how the industrial sourcing system in Japan has evolved from laissez-faire to collaborative subcontracting relations, which in turn helped ensure the continuous output and large variety of high-quality, low-cost products. On the one hand, we found the socioeconomic and technological infrastructure at different historical periods to have provided the necessary conditions for the emergence and continuation of various forms of subcontracting, or the lack thereof, in Japan. But we also discovered that there is no determinate "national" predisposition that accounts for particular forms of contractual relations. The political influence on stabilizing this small sector of the economy is also highlighted. Part II distinguishes the contemporary sourcing system in Japan from the traditional "bargaining-oriented" practices in the United States and Europe. Quantified evidence demonstrates the advantages of the Japanese practice, and the accompanying qualitative analysis reveals the system's underlying "problem solving–oriented" logic that pulls together various agents and allows them to collaborate, supported by a range of institutional arrangements.

Through a long evolutionary process of socioeconomic, technological, political, and producer-level strategic interactions, Japanese manufacturers have created a new and distinct system of industrial sourcing, elements of which have been adopted by their international competitors. The interpretation of strategic industrial sourcing in Japan presented in this book constructs a powerful paradigm of a new economic organization that has profound implications for the future performance of all industrial societies.

While writing this book, my affiliations shifted from Nuffield College of the University of Oxford, where I was a doctoral student, to the Massachusetts Institute of Technology as a research fellow, to INSEAD in France as a postdoctoral fellow.

Currently, I am an assistant professor of management at the Wharton School of the University of Pennsylvania.

Like any work requiring years of research and thinking, this study owes a great deal to a number of individuals. John H. Goldthorpe read some earlier drafts of this work; my notes on his comments are still among the most esteemed in my intellectual inventory. Ronald P. Dore, who read the whole draft, not only helped shape its writing and organization but also planted the seeds for my academic development. These two scholars were also the official supervisors of my doctoral dissertation submitted to the University of Oxford, from which this book eventually emerged. The Massachusetts Institute of Technology, where the bulk of the draft was in fact written, provided an ideal environment for its completion as a doctoral thesis. Charles F. Sabel offered extremely insightful critiques, and Michael A. Cusumano provided feedback of the most thorough kind. Both read the entire draft, and their encouragement constantly furnished both fuel to keep this study running and water to cool it off from time to time. Richard Locke, who read parts of the draft, also offered stimulating comments. Daniel Roos and James P. Womack kindly relieved me from many of the administrative tasks at the International Motor Vehicle Program for which I worked as a research fellow. Outside MIT, Michael Smitka read parts of the earlier draft and offered useful comments.

From Japan, Professors Masayoshi Ikeda and Shoichiro Sei were indispensable to the progress of this study. I shared with them substantial parts of my field research in many parts of the world (Europe, North America, Japan, Mexico), and we spent many hours together discussing the issues treated in this book. It is impossible to express adequately my gratitude to them.

At various stages of this study, many others, listed below with thanks, were also helpful: Herbert J. Addison, Bruce Ahlstrand, David Allen, Yasunori Baba, the late Eric V. Batstone, Robert E. Cole, Eiichi Eguchi, Helen Fawcett, Duncan Gallie, Frank E. Gillett, Andrew Graves, Shigeru Hayakawa, Masaki Hayashi, Susan R. Helper, Gary Herrigel, Tsutomu Hyodo, Takeshi Inagami, Hiroshi Ishida, Motoshige Ito, Daniel T. Jones, Tsutomu Kagawa, Yukinobu Kitamura, Toshiya Kitayama, Tadao Kiyonari, Andrew Knapp, Kazuo Koike, John F. Krafcik, Richard Lamming, Harold Lydall, John Paul MacDuffie, John McMillan, Toru Minato, Itsutomo Mitsui, Hideichiro Nakamura, Masanori Nishi, Mitsuko and Kaoru Nishiguchi, Kentaro Nobeoka, Nobutaka Ohnishi, Taku Ohshima, Yoichi Ohta, Hiroshi Ohyama, Kinetaro Ono, Hugh T. Patrick, Ann Rowbotham, John Rutter, Mari Sako, Richard J. Samuels, Haruo Shimada, Koichi Shimokawa, Toshimasa Shiraishi, Barry Supple, Mary Sutherland, Yasuo Suwa, Kenji Takasu, Akira Takeishi, Keith E. Thurley, Konomi Tomizawa, Hideo Totsuka, Gordon B. M. Walker, Yukio Watanabe, Hugh Whittaker, Melinda Wirkus, Stephen Wood, Takashi Yamabe, and Motonari Yamada.

In addition, this book benefited greatly from more than one thousand field interviews with eight hundred persons at four hundred organizations in fourteen countries over nearly a decade. Those interviewed in the field gave invaluable information and inspiration for this research. Collectively, they provided overwhelming evidence that the traditional framework of exploitative contractual relations needs to be reviewed in a new light. A list of their names can be found in Appendix A. The usual disclaimer applies.

Finally, the consistent care and support from my parents, Mitsuko and Yuzuru Nishiguchi, throughout the long and often trying fieldwork and writing of this book can be compared to *basso continuo* in a piece of music—sometimes subdued, sometimes pronounced—and yet I was always aware of their comforting support that constantly sustained my efforts. Naturally, this book is dedicated to them.

Philadelphia   TOSHIHIRO NISHIGUCHI
April 1992

CONTENTS

8. Conclusion, 209

ABBREVIATIONS

CAD	Computer-aided design
CAM	Computer-aided manufacturing
CEO	Chief executive officer
CNC	Computer(ized) numerical control
Denki Roren	Federation of Electrical Machine Workers' Unions
EIA	Engineering Industries Association
EIAJ	Electronic Industries Association of Japan
FMS	Flexible Manufacturing System
FTC	Fair Trade Commission
GM	General Motors
IBM	International Business Machines
IC	Integrated circuit
IMVP	(MIT's) International Motor Vehicle Program
JAPIA	Japan Auto Parts Industries Association
JAMA	Japan Automobile Manufacturers' Association
JAW	(Confederation of) Japan Automobile Workers' Unions
JETRO	Japan External Trade Organization
JIT	Just-in-time
JSC	Japanese Stereo Company (a pseudonym)
LDP	Liberal Democratic party
LSI	Large-scale integrated circuit
MCI	Ministry of Commerce and Industry
MEMA	Motor and Equipment Manufacturers' Association
MIT	Massachusetts Institute of Technology
MITI	Ministry of International Trade and Industry
NC	Numerical control
NICs	Newly industrialized countries
OEM	Original equipment manufacturer
OJT	On-the-job training
PCB	Printed circuit board
PPM	Parts per million
QA	Quality assurance
QC	Quality control
R & D	Research and development
SCAP	Supreme Commander for the Allied Powers
SMEA	Small and Medium Enterprise Agency
SQC	Statistical quality control

TQC   Total quality control
VA   Value analysis
VCR   Video cassette recorder
VE   Value engineering
VLSI   Very large-scale integrated circuit

TABLES AND FIGURES

Tables

Figures

ACKNOWLEDGMENTS

Table 2-4; Figures 2-1 and 2-3. Reprinted from Hyodo, 1971. Copyright © 1971 by the University of Tokyo Press, Reprinted by permission of the publisher.

Tables 2-5 and 2-7. Reprinted from the Society for Promotion of the Machinery Industry (Kikai shinko kyokai), 1986. Copyright © 1986 by the Society for Promotion of the Machinery Industry. Reprinted by permission of the publisher.

Tables 2-9, 2-10, 2-11, and 2-12. Reprinted and adapted from Fujita, Keizo, 1985. Copyright © 1965 by Iwanami shoten, Tokyo. Reprinted by permission of the publisher.

Table 3-1; Figure 4-7. Reprinted and adapted from Nakamura, Takafusa, 1981. Copyright © 1981 by the University of Tokyo Press. Reprinted by permission of the publisher.

Table 3-2. Reprinted from Nakamura, Hideichiro et al., 1981. Copyright © 1981 by Nihon Keizai Shinbunsha. Reprinted by permission.

Tables 3-6, 3-7, 3-8, 4-7, and 4-18. Reprinted from Suitsu, 1979. Copyright © by Moriyama Shoten. Reprinted by permission of the publisher.

Figures 3-5 and 3-7. Reprinted from Friedman, 1988. Copyright © 1988 by Cornell University Press. Reprinted by permission of the publisher.

Table 4-5. Reprinted from Fujita, Eishi, 1980. Copyright © 1980 by the Japan University of Social Welfare (Nihon fukushi daigaku). Reprinted by permission of the publisher.

Table 4-6. Reprinted from Gordon, 1985. Copyright © 1985 by the Council on East Asian Studies, Harvard University. Reprinted by permission of the publisher.

Table 4-10. Reprinted from the Society for Promotion of the Machinery Industry (Kikai shinko kyokai), 1980. Copyright © 1980 by the Society for Promotion of the Machinery Industry. Reprinted by permission of the publisher.

Tables 4-14 and 4-16. Reprinted and adapted from Kiyonari, 1970. Copyright © 1970 by Kiyonari. Reprinted by permission of the author.

Tables 4-15 and 4-19; Figures 4-10 and 4-12. Reprinted and adapted from Ikeda, 1968, 1975, and 1986. Copyright © 1968, 1975 and 1986 by Ikeda. Reprinted by permission of the author.

Tables 4-17, 4-19, 4-21, and 4-22; Figures 4-13 and 4-14. Copyright © 1971, 1977 and 1983 by the Central Bank for Commercial and Industrial Cooperatives (Shoko kumiai chuo kinko). Reprinted by permission of the publisher.

Table 4-20. Adapted from Clark et al., 1987. Copyright © 1987 by Clark et al. Reprinted by permission of the lead author.

Figure 4-9. Reprinted from the MIT International Motor Vehicle Program, a bound copy of Policy Forum papers, 1989. Copyright © 1989 by the MIT International Motor Vehicle Program. Reprinted by permission of the director of the program.

Strategic Industrial Sourcing

1

Overview

Problem Setting

This book discusses subcontracting[1] in manufacturing industries, focusing on the description and analysis—both historical and contemporary—of the Japanese automotive and electronics industries. It also offers a comparative analysis of different modes of subcontracting in advanced economies, with special reference to British–Japanese electronics subcontracting and the flexible manufacturing capabilities of automotive components suppliers in Japan, the United States, and Europe.

Why does subcontracting persist? This central question leads to other, related questions that this book also addresses. Why is subcontracting maintained to a greater degree in certain economies or industries compared with others, when alternative modes of transaction might have been adopted? Do the economic agents' cultural attributes matter? What leads the managers of prime contractors[2] to resort to outside purchasing rather than in-house manufacturing? Is one reason a desire to protect profits in the face of external uncertainty? Is this determinant simply a cost calculus in which putting out appears lucrative? Could the reason be an attempt to divide the workers against one another? Is the decision to subcontract based on the technologies used in manufacturing? And do these considerations differ depending on the properties of the product markets? Has the mode of subcontracting changed over time? Are changes in producers' strategies responsible for the emergence of novel modes of subcontracting? Does the recourse to subcontracting differ according to the subcontractors' size, skills, and technical expertise? If so, how are

1. In this study, *subcontracting* is defined as contracting that partially contributes to carrying out a major contract. Usually, it takes the following form: The prime contractor commissions the subcontractor to fulfill a part of the major contract, by manufacturing parts and components (usually, but not necessarily, of the prime contractor's own design and specifications), producing finished products, providing assistant capacity and/or labor for performing a given production process, or providing other miscellaneous services that may not necessarily be directly concerned with manufacturing. The term *subcontractor* refers to the agent, either the firm or the individual, which undertakes the subcontracting.

2. Throughout this study (unless other terminologies seem to be contextually unequivocal), I use the term *prime contractors* to refer to firms that award contracts to subcontractors. I use this term more often than others such as original equipment manufacturers (OEMs), assemblers, customers, purchasers, top firms, principal employers, and primary manufacturers, because depending on the context and the way in which they are used, these other terms tend to be too narrow, broad, or confusing, whereas *prime contractors* is the most consistently unequivocal.

3

contractual relationships affected when markets shrink? Can differences in the prime contractors' behavior be explained by the amount of asset specificity in contractual relations? How does government policy influence small firms and/or subcontractors? Furthermore, if there are national differences in the organization of subcontracting and in-house manufacturing, what socioeconomic and historical factors account for these differences? Is there a correlation between firm-level or international competitiveness and the way that subcontracting is organized by certain firms or national economies?

Several theories try to answer these questions. I argue, however, that all of them have critical shortcomings. Because the historical origins, economic rationale, and organizational functions of subcontracting differ from society to society, no single theory may be sufficient to explain it fully.

This study of subcontracting has three levels of analysis: theoretical, empirical, and pragmatic. At the theoretical level, it exposes the inadequacies of existing theories explaining subcontracting. At the empirical level, it examines the detailed historical and contemporary evidence regarding the evolution of Japanese industrial sourcing toward a collaborative manufacturing model based on problem-solving principles. This evidence serves to clarify the shortcomings of traditional accounts, and so at the pragmatic level, I provide case examples that may help form new strategies for ongoing manufacturing and subcontracting activities.

Research Approach

Traditional secondary sources are the basis for this book's accounts of the early historical period. To analyze recent history and the current situation, especially the origins and persistence of subcontracting in Japan, I conducted 1,035 field interviews between 1983 and 1989, including 813 persons at 394 organizations in fourteen countries. I logged a total of 2,169 interview hours, or approximately 3 hours per interviewee, on average. These visits ranged from General Motors' headquarters in Detroit to a one-man subcontractor on the outskirts of Tokyo. Appendix A lists the establishments, interviewees, titles, dates, and time spent, and Table 1-1 summarizes this schedule, with the organizations grouped into fifteen categories.

The core of my field research is the discussions with 251 interviewees in 71 prime contracting firms and 320 interviewees in 172 supply and subcontracting firms for the automotive and electronics industries in ten countries. Generally I used a set of questionnaires to create a semistructured interview format,[3] though I did not use all of the interview materials for this study.[4] The reason is partly the particular

---

3. Appendix B provides questionnaire/interview questions, the responses to which led to the results reported in this book.

4. Four months were required, once the interviews were completed, to organize the large amount of data collected. Ultimately, the interview results were reduced to nine thousand (4 × 6 inch) index cards. The material has been organized using six broad categories: (1) purchasing (e.g., organization, control, grading, pricing, quality assurance, contracts, product development), (2) dualism (e.g., measures taken against fluctuations in demand and temporary workers), (3) manufacturing practice (e.g., changeover time, lead time, delivery, batch size, product variation, layout, design change, self-developed technology, flexible labor), (4) personnel (e.g., recruitment, labor turnover, absenteeism, training, wages, welfare programs, working hours, promotion), (5) products and customers (e.g., types and range

TABLE 1-1. Interviews, 1983–89

Category	No. of Establishments	No. of Interviewees	Time Spent[a]
1. National governments	7	8	11hrs.
2. Local authorities	10	21	37
3. Trade associations	11	24	38
4. Industrial cooperatives	7	20	43
5. Trade unions	4	8	11
6. Public research organizations	9	20	37
7. Prime contractors	71	251	567
8. Suppliers and subcontractors	172	320	909
9. Business consultants and private research organizations	27	31	73
10. Trading companies	3	5	10
11. Transportation companies	1	1	2
12. Car dealers	4	6	6
13. Banks and security companies	3	4	13
14. Journalists	8	10	20
15. Academic institutions	57[b]	84	392
Total:	394	813	2,169hrs

[a]Hours spent with individual interviewees, with no adjustment for group (or otherwise overlapping) interviews.
[b]Counted by department, college, program, or research unit, whichever was deemed appropriate.

scope of the study and partly the incompleteness of some of the data I collected. Part II gives detailed accounts of my research methodologies, including sample selection and attributes, definitions of technical terms, data collection methods, and coding. Chapter 4, on the historical evolution of Japanese subcontracting between 1960 and 1990, also draws heavily on the results of my field interviews.

Another part of my research was a mail questionnaire, which was distributed in 1986. The subject was reasons for subcontracting, as perceived by twenty large automotive and twenty large electronics firms in Japan. The results are reported and discussed in Appendix B. This survey supplements the historical and other empirical components of this book.

A New Explanation of Japanese Subcontracting

Today the productivity and quality levels at Japanese engineering and manufacturing firms are setting new standards of performance worldwide. For example, Japanese automotive producers spend an average (after adjusting for different types of models and work content) of 17 hours to assemble a car, whereas the U.S. and European figures are 25 and 37 hours, respectively (Krafcik & MacDuffie, 1989). Japanese assemblers can develop a new car in 43 months, whereas comparable lead times for U.S. and European assemblers are, respectively, 62 and 63 months (Clark, Chew, &

---

of products, number of regular customers), and (6) figures (e.g., output, defect rates, part numbers). Because the focus of this book is on interfirm contractual relations, the data related to this topic are the most frequently used, although their usefulness has not yet been exhausted. Indeed, I intend to produce other empirical studies drawing on these materials, to deal with issues not covered in this study.

Fujimoto, 1987; Clark & Fujimoto, 1987, 1988). On a production line Japanese automotive components suppliers change over from one product to another fifteen times more quickly than U.S. and European suppliers do. They carry one-fifth and one-tenth of the in-plant inventory levels of their U.S. and European competitors, respectively (see Chapter 7). In regard to the quality of products in use, Japanese cars exhibit approximately 30 percent fewer defects than U.S. and European cars do (J. D. Power and Associates, 1987). Another industry has produced some striking evidence: The best Japanese air conditioners have between five hundred and one thousand times fewer defects than do the worst U.S. air conditioners (Garvin, 1983). These data indicate how Japanese producers spend less time on development and still manufacture better-quality products, more flexibly, than do their world competitors.

One important reason for the competitiveness of Japanese producers is the nature of Japanese subcontracting, which emphasizes synergistic problem solving, rather than antagonistic bargaining, between organizations. Traditionally, it has been argued that behind the prosperity of Japanese industry, particularly in the automotive and electronics sectors, lies the sacrifice of many subcontractors. They are characterized as "sweatshops" with cheap labor and labor-intensive technologies (Ito, 1957; Fujita, 1965). If this claim were correct, the competitiveness of Japanese industry might have declined when interscale wage differentials substantially narrowed in the mid-1960s to international levels (see Chapter 4). If the position of Japanese subcontractors were only that of an exploited group, they might have withered away, as the dualists predicted (Edwards, 1979). A la Galbraith, there might have been a large-firm industrial system, with little room for small, inefficient firms (Galbraith, 1972).

Empirical evidence rejects these contentions, however. Over the last three decades, small Japanese firms have consistently contributed one-third of the value added in the Japanese economy. Their share of the total working population has been three-fourths of the total. Moreover, the number of small firms subcontracting for manufacturing industries has steadily risen from slightly over 50 percent to now 65 percent (see Chapter 4). These data indicate that small firms in Japan have grown not only parallel to but also connected with large firms by means of subcontracting throughout the period of high and stable growth between 1960 and 1990.

This book argues that Japanese automotive and electronics producers have achieved notable growth not by unilaterally exploiting subcontractors but by strategically creating, and benefiting from, distinctive institutional arrangements in subcontracting based on problem solving. These new arrangements institutionalized the goal of continuous improvement with the aid of systematic checking mechanisms (e.g., grading, self-certified subcontractors, "bonus–penalties" for deliveries). Prime contractors benefit from the subcontractors' enhanced performance, and the result is better design, higher quality, lower cost, and timely delivery. At the same time, the establishment of rules to share fairly the profits from collaborative design and manufacturing has encouraged the subcontractors' entrepreneurship and their own symbiotic relationships with their customers. Benefits from the subcontractors' commitments have reached their customers as well; thus a virtuous circle has emerged.

A comparative study of British–Japanese electronics subcontracting (see Chapter 5) also shows that contemporary Japanese subcontracting relations are characterized by high asset specificity, compared with those of the United Kingdom.[5] This is a historical product of the strategies of large Japanese manufacturers from the 1960s onward. In the face of increasing manufacturing complexity concomitant with product proliferation in the rapidly growing competitive domestic market, these firms over time converted many of their subcontractors—previously used chiefly for instrumental reasons and for simple processing tasks (such as machining and treating the surface of metals)—into "contract assemblers" and "systems-components" manufacturers (see Chapter 4).

In this process, technologies were transferred among firms. Customers taught a variety of skills to their subcontractors in the interest of maintaining product quality. Asset-specific features of contract-assembly and systems-components manufacture contributed to stabilizing contractual relations, which provided further incentives for the subcontractors to grow. Over time, the proportion of development and design input from subcontractors increased (e.g., "black box" design), and subcontractors even began to offer their own technologies to their customers (see Chapter 4). For prime contractors, these new arrangements secured continuing sources of production for some of their own products (frequently small-lot, specialized, and mature) without having to invest heavily themselves. In this way, they were able to allocate their newly freed resources to state-of-the-art technologies and the development of new products. The simultaneous diffusion of various production and development activities to external organizations shortened overall lead times and product cycles while maintaining the "full-product-line" strategy that many Japanese producers pursued in the wake of a high-growth economy. Prime contractors thus benefited from the new arrangements by being able to adjust to shifting demand and so pulled ahead of the competition; subcontractors enjoyed relatively stable contractual relations, together with more responsibilities and greater commitment from their customers.

Along with the development of contract-assembly and systems-components manufacture, a well-defined "clustered" structure for manufacturing control, or *clustered control,* was created. For instance, the procurement of parts for particular systems components or contract-assembly products may be delegated to "select" first-tier subcontractors that assemble these products. Such a first-tier subcontractor would act on behalf of the prime contractor, but the control function would reside with the subcontractor that managed that function for the other subcontractors in the pyramid's lower tiers. In this way, the subcontractors form a series of clusters for controlling the manufacturing and purchasing functions. Again, this new organization relieved the prime contractor from having to cope with the increasingly complex control functions accompanying product proliferation and rapid technological progress; at the same time, first-tier subcontractors could look toward stable growth and enhanced responsibilities.

5. *Asset specificity* is defined as durable investments that are undertaken in support of particular transactions (Williamson, 1985:55) and that are not readily applicable, without substantial alterations, to other customers. For more discussion on the concept and measurements of asset specificity, see Chapter 5.

Politics has historically played an important role in the emergence, promotion, and stabilization of Japanese subcontracting. A prototype of the Japanese subcontracting institution can be traced back to the wartime economy of 1931 to 1945. When the demand for munitions surged, the government tried to convert small firms, which had proliferated during the 1920s with the rise of a dual economy, into "dedicated" subcontractors serving large manufacturers in dire need of capacity. But because of a structural mismatch between the productive linkages in this particular style of subcontracting and the aims of mass production—exacerbated by a critical shortage of various natural, human, and facilities resources—this attempt failed (see Chapter 3).

Japanese subcontracting institutions rebounded with the civilian economic boom in the late 1950s, after benefiting from new demand for munitions during the Korean War. But the harsher side of contractual relations also emerged. The subcontractors' prices were beaten down, and payments were withheld, reflecting the asymmetrical balance of power between large purchasers and small sellers. In the interest of securing a source of electoral support and also reducing political pressures from small-business organizations, the Japanese government introduced a series of laws to protect and promote small subcontracting businesses. Periodic government investigations discouraged and thwarted unfair subcontracting practices, and small-business financing organizations and cooperatives provided a framework dedicated exclusively to small firms. Thus, the infrastructure of the small-business sector was, in significant part, politically shaped. The new strategies of large Japanese producers—to convert many of the existing subcontractors into contract assemblers and systems-components manufacturers—were developed and built on such socioeconomic, political, and infrastructural bases as were available to them during the high-growth era of the 1960s. In the 1970s and 1980s, Japanese subcontracting institutions continued to flourish and evolve as a successful organizational response to changing and rapidly internationalizing markets (see Chapter 4).

From the mid-1970s onward, an international cross-cultural transfer of Japanese manufacturing organization, including subcontracting relations, got under way. This has produced, and still is producing, interesting outcomes in other industrial societies. The adoption by major Western automotive producers of "Japanese" institutional subcontracting practices (e.g., subcontractor grading, black box design, resident engineers, and clustered control, as detailed in Chapter 4) and successful British electronics subcontractors' acceptance of and commitment to the Japanese subcontracting system, as executed by Japanese "transplants" in the United Kingdom (see Chapter 6) demonstrate that its principles are applicable outside Japan. The results of this book are thus consistent with the claim that the major advantages of Japanese subcontracting organization lie chiefly in the economic benefits derived from interfirm problem-solving mechanisms to ensure the continuous production of high-quality, low-cost products.

In this context, the following remarks by high-ranking managers of Japanese and U.S. manufacturers are indicative of the logic underlying contemporary Japanese subcontracting relations:

> Wherever you may go in the world, it is never inappropriate to approach subcontractors with the principle of long-term, mutual commitments based on trust. It

cannot be unreasonable to ask any manufacturer for joint efforts and cooperation to try to produce better-quality products at a lower cost. In the United States, Europe or Japan, it's the same. But the real test is whether you can maintain this principle through ups and downs. Our thirty years of experience have proved that we can.[6]

Good subcontractor management demonstrates a prime contractor's ability. It directly concerns its business performance. Why aren't our products competitive, and why are we losing market share? Because our subcontractor management has been so poor.[7]

When we first met our Japanese customers [when we decided to supply their assembly operations in the United States], we thought they were crazy because they demanded our cost tables—our proprietary information. But as we continued doing business with them, we soon realized that what they are really interested in is not just their own profits but the viability of our business as well. They help us technically, to reduce our cost at the source, and are worried about level ordering to us, for several years to come. This is surprising—because in my thirty years of experience, I have never been treated like that by our American customers.[8]

Four Theories of Subcontracting

Dualism

The core of the dualist theory is that economic agents located in different segments of the economy are treated unequally, regardless of their objective worth. These segments can be labor markets (Kerr, 1954; Doeringer & Piore, 1971; Piore, 1975; Wilkinson, 1981) or dual economies (Averitt, 1968), and the economic agents may be workers (the former literature) or firms (the latter literature). Whatever the differences in conceptual formation and terminologies, dualists see inequality between the internal and external labor markets, between the primary and secondary sectors, or between the core and peripheral economies.

Applied to the language of subcontracting, these dualist theories can be interpreted as follows: Neither workers—often with a temporary status and/or in peripheral firms in the external labor market or the secondary sector—nor small firms—frequently subcontractors in the peripheral economy—receive what they are worth. That they do not earn what the market dictates is built into the structure of dualism rather than based on their individual skill levels.

Screening thresholds, called "points of entrance" (Kerr, 1954:101) or "ports of entry and exit" (Doeringer & Piore, 1971:2), at the boundary of the two labor markets effectively discriminate outsiders from insiders. Internal workers are promoted according to administrative rules governing clearly defined mobility clusters. Through stabilizing institutional arrangements, they are largely protected from external shocks. Their wages are relatively high and well defined by wage scales

6. Based on my interview with a purchasing general manager of a Japanese automotive assembly transplant in the United States, in March 1989.

7. Based on my interview with a purchasing manager of a Japanese automotive assembler in March 1986.

8. Based on my interview with a president of a U.S. automotive components supplier in September 1988.

based on length of service. Amenities and fringe benefits are ample. Working environments are generally good. The workers'/firms' skills are—albeit arguably—relatively high and often firm specific. Jobs are usually secure. This situation is reversed for external workers. Similarly, small firms in the peripheral economy are discriminated against in terms of access to technologies, capital, and human resources, which are readily available to large firms in the core economy. Furthermore, workers and firms in the external and/or peripheral sectors are largely subject to the laissez-faire competition of the market. When the economy is booming, they are used extensively, but when it contracts, they are the first to be forced out.

Berger and Piore (1980) proposed a dynamic theory of dualism in which the strategic use of subcontracting, by shifting many of the productive processes—and therefore the risks—to the secondary sector would help large firms survive in a world of uncertainty and flux. They cited French and Italian cases in which the origins of this strategy are seen as a corporate response to the massive wave of strikes in the late 1960s in both countries that halted production and, through subsequent legislation, made labor contracts in the primary sector more rigid. A flexible recourse to subcontracting is seen to have resolved the problem.

The impetus for large French and Italian firms to use subcontracting more extensively was fourfold: (1) increased legal and administrative restraints on employers' discretion to lay off, fire, or use workers for purely economic (as opposed to disciplinary) reasons; (2) the work force's legal right to organize in the workplace; (3) the exemption of small firms (fewer than sixteen employees in Italy and fewer than fifty in France) from this plant-level representation; and (4) an abundance of workers in the secondary sector who, because they were exempt from the preceding constraints, could be flexibly utilized as low-wage, buffer workers through subcontracting (Berger & Piore, 1980:28–41).

Interestingly, there is a similarity, superficially at least, between this European adaptation and the Japanese corporate response to the economic upheaval in the 1950s following the impact of the Dodge Plan and the subsequent Korean War boom, although the latter yielded markedly different outcomes that may or may not be explained simply in these dualistic terms. (This point will be discussed in Chapters 3 and 4.)

From a labor control perspective, Edwards (1979) proposed the radical idea that differentiated labor markets were a result of employers' attempts to break up the working class in a capitalist economy, through the evolution of three forms of labor control: simple or direct, technical, and bureaucratic. Simple or direct control relies on personal supervision in a small unit of production, whereas technical and bureaucratic controls are built into the organization of work tasks and rules systematically crafted along with the development of the modern corporation. These different control structures emerged not only as a response to the expansion of size and technological development but also to the resistance from, and the unionization of, the work force. Hodson and Kaufman (1982:730) summarized the consequences of control structures as interpreted by the radicalist school: "Beyond their function as a means of coordinating work and delegating authority, both the technical and bureaucratic control structures promote fragmentation of the working class within the firm as well as between firms by creating artificial inequalities and gradations between different fractions of the working class."

Defined in this way, both the liberal and radical schools of dualism see inequalities between the segmented labor markets. The emphases of their arguments are strikingly different, however: The liberal school sees value in the flexible use of subcontracting[9] as a response to uncertain externalities, and the radical school emphasizes a class conflict aspect of dualist strategy from a Marxist perspective. Lacking in both is a consideration of the properties of products, product markets, and producer strategies that dictate and circumscribe the differentiated use of subcontracting and workers in more realistic terms. Neither school offers systematic evidence or even argument in this regard.[10] Furthermore, both theories ignore a technological factor at variance with the manufacture of different types of products: Building an automobile obviously requires different types and scales of technologies from those needed to manufacture a microphone. Similarly, assembling a video cassette recorder (VCR) requires a combination of skills and equipment radically different from those needed simply to place certain metal parts in it, which demonstrates that technological requirements differ even for the same product, depending on which part of processing is considered. And these differences affect the mode of production organization, including subcontracting. Neither Berger and Piore nor Edwards addresses this issue.[11] Moreover, some of the dualist literature uncritically assumes that opportunities to exploit advanced technology are unequivocally limited to the primary sector. For example, Edwards (1979:77) claims:

> The increasing relative and absolute size of the typical core firm equips it with many advantages. One of the most important is the ability to capture the benefits of new technology. Innovation may come either from within the core sector's own research labs or from outside (small businesses or individual inventors). But generally such technology can only be profitably *exploited* by firms of sufficient scale to produce, market, and advertise for the national market, leaving no uncontested markets to potential competitors. (Emphasis in original)

One of the ramifications of this assumption is the hypothesis of the small sector's retreat paralleling the larger sector's domination: "The core of the economy expands as core firms spill over into new markets and new industries, and the economy's competitive, small-business periphery declines and recedes" (Edwards, 1979:84). The limitations, and in part the failure, of this analytical framework will be made clear when empirical materials are examined in subsequent chapters.

Obligational Contracting

Williamson's arguments (1975, 1985) constantly refer to the assumption that human nature tends toward opportunism and bounded rationality. Opportunism here is defined as the fulfillment of one's own interests by means of guile, including lying,

---

9. Chapter 7 challenges the traditional idea of this "flexible use" of subcontracting as a response to external uncertainties, drawing on original data on the flexible manufacturing capabilities of automotive components suppliers in Japan, the United States, and Europe.

10. Chapter 4 does provide them, however, with reference to the historical evolution of Japanese subcontracting between 1960 and 1990. Chapter 5 offers a case study of how the different subcontracting strategies of two plants led to considerably different outcomes even within the same Japanese electronics firm.

11. Chapters 3 and 4 and Appendix A directly address these issues, using empirical evidence.

stealing, cheating, an incomplete or distorted disclosure of information, and, especially, calculated efforts to mislead, distort, disguise, obfuscate, or confuse. It is held "responsible for real or contrived conditions of information asymmetry, which vastly complicate problems of economic organization" (1985:47–48). Bounded rationality is referred to as the human mind's limited capacity for rationally formulating and solving complex real-world problems. This concept was originally proposed by Simon (1957:198) in his attempt to construct a behavioral theory of the firm.

This pairing of opportunism with uncertainty and/or complexity and of bounded rationality with small-numbers exchange, or bilateral monopoly, is assumed to be responsible for the rise of what Williamson calls "information impactedness," which occasions exchange difficulties, or market failure. To cope with this problem in the mechanism of market contracting, an organizational recourse to hierarchies, rather than markets, is prescribed, which theoretically accounts for the genesis of vertical integration. A merger agreement is held to foreclose costly haggling between parties in the marketplace and thus to economize hierarchically on transaction costs (Williamson, 1975).

This dichotomous formalization of markets and hierarchies, however, has been criticized for its failure to explain the continuation of the contracting mode of transaction. Williamson's lack of empirical evidence to support his contentions has also been pointed out (e.g., Ohta, 1985).

Persuaded that transactions in the middle range—that is, continual "obligational contracting" (as between vertical integration and spot contracting)—are more common than assumed in his original framework, Williamson then named asset specificity as the best way of describing such transactions (1985:30, 83). His tightly knit argument regarding asset specificity is germane to our study of subcontracting and so deserves further examination.

Asset specificity refers to durable investments undertaken in support of particular transactions (Williamson, 1985:55). Williamson distinguishes four types of asset specificity: site, physical, human, and dedicated. *Site specificity* means that successive, but immobile, stages are physically located close to one another so as to economize on inventory and transportation expenses. If setup and/or relocation costs are great, a bilateral exchange may be established between the parties for the useful life of the assets. *Physical asset specificity* refers to an asset's mobile and physical features, such as specific dies, molds, and toolings for the manufacture of a component. Lock-in problems can be avoided if, as is often the case in the West, the purchaser owns the assets, for then he or she can reclaim them and reopen the bidding in case of trouble with the contract. *Human asset specificity* arises in a learning-by-doing fashion through long-standing customer-specific operations. *Dedicated asset specificity* represents a separate and/or additional investment in generalized (as opposed to specific) production capacity in the expectation of significant product sales to a particular customer. Although this type of specific asset is assumed to be placed at hazard by unilateral long-term trading, a reciprocal long-term exchange agreement supported by separate but concurrent investments by both parties (i.e., buyer and supplier) provides a mutual safeguard against the following two risks of trading: premature termination of the contract by the buyer and the supplier's expropriation of a bond required from and posted by the buyer (Williamson, 1985:95–96, 194–95). These four types of asset specificity provide pertinent analytical leverage for an analysis of subcontracting.[12]

Goodwill and Benevolence

In contrast with Williamson's analysis of obligational contracting, Dore (1987) offers a distinctively cultural explanation. He maintains that the extent to which the Japanese economy is characterized by and dependent on obligational (or in his preferred term, "relational") contracting cannot be explained—as Williamson does—by means of asset specificity alone. Rather, an extraeconomic factor particularly strong in Japanese culture is assumed to be responsible for the continuation and prevalence of subcontracting in Japan. This extraeconomic factor, Dore suggests, can be termed either *benevolence*, defined as "something shown in relations between unequals, by superior to inferior, the reciprocal of which is usually called loyalty"; or *goodwill*, which has a more neutral connotation and a broader meaning, defined as "the sentiments of friendship and the sense of diffuse personal obligation which accrue between individuals engaged in recurring contractual economic exchange" (Dore, 1987:170).

To be sure, Dore recognizes the importance of economic factors such as interscale wage differentials, taxation differentials, constraints of economies of scale or scope within a single firm, and a high level of education; all these are common to industrial societies other than Japan's and thus explain the continuation of relational contracting in general (Dore, 1987:172–73). But Dore also cites another factor that applies especially to Japan: a cultural trait of the Japanese, or *goodwill*, which makes Japanese trading relations somewhat singular in capitalist economies:

> Here is another of those timeless generalizations concerning "capitalist economies" about which Japan gives pause. Transaction costs for large Japanese firms may well be lower than elsewhere. "Opportunism" may be a lesser danger in Japan because of the explicit encouragement, and actual prevalence, in the Japanese economy of what one might call moralized trading relationships of mutual goodwill. (Dore, 1987:173)

The importance that Dore attaches to the cultural factor goes beyond a matter of emphasis. In his formalization, he also assumes the cultural dispositions of the Japanese to include four significant elements: collective risk sharing and long-term advantage, dutifulness, friendliness, and economic efficiency of a nonallocative kind.

---

12. Chapter 5 offers direct and systematic evidence regarding the four types of asset specificity, drawing on comparative data on British–Japanese electronics subcontracting. Chapter 4 gives a historical account of how asset-specific contractual relations emerged in Japan after the 1960s as the result of distinctive producer strategies.

Although Williamson (1985:9, 22) tangentially refers to cultural and/or societal variation of transactions, he never directly addresses this question. He does briefly mention Toyota and the prominent Japanese reliance on subcontracting in general. But he reduces the issue to a marginal factor in the degree to which Japanese and the U.S. societies, for example, are exposed to the hazards of trading because of differences in cultural and institutional checks on opportunism (1985:120–23).

First, the Japanese are assumed to be "generally very long-term-future-ori-ented," in the sense that the central government maps out a vision of the world economy more than a decade in advance and Japanese industrial groups sacrifice overall as well as individual firm efficiency in the interests of collective risk sharing and greater equality.

Second, benevolence in Japan is held to be a duty, a sense of diffuse obligation to the individual trading partner over and above written contractual terms, providing the assurance of a payoff that enables obligational contracting.

Third, the "friendliness" of the Japanese, that is, their inclination to shun openly adverse bargaining relationships, is seen as responsible for the continuing viability of subcontracting. These three cultural values also explain the normative parallel between relational contracting in the intermediate goods market and in the labor market in Japan. Relational contracting in the internal labor market is de-scribed as an organization-oriented employment system geared toward long-term and career-formulating relations, replacing the spot contracting and easy hire/easy fire assumptions of the external labor market.

Fourth, economic efficiency in Japan is not allocative but "X-efficiency" (as proposed by Leibenstein, 1966) and is held to more than offset the assumed price-distorting consequences of relational subcontracting (Dore, 1987:17–18, 184–185).

Dore also maintains that there are three advantages to relational subcontracting. First, the relative security of such relationships is conducive to investment in sup-plying firms. Second, through such high-trust and interdependent relationships, information can flow more easily. Third, as a by-product of the system, product quality is emphasized, which is an indicator of the suppliers' efforts to provide the best buy for the purchaser (Dore, 1987:186).

Having formulated this cultural explanation of the greater use of relational contracting in Japan, Dore then asks: How uniquely Japanese is it? His answer is that although the Japanese are believed to have an unusual preference for relational contracting, they are not uniquely susceptible to it. Referring to evidence in British civil construction, textile, and retail industries that demonstrates the existence of a similar mode of contracting in the United Kingdom, Dore further hypothesizes that relational contracting is a phenomenon of affluence. When well-off consumers become more quality conscious than price conscious, relational contracting is held to come into its own, for two reasons. First, quality assurance, demanded by affluent consumers, depends largely on trust. Second, when affluence reduces price pressures, the tendency to prefer a stable and friendly relationship to an adverse bargaining one emerges. Having referred to a stronger emphasis on quality over price in Japan's consumer markets than in Britain's, Dore (1987:188) concludes: "Japan's difference from Britain, then, is explained both by the fact that the cultural preferences, the suppressed tendencies, are strong, *and* by the fact that the price pressures have been more reduced by a much more rapid arrival at affluence, and consequently a greater subjective sense of affluence" (emphasis in original).

The differences between Williamson's and Dore's approaches to relational con-tracting are clear. Williamson starts with the assumption that "man" is essentially opportunistic and that this fact makes market contracting difficult, resulting in a hierarchical option of organization that is relatively free of risks. When a range of interfirm contracts involves asset specificity (defined as durable investments in support of specific transactions), however, obligational contracting can be maintained. Although asset specificity is claimed to be the key to explaining transactions, social and/or cultural variations in contracting are reduced to marginal differences in cultural and institutional checks on trade risks resulting from opportunism.

By contrast, Dore insists that the strikingly nonopportunistic characteristic found in Japanese culture is what mainly explains the Japanese reliance on relational contracting. Benevolence and goodwill as exhibited by and prevalent among the Japanese are responsible for not only holding together the general social fabric but also maintaining more specific long-term contracting relations. Neither proponent really debates what his opponent offers. In the final analysis, however, a fundamental difference in the assumptions remains: hard-nosed and opportunistically profit-maximizing "man," as opposed to trusting Japanese traders in the world of relational contracting.

There emerge two interesting empirical questions in regard to Dore's theory. First, given the values of risk sharing, dutifulness, friendliness, and X-efficiency that is thought to characterize Japanese culture and given the resulting advantages of investment incentives, a more rapid flow of information, and a general emphasis on product quality that the Japanese high-trust contracting system is held to yield, one might ask: Has the institution of subcontracting always been an essential feature of the Japanese economy, say, between 1900 and 1990? Second, what would be the consequence of moving the current Japanese subcontracting system to an entirely different cultural environment, say, the United States or the United Kingdom? Would the transference immediately hamper the system because of a general lack of benevolence and goodwill in these societies? Would the competitiveness of the Japanese system wither away as a consequence of investment disincentives, "information impactedness," and the inferior quality of materials supplied locally, none of which is a problem in Japan? Or could it succeed despite the foreign environment's apparent lack of cultural values that are claimed to be determinants of the "Japanese success"?[13]

Flexible Specialization

Piore and Sabel (1984) argue in regard to the resurgence of flexible specialization that today the mass production technology and existing regulatory institutions based on mass production principles are crumbling because of their diminishing adaptability to emerging externalities. If industrial society is to become prosperous again, it must instead adopt institutions and production methods based on the principles of flexible specialization: a derivative of the craft mode of production that lost out to the mass production model at the first industrial divide in the nineteenth century.

Piore and Sabel claim that we are living through the second industrial divide in

---

13. These questions suggest fascinating empirical tests of the importance of Dore's cultural factors to relational (or obligational) contractual relations. Chapters 2, 3, and 4 provide extensive historical answers to the first question, and Chapter 6 answers the second question through an examination of British subcontractors' reactions to "demanding" Japanese electronics "transplants" in the United Kingdom in the late 1970s and the 1980s. Chapter 4 also addresses the "Japanization" of Western producers' subcontracting institutions.

which two alternative strategies are available. The first builds on mass production technology. But the latter is inherently inflexible with its use of dedicated machines and semiskilled labor to produce standardized goods. As the failure of the "world car" strategy shows, this option is not promising. The second strategy is to adopt flexible specialization technology, which allows skilled workers to use general-purpose machinery to turn out a wide and constantly changing assortment of goods for constantly shifting markets. Evidence from various regions in the world (or whole nations, as in the case of Germany and Japan) indicates this strategy's resilience to changing externalities.

Piore and Sabel (1984:206) further believe that a reversal of roles between the hitherto dominant and subordinate sectors is taking place as a result of the diffusion of flexible specialization in the small sector: "This model stands the regnant paradigm of production on its head. Dominant sectors of the established system were subordinated, subordinate ones dominated. As in any revolution, it was this reversal of roles—and the revelation of surprises in familiar structures—that disconcerted participants and observers."

Some of their claims may or may not be tenable. But they have identified three important dimensions: dynamic linkages between product markets and the technologies concerned, a macro socioeconomic context in which adaptation takes place, and technology as a key variable for success or failure, rather than attributes of inequality, bargaining, or culture. But there is a problem with this flexible specializationalist account: its assumption of a rather dichotomous division, and a reversal of roles, between large and small firms and its assumption of the confrontational positioning of the two technological paradigms.

I

THE HISTORY
OF SUBCONTRACTING
IN JAPAN

2

The Origins of Dualism and the Rise of Subcontracting in Japanese Manufacturing Industries, 1900–1945

Subcontracting in Japanese manufacturing industries cannot be separated from its historical context. As with any economic institution, it is a complex product of both idiosyncratic developments and common features of a capitalist society. The aim of this chapter is not to trace Japanese economic developments in general, but to examine the particular historical and socioeconomic conditions that determined why subcontracting in Japan developed as it did.[1]

Labor Mobility and Stabilization

There is wide agreement in the literature that the origins of the segmented labor markets in Japan can be traced back to the post–World War I period (see Fujita, 1965:322–23; Sumiya, 1966: 132–35; Nakamura, Takafusa, 1967:273–75, 1983:134, 220–31; Hyodo, 1971:404–79; Hirschmeier & Yui, 1975:155; Nariai, 1977:18; Hazama, 1978:106–7; Clark, 1979:44; Shoya, 1979:1015; Nakamura, Tsutomu, 1983:103). In the nineteenth century the Japanese labor market was characterized by substantial regional wage differentials based on interregional labor immobility (Nakamura, Takafusa, 1983:131). Beginning with the turn of the twentieth century, however, regional wage differentials narrowed because of increased labor mobility. For example, regional wage differentials (expressed as the ratio between maximum and minimum wages) for metalworkers in Kochi, Hiroshima, Nagoya, Kanazawa, Tokyo, and Sendai continually decreased: 2.0 (1900), 1.8 (1907), 1.6 (1914), and 1.5 (1920) (see Nakamura, Takafusa, 1983, Table 4.10, pp. 132–33). The labor market situation in Japan came to resemble the unstructured

1. Although our focus will be narrowed to the electrical and automotive industries in subsequent chapters, Japanese manufacturing industries overall will be covered in this chapter, as the shipbuilding and iron and steel industries, followed by machinery, set institutional precedents that had a major impact on the subsequent development of both the electrical and automotive industries.

TABLE 2-1. Length of Service of Skilled Workers, 1903

No. of Years	Metalworkers		Printing Workers	
	Number	Percent	Number	Percent
Under 0.5	1,258	12.9	650	23.8
0.5–1	3,853	39.6	498	18.3
1–2	645	6.6	511	18.8
2–3	1,730	17.8	323	11.8
3–5	1,113	11.4	310	11.4
5 or more	1,134	11.7	433	15.9
Total:	9,733	100.0	2,725	100.0

Source: Sumiya, 1966:50. Original Source: Ministry of Agriculture and Commerce (1903), *Shokko jijo* (Conditions of workers), vol. 2, p. 223.

model of neoclassical economics. Workers with a spectrum of skills began to move frequently from one employer to another, seeking better working conditions within the constraints of what the market situation and their individual skills afforded. For example, a pool of skilled labor consisting of *watari shokunin,* or "artisans of passage," who, having completed an apprenticeship of approximately three years, became professional job-seekers in the marketplace (Sumiya, 1966: 49–50; Nakamura, Takafusa, 1967:274). According to Katayama (1899): "They constitute a society of their own. Wherever they go, they can always find somebody they know. . . . They are everywhere in Japan."[2]

An investigation by the Ministry of Agriculture and Commerce (1903) showed that the annual labor turnover for *tekko* (metalworkers) and *insatsuko* (printing workers) were, respectively, 52.5 and 42.1 percent. Among skilled workers, a homogeneous, national labor market was being formed, covering Kyushu, Osaka, Tokyo, Tohoku, and Hokkaido (Sumiya, 1966:50). Table 2-1 shows the distribution of length of service for metalworkers and printing workers at the turn of the twentieth century. The fluidity revealed in Table 2-1 was also characteristic of unskilled labor. Women from the countryside, for example, often were attracted to working in the cotton mills, but because they were exploited and dissatisfied, they frequently left after a short period. An investigation by the Japan Cotton Spinners' Association in 1919 showed that 45 percent of these women remained at the mills less than a year and that only 21 percent remained for more than two years, with the average length of stay being one year and five months.[3]

2. Quoted in Sumiya, 1966:50. These skilled workers were generally trained as *kokata* (apprentices) by *oyakata* (master workmen or independent labor contractors). The *oyakata* contract system was particularly prevalent in engineering trades. In earlier days firms did not directly control skilled labor but usually made lump-sum contracts with *oyakata*. The latter would "then find the labour, determine methods of work, supervise the work process, provide payment to the workers, and meet any production deadlines" (Littler, 1982:149). The early prevalence of the *oyakata* system was later replaced by direct labor control by employers. Direct labor control was necessitated by technological change and the emergence of firm-specific skills. This point will be discussed later. For more on the *oyakata* system, see Sumiya, 1966: 7, 19, 51–53, 69–71; Littler, 1982:149–55.

3. Orchard, 1930:244–45. Note that these figures are still a result of labor stabilization in relative terms. Earlier, the labor turnover in the textile industry was much higher. In 1900, for example, the Hyogo branch of a large spinning firm had a turnover rate of 192 percent per year, including 6.5 percent

FIGURE 2-1. Labor Turnover at Large Manufacturers, 1919–30

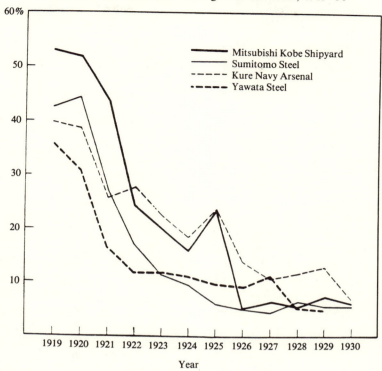

Year

Source: Hyodo, 1971:405. Original Sources: *Fuso kinzoku kabushiki gaisha goju nen shi* (A fifty-year history of the Fuso Metal Company), 1951, vol. 2, *Fuhyo* (Attached tables); Mitsubishi Kobe Shipyard, *Sogyo irai shokko tokei* (Statistics on workers since foundation); Hashimoto, "Honpo seitetsu gyo rodo jijo gaisetsu" (An outline of working situations in the iron & steel industry), in *Shakai seisaku jiho* (Social policy bulletin), June 1926, p. 98; Yawata Steel, *Seitetsusho kojo rodo tokei* (Statistics on steel mill labor), 1924–29; *Kure kaigun kosho zosenbu enkaku shi* (A historical outline of the Kure navy arsenal), 1925, *Fuhyo* (Attached tables); Ministry of Internal Affairs, Bureau of Social Affairs, *Kangyo rodosha ido shirabe* (Labor mobility survey of the public sector), 1930; Bank of Japan, *Rodo tokei* (Labor statistics).

This evidence indicates that there was at that time no lifetime commitment in those sections of the Japanese economy that came to be known in later years for their job stability. Furthermore, the frequent job shifts of skilled workers suggest that there were no substantial differences in working conditions among firms.

During the 1920s, however, there was a significant departure from this labor mobility pattern, specifically in the large-scale manufacturing sector of the economy, for instance, the shipbuilding and iron and steel industries. Figure 2-1 shows a dramatic decrease in labor turnover at four large manufacturers during this decade, from almost 50 percent on average to less than 10 percent per year.

This decrease in labor turnover was largely restricted to large firms in the heavy

of the layoffs due to illness and 0.7 percent to deaths. Among those who left, 79 and 83 percent of male and female workers were "runaways" (Ministry of Agriculture and Commerce, *Shokko jijo,* vol. 1, pp. 69–70, quoted in Hazama, 1978:277).

TABLE 2-2. Length of Service at an Electrical Equipment Firm in Tokyo, 1926

No. of Years	Males[a]	Females[b]	Total
Under 1	34.6%	66.2%	48.9%
1–3	42.6	29.0	36.4
3–5	7.9	1.2	4.9
5–10	11.9	2.4	7.6
10 or more	3.0	1.2	2.2
Total	100.0	100.0	100.0

[a]$n = 101$

[b]$n = 83$

Source: Adapted from Orchard, 1930:345.

manufacturing industries, which can be seen from the national data from the 1920s, showing a higher average turnover than indicated in Figure 2-1. According to the government's Bureau of Social Affairs, the average labor turnover (for all establishments, small or large) for 1925 was still 35 percent in the chemical industry, 42 percent in engineering, and 65 percent in miscellaneous industries (Harada, 1928:109, quoted in Orchard, 1930:344–45). Similarly, the labor turnover in 1930 was still around 30 percent at mining firms employing more than fifty people (Ministry of Internal Affairs, 1930, quoted in Hyodo, 1971:406). Table 2-2 uses as an example a small electrical equipment firm in Tokyo (with 101 male and 83 female workers) where the labor turnover was still fairly high in the mid-1920s. This table shows that the sharp decrease in labor turnover in large firms, as seen in Figure 2–1, did not apply equally to small firms.

The Rise of Internal Labor Markets

The foregoing evidence indicates that during the 1920s the Japanese labor markets, which had been characterized by fluidity and a lack of structure, acquired two distinctive segments—one for large firms, especially those in the heavy manufacturing industries, and the other for the rest of the economy. For the latter, the labor turnover remained essentially the same, but for the former, it dropped abruptly. As we shall see, the stabilization of labor at large firms did not simply happen[4] but instead was in large part the product of a deliberate strategy by management. The

4. One could argue that the labor stabilization was a result of the postwar recession. To the extent that finding alternative jobs became harder, it may well be true that workers stayed with their jobs. There are two problems with this recession thesis, however. First, it does not explain why labor stabilized primarily in the large-scale sector of the economy, whereas there was little change at small firms. Second, the recession thesis cannot explain why labor instability did not resume at large firms when the recession ended. Unless there were other powerful factors operating separately—or in addition to—the recession, the labor mobility pattern at small firms should have looked much the same as it did at large firms during this period. Further, labor instability would have resumed in the large sector when demand resumed. But neither has been found to be the case. It is in this context that the strategic creation of new institutions at large firms is deemed important to effectuating—or even perpetuating—disparity in stabilization.

strategy involved the creation of a series of institutions: in-house training and promotion, systematic recruitment, refined job classifications, seniority-based pay, bonuses, and formal retirement age and retirement pay. Most of these are familiar attributes of the internal labor markets of today (e.g., see Doeringer & Piore, 1971; Osterman, 1984; Piore, 1975).

But why did that all happen in Japan in the 1920s? What socioeconomic and technological factors were responsible for the rise of the new institutional arrangements?

In-House Training

After World War I, large Japanese manufacturers devised more in-house and firm-specific job classifications, concomitant with the breakup of the traditional hand-icraft mode of production. The sheer size of the business expansion during the wartime economic boom made it imperative that along with extensive investments in facilities, labor be more finely differentiated. Instead of having a shipbuilder do all of the tasks of ironing, drilling, riveting, and welding, for example, an iron worker, a driller, a riveter, and a welder were hired. This practice had already been adopted at the navy arsenals (*kaigun kosho*) and Mitsubishi Shipbuilding around the time of the Russo-Japanese War (1904–5) and became common during World War I. Moreover, several new jobs were created that required intellectual skills, such as those of experimenter, analyst, and draftsman, during wartime in the shipbuilding and iron and steel industries. During the period of rationalization after the war, various skilled trades responsible for process management also were created: *koteiko* (process workers), *kikakuko* (planners), and *kirokuko* (recorders). As a result of this job differentiation, a shipbuilder's job, which in an earlier period had been based on handicraft and leaned toward being a jack-of-all-trades, was broken down in the late 1920s into 21 job classifications at Kawasaki Shipbuilding and 27 each at Mitsubishi Kobe Shipbuilding and the navy arsenals. Similarly, Yawata Steel increased the number of its job classifications from 60 to 116 in 1924 (Hyodo, 1971:220–25, 409–11).

Along with the division of labor came the expansion of firm-specific skills. Unlike shipbuilders in the late nineteenth century, shipbuilders in the 1920s were required to do fewer tasks, according to specifications set by the firm. Moreover, how jobs were classified and tasks defined differed substantially from one firm to another (Hyodo, 1971, esp. Table III-10). It was therefore a prerequisite that workers in similar job categories be trained according to the new, firm-specific requirements. It is not difficult to see why the employment policies of the heavy manufacturers shifted from relying on *watari shokunin* to fostering in-house, dedicated workers in this period.

Large firms also set up company training schools and started providing in-house technical education for their workers and apprentices during working hours. As a result, the haphazard practice of hiring workers as necessary from the general job market was replaced by the periodic recruitment of elementary school leavers as apprentices. These apprentices were also taught non-job-related subjects at the company schools and were trained according to a disciplinary regime designed to enhance their dedication to the firm.[5]

Pay, Bonuses, and Retirement Pay Based on Length of Service

However effective this in-house training may have been, it would have made no economic sense if the trained workers had left for better opportunities after acquiring their skills. The cost of their education needed to be met by stabilizing the labor situation and making full use of the trained workers. As the pattern of pre–World War I labor mobility clearly shows, Japanese workers were no exception to being calculating and discerning: Whenever they found better job opportunities, they simply switched employers.

A powerful incentive to stabilize this precarious labor situation was to institute a linkage between length of service and incremental pay. Accordingly, periodic pay increases (once or twice a year) based on length of service became widespread among large Japanese firms during the 1920s (Hazama, 1978:520–24). By the mid-1920s, wage curves with an upward slant to the right—like those frequently seen today—became common; see Figure 2-2.

In addition, perfect attendance and seasonal bonuses, introduced during World War I to encourage continuous employment, became standard practice after the war (Hyodo, 1971:414). The culmination of this incentive system was the introduction of retirement (or severance) pay schemes, in which the amount of retirement pay was proportional to the length of service, together with a formal retirement age requirement (normally either fifty or fifty-five years of age). This retirement/severance pay plan was designed to mobilize labor to the firm's advantage. On the one hand, it paid either no or little money to those leaving the firm on their own initiative, before the formal retirement age. On the other hand, it paid extra money to those leaving at the firm's request. Thus, while avoiding possible unrest from dismissals, large Japanese firms were able to stabilize the work force in which they were investing so much. Because national unemployment insurance was virtually nonexistent at that time, the attraction of the retirement severance scheme for workers was considerable (Hyodo, 1971:415–16). These employment policies, along with the postwar recession in the 1920s, dramatically increased the workers' commitment to large firms. From these developments emerged the prototype of the lifetime employment system that characterizes the modern Japanese economy—at least in regard to the big corporations.

As a result of these developments, wage differentials in the various segments of the economy expanded. The economic downturn during the decade after World War

5. Such moves were initially made by the traditional heavy manufacturers. But the emergent electrical equipment manufacturers such as Hitachi followed suit. Started in 1908 by Namihei Odaira, Hitachi grew rapidly, manufacturing items ranging from heavy industrial equipment to consumer electrical appliances. The rapid expansion of its product range necessitated the fostering of workers equipped with a diversity of technical expertise pertinent to in-house purposes. In 1928 Hitachi formally founded the Hitachi Technical College (Hitachi kogyo senshu gakko), which grew out of its apprentice school (totei yoseijo) (Hitachi, 1949:168). Over time, technical education at these company training schools replaced the previous practice of sending workers out to night schools, which were no longer adequate to changed requirements.

FIGURE 2-2. Wage Curves at Two Shipyards, circa 1925

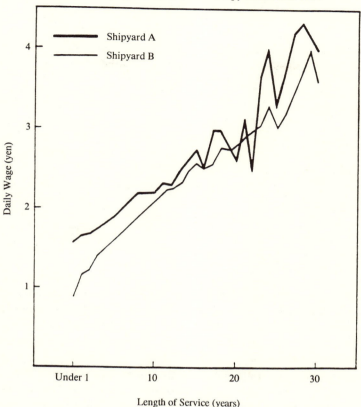

Length of Service (years)

Source: Hazama, 1978:522. Original Source: *Shakai seisaku jiho* (Social policy bulletin), vol. 77, pp. 81–82.

I created a large surplus of labor competing for limited job slots. Whereas the wages of workers at large firms remained unchanged, the wages of peripheral workers declined significantly. Table 2-3 shows the widening wage differentials between small and large establishments from 1908 to 1930. It also reveals the striking increase in average employment size per establishment in the big corporations, with the advent of huge factories, particularly for shipbuilding.

With the labor markets thus structured differently, the emergence of a dualist system was now complete. And it is in this new socioeconomic context that the strategic use of those in the peripheral sector, as either temporary workers or subcontractors, came to make economic sense.

The Rise of Temporary Workers

Before the 1920s, Japan's heavy industries already were using temporary workers. Because of the general high turnover of regular workers (*shokko*), however, the

TABLE 2-3. Interscale Wage Differentials, 1908 and 1930

	Average No. of Workers per Factory	Wage Index (Estimates)
1908		
Shipbuilding	285	100
Vehicles	102	94
Machinery	77	87
Cutlery	33	85
Metal kitchenware	23	80
1930		
Shipbuilding	859	100
Railway vehicles	231	88
Electrical equipment	61	72
Prime movers	31	72
Machine tools	14	50

Source: Hazama, 1978:57. Original Source: Ministry of Agriculture and Commerce/Ministry of Commerce and Industry (1908/1930), *Kojo tokeihyo* (Statistics on factories).

distinction between the two tended to be blurred. Moreover, employers did not depend on temporary workers to a great extent. In 1910, for example, Mitsubishi Nagasaki Shipyard employed 7.7 percent of its total labor force as *rinjiko* (temporary workers), and at Shibaura Seisakusho (later Toshiba) the figure was 10.8 percent (see Hazama, 1978, Table 85, p. 453).

The development of the distinctive internal labor markets in the 1920s, however, necessitated new policies to compensate for the rigidity of long-term employment relations. As pointed out, there was a substantial surplus of workers in the external labor markets during the postwar period. Legislation such as the Kojoho (Factory Act), implemented in 1916, and other labor protection acts applied primarily to regular workers but not to casual labor. The once-flourishing *watari shokunin* (artisans of passage) system had faded away with the abolishment around 1910 of the *oyakata* (master workmen) system on which it was based (Hazama, 1978:453).

It is in this context that large firms extensively employed temporary workers during the 1920s. Unlike their predecessors in the 1910s, who did simple tasks and miscellaneous odd jobs, the temporary workers in this decade were required to do more complex jobs like metalwork or smelting, similar to those of regular workers (Hyodo, 1971:431). Despite this, their pay remained the same or rose only slightly, irrespective of their length of service. Temporary workers were hired and fired in response to fluctuating demand; they received neither severance pay nor seasonal or perfect attendance bonuses. But the disparity between the labor markets and the general difficulty of finding a job led many workers to accept these disadvantageous job opportunities in the large firms as long as they could hold onto them (Hyodo, 1971:432–33). Thus, the large Japanese heavy manufacturers in the 1920s found a way to respond to uncertainties in the deliberate creation of a regulatory labor mechanism: temporary workers.

FIGURE 2-3. Employment Fluctuations of Regular and Temporary Workers at Yawata Steel, 1920–31

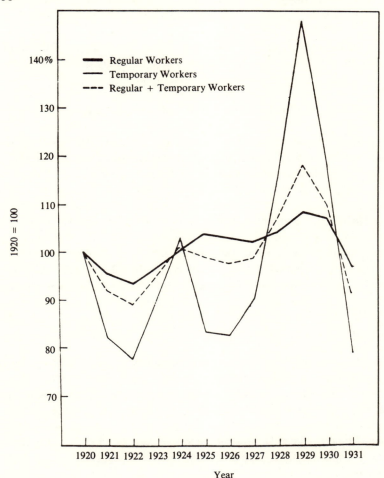

Source: Hyodo, 1971:432. Original Source: *Yawata seisakusho goju nen shi* (A fifty-year history of Yawata steel), 1950, *Fuhyo* (Attached tables).

Figure 2-3 shows that Yawata Steel followed such a dualist strategy throughout the 1920s. Whereas its employment of regular workers fluctuated by only about 10 percent, that of its temporary workers was about 70 percent! The sharp rise and fall of temporary worker employment during the Great Depression is particularly striking.

The use of temporary workers increased throughout the 1920s and 1930s among a variety of firms. Evidence shows that in 1934, for example, the percentage of temporary workers in the work force ranged from 73.7 at Nippon Steel's Hiroshima factory to 43.1 at Hitachi's Hitachi factory to 31.6 at Fuji Electric Manufacturing.[6]

6. From Employment Research Institute (Rodo jijo chosajo), 1935:16–20, quoted in Hazama, 1978:496–97. All these firms had more than five hundred workers, including temporary workers.

Including all establishments employing more than one hundred workers, the average percentage of temporary workers in the total work force in the Japanese machinery industry was 24.6 in 1934 (Bureau of Social Affairs, Labor Section, 1935:8, quoted in Hazama, 1978:64).

Thus, temporary workers came to constitute an essential part of the work force in the large manufacturing sector of the Japanese economy during the 1920s.[7]

The Emergence of Subcontracting

Subcontracting in Japan as we know it today is a distinctive product of the wartime economy that started with the outbreak of the Manchurian Incident in 1931. Along with Japan's expansionist involvement in the Sino-Japanese War in 1937 and World War II in 1941, military demand skyrocketed. At first, large Japanese manufacturers turned to subcontracting as a convenient means of meeting rapid surges in demand. Then the Japanese government introduced a series of laws intended to mobilize a large part of the nation's industrial resources for war purposes. Part of the program was organizing small firms as subcontractors serving large munitions manufacturers. Before considering this issue further, however, we should review the socioeconomic background of these developments in relation to the foregoing discussion of dualism.

Before 1920

Subcontracting was not extensively used in Japan before the Manchurian Incident.[8] Before World War I, machinery and components for the manufacture of goods were largely imported. During the war, owing to the decrease in imports, Japanese manufacturers started to make industrial equipment (e.g., pumps, motors, and construction facilities) and machine tools (e.g., milling machines and grinders) on their own (Minato, 1986:53). Most of the work was done in-house; only raw materials and some specific items were purchased, such as cases, chemical insulators, and castings (see, e.g., Hitachi, 1949:12–13, 15, 20–21, 184).

---

7. The efficacy of temporary workers, by providing both flexibility and lower fixed costs, proved so great that on-site temporary workers (increasingly employed by subcontractors rather than directly by the prime contractor) have over time become a permanent feature of employment practices in the Japanese shipbuilding and iron and steel industries. The term *shagaiko,* or on-site subcontractors' employees, is used to describe them. This is a clear manifestation of a dualist strategy.

8. For example, see Komiyama, 1941:41; Fujita, 1965:20, 33; Minato, 1986:56. In contrast with temporary workers, there is a curious lack of systematic empirical evidence as to what extent subcontracting was or was not implemented during this period. Company histories, for example, start referring to subcontracting only after the late 1930s. Furthermore, there appear to be—as Fujita (1965:56) indicates—few statistics on subcontracting at this time, in contrast with the abundant documentation in the post–World War II period. The scarcity of the data may well suggest that subcontracting before the 1930s did not constitute an important part of business activities among Japanese firms. In this connection, it is interesting that in 1937 a researcher remarked: "By the way, it is relatively recent that the word *shitauke* [subcontracting], as in the sense of *shitauke* industries, came to be used" (Fujita, 1965:34). Thus we should at least attempt to discover what the purchasing situation was like in this earlier period.

Without any effective labor regulatory mechanisms, Japanese firms—both large and small—suffered from the fluctuations in this period. When demand fell, workers were generally laid off or discharged, but when the economy was booming, the firms simply could not meet the increased demand. Deliveries of parts often were delayed because of the lack of labor capacity and poor materials control. Intrafirm and interfirm coordination was negligible. The following example is of Hitachi.

In the summer of 1914, immediately after the outbreak of war, orders sharply decreased, and so Hitachi laid off its idle workers. In 1915, as a result of a sharp decline of imports, both Hitachi and its competitors enjoyed an increase in orders. Only some sections of Hitachi's factory were busy, however, whereas others were not. Moreover, it was extremely difficult to procure the necessary materials. The delay of incoming goods such as castings and copper materials inhibited production. In 1916, orders soared further, and workers worked day and night to meet strict deadlines. But the flow of incoming goods was so unpredictable that the in-house manufacturing process was badly affected. By the end of the year, the factory was filled with huge stocks of unfinished goods. The difficulty in procurement worsened: In January 1917, one could not even walk around the factory, which was jampacked with undeliverable motors and transformers. Customers were castigating Hitachi for unacceptable delivery delays. But even the smallest lack of components due to ineffective procurement disabled production. The morale of workers deteriorated as a result of the many overtime hours, including all-night shifts, over the year. By mid-1917, however, the boom was over, and demand dropped. Manufacturing operations were further disrupted. Although some parts of the operation were still busy, in other divisions, idle workers had to be laid off again. Management feared that the idle workers would disrupt the activities of the busy workers and might stir up labor discontent. When World War I was over, the recession deepened, and the factory shut down completely (Hitachi, 1949:20).

As is clear, except for layoffs, there were no regulatory mechanisms—either intrafirm or interfirm—in the face of fluctuations in demand. In addition, the absence of such a regulatory system caused a host of quality problems due to design defects, uncertain schedules, and poor materials control (Hitachi, 1949:21).

What are the implications of these historical facts? One finding is that neither dualism nor the use of temporary workers or subcontractors had been essential to the Japanese economy earlier in the twentieth century. As we have seen, the labor markets were fairly fluid, and interscale wage differentials were limited. Whether or not the cultural characteristics of the Japanese facilitated trust and relational contracting (as Dore argues), there were few socioeconomic conditions in pre–World War I Japan conducive to the emergence of subcontracting. The postwar situation created the internal labor markets in large Japanese firms. The use of temporary workers also increased during the 1920s and 1930s, but still subcontracting was not widely relied on,[9] or more precisely, for technological and other infrastructural reasons, subcontracting could not be relied on.

---

9. Referring to this period, Komiyama (1941:41) observed: "These large factories do almost everything in-house, sometimes including those jobs requiring raw materials, and they carry out a variety of complete tasks."

TABLE 2-4. Number of Male Workers per Factory in Private
Heavy Manufacturing Industries, 1920 and 1930

No. of Workers per Factory	Total Number of Workers			
	1920		1930	
500 or more	122,700	(50.2%)	80,000	(34.0%)
100–499	40,400	(16.5)	46,100	(19.6)
50–99	18,000	(7.4)	19,600	(8.3)
30–49	12,400	(5.1)	18,700	(7.9)
5–29	50,800	(20.8)	70,900	(30.1)
Total:	244,300	(100.0)	235,300	(100.0)

Source: Adapted from Hyodo, 1971:418, Table III-11. Original Source: Ministry of
Agriculture and Commerce/Ministry of Commerce and Industry (1920/1930), *Kojo
tokeihyo* (Statistics on factories).

The 1920s

The emergence of dualism in the 1920s, however, provided the fertile industrial soil
in which extensive subcontracting was to grow later. In this decade a significant
proportion of the working population—those either expelled from or unable to enter
the internal labor markets of large manufacturers—drifted into employment in the
small firms. A general decrease in the demand for ships, the treaties of the 1921–22
Washington disarmament conferences, and the reentry of Western shipbuilders into
the market all contributed to a serious slump in Japan's shipbuilding industry. The
iron and steel and related industries also were affected. Demand did not substantially pick up throughout the 1920s, and employment by the large manufacturing
sector did not recover to the level of 1919–20 (Hyodo, 1971:417–18). In the
meantime, the male working population showed a steady annual increase of more
than 200,000 (Ohkawa, 1956:127). Thus, the structure of the national economy was
such that only the peripheralization of the surplus labor could alleviate the problem.[10]

Table 2-4 shows this distinctive trend in the heavy manufacturing industries in
the 1920s. The upsurge of the smallest sector (employing from five to twenty-nine
workers), which raised its employment share from 20.8 to 30.1 percent, is notable.
The employment level of the "miniature" firms in the metal and machinery industries (employing fewer than 5 workers and not covered by the government's statis-

10. From a different perspective, one could ask: Why, then, didn't the manufacturers lower the wages
of their core workers (and discard the fringe benefits), to enable them to compete with the peripheral
workers? If they had done that, however, it would have been self-defeating. It was precisely because the
quality of core labor had risen because of firm-specific training and skills that the internal working
conditions were differentiated to enable stabilization. Short-run profits from economizing on labor were
thus calculated to be less desirable than long-term gains in maintaining and making full use of quality
labor in which they had a paid stake. Accordingly, firms neither lowered the wage levels of their core
workers nor exchanged high quality for cheap labor. Instead, they chose a middle way: While maintaining the structure of the internal labor markets, they resorted to temporary workers for those jobs requiring
fewer firm-specific skills. The economic puzzle, then—to which the behavior of the large Japanese firms
in the 1920s provides a clue—is not why wages in the periphery were low, but why wages in the core
were high.

TABLE 2-5. Number of Industry Start-ups, 1904–33

Year	Machinery	Metal	Manufacturing Total
1904–8	368	245	3,826
1909–13	605	396	5,683
1914–18	992	762	8,315
1919–23	1,606	1,064	14,052
1924–28	1,713	1,227	13,769
1929–33	1,780	1,248	13,436
Total:	7,850	8,542	71,940

Source: Minato, 1986:55. Original Source: Ministry of Commerce and Industry (1933), *Kojo tokeihyo* (Statistics on factories).

tics on factories) also rose, according to Hyodo's estimate, from 330,000 to 359,000 workers between 1920 and 1930. (Hyodo, 1971:419). What is interesting is not only that those in the surplus labor market were peripheralized as workers but also that many started their own small businesses. Table 2-5 shows the high number of start-ups in the 1920s.

The Great Depression helped dampen the wages of peripheral workers. Furthermore, the income level of entrepreneurs with capital of less than ¥2,000 was below that of workers in large firms (Hyodo, 1971:419). As Table 2-3 demonstrates, the wage differentials widened in this period. Taking into account all the foregoing, then, the situation was ideal for the large manufacturers in the core economy to profit, in ways that created a dualistic structure. The restructuring of the economy throughout the recession of the 1920s thus prepared for the rapid development of subcontracting systems in Japan from the 1930s onward.

The Wartime Economy, 1931 to 1945

The wartime economy between 1931 and 1945 marked the rise of subcontracting in Japan. Although the subcontracting systems that developed in this period may not have achieved their original aims, they did leave a range of institutional prototypes on which the postwar evolution of Japanese subcontracting is based. Apart from the availability of cheap labor and the pool of small firms already mentioned, four other factors were responsible for the development of subcontracting in Japan in the 1930s: economic, technological, infrastructural, and political. (The political factor will be treated separately in the section Politics and Prototypes.)

The first economic factor is the most obvious: the burgeoning demand for munitions. Japan's involvement in the Manchurian Incident, the Sino-Japanese War, and World War II all necessitated a steady rise in munitions output, and the capacity of the existing large manufacturers simply could not meet this demand. The situation was exacerbated by the Sino-Japanese War in 1937, and Table 2-6 shows the enormous leap in demand for munitions in this period. The number of munitions orders to the private sector of the machinery manufacturing industry quadrupled in only one year, from 1936 to 1937, and the share of munitions in the industry's entire output jumped from 38.5 to 66.3 to 75.3 percent from 1936 to 1938. Table 2-7

TABLE 2-6. Influence of Munitions Demand on Machinery Industry, 1932–38

(Millions of yen)

Year	(a) Munitions Order	(b) Munitions Order to Private Sector of Machinery Industry	(c) Machinery Industry Output	b/a	b/c
1932	686	364	543	53.1%	67.1%
1933	872	432	805	49.5	53.6
1934	946	445	1,082	47.0	41.1
1935	1,032	528	1,380	51.1	38.2
1936	1,078	532	1,609	49.3	38.5
1937	3,766	2,152	3,248	57.1	66.3
1938	6,016	3,283	4,359	54.5	75.3

Source: Yamada, 1943:152.

TABLE 2-7. Value of Backlogged Orders at Major Manufacturers, 1937–38

(Millions of yen)

Firms	1937 (First Half) (a) Value of Backlogs	(b) Production Capacity	a/b	1938 (First Half) (c) Value of Backlogs	(d) Production Capacity	c/d
Mitsubishi Heavy Industries	178.0	58.0	(307%)	270.0	64.0	(422%)
Hitachi	32.0	34.0	(94)	85.3	68.5	(125)
Shibaura Seisakusho	27.8	18.7	(149)	50.0	23.0	(217)
Mitsubishi Electric	15.0	13.3	(113)	40.0	20.0	(200)
Ikegai Tekko	10.0	5.0	(200)	20.0	6.0	(333)
Tokyo Gas Denko	12.0	6.0	(200)	20.0	9.0	(222)
Ishikawajima Shipbuilding	25.0	9.2	(272)	29.7	15.0	(198)
Tokyo Automotive Industry	55.0	4.5	(1222)	80.0	15.0	(533)
Total:	354.8	148.7	(239)[a]	595.0	220.5	(270)[a]

[a] Average.

Note: The original percentage figures that appeared to be miscalculations have been corrected.

Source: Minato, 1986:58.

shows the sharp increase in order backlogs resulting from the higher demand for munitions between 1937 and 1938.

To alleviate this problem of insufficient capacity, the large manufacturers found it necessary to externalize part of their production activities. As pointed out, there was surplus capacity in the peripheral economy, and wage differentials between the core and the peripheral sectors were substantial.[11] Further, the "lessons that large manufacturers learned immediately after World War I through failures in wartime overinvestments made them cautious about further investments" (Isobe, 1942:253). Thus, the use of subcontracting arose as a convenient means to fulfill the gap between the skyrocketing munitions demand and the faltering supply.

One of the government's earliest statistics on subcontracting shows that in 1934 the average percentage of subcontracting in the total output of prime contractors was 17.5 percent in the machinery industry.[12] More specifically, the subcontracting percentages for the automotive and electrical industries were, respectively, 11.7 and 15.8 percent. However, these figures do not include purchases of finished products (*kiseihin*). Including these, purchasing percentages for the automotive and electrical industries were, respectively, 51.6 and 25.6, the former being double the latter. In other words, automotive prime contractors purchased 39.9 percent of their output as finished products (probably components), whereas electrical equipment manufacturers purchased only 9.8 percent.

From the standpoint of the subcontractors, then, how much of their output was accounted for by subcontracting? In 1937, dependence on subcontracting was 89.4 percent among the "miniature" firms (employing fewer than ten workers) in the machinery industry in Tokyo.[13] Although the data cover only the smallest firms, it can be reasonably inferred that the use of subcontracting in the machinery industry was substantial.

The second factor in the surge of Japanese subcontracting in the 1930s is tech-

11. In 1937, for example, between the smallest subcontractors (employing fewer than five workers) and large, independent firms in the Taisho District in Osaka (where the transportation equipment, spinning machinery, machine tools, and vehicles industries were concentrated), wage differentials were 49.8 versus 100 by index. It is also striking that even the entrepreneurs of "miscellaneous machined parts" firms (which most likely overlapped with the smallest subcontractors) earned less than did workers in independent firms: 92.6 versus 100 by index (see Fujita, 1965:54–55, 64, 70–71).

12. The data cover 571 prime contractors and 8,401 subcontractors in five prefectures, including Tokyo, Osaka, and Nagoya. On average a prime contractor had 14.7 subcontractors (Ministry of Commerce and Industry, Minister's Secretariat, Statistics Section, 1936, *Kikai kigu kogyo gaichu jokyo shirabe* [An inquiry into the subcontracting conditions of the machinery and equipment industry], quoted in Fujita, 1965:38). The same statistics do not specifically list figures for secondary or tertiary subcontracting, though Fujita assumes that the preceding figure includes some overlap with secondary or tertiary subcontracting (p. 40).

13. Calculated from Tokyo City (1937), *Tokyo shi shokojo chosasho* (An investigation of small factories in Tokyo), quoted in Fujita, 1965, Table 3, p. 40. The figure consists of 51.6 percent of their output bought by factories alone, 27.2 percent by brokers alone, and 10.6 percent by both factories and brokers (no overlapping with the former two figures). Other figures were omitted from this calculation because of overlapping: that is, 2.3 percent bought by brokers, retailers, and the general public; 1.9 percent by factories, retailers, and the general public; 0.6 percent by factories and the public sector; and 0.1 percent by brokers and the public sector.

nological. Unlike their predecessors, small firms in this decade came to be equipped with at least a set of small *gendoki,* or prime movers (electrical or gasoline powered), lathes, and drilling machines—however primitive (Fujita, 1965:35, 60–61). This was a quantum leap from those days when large-scale steam-powered prime movers could be seen only at large factories, whereas the small firms operated using only labor power. This lack of prime movers had slowed the earlier adoption of subcontracting in the machinery industry.

The technological development in machine tools now changed the situation. Even the smallest subcontractor with a family operation could now be linked with large, advanced firms. The standardization of manufacturing processes, along with mass production methodologies, promoted the division of labor among varied manufacturing units, thus giving rise to jobs like simple machining and drilling that could be easily and cheaply done by subcontractors.

The third factor in the development of subcontracting was infrastructural. The expansion of national transportation and communication systems now largely removed geographical barriers to a workable division of labor between prime contractors and subcontractors, which enhanced the marketability of the small subcontracting firms output.[14] Also important was the spread of electric power. In 1922, for example, the use of electric power in factory operation was 50 percent in the Japanese textile industry, but in 1929 the figure amounted to 88 percent. This compares with 19 percent in England and 59 percent in Germany and the United States in the same period (Hazama, 1978:325). It is not difficult to imagine that the small subcontractors also greatly benefited from using electric-powered lathes and drilling machines, which brought them technologically closer to the large manufacturers.

Thus the historical evidence has demonstrated that neither a specific national culture nor the advent of dualism was a sufficient condition for subcontracting to emerge in Japan. There had to be a sudden leap in demand that necessitated a quick solution to undercapacity problems and technological and infrastructural advances that made it possible to connect large and small manufacturers through subcontracting. This reconfirms that the dualist tendencies of the Japanese economy and the spread of subcontracting are relatively recent phenomena in Japanese history.

So far, our discussion has concerned the macrostructure that defined the rise of subcontracting in Japan. Next we shall narrow our focus to more specific operational issues concerning subcontracting. This knowledge of the microstructure should, in combination with the preceding macroanalysis, provide a comprehensive picture of wartime subcontracting in Japan.[15]

---

14. Fujita, 1965:35–36. It is not difficult to see why the developing mode of subcontracting marked an important divide between coexisting dualism and interrelated dualism. *Coexisting dualism* is a phenomenon usually seen in developing nations in which the modern industrial sector and the traditional handicraft sector coexist with remote mutual relationships. By contrast, *interrelated dualism* signifies a useful economic marriage between the two, although its stability or divorce rate is largely determined by the context.

15. Due to the scarcity of prewar and wartime empirical materials, however, the examination is confined to extremely few sources, which may limit the generalizability of these findings.

Modes of Subcontracting

The Rise of Purchasing Organizations

As purchasing became more important, prime contractors began establishing independent purchasing sections or departments. In 1937, for example, factories had subsections (*kakari*) of purchasing (*kobai gakari*) or subcontracting (*gaichu gakari*) within a variety of sections (*ka*) such as production (*komu*), utilities (*yotaku*), or general affairs (*somu*). In the purchasing subsection, an engineer supervised a few purchasing agents responsible for all aspects of purchasing except for payments and inspection. For example, they investigated, selected, and supervised suppliers and subcontractors on technical matters, and they also determined delivery deadlines and urged subcontractors to observe them (Fujita, 1965:37).

As the amount of purchasing grew, however, such a small operation could no longer manage the greater workload. Purchasing organizations began to be upgraded. In 1939 at Toyota, for example, the purchasing department (*kobai bu*) was newly established, outgrowing its predecessor, the purchasing subsection (*kobai gakari*), which had been under the administration department (*jimu bu*).[16]

Similarly, in 1938, Hitachi set up at its headquarters a new materials department (*shizai bu*) to which the purchasing section was now transferred from the general affairs department. The investigation section (*chosa ka*), responsible for interpreting the laws and regulations for purchasing and investigating materials control, was also put in the same department. Owing to the greater importance of purchasing activities because of the military involvement in materials control, the purchasing department was then expanded. In 1942, it had seven different sections, and by January 1944, there were two hundred people working in the department (Hitachi, 1960:19, 20, 32).

By the same token, in 1937 Nissan upgraded its purchasing subsection to a section and in 1940 to a department (Nissan, 1965:69, 70, 86). At Toyo Kogyo (then a manufacturer of three-wheel vehicles and machine tools; later Mazda) a purchasing department was established in 1943 (Toyo Kogyo, 1972:156).

At some firms, process subcontracting and other purchasing were distinguished in the purchasing organization. At Isuzu, for instance, in 1937 the purchasing section, under the general affairs department, had three subsections: products (*seihin*), materials (*sozai*), and preparations (*seiri*). By 1940, however, a new subsection of process subcontracting (*kako gaichu*) had been added to the purchasing section, and the section itself had been transferred to the finance department (Isuzu, 1957:199, 202).

---

16. Toyota, 1967:42, 110, 167–68. Risaburo Ohshima, the managing director, became the first department manager, supported by Shuji Ohno as the manager of the new section. Two years before the new purchasing department was set up, procedural rules concerning purchasing had already been put in writing at Toyota: memoranda for purchasing agents (*kobai gakari kokoroecho*), memoranda for warehouse agents for purchased materials (*gaichu hin soko gakari kokoroecho*), memoranda for materials control (*zairyo gakari kokoroecho*), rules for supplier financing and investment (*gaichu kojo kin'yu toshi kitei*), and internal rules for ordering to subcontractors (*shitauke kojo chumon hoho naiki*) (p. 112).

The Division of Labor

Besides purchasing finished products, the content of subcontracting in the machinery industry was mainly concerned with processes such as machining, drilling, forging, and casting, and the manufacture of simple, small parts (*komono*) was often subcontracted out. These tasks generally required few skills. In principle, only parts allowing substantial tolerances in dimension and finish were contracted out (Fujita, 1965:41; Oshiro, 1970:152).

The Origins of Gradational Subcontracting

A closer look at specific industries reveals the range of subcontracting arrangements during this period. For example, the Japanese automotive industry was becoming established in the 1930s.[17] The first Toyota car, the 1935 A1 prototype passenger car, consisted of a body, cylinder heads and blocks, housings, and a transmission case—all made in-house. Other than these, nearly all the gear and chassis components were Chevrolet imports. Steel materials and steel pipes were brought in from Yawata Steel and Sumitomo Metal. Forgeable castings were purchased from Tobata Castings (later Nissan) and other components from local Nagoya suppliers (Toyota, 1967:56, 61). All bus bodies were purchased from automotive body specialists like Shibaura Automotive Industries in Tokyo, Kurata Heavy Industries in Yokohama, and Nagoya Automotive Manufacturers in Nagoya (Toyota, 1967:66). Because of the government's restrictions on imports, Toyota motor vehicles' local content increased, whereas in-house manufacturing did not. Toyota's reliance on purchasing also increased. In November 1936 a mere two hundred Toyota motor vehicles were produced (Toyota, 1967:767), with 51 percent of the manufacturing cost per vehicle spent on purchased parts (see Toyota, 1978:63). In 1939, when twelve thousand units were manufactured (Toyota, 1967:767), a Toyota motor vehicle consisted of 66 percent purchased components, excluding raw materials. Table 2-8 shows the breakdown. The purchased components and materials, plus raw materials, accounted for well over 70 or even 80 percent of the manufacturing costs at Toyota when it began to produce in large quantities.

In fact Kiichiro Toyoda, the founder and then vice-president of Toyota, assumed that the company's overwhelming dependence on purchasing was the reason for the

17. After the Kanto earthquake in 1923, motor vehicles came to be widely recognized by the Japanese public as a convenient means of transportation. Seeing great opportunities in the Japanese market, Ford and GM established their Japanese subsidiaries in 1925 and 1927, respectively, and started to mass-manufacture knock-down motor vehicles competitively. Japanese motor vehicle assemblers, which had slowly been appearing, were virtually forced to withdraw from the scene. However, the Japanese government introduced a series of acts—the most important being the May 1936 Motor Vehicle Manufacturing Business Act (Jidosha seizo jigyo ho)—intended to encourage domestic motor vehicle manufacturers. This was deemed essential for both economic and military reasons. In 1936, Toyoda Automatic Loom Works (whose automotive department became independent as Toyota in 1937) and Nissan became the first licensed producers under the act. Isuzu followed suit shortly afterward. In the meantime, GM's and Ford's Japanese operations had to cease operating in 1939 as a result of measures such as a ceiling on production, increased import duties, and revised foreign exchange regulations. For an excellent history of the Japanese automotive industry, see Cusumano, 1985. Also see Kumaki, 1959; Chang, 1981; Amagai, 1982; and Nakamura, S., 1983.

TABLE 2-8. Manufacturing Costs[a] of a Toyota Motor Vehicle in 1939

Item	Cost	
Purchased parts	¥2,300	(66.1%)
Labor	180	(5.2)
Overhead	1,000	(28.7)
Total:	3,480	(100.0)

[a]Excluding raw materials.

Source: Adapted from Toyota, 1967:174–79.

higher cost, and so in February 1940 he issued a fiat to switch, in large part, from purchasing to in-house manufacturing. Moreover, he tried to structure Toyota's purchasing practices, by clearly differentiating three categories of components by origin: (1) in-house components fabricated by Toyota itself, (2) quasi–in-house components manufactured by Toyota's affiliates such as Toyoda Automatic Loom Works (from which the Toyota Motor Corporation spun off in 1937), and (3) purchasing. The third category was further divided into three groups according to their production technologies and financial ties. In the Internal Rules for Automotive Components Control, issued in conjunction with the aforementioned fiat, Toyoda stated:

Purchased components are divided into the following three types:

(a) General purchasing (*Ippan gaichu*)
Components of this type can be made by and brought in from any factory, or they can be manufactured by ordinary facilities. Therefore, these subcontractors may be switched as necessary.

(b) Special purchasing (*Tokushu gaichu*)
The manufacture of components of this type requires a certain degree of facility and training. We specifically allocate the manufacture of these components to factories with which we have close capital or financial ties; we thus regard them as Toyota's special subcontracting factories. Therefore, prototypes and items to be studied should, preferably, be ordered from these factories. Only in unavoidable cases should these things be ordered from the subcontractors in item (a).

(c) Specialty factory purchasing (*Senmon kojo gaichu*)
The manufacture of special components of this type requires special facilities. Therefore, we will consider establishing in the future close capital and financial ties with those subcontractors with such facilities. (Toyota, 1967:182)

That this arrangement was not temporary but strategic in intent can be seen in Toyoda's remark in the same Internal Rules: "In the future our purchasing relations shall proceed according to the above policies (Toyota, 1967:182). The criteria for the different categories were technological expertise and financial ties. This indeed was typical of Toyota's—and in this regard Japan's—approach to gradational subcontracting. This approach to subcontracting, as exemplified by prewar Toyota, later materialized on a larger scale among large Japanese manufacturers after the war, with the introduction of the subcontractor grading system (see Chapter 4).

Toyota's criteria also presaged a tendency toward more asset-specific investments, as Williamson defined them.

Control

In general, during wartime, even those subcontractors supplying one or two firms received neither financial nor managerial support from their customers. Subcontracting entrepreneurs who had previously been employed by their customers also received nothing. Technical control over subcontractors was haphazard as well, with no long-term plan (Fujita, 1965:43).

Furthermore, at least until the government began to rationalize subcontracting practices, much of the subcontracting was arranged by brokers who charged large commissions and had little interest in the technical aspect of their clients' business (Komiyama, 1941:56). But when the government entered the picture, the brokers were gradually driven out, and direct control of the subcontractors by the prime contractors was encouraged instead.

Reasons for Subcontracting

The prime contractors resorted to subcontracting because of sudden surges in demand. Subcontractors were used mainly for the short term, though their primitive technologies often inhibited production. The abundance of competitors weakened the subcontractors' bargaining position, and without access to a final product market of their own, many subcontractors succumbed to pressures to lower costs or leave the market. Indeed, referring to their inherent instability in the market, Komiyama (1941) once called them "floating subcontractors" (*fudoteki shitauke*).

Employment Conditions

The two criteria for selecting subcontractors were their technical performance and costs.[18] For the former, the subcontractors' facilities and technologies were investigated, and for the latter, bids were often sought. When the prime contractors determined the price, they simply chose the subcontractors they were already using (Fujita, 1965:42). Generally, prime contractors were not concerned with planning their subcontracting in advance, which was why they found it so convenient to adjust their production through the variable use of subcontractors in the face of fluctuations. Accordingly, as a general practice, prime contractors generally discarded the subcontractors during recession.[19]

The subcontractors' responses to this instability were twofold. First, they could either reallocate jobs among themselves or employ their own subcontractors, that is, second-tier subcontractors (from the standpoint of the primary contractor), though

18. Delivery performance was not yet on their priority list.

19. Fujita, 1965:44, 75. Prime contractors in this period tended to conceal the fact that they were using subcontractors (p. 21). This may mean that they did not want to disclose their possibly harsh treatment of subcontractors, particularly during a recession.

TABLE 2-9. Sub-subcontracting at Large Subcontractors in the mid-1930s

Subcontractor	No. of workers	No. of Sub-subcontractors
A	120	10
B	80	10
C	50	5

Source: Fujita, 1965:45.

this latter option was limited to fairly large subcontractors. Table 2–9 explains this use of sub-subcontracting. Second, subcontractors could find more customers. This strategy was effective when one or two of their major customers suddenly pulled out. Despite their primitive production capabilities, subcontractors in the 1930s had a fairly wide customer base, with those trading with three or more customers accounting for more than half their accounts, as seen in Table 2-10.

Associations of Subcontractors

Subcontractors' associations (*kyoryokukai*) were a deliberate product of the government's wartime program to organize the subcontractors into *keiretsu* (channeled groups). In *keiretsu,* subcontractors served the same contractor(s). Toyota's *kyoryokukai,* officially renamed the Kyohokai in December 1943, has an interesting history. First, it was established in the first roundtable conference of Toyota Motor's subcontractors (Toyota jidosha shitauke kondankai), which took place in November 1939, more than one year before the announcement of the government's Rationalization Outline. Second, the association was aimed at promoting mutual friendship (*shinboku*)—rather than hierarchical control relationships—between Toyota and some twenty key subcontractors who participated in the conference. Third, principally at the subcontractors' own initiative, the assembler–subcontractor relationship was strengthened in 1943 in order to secure materials and exchange technical information through interfactory inspections (Toyota, 1967:253). Throughout the process, Toyota's actions preceded the government's coercive measures.

TABLE 2-10. Number of Customers for Machinery Subcontractors in the Taisho District, Osaka, 1937

No. of Customers	No. of Subcontractors	
1	47	(23.9%)
2	44	(22.4)
3	30	(15.3)
4	17	(8.7)
5	21	(10.7)
6–10	26	(13.3)
11 or more	6	(3.1)
Unknown	5	(2.6)
Total:	196	(100.0)

Source: Fujita, 1965:74.

TABLE 2-11. Number of Prime Movers and Their Working Horse Power per Worker in the Machinery Industry, 1936 and 1937

No. of Workers per Factory	No. of Prime Movers per Worker	Working Horse Power per Worker
Fewer than 5 (Osaka) (1936)	0.349	0.427
More than 200 (countrywide) (1937)	1.873	2.604

Source: Fujita, 1965, Table 10, p. 61.

Tooling

Prime contractors often sold, on credit, their used equipment to their subcontractors. In Osaka and Nagoya, payments for subcontracted jobs sometimes went toward this (Fujita, 1965:42).

On the whole, subcontractors' production facilities could at best be described as primitive. Further, they lacked tooling: In 1937 among 287 machinery subcontractors in the Taisho District in Osaka, there were on average 8.66 machines per factory, comprising 2.9 lathes, 1.71 drilling machines, and a few other machines (Fujita, 1965:59). Table 2-11 compares the number of prime movers and their working horse power per worker at the smallest and medium-to-large factories. The types of machines that these subcontractors operated were predominantly general purpose and did not require much technical sophistication. Indeed, these machines, many of them bought from machinery traders in Kamimachi, were notorious for their inferior quality (Fujita, 1965:60).

In the mid-1930s the Japanese machine tool industry had only a 50 to 60 percent share of the domestic machine tool market. Usually, the high-tech and high-precision machine tools were imports. In 1937, some 80 percent of Japan's machine tool manufacturers were, not surprisingly, very small firms with fewer than thirty workers producing small, low-grade, and inferior-quality lathes and other turning machines.[20] According to a Japanese army officer, "The composition of machine tools in a country's manufacturing industries generally reflects the degree of its manufacturing industries' development. For example, simple lathes prevail in primitive countries. Unfortunately, the state of affairs in our country is not far from this" (Fujita, 1965:60–61).

Materials Supply

The practice of prime contractors' directly supplying materials to their subcontractors was quite common. On April 15, 1937, for example, it was agreed at the meeting of Osaka's subcontracting industries that a direct materials supply system would be formally established (Fujita, 1965:65).

20. Toyo Kogyo, 1972:116. The Japanese government's involvement in rationalizing the machine tool industry is discussed later.

Drawings and Design Capabilities

Subcontractors in this period generally had no design capabilities of their own; they simply machined, cast, forged, or manufactured parts according to drawings and specifications provided by prime contractors. Seldom were such tasks divided between prime contractors and subcontractors (Oshiro, 1970:152–53). Compared with the market after the war, particularly after the mid-1950s, model and design changes were much less frequent, and subcontractors were seldom asked to innovate.

Quality Assurance

Compared with the current practice in Japan, quality assurance during wartime was very weak. Usually, unskilled workers in the prime contractor's inspection subsection were responsible for inspecting incoming goods.[21] Owing to the subcontractors' primitive technical capabilities, however, the parts they provided had various problems regarding interchangeability, tolerance, and dimensions. This weak supply base from such unreliable subcontractors posed a near-fatal barrier to the mass production of modern armaments, with the result being an array of defective aircraft and motor vehicles.[22] Toward the end of World War II, despite an increase in output, the Japanese aircraft industry had degenerated into slipshod manufacturing, and the prime contractors continuously had to replace and readjust incoming parts.[23] Some of these problems with quality can be attributed to the inferior machine tools that turned out these products, and the absence of quality assurance mechanisms in subcontracting only made the situation worse.

Ordering and Delivery

By the latter half of the 1930s, purchasing contracts contained some penalty clauses for late delivery, though in practice they were rarely invoked. As World War II wore on, the incidents of late or nondelivery increased and became a widespread problem in the Japanese economy (Fujita, 1965:42, 179).

Payments

Process subcontractors usually received payment for their service half a month after the ordered goods were delivered. Depending on the content of the job, however,

21. Fujita, 1965:43. This contrasts with the establishment of "self-certified" subcontractors from the mid-1960s onward, which were made wholly responsible for having zero defects in the components they supplied.

22. Ironically, Japanese motor vehicle manufacturers, which lacked both in-house capacity and a purchasing supply base, had to resort to a substantial amount of imports—particularly some key engine components—in the midst of the war (Komiyama, 1941:40–43).

23. Oshiro, 1970:153, 178. It is well documented that some late-war Japanese fighters, such as the Hayate and the Shidenkai, often could not achieve expected performance, owing to engine and other miscellaneous mechanical problems. When U.S. B-29s were bombing Japan, many of these brand-new fighters were either glued to the ground or took off but soon had to land without engaging in aerial combat, owing to mechanical troubles. After the war, American pilots who test-flew these planes unanimously praised their design and performance features—but they were of little value because of poor manufacture.

interim payments or, for those subcontractors closer to (or bigger than) the customer, advance payments could be made. That is, the balance of power or the degree of closeness between the parties dictated the method of payment.[24]

Career Patterns

The 1930s followed the 1920s pattern of start-ups (see Table 2-5). Between 1932 and 1936, for example, there was a 115 percent increase in the number of machinery firms in Osaka, with 1,424 start-ups, making the total number of firms 2,661. Of these start-ups, 86.5 percent (1,231 firms) were small firms employing fewer than thirty workers (Fujita, 1965:73).

Most of the entrepreneurs at subcontracting firms had at one time worked for other firms in the same industry.[25] With modest severance pay, savings, and loans from relatives, they had started their own businesses, with usually just enough capital to buy minimal facilities (Fujita, 1965:61–62).

Composition of Labor Force

In general, the smaller the subcontractor was, the more it relied on family labor and apprentices (*totei*) rather than full-status workers. The following example concerns the machinery industry in Tokyo and Osaka in the late 1930s.

In 1937, in the four districts (Shinagawa, Toshima, Arakawa, and Joto) in Tokyo where these small firms were concentrated, the breakdown of firms with fewer than 10 workers was—out of a total of 5,601 workers—2,676 workers (47.8 percent), 1,897 apprentices (33.9 percent), 963 family employees (17.1 percent), and 65 "others" (1.2 percent), and the average employment of these firms was 5.1 persons per establishment (Tokyo City, 1937, quoted in Fujita, 1965, Table 8, p. 46).

The Taisho District of Osaka in 1936 shows a similar pattern. The labor composition of 287 subcontractors employing a total of 2,592 people was 1,320 workers (50.9 percent), 956 apprentices (36.9 percent), and 316 family employees (12.2 percent), and the average employment of these firms was 9 persons per establishment.[26] In both Tokyo and Osaka in the late 1930s, approximately half the workers at small firms were family members and apprentices. Table 2-12 shows that small firms employing fewer than 10 persons relied heavily on family members and apprentices.

24. Fujita, 1965:43. Compared with the postwar practice of payment delays of up to six months (or more!), the prewar practice appears rather benign. The severity of the subcontractors' plight due to payment delays in the 1950s persuaded the government to pass the Law on the Prevention of Delay in the Payment of Subcontracting Charges and Related Matters (Shitauke daikin shiharai chien to boshi ho) in 1956.

25. In 1937, in the Taisho District of Osaka, for example, 80.5 percent (231 people) of entrepreneurs at all the 287 machinery factories were found to be ex-workers who had once served in the same machinery industry, followed by 10.5 percent (30 people) who had taken over the family trade (Fujita, 1965:73).

26. Fujita, 1965:69–70. These data contrast with thirty-six independent firms (employing 104 persons on average) in the same district, whose labor composition for a total of 3,759 people was 3,598 workers (95.7 percent), 157 apprentices (4.2 percent), and 4 family employees (0.1 percent) (Table 21, p. 70).

TABLE 2-12. Differences in Labor Composition Among Machinery Subcontractors in the Taisho District, Osaka, 1936

No. of Workers	No. of Factories	Family Members	Apprentices	Regular Workers	Total
Under 5	94	41.6%	41.3%	17.1%	100%
5–9	116	15.2	50.7	34.1	100
10–29	64	7.0	31.1	61.9	100
30–49	12	1.2	21.4	77.4	100
50–99	1	0.0	46.3	53.7	100
Average:	287[a]	12.2	36.9	50.9	100

[a]Total.

Source: Adapted from Fujita, 1965, Table 22, p. 70.

Terminology

The word *shitauke* (subcontracting) began to appear in the 1930s just as subcontracting itself was beginning to be widely used. While the word was being established as a generic term,[27] it also assumed a connotation of "social dumping," in the sense that subcontractors were obliged to sell their products at a cost below what it would be if they paid their employees a decent wage. As part of the government's program to rationalize subcontracting, alternative terms, *kyoryoku kojo* (cooperating factory) and *kyoryoku kogyo* (cooperating industry) were officially recommended in 1941.[28]

The two terminologies have persisted. As I found out during my field research in the 1980s, the interviewees—both major employers and subcontractors—appeared reluctant to use the word *shitauke* formally, though they often used it informally as a term of disparagement. Today, *kyoryoku kojo* or *kyoryoku gaisha/kigyo* (cooperation firms/enterprises) are invariably used on formal occasions.

Discussion

One striking observation of modes of subcontracting during wartime is that there were very few institutional mechanisms to stabilize subcontracting relations. Subcontractors were merely asked to undertake simple processing or parts manufacture in a competitive environment. They were used primarily for short-term instrumental reasons. Prime contractors were not concerned with the long-term mobilization of

27. In December 1939, for example, Kiichiro Toyoda, the founder of the Toyota Motor Corporation, clearly used the word *shitauke kojo* (subcontracting factories) in Toyota's house magazine, *Ryusenkei* (Streamline), (Toyota, 1967:152–53). The 1940 MCI (Ministry of Commerce and Industry) Rationalization Outline of the Machinery and Iron and Steel Industries officially defined subcontracting as "the manufacture or general processing of nonuniversal components specific to the product(s) concerned" (Minato, 1986:66).

28. An MCI notification of November 1941 stated: "The term subcontracting is not appropriate. Henceforward, the so-called subcontracting industry and subcontracting factories, as in the Rationalization Outline of the Machinery and Iron and Steel Industries, are to be called the cooperation industry and cooperation factories." Since then, the word *subcontracting* disappeared from governmental documents until the end of the war. For more discussion of this, see Fujita, 1965:180–195.

subcontractors as an external manufacturing organization. Subcontractors whose skills and machines were primitive were subjugated to market forces. They made few innovations; their products were bad; their delivery performance was unimpressive; and their labor consisted mainly of family labor and apprentices. All this suggests (as the radical dualists have predicted) that these small entities would have been driven out of existence if the observed laissez-faire tendencies of this period had continued. The very fact that there were no harmonious, trusting relations in prewar Japanese subcontracting (in contrast with Dore's description of today's practices) indicates that cultural explanations are not consistent with the facts.

Politics and Prototypes

It is interesting to imagine what the outcome would have been if certain powerful influences had been absent in regard to subcontracting in Japanese manufacturing industries over the last fifty years. Perhaps the situation today would have been quite different if the Japanese government—led by the Ministry of Commerce and Industry (MCI) which later became the Ministry of Munitions[29]—had not intervened and tried to rationalize subcontracting systems between 1940 and 1945.

The five years before Japan was defeated in 1945 were characterized by a desperate struggle to establish an autarkic economy. With the wartime bans and restrictions on imports imposed by both the Japanese and foreign governments and with the accelerating depletion of resources due to Japan's losses in the war, the Japanese were obliged to look inward industrially.

In June 1940, for example, all American machine tool imports, which had accounted for 83.5 percent of all machine tool imports to Japan in 1939, were banned by the U.S. government. German machine tool imports had fallen from 30.9 percent in 1936 to 8.8 percent in 1939 as a result of the outbreak of World War II. Before this, the Japanese government had passed the Machine Tool Manufacturing Business Act in 1938 to encourage domestic machine tool manufacturers to close the expected imports gap. This legislation provided licensees with various tax exemptions and promotional schemes. At first, six large machine tool manufacturers, including Ikegai and Ohkuma, became licensed producers under the act. Toyo Kogyo, Toyoda Machine Tools, and others followed suit, with the number of licensees rising to twenty-one firms with twenty-four factories. The internal supply of machine tools, which in 1935 had been slightly more than 50 percent, increased to 83 percent in 1940 and to 95 percent in 1941 (Hitachi, 1960:3; Toyo Kogyo, 1972:116-17). But because the industrial base of Japanese machine tool manufacturers was rather precarious, much unusable "scrap" was produced, especially by the smaller new entrants (Fujita, 1965:169).

The situation was similar in other industries. Japanese-made military motor vehicles had often been reported to fail at critical moments in Japan's war with China, partly because the Japanese content had been increased in these vehicles, according to the MCI's 1936 recommendations that "unless unavoidable, materials and components for [the manufacture of] motor vehicles should not be imported,

---

29. This organization preceded the postwar Ministry of International Trade and Industry (MITI).

and, after 1938, efforts should be made to use domestic products" (Nissan, 1965:60).

Under these circumstances, the Japanese government finally determined that industry-by-industry measures could no longer resolve those quality problems related, among other things, to components. In December 1940, the MCI issued the Rationalization Outline of the Machinery and Iron and Steel Industries, which was aimed at structuring for the first time the existing "anarchic" state of subcontracting in Japanese manufacturing industries. The issues addressed in the Outline that were directly concerned with subcontracting were twofold: demarcation of production and rationalization of subcontracting institutions.

First, in order to improve quality and close the imports gap, production was to be divided according to the specific expertise needed. In particular, components specialists were to be promoted, and the production of overlapping components by major contractors was to be gradually phased out. Further, major contractors were required to use subcontractors "as much as possible" for those items suitable for subcontracting manufacture or processes.

Second, the idea of designating subcontractors was introduced. Designated subcontractors with good technological expertise and facilities were required to maintain regular and interfunctional relationships with—and to be exclusively dedicated to—particular "parent" contractors in the private sector. The latter, on the other hand, were required to support their subcontractors technically, managerially, and financially and to be responsible for giving them regular orders. When necessary, subcontractors were authorized to amalgamate or run businesses collectively under the guidance of their major contractors and the local authorities concerned. Provision was made for establishing subcontractors' organizations, to be controlled by their prime contractors (thus the origin of the term *kyoryokukai* in today's sense). In order to promote rationalization, local subcontracting industries associations were also to be formed in seven national geographical regions.

The Outline also determined the following:

Production categories and items at each factory were to be approved through its industrial bodies by the MCI.

Items produced by component specialists were to be selected by the MCI, which would take into account the opinions of the industrial bodies concerned.

Designated subcontractors in the private sector were to be selected by the prime contractors concerned, with the MCI's permission.

In principle, the designated subcontractors were supposed to undertake nothing other than their subcontracting jobs, although in certain cases, they could manufacture other products with the permission of the prefecture.

In principle, subcontracting orders were not to be given to those other than the designated subcontractors.

In principle, prime contractors were responsible for directly providing the incumbent subcontractors with all necessary materials.

The number of obligatory subcontracting orders was to be determined when the materials were distributed.

In principle, second-tier (and lower) subcontractors were not permitted. But when indispensable for technological and other reasons, they were required to be designated while at the same time clarifying their relationships to first-tier subcontractors and prime contractors.

Intermediaries such as brokers and wholesale dealers were not permitted.

Finally, inefficient small or medium-sized firms that were unable to keep up with the aforementioned rationalization were to be eliminated (Ministry of Commerce and Industry, 1940, quoted in Minato, 1986:64–68).

The Rationalization Outline marked an important divide between laissez-faire and structured subcontracting. Furthermore, it signified the government's intervention in existing subcontracting practices by introducing restrictions, providing approval, and monitoring oversight through local subcontracting industries associations that army and navy purchasing officers, local authorities' officials, private-sector prime contractors, subcontractors, and academics all joined.

How well was the Outline implemented? Not very well. There still was little coordination between major contractors and subcontractors. Technological gaps between the two remained problematic. Sub-subcontracting continued to be widely practiced.[30] Supposedly "dedicated" subcontractors often switched or served other customers. But the major contractors also switched subcontractors. Because of these frequent switches by both customers and subcontractors, "unfinished products"—which could not be used because they lacked certain components—became a widespread problem (Fujita, 1965:179). In February 1943 an Osaka prefectural official remarked: "It is not unusual for prime contractors to use subcontractors only when they need them and only on the most convenient terms. . . . There was mutual dissatisfaction and both parent and child factories did not behave as their names suggested.[31]

In August 1943 when the war was stalemated, the government took further action to transform the original purpose of the 1940 Outline into the creation of enterprise groups (*kigyo shudan*).[32] In order to concentrate on the mass manufacture of airplanes, the increase of machine tool production was carefully mapped out. In October of the same year, the first enterprise groups, comprising eleven lathe and eight milling machine–manufacturing groups, were established. The institution of enterprise groups soon spread to the aircraft and other industries. Meanwhile, in the same month the Munitions Firm Act was passed. In November 1943, the MCI and the Planning Agency (Kikaku in) merged into the Ministry of Munitions, which took central control of the aircraft industry. The first designation of 150 munitions firms, including Hitachi, Toshiba, Toyota, Nissan, and Toyo Kogyo, which were now to be directly controlled by the Ministry of Munitions, was made in January

30. The MCI's original disapproval in 1940 of secondary or lower subcontracting soon receded. The MCI's November 1941 notification altered its remark on sub-subcontracting from "not permitted" to its "rationalization" (MCI, November 1941, "On the rationalization of the cooperation industry based on the rationalization outline of the machinery and iron & steel industries," quoted in Fujita, 1965:180–81).

31. Fujita, 1965:158. For the prime contractors' distrust of the subcontractors' technical capabilities, see also Tsuru, 1943:204.

32. The idea is proposed in the cabinet's agreement in August 1943 on the urgent measures for machine tools required to increase the production of airplanes. For more details, see Fujita, 1965:162.

1944 (Hitachi, 1960:5; Fujita, 1965:161–63, 186; Nissan, 1965:123; Toyota, 1967:219–20; Toyo Kogyo, 1972:141). The second and third designations came in April and December of the same year, naming 424 and 109 firms (Hitachi, 1960:5). Regardless of their previous production items and expertise, these munitions firms were now ordered to manufacture aircraft components and other armaments.

Following this move, the government rationalized vertical enterprise channels (*kigyo keiretsu*) in 1944.[33] That is, the vertical hierarchy between prime contractors and subcontractors was once again imposed. *Keiretsu* subcontractors (defined as those equipped with more than ten major machines) were required to be as "dedicated" as possible, and they were classified according to the degree to which their production was dedicated. Those with 80 or more percent dependence on a major customer were called *dedicated cooperation factories* (*senzoku kyoryoku kojo*), and those with 30 to 80 percent dependence on a major customer were called *collaborative cooperation factories* (*kyodo kyoryoku kojo*). In 1945 the former numbered 18,910 and the latter 12,404, serving a total of 5,191 designated prime contractors, whose locations extended from Karafuto to Okinawa.[34]

Kyoryokukai, or subcontractors' organizations dedicated to a major customer, became widespread. At Hitachi's Kameari plant, for example, a *kyoryokukai* was established in March 1944, with four divisions—armament, machinery, materials, and special items—and 211 subcontractors—190 in Tokyo and 21 in other prefectures. The association promoted both horizontal and vertical communications. The prime contractor provided the subcontractors—who had an average of 12.5 machines—with assured minimum orders, technical teaching, and machinery on loan (Hitachi, 1960:34–35). These institutions also spread to second-tier (and lower) subcontractors. Designated prime contractors were made "responsible factories" for controlling their own enterprise groups (Fujita, 1965:163, 188; Oshiro, 1970:174–75).

These new institutions had two important effects. First, when subcontractors were dedicated to certain prime contractors, this, by definition, necessitated an extensive transfer of technology from the latter to the former—in the form of technical instruction, jigs, gauges, fixtures and machines on loan, specialization of production, and so on—without which the system would have been meaningless. As a result, the technological level of the subcontractors, which developed specialized expertise, rose.

Second, with the spread of hierarchically structured enterprise groups, or *keiretsu,* a distinctively pyramidal mode of subcontracting appeared. Responsible factories at the peak were assemblers, and subcontractors became components or process specialists. In July 1943, Nobusuke Kishi, Minister of the MCI, commented: "MCI plans to make child factories dedicated to parent firms, and grandchild factories to child firms. Child and grandchild factories must stop manufacturing finished products and must manufacture components principally for their parent factories. Parents and children must share labor management, materials, and capital" (*Nippon Sangyo Keizai,* July 8, 1943, quoted in Fujita, 1965:186–87). Furthermore, the production

---

33. With the Implementation Outline of Rationalizing the Machinery and Other Industries introduced in February 1944.

34. Hosono, 1950:18–19. On average, one prime contractor had six subcontractors.

methodology of enterprise groups was defined as the division of labor "between responsible factories on top and a body of subcontractors in a pyramidal structure [*keiretsu ka*]."[35]

Toward the end of the war, in a desperate struggle to attain economies of scale, a variation of the foregoing strategy was pressed into service: government-promoted subsidiary structuring through merger and amalgamation. This usually took the form of a core firm's (such as Hitachi or Toshiba) buying out existing medium-sized firms (usually subcontractors) and making them dedicated subsidiaries. In so doing it was hoped that the managerial, capital, and technological transfer would be further expedited. As a result of this government policy, the number of Toshiba's subsidiaries, for example, had reached 104 at the end of the war (Toshiba, 1963:129–33, 1977:51–52). Similarly, Hitachi had 53 subsidiaries when it had to dissolve them after the war (Hitachi, 1960:112).

The situation in Japan near the end of the war—characterized by mutilated transportation systems, severe shortages of materials and skilled labor, long but unproductive working hours, geographical dispersion of factories, scarce resources, incessant bombing by U.S. B-29s—all made it impossible for any system or institution to work. It took the defeat, the subsequent socioeconomic turmoil, and the leap in demand after the outbreak of the Korean War for the Japanese to find new uses for the remains of their wartime institutions. These institutions had virtually eliminated such features of earlier periods as subcontracting brokers and wholesale dealers and had replaced laissez-faire with structured subcontracting mechanisms. Like the rise of the internal labor markets in the 1920s, the rise of subcontracting institutions in Japan in wartime, necessitated by the demand for munitions, clearly marked a prototype, a framework, a mold, from which the new model of the postwar Japanese subcontracting would be formed. What had seemed to die out—the product of an anachronistic struggle—reappeared in a new guise, making perfect economic sense in a fundamentally changed postwar environment.

Summary and Conclusions

This chapter traced the origins of dualism and the evolution of subcontracting in Japanese manufacturing industries from 1900 to 1945. We found that earlier in this century neither dualism nor subcontracting was an essential feature of the Japanese economy. Labor markets were fluid, and interscale wage differentials were minimal. The period after World War I saw the rise of the internal labor markets in large Japanese firms and the heavy utilization of temporary workers. But subcontracting was still not widely practiced. It was primarily the dramatic increase of munitions demand from the late 1930s through the end of World War II that led subcontracting to emerge in the Japanese economy, building on various socioeconomic and technological factors that laid the groundwork for such a move. Politics also played a part. To advance the war effort, the Japanese government promoted "dedicated"

35. *Nippon Sangyo Keizai*, September 23, 1943, quoted in Fujita, 1965:187. Evidence of the extent to which the government's 1944 subcontracting reshuffle was implemented is, unfortunately, scarce owing to the devastation of the war (p. 163).

subcontracting institutions by means of coercive measures, though this had little effect, and the irregular subcontracting practices persisted. There was no harmony, no trust. Ultimately the war paralyzed the national economy, which made it impossible for any institution to work.

What are the implications of these historical facts? The Japanese, whose economy relies heavily on subcontracting systems today, did not have similar arrangements earlier in this century, and so it appears that there is no national predisposition that accounts for particular forms of subcontracting. Rather, socioeconomic conditions (e.g., widening interscale wage differentials, the increase in small firms, a sudden demand surge) and technological and infrastructural factors (e.g., subcontractors in possession of lathes, the spread of electric power, the expansion of national transportation and communication systems) were crucial to the emergence and prevalence of subcontracting practices. Furthermore, politics did matter. Despite its questionable efficacy, the strong wartime government intervention structured the previously laissez-faire subcontracting practices and provided an institutional framework from which postwar subcontracting mechanisms later developed. This chapter, therefore, supports the claim that the major determinants of subcontracting organization lie chiefly in the domain of socioeconomic, technological, infrastructural, and political factors and not necessarily in the economic agents' cultural attributes.

3

The Emergence
of Postwar Subcontracting,
1945–1960

The following two chapters will cover the forty-five years after World War II in Japan, a time that may be described as epoch making, because it produced a profusion of new subcontracting institutions in Japanese manufacturing industries. The institutions rapidly evolved, building on one form after another and constantly adapting to radical external changes. The end result is something beyond what traditional accounts usually discuss.

Until the late 1950s, there were, on the whole, few events that could not be explained in conventional dualist terms. By contrast, developments in the high-growth 1960s and later require—I shall argue—a new framework of industrial sourcing, for it is during this period that subcontracting relations in Japanese manufacturing industries underwent a major transformation.

Postwar Turmoil

The end of World War II marked a fundamental break in the Japanese economy. The demand for munitions abruptly disappeared, and the facilities producing munitions were in ruins. Although 44 percent of Japan's territory, including Korea and Taiwan, was lost along with the investments in them, there was a huge influx of demobilized soldiers returning to mainland Japan.[1] This shift of territory and population had two effects: First, there was a sharp decline in, or more precisely a paralysis of, the nation's manufacturing capacity, which dropped below, temporarily at least, 10 percent of the 1935–37 average when the war ended (Hitachi, 1960:119). Second, what was more problematic was the enormous scarcity of basic materials, including food and clothing, due to the substantial loss of natural and manufactured resources.[2]

1. Nissan, 1965:137. Over two years after the war, more than 6 million people returned from abroad, adding to the 72 million people already in mainland Japan in 1945 (Toyota, 1967:233).

2. Compared with the 1934–36 average of 100, 1945 production indices for commodities were 66.5 for rice, 58.0 for coal, 44.5 for marine products, 35.6 for iron and steel, 12.8 for raw silk, 4.2 for cotton yarn, and 1.4 for cotton textiles (Nissan, 1965:137).

In September 1945 the supreme commander for the Allied Powers (SCAP) ordered the Japanese government to promote the production of basic commodities, thereby making way for the war-shattered munitions manufacturers to shift to non-military manufacturing (Nissan, 1965:137). Using whatever leftover materials and facilities were available, manufacturers—small and large alike—started to produce the necessities of everyday life, though production was limited owing to the lack of raw materials, capital, electric power, and food.[3] There was also a good deal of business uncertainty while SCAP was trying to make up its mind how far, in the interest of equality and competition, it would proceed in breaking up the *zaibatsu* (prewar industrial cliques). This meant that the wartime subcontracting institutions—that the government had used for armament production under the *keiretsu* arrangement—were no longer functional. Manufacturing activities went back to a state of laissez-faire (Ito, 1957:107, 231, 264; Mitsubishi Heavy Industries, 1967a:96).[4]

Among the many things that happened within a decade after the war, of particular importance to us are the rise of enterprise unions, the Dodge Plan and the resulting labor strife, the influence of the Korean War boom, and the subsequent widening interscale wage differentials and decline in union membership.

Unionism

The two important characteristics of Japanese unions after the war were the heavy legislative protection and the rise of firm-specific unions to which both blue-collar workers and white-collar staff belonged, as employees.

First, unlike their prewar predecessors, which were crushed by the government after the Sino-Japanese War,[5] the unions after World War II were heavily protected by a series of labor laws. In December 1945 the first Labor Union Law in Japan (amended in 1949) was passed, guaranteeing workers (including government em-

3. For more details on the difficulty in production in the immediate postwar period, see Nissan, 1965:156–60; Hitachi, 1960:120–21; Nippondenso, 1984:13, 15.

4. "In the immediate postwar period when large firms were still rebuilding their production facilities and preparing for a new start, small firms flourished by quickly fulfilling people's demands for consumers' goods. They shrewdly got round economic control, took advantage of the black market and inflation, and produced commodities using leftover or locally produced materials" (Nakamura, Hideichiro, et al., 1981:14).

5. Sumiya, 1966:179–87. Although it goes beyond the scope of this book, labor movements in prewar Japan are an interesting issue, particularly in view of the wartime government's political and economic needs. Furthermore, prewar unionism was characterized by low density (a peak of 7.9 percent in 1931 at best), volatility of unions and union memberships (unions and union members were visible only when they disagreed), the small numbers participating in disputes (37.4 percent of the disputes in 1932 were fought by fifteen or fewer workers per dispute), lack of labor legislation (the right of collective bargaining, if any, was a product of individual agreements between individual firms and individual unions), and the rise and diffusion of enterprise organizations such as works councils (*kojo iinkai*) in large firms, which functioned more like communication gatherings (*kondan kai*) than unions. For these and other historical accounts of Japanese labor movements since the late nineteenth century up to the end of World War II, see Sumiya, 1966:3–187, and for more specific arguments on prewar works councils, see Totten, 1967:216–33; and Hyodo, 1971:367–403.

ployees[6] except for policemen and firemen) the rights of organizing, collective bargaining, and striking. Article 28 of the Constitution, enacted in 1946, also guaranteed to workers these three basic rights. And in 1947 came more labor-related legislation.[7] Together, these labor laws gave Japanese workers unprecedented protection, even compared with that of other industrial societies (Shirai, 1988:55).

Released from wartime oppression and supported by labor legislation, there was an explosion of new unions immediately after war, so that by the end of 1945 there were 507 unions and 380,000 union members nationwide, already reaching the prewar levels. Following the enactment of the Labor Union Law in December 1945, the number of unions totaled more than 10,000, with 3.3 million members within the first six months of 1946. By June 1946, 40 percent of Japan's workers had joined unions, with the majority of employees in large firms belonging. The unionization boom expanded to small firms, and by the end of 1947 there were 28,000 unions and 6.27 million union members, or 51 percent belonging to unions. This rapid pace of unionization within such a short period is perhaps unprecedented. (Sumiya, 1966:190–91).

A second important feature of Japan's postwar unionism is the extensive diffusion of enterprise unions and their stable and monolithic membership.[8] The prewar

6. In 1948, SCAP deprived government employees of their right to strike, as a result of changes in its labor policies (Nakamura, Takafusa, 1981:40).

7. Namely, the Law on the Regulation of Labor Relations (Rodo kankei chosei ho), which regulated procedural rules for strikes, the Labor Standards Law (Rodo kijun ho), which set the standards for working conditions, the Occupational Stabilization Law (Shokugyo antei ho), the Unemployment Insurance Law (Shitsugyo hoken ho), and the Law on Compensation Insurance for Workers' Accidents (Rodosha saigai hosho hoken ho) (Shirai, 1988:53–54).

8. Japanese enterprise unions, such as they are, are a product, both qualitatively and quantitatively, of the postwar period. The prewar enterprise unions were nothing more than management's pawns deprived of the right of collective bargaining and strike (Sumiya, 1966:168). They were found primarily in the public sector and the large-scale private sector and were rarely involved in industrial disputes, which took place mainly in the small sector of the economy (Sumiya, 1966:155–57, 165–68). Moreover, the density of prewar enterprise unions—in terms of both the number of unions and the size of the union memberships—was fairly low compared with their postwar counterparts (see Table 3-F1).

TABLE 3-F1. Enterprise Unions, 1926–30 and 1947–75

Year	No. of Enterprise Unions		No. of Enterprise Union Members	
1926	85	(17.4%)[a]	116,663	(41.0%)[a]
1927	77	(15.2)	108,302	(35.0)
1928	88	(17.6)	121,197	(39.2)
1929	101	(16.0)	128,132	(38.7)
1930	116	(16.3)	127,463	(36.0)
1947	24,655	(88.0)	5,119,690	(81.7)
1948	30,683	(90.4)	5,498,165	(82.3)
1962	42,984	(89.9)	7,547,616	(85.9)
1964	48,386	(94.0)	8,819,041	(91.4)
1975	65,337	(94.2)	11,361,378	(91.1)

[a]Density as a percentage of the total number of trade unions or trade union members.

Source: Labor Minister's Office, Statistics and Information Bureau, 1978:88–89, 118–19.

The extensive and stable state of enterprise unions throughout the postwar period is impressive, as is the disparity in absolute numbers of unions and union memberships between the prewar and postwar periods.

distinction between the white-collar staff (*shokuin*) and blue-collar workers (*koin*) in the same firm was largely abolished a few years after the war.[9] Now both were called employees (*shain* or *jugyoin*). Blue-collar workers now received—as their white-collar colleagues did—monthly salaries instead of daily or weekly wages. Union membership was defined as a monolithic status. All regular employees— irrespective of their "trades" and excluding those at the level of section managers (*kacho*) or above—became union members unless otherwise specified.

These two features of Japan's postwar unionism had two important implications for the later development of its subcontracting systems. First, because the unions were so well protected, management no longer could arbitrarily fire their employees, for fear of being accused of unfair labor practices.[10] This in turn greatly limited management's freedom to move around or lay off employees. Therefore, it seemed only logical to have buffer labor resources—either temporary workers or subcontractors—that could be used and discharged without infringing on their rights.

Second, the rise of firm-specific unions and companywide membership in them marked a significant departure from the traditional demarcation of interests—or, if you will, classes.[11] The unification of different types of staff and workers under one roof as one entity (i.e., employees) and their relatively equal treatment in terms of working conditions,[12] payment methods and scales, fringe benefits, and so on had a tremendous impact on the unions' conduct. Moreover, these so-called enterprise unions were greatly influenced by such institutional arrangements as bonus schemes based on the firm's performance or a pay cut for the directors (not for the employees, at least initially) in case of poor business results, which was then used by management as a bargaining tool in asking for concessions by the union. These arrangements encouraged a mutual sharing of interests, rather than a disorderly skirmish, between management and employees. For employees, the traditional "them"—in a Western sense—came to mean, institutionally, either their outside competitors or, more broadly, any entities outside the firm. For employees, "us" came to mean everybody in the firm, including management. Enterprise unions provided mechanisms that encouraged interfirm competition in business perfor-

9. Until the end of the war there was generally a clear demarcation of *shokuin* and *koin* (or the more archaic term, *shokko*) in Japanese firms. They were treated differently in terms of payment, working conditions, and fringe benefits. The distinction between the two was abolished, for example, at Toyota and Nissan in 1946 and at Hitachi in 1947 (Nissan, 1965:163; Toyota, 1967:262–63; Okamoto, 1979a:93–94).

10. Article 7 of the Labor Union Law forbids employers to violate workers' right of organization to defend against unfair labor practices. The latter concept was borrowed from the U.S. National Labor Relations Act of 1935 (Shirai, 1968:54–55). Before the war, workers could be fired at the employer's discretion if they accused the firm of unfair labor practices. For more information on the prewar practices, see Sumiya, 1966:3–187.

11. It is debatable if the "them versus us" feeling common in the West ever existed in Japan with the same force. But surely the prewar differential treatment of *shokuin* and *koin* in the same firm influenced their perception of hierarchical order within the firm. Among the common slogans of the unions' early postwar struggle was the "abolishment of *mibun sei* (social status)" in the firm. See, for example, Okamoto, 1979a:92–96.

12. Koike (1983:31) demonstrates that today the wage increase curve of Japanese blue-collar workers is similar to that of the white-collar staff.

mance: More work and better performance in our firm will bring more pay and bonuses for us.[13] In contrast, the idea of the interfirm unification of the "working class," especially between the unionized and nonunionized sectors, nearly disappeared.[14] It is debatable whether management designed these mechanisms with a view to the future.[15] But later, the large firms found it extremely convenient to use small subcontracting firms, which were generally not unionized after the 1949–50 recession. Insofar as their jobs were secure, union members had no reason to sympathize with those in the nonunionized sector.

Thus the protection of the unions and the interfirm demarcation of interests along the lines of enterprise unions provided the conditions for the postwar development of subcontracting. Before management would use subcontracting as one of its principal strategies, it took the fierce labor strife after the Dodge Plan and the subsequent Korean War boom that put the existing institutions in turmoil.

The Impact of the Dodge Plan

With the deepening cold war, American policy toward Japan changed quickly. In October 1948 the U.S. National Security Council adopted Resolution 13/2 regard-

13. This by no means indicates that enterprise unions were—as in the prewar period—merely management's pawns. Labor legislation provided a legal framework through which postwar enterprise unions collectively bargained for a fair distribution of profits within the firm. In fact, the five years or so after the Labor Union Law was passed were filled with disputes by enterprise unions trying to establish new rules for the fair distribution of power, prerogatives, and profits within the firm.

14. For the first several yeas after the war, the "class struggle" principle was largely adopted by labor movements nationwide. But it soon receded with the diffusion of enterprise unions and was killed in the 1949–50 recession. The focus of national labor movements then shifted to a more pragmatic arena, from which an important macroeconomic regulatory mechanism, the *shunto* or the spring offensive, was devised.

15. One could argue, as radicals such as Edwards (1979) certainly would, that Japanese postwar enterprise unionism was a deliberate creation of the managements of core firms with the intention of, on the one hand, molding the regular work force to their own ends and, on the other hand, breaking up the "working class" in general. This contention, however, meets two technical difficulties in providing convincing empirical support for the postwar Japanese situation.

First, enterprise unionism in Japan appeared as soon as the unions were liberalized, in the immediate postwar period, when labor was the strongest. As Table 3-F1 shows, enterprise unions and union memberships accounted for 90.4 and 82.3 percent, respectively, of all trade unions and their members as early as 1948. This suggests that labor chose enterprise unionism. Shirai (1983:121–24), for example, provides explanations consistent with this view.

Second, my survey of the forty largest Japanese automotive and electronics manufacturers in 1986 revealed that only a few respondents chose "dividing up the work force" among their firm and their subcontractors as a reason for subcontracting out, and more intriguingly, they did not seem to understand what this meant. This fact was further confirmed in my interviews with the purchasing and personnel managers of six of the responding firms, in which they reported difficulties in understanding—and therefore asked for an explanation of—the meaning of that answer. After I gave them a full account of the radical view that the managements of core firms used subcontractors so as to prevent the working class from uniting, they still remained puzzled. A high-ranking purchasing manager of Fuji Electric commented: "The radical view is intriguing. But I don't think we deliberately created the mechanism [of enterprise unionism]. The truth is that long before we started to use subcontractors extensively, workers had divided themselves [between unionized and nonunionized sectors along the border of enterprise unionism]" (based on my interview with A. Kubota, general manager, Purchasing Department, Fuji Electric, March 6, 1986). This will be further discussed in Appendix B.

ing Japan, which stated that Japan's economic recovery using its own resources would be expedited so as to create a "bulwark against Communism" (Nakamura, Takafusa, 1981:35, 38; Toyota, 1967:287).

In February 1949 Joseph Dodge came to Japan with the ministerial rank of financial adviser to General Douglas MacArthur. Using classical monetarist ideas, he advanced three basic policies consisting of a balanced budget, the suspension of new loans from the Reconstruction Bank, and the reduction and/or abolition of subsidies to Japan. His deflationary policies—known as the Dodge Plan—were immediately implemented by the Occupation forces (Nakamura, Takafusa, 1981:37–39; Nissan, 1983:82; Toyota, 1967:287–89).

The Dodge Plan had a great impact. The suspension of loans from the Reconstruction Bank paralyzed many firms' cash flow, and delays in retrieving sales credits became a matter of everyday life. Between February 1949 and March 1950 there were more than 1,100 bankruptcies and more than 510,000 redundancies (Toyota, 1967:289). The unions fought back, but there was little that they could do to stop the trend.[16]

The management "victory" during this period produced a new equilibrium of power, and the five-year postwar turbulence in Japanese industrial relations came to a halt (albeit temporary).[17] Management's successful fight for incontestable discretion in areas of "management rights" was often reflected in the clauses of new labor–management agreements that emerged after the settlement of disputes.[18] But the Dodge Plan was soon superseded by the Korean War, which heralded a new era for Japanese industry.

The Korean War Boom and After

It is ironic that on the heels of a multitude of redundancies, the Korean War broke out on June 25, 1950. The demand for munitions for the United Nations forces skyrocketed, and with it came an economic boom to Japan. Japanese industry, which was close to dying, owing to the difficult demands of the Dodge Plan, experienced an immediate rejuvenation. The large new demand invigorated production, with the 1950 production index of the mining and manufacturing industries outperforming the prewar level of 1934–36 (*Economic White Paper, 1956*, quoted in Ito, 1957:160; also see Hitachi, 1960:134).

The boom started with the munitions procurement. Toyota, Nissan, and Isuzu received a total order of 11,920 military trucks (Nissan, 1965:226), accounting for approximately one-eighth of the total munitions procurement of $222 million in

16. Various sources describe the ferocity of the 1949–50 labor strife in Japan. For example, see Hitachi, 1960:132–33; Nissan, 1965:213–15; Toyota, 1967:293–302; and Okamoto, 1979a:100–13.

17. In this reshuffle, left-wing activists, particularly Communists, were openly dismissed, similar to the Red Purge, which helped reshape later industrial relations in Japan (Nakamura, Takafusa, 1981:40). I am grateful for Prof. Ronald Dore's comment that this point should be stressed here, as the composition of the labor force after the 1949–50 strife was so different from that of the immediate postwar period.

18. For example, Hitachi's new labor–management agreement of March 1951 emphasized the reestablishment of management's prerogatives to control business affairs and personnel administration. A Hitachi union leader remarked: "When the 1951 new labor agreement was reached, there remained few things inconvenient for management" (Okamoto, 1979a:111–13).

TABLE 3-1. Economic Indicators, 1949–56

(1949 = 100)

Year	Mining and Manufacturing Production	Consumer Price	Nominal Wage for Manufacturing Industries	Real Wage for Manufacturing Industries
1949	100.0	100.0	100.0	100.0
1950	122.5	93.1	121.5	130.5
1951	169.2	108.4	155.9	143.9
1952	181.3	113.8	183.4	161.2
1953	221.4	121.2	205.7	169.7
1954	240.1	129.1	216.6	167.8
1955	258.2	127.7	225.1	176.5
1956	315.9	128.1	261.0	191.9

Source: Adapted from Nakamura, Takafusa, 1981:42. Original Sources: Production indices from Ministry of International Trade and Industry; consumer price indices from Prime Minister's Office, Statistics Bureau; wage indices from Ministry of Labor.

Japan between the outbreak of World War II and June 1951 (Nissan, 1983:83). The iron and steel, heavy machinery, and electric power industries benefited from the enormous ripple effects. Aggressive investments in various industries for facilities, technologies, and innovations followed. Productivity increased. With the domestic market thus invigorated through capital goods production, the heavy chemical and machinery industries became the core of the postwar Japanese economy (Hitachi, 1960:134).

As firms' earnings and productivity rose, their employees also profited. Table 3-1 shows the 1949–56 indices of production for the mining and manufacturing industries, consumer prices, and nominal and real wages for the manufacturing industries. Wages for employees of manufacturing industries relative to consumer prices showed a steady and sizable increase. The workers as consumers now had considerable purchasing power, and a large part of their disposable income was spent on household goods, including electrical appliances.

There was a boom in radio sales in the early 1950s. Then, beginning around 1953, came an "electrification" boom (*denka bumu*). A substantial new market was now waiting for electrical appliances such as fans, refrigerators, washing machines, and television sets. Recognizing the great opportunity, traditional manufacturers of heavy electrical equipment, like Toshiba, Hitachi, and Mitsubishi Electric, hurriedly joined an array of consumer appliance firms such as Matsushita Electric and Sanyo. The growth of the consumer electrical appliances industry was apparent by the mid-1950s (Okamoto, 1979a:64–66, 218–19).

The expanding demand necessitated expanding capacity, and it was from the mid-1950s onward that electrical manufacturers began to set up mass production facilities of their own or subsidiaries dedicated to the assembly of major household appliances (Suitsu, 1979:63–64). Supply did not, however, catch up with demand. As in the late 1930s, the major electrical manufacturers also expanded their subcontracting base. In the mid-1960s, the automotive manufacturers followed suit in response to a rising demand for private-use passenger cars (as opposed to commercial vehicles such as taxis and trucks).

Before delving further into industry-specific examinations, however, we should look at differentiation in wages and unionization. According to a dualist formula, it should be cheaper to subcontract out, and subcontractors should, preferably, be nonunionized so as to avoid the strictures of the labor agreements. As we shall see, the rapid development of Japanese subcontracting after 1950 can in large part be attributed to and was enabled by the changing socioeconomic conditions. In addition, technology facilitated the connections between large and small firms.

Changing Socioeconomic Conditions

The aftermath of the 1949–50 labor strife had two significant effects on the development of subcontracting systems: The interscale wage differentials widened, and the number of union members declined, particularly in the small manufacturing sector.

Although the postwar turmoil produced little tangible evidence, one observer reports that not only were there few interscale wage differentials in the immediate postwar period but some wage differentials were even reversed (i.e., better earnings for small entities), owing to the small firms' maneuverability in the black market (Ito, 1957:60, 107, 217). The earlier state of wage differentials began to be restored around 1948 and persisted after the 1949–50 disputes (Ito, 1957:60). Table 3-2 shows the steadily widening interscale wage differentials between 1950 and 1955. Following the precedent of the 1920s and 1930s, there was a resurgence of wage disparity in the economy, which provided a great incentive for large firms to use small subcontractors. Thus the first condition of reducing manufacturing costs through subcontracting was met in a macroeconomic context.

The second condition of unionization, union density, is analyzed in Table 3-3. Union density steadily declined after peaking in 1949, from 56 percent in that year down to 32 percent in 1960. Union density refers to the percentage of union members in the total population of employees. If the total number of employees remains constant, a decline in this figure means a relative increase in the nonunionized sector. In fact, the total number of employees jumped from 12.5 million to 23.8 million between 1950 and 1960 (Labor Minister's Office, Statistics and Information Bureau, 1978:31, 42). Therefore, the expansion of the nonunionized sec-

TABLE 3-2. Interscale Wage Differentials (in cash) in Manufacturing Industries, 1950–55

(500 or more = 100)

Year	No. of Employees per Establishment		
	500 or More	100–499	30–99
1950	100.0	83.1	67.3
1951	100.0	79.5	61.3
1952	100.0	79.1	58.8
1953	100.0	79.3	59.8
1954	100.0	77.8	60.0
1955	100.0	74.3	58.8

Source: Nakamura, Hideichiro, et al., 1981:74. Original Source: Ministry of Labor, *Maitsuki kinro tokei chosa* (Monthly statistical survey of labor).

TABLE 3-3. Union Density, 1946–60

(As of June of each year)

Year	Percent
1946	39.5%
1947	45.3
1948	53.0
1949	55.8
1950	46.2
1951	42.6
1952	40.3
1953	36.3
1954	35.5
1955	35.6
1956	33.5
1957	33.6
1958	32.7
1959	32.1
1960	32.2

Source: Labor Minister's Office, Statistics and Information Bureau, 1978:31, 42.

tor—an inverse of the decline of union density—was larger in absolute terms for the period than Table 3-3 indicates. Did the drop in unionism occur evenly in various sectors of the economy? If not, which sectors of the economy became more nonunionized? Table 3-4 provides some of the answers.

Between 1948 and 1956, total union membership in all industries fell by 4.9 percent, from 6,677,427 to 6,350,357 (Labor Minister's Office, Statistics and Research Bureau, 1978:50). As Table 3-4 shows, union membership of manufacturing industries decreased by 9.9 percent during the same period. Therefore, manufacturing industries had more of a decline in union membership than the average. The distribution of union membership by size, however, fundamentally changed for the

TABLE 3-4. Distribution of Union Members According to Size of Manufacturing Industry, 1948 and 1956

	No. of Union Members			
Size[a]	1948		1956	
1,000 or more	781,503	(35.5%)	1,233,056	(62.2%)
500–999	359,996	(16.4)	189,013	(9.5)
100–499	700,344	(31.8)	379,155	(19.1)
99 or less	357,935	(16.3)	179,717	(9.1)
Total:	2,199,778	(100.0)	1,980,941	(100.0)[b]

[a]Refers to the number of union members per union in 1948 and the number of employees per firm in 1956. Owing to the high density of enterprise union memberships (82.3 percent of all trade union members in 1948) and the immediate postwar practice of including entry-level managers (*kacho* and sometimes even *bucho*) as union members (whose presence was significant), the 1948 definition of size is very close to that of 1956 and will suffice for comparison.

[b]This total is actually 99.9 but has been rounded off.

Sources: Constructed from Ministry of Labor, Labor Statistics and Research Bureau, 1948:26–27; Labor Minister's Office, Labor Statistics and Research Bureau, 1957b:274.

manufacturing industries. In all firms with fewer than one thousand employees, union membership fell by half between 1948 and 1956 in both number and percentage,[19] whereas it nearly doubled in those with one thousand or more employees. This disparity in unionization between small and large firms came to be structurally defined in manufacturing industries and must also have given large firms a considerable incentive to subcontract out to the nonunionized, small sector. The second condition of nonunionized subcontractors was thus met.

The State of Technology

In addition to these two socioeconomic conditions, the third factor that facilitated the rapid expansion of subcontracting after the 1950s is technological. Much of the old equipment that the large firms replaced found its second home at small firms during this period, and Table 3-5 shows the 1954–59 national data on the purchase rate of used equipment in fixed investments, by size of firm.

There is a distinctive hierarchy by size of firm in equipment investment patterns. This period was marked by the leading manufacturers' aggressive investments in new equipment and facilities for mass production. At the same time, large firms disposed of their old equipment dating from the war, which is reflected in their low expenditures on used machinery. These figures are based on the purchase value of used machines in the overall fixed investment. In general, secondhand equipment depreciates very rapidly even if its capability remains constant. Therefore, even though the purchase value of this secondhand equipment was around 40 percent for the smallest sector, it nonetheless made up around 70 to 80 percent of the actual equipment used (Shinohara, 1961:127). More important, there was a substantial market in Japan for these discarded machines. Put differently, there was a macrostructural incentive for entrepreneurs with little capital to start or expand their

19. The reader may wonder whether the overall employment size of the small sector itself decreased much during the same period, which may well account for the small-sector decline in unionization: See Table 3-F2.

TABLE 3-F2. Percentage Increase in Number of Employees According to Size of Firm, 1952–55

No. of Employees per Establishment	Percent
1,000 or more	0.2%
200–999	15.3
30–199	22.7
4–29	16.3
3 or less	14.9
Total:	14.6

Source: Labor Minister's Office, Labor Statistics and Research Bureau, 1957b:72. Original Source: Ministry of International Trade and Industry, *Kogyo tokei hyo* (Census of manufacturing).

Clearly, the employment size of the small sector did not decrease; in fact, for all firms with fewer than 999 employees, it increased, and that of firms employing 1,000 or more remained constant.

TABLE 3-5. Purchase Rate of Used Equipment in Fixed Investments, by Size of Firm, 1954–59

No. of Employees per Firm	1954	1955	1956	1957	1958	1959
4–9	48.8%	40.2%	34.3%	41.0%	—	—
10–19	44.1	40.8	29.9	35.0	—	—
20–29	39.5	34.3	28.7	30.5	—	—
30–49	35.0	28.9	26.1	26.4	26.5	20.5
50–99	31.5	22.0	22.3	22.1	20.9	17.1
100–99	23.0	16.3	16.8	15.2	13.8	12.8
200–99	15.2	9.1	9.9	9.3	10.0	9.5
300–499	13.9	10.1	9.1	7.4	7.6	7.6
500–999	11.2	5.2	4.2	4.6	6.3	9.6
1,000 or more	4.6	4.1	4.9	3.3	3.1	4.1
Average	18.3	14.3	12.3	10.9	—	—
30 or more	—	—	9.7	8.2	8.2	8.4

Source: Shinohara, 1961:127. Original Source: Ministry of International Trade and Industry, Statistics and Research Bureau, *Kogyo tokei hyo* (Census of manufacturing).

operations by purchasing and using secondhand machines. These machines reflected the state-of-the-art technology of just a decade or so earlier. Whether or not entrepreneurs bought used machines from their customers directly[20] or from the general market, the technological base of Japanese subcontractors developed in a complementary fashion.

The Postwar Rise of Subcontracting Systems

Electrical Appliances Subcontracting

Following the "electrification" boom beginning in the early 1950s, most of the electrical appliances firms, seeing great opportunities, adopted a strategy of "full product lines" (*zenten kyokyu*) and fiercely competed for a larger share for each item (Suitsu, 1979:62). By 1957 Hitachi, Toshiba, and Mitsubishi had plunged into the consumer electrical appliances market; in 1958 Hitachi had more than ten thousand products of its own. The traditional appliances manufacturers were not far behind. Between 1950 and 1959 the number of Matsushita Electric's product divisions jumped from three to eighteen responsible for radios, television sets, electric fans, refrigerators, washing machines, rice cookers, stoves, heaters, lights, torches, batteries, special-purpose light bulbs, storage batteries, distributors, tubes, components, and electrical machinery.[21] Because of this great competition, the multiplica-

20. In this connection it is interesting that in its third postwar disposal of old machines between 1956 and 1957, Toyo Kogyo (later Mazda) preferred selling them to its suppliers and subcontractors (Toyo Kogyo, 1972:281).

21. Suitsu, 1979:62, 68. As early as 1933, Matsushita Electric established a multidivisional structure for each of its product lines, consisting of three divisions of radios, lights and batteries, and wiring

TABLE 3-6. Years of Subcontractors' Business with Matsushita Electric, 1961

No. of Years of Business	No. of Subcontractors	Percent
5 or fewer	329	57.6%
6–10	127	22.2
11–20	59	10.3
21 or more	10	1.8
Unknown	46	8.1
Total:	571	100.0

Note: Errors in the original calculation have been corrected.

Source: Suitsu, 1979:70. Original Source: Osaka Prefectural Research Institute of Commerce, Industry and Economy, 1961b:10.

tion of products, and the macroeconomic change, electrical appliance firms began to use subcontractors extensively.

Between 1950 and 1960, the volume of materials that Hitachi bought increased sevenfold, and the number of its subcontractors doubled. The subcontractors formed associations (*kyoryokukai*) and/or cooperatives (*kyodo kumiai*) and began systematically to serve Hitachi (Hitachi, 1960:147). Toshiba also subcontracted out various processes in this decade (Suitsu, 1979:63–64), but Matsushita Electric subcontracted out even more extensively, as illustrated in Table 3-6. Matsushita increased by five times the number of its subcontractors during the 1950s, and moreover, nearly 60 percent of them started working with Matsushita only in the latter half of the decade. In terms of the value of shipments from its subcontractors, an increase of 82.8 percent—from ¥1,722 million to ¥3,147 million—was recorded in the two years between 1958 and 1960 (Suitsu, 1979:70).

Table 3-7 shows that in the Kansai region—where Matsushita, Sanyo, and Hayakawa (later Sharp) are based—there was a steady rise in purchasing and subcontracting shares for *jakuden* (electronics, electrical appliances, and communication equipment) between 1955 and 1959.

Most of the subcontracted jobs during this period required only general-purpose technologies and low asset specificity, such as simple processing and simple parts manufacture (e.g., machining, milling, stamping, molding, painting, plating, welding, heat treatment, wiring, casting, die making, nuts, coils and springs, metal parts, wood, rubber and paper products, other various parts, components, and attachments).[22] It was not until the 1960s that closer and longer-term subcontracting relations supported by high asset specificity resulted from distinctive producer strategies.

As subcontracting grew in the Japanese electrical appliances and other industries in the 1950s, its harsher side also became apparent, primarily in lower prices and

---

equipment and heaters. This compares with Westinghouse's adoption of a multidivisional structure in 1935 (Okamoto, 1979a:42). The number of Matsushita's divisions later increased to forty-six in 1969 and fifty-one in 1977 (Suitsu, 1979:68).

22. For a comprehensive list of items that Matsushita subcontracted out during this period, see Suitsu, 1979:65–66.

TABLE 3-7. Percentages of Output by Electrical Suppliers
and Subcontractors for Electronics, Electrical Appliances,
and Communication Equipment, 1955–59

Year	By Suppliers of Products and Parts	By Subcontractors
1955	59.9%	62.3%
1956	58.3	65.8
1957	59.3	72.1
1958	66.5	80.8
1959	70.0	84.3

Source: Suitsu, 1979:74. Original Source: Osaka Prefectural Research Institute of
Commerce, Industry and Economy, 1961a:91.

deferred payments. And this is where the government eventually intervened with a
series of laws, including the Law on the Prevention of Delay in the Payment of
Subcontracting Charges and Related Matters.

In order to survive in such a competitive market, prime contractors often unilaterally required low prices from their subcontractors, and they generally got them.
Likewise, a multiple sourcing strategy—which Matsushita, for example, adopted in
the 1950s—strengthened the prime contractors' bargaining power over price (Suitsu, 1979:75). In 1959, of 209 subcontractors serving 5 oligopolistic electrical prime
contractors, 130 (62.2 percent) were asked to lower their prices, and 110 (52.6%
percent) agreed.[23]

The practice of delaying payments to subcontractors—which started in many
industries in the midst of the 1949 recession so as to avoid capital flow problems—
became widespread, as if it were the prime contractors' legitimate right (Ito,
1957:269). The investigation by the Small and Medium Enterprise Agency (Chusho
kigyo cho, or SMEA) shows, for example, that the longest after-due days for bills
issued between 1959 and 1962 were 180 days for electrical equipment, 190 for
motor vehicles, 200 for printing and publishing, and 240 for textiles and spinning
and weaving equipment (Fujita, 1965:311–12).

In order to cope with these pricing and payment problems and also to pass on
part of the burden arising from these fluctuations, the first-tier subcontractors divided their jobs into segments and assigned the simple, messier, and more labor-
intensive tasks to the second-tier subcontractors. In so doing, the first-tier subcontractors managed to earn a small profit, owing to the widening interscale wage
differentials. As illustrated in Table 3-8, Matsushita's subcontractors substantially
increased their secondary subcontracting in the late 1950s.

The increase in the rate of secondary subcontracting was greater than that of
primary subcontracting. In addition, depending on the items, technologies, and
availability of labor, tertiary contracting also became a possibility. The further down
the subcontracting level was, the more tedious the tasks were, and the simpler the
technologies that were needed. At the lowest tier, semiskilled or unskilled workers

23. Osaka Prefectural Research Institute of Commerce, Industry and Economy, 1961a:105, quoted in
Suitsu, 1979:73. Unlike developments after the 1960s there is little evidence for this period showing that
the prime contractor and subcontractor had problem-solving orientation through joint efforts to reduce
costs. More on this in Chapters 4 and 6.

TABLE 3-8. Secondary Subcontracting by Matsushita Electric's First-Tier Subcontractors, 1957–59

(Thousands of yen)

Year	(a) Output Value per First-tier Subcontractor	Index	(b) Contracted Value from First-tier to Second-tier Subcontractors	Index	b/a
1957	¥8,622	100	¥1,855	100	21.5%
1958	13,220	153	3,492	188	26.4
1959	24,412	283	6,907	372	28.4

Source: Suitsu, 1979:77. Original Source: Osaka Prefectural Research Institute of Commerce, Industry and Economy, 1961b:22.

undertook the simplest manufacture of parts and/or the simplest processes, either by hand or by using simple tools (e.g., soldering irons) and machines (e.g., lathes, simple special-purpose machines). As the number of prime contractors' production items rose, the subcontracted parts and processes also varied. This necessitated a finer-tuned division of labor among "clusters" of interrelated manufacturing units, which in turn enabled those with a small amount of capital to start their own subcontracting businesses.[24]

Automotive Subcontracting

Compared with electrical appliances, Japanese automotive subcontracting developed the mechanisms of *kyoryokukai* differently from the start, by disseminating and sharing technical information. The automotive industry also began using some embryonic forms of problem solving (as opposed to bargaining) in regard to its subcontracting relations, concerning pricing, ordering, quality assurance, and resident engineers, and this later gave the industry a distinctive competitive edge. Motor vehicles in the 1950s were still, however, a luxury item beyond the reach of most Japanese consumers, and it was not until the prosperous 1960s that Japanese motor vehicle assemblers began to develop a full-fledged components supply base.

Although the Korean War played a significant role in revitalizing the Japanese automotive industry, the boom lasted for only a year. Motor vehicle assemblers were able to meet the extra demand through *haichi tenkan*, or the internal mobilization of regular workers, overtime work, and, in the case of Nissan, temporary workers.[25] Between 1950 and 1955 the industry's growth was rather slow, from an annual output of 11,706 to 22,786 vehicles at Toyota and from 12,458 to 21,767

24. Suitsu, 1979:78. In this connection, 43.9 percent of subcontractors and 35.1 percent of products and parts suppliers in the electrical industry in the Kansai region were started up after 1951 when the demand for subcontractors surged (Osaka Prefectural Research Institute of Commerce, Industry and Economy, quoted in Suitsu, 1979:71).

25. For example, Toyota adopted a threefold strategy: hiring no new workers, mobilizing regular workers internally, and instituting two-hour overtime work (Toyota, 1967:324). Nissan followed suit with 399 regular workers temporarily assigned to its factories, for a total of 1,893 *oen* (temporary help) days in 1950. In addition, Nissan employed 667 temporary workers primarily for machining and assembly operations between August and December 1950 (Nissan, 1965:227–79).

vehicles at Nissan. By 1960, however, annual production had jumped to 154,770 and 115,465 vehicles at Toyota and Nissan, respectively (Toyota, 1967:767; Nissan, 1983:271). It is in this context that subcontracting became an important issue for motor vehicle assemblers, as seen in three indicators reminiscent of the wartime institutions: a quantitative increase in subcontracting, a qualitative change in assembler–subcontractor relations, and the rise, or resurgence, of subcontractors' associations.

In regard to the quantitative increase in subcontracting, the bought-in rate (*gaichu izon ritsu*, or the purchased components as a percentage of total manufacturing cost, as reported by each manufacturer to the Ministry of Finance) rose at Toyota from 57 to 71 percent between the second halves of 1955 and 1961, and Nissan's from 50 to 64 percent between the second half of 1957 and the first half of 1961.[26] Similarly, Toyo Kogyo's subcontracting rate—calculated as a percentage of subcontracted processes (*kosu*) in the total processes—increased from 29.1 percent in 1951 to 47.5 percent in 1955 and then to 54.6 percent in 1960. Reflecting the three-wheel vehicle boom in the latter half of the 1950s, Toyo Kogyo, then one of the leading manufacturers of three-wheel vehicles, aggressively increased the number of its subcontractors as well, from 43 in 1950 to 55 in 1955 and then to 104 in 1960. The value of shipments from its subcontractors to Toyo Kogyo jumped from ¥67 million to ¥540 million and then to ¥4,650 million for the same years (Toyo Kogyo, 1972:309).

This rapid expansion in external capacity entailed a qualitative change in assembler–subcontractor relations. The weak components supply base of the Japanese automotive industry was increasingly felt to be problematic. Small subcontractors had little capital, and they could do little to expand capacity on their own. Furthermore, quality problems were felt to be prohibitively costly (Iwakoshi, 1968:279).

Under these circumstances, the assemblers began to pursue systematic strategies vis-à-vis their subcontractors. First, they encouraged their subcontractors to modernize their facilities and provided them with technical assistance and, if necessary, helped them financially.[27] Moreover, pricing and quality assurance came to be ascribed more to the source than to the downstream purchaser. That is, the locus of pricing began to shift from the negotiators' bargaining based on their "sixth sense" and ongoing market prices to codetermination based on standardized cost calculations and process rationalization. Toyota was particularly quick to move in this direction. In 1953, it applied cost calculation methods based on standardized opera-

26. Ministry of Finance, *Yuka shoken hokokusho* (Report on securities), for each firm, each year. Toyota's bought-in rate (*gaichu izon ritsu*) refers to that for a standard truck for these years. For Nissan, the 1957 figure refers to a standard car and the 1961 figure to a small car. Incidentally, Toyota provides a rare breakdown of its *gaichu izon ritsu* for the second half of 1955: 52 percent for finished purchased components (*kansei konyu bubunhin*) and 5 percent for subcontracted products (*gaichu hin*). Further, as its suppliers of finished components, Toyota names Nippon Battery, Mitsubishi Metal, Nippon Spring, Toyo Radiator, and Nippondenso.

27. For example, Shin Nihon Mitsubishi Heavy Industries (part of which later became Mitsubishi Motors) invested and/or financed a total of ¥1,144 million for its sixty-five automotive subcontractors between 1958 and 1963. The core of this investment and financing was related to the introduction of a strategic product, the Mitsubishi 500, with which Mitsubishi entered the nonmini four-wheel passenger car market (Mitsubishi Heavy Industries, 1967b:271, 553). At that time "mini cars" were defined as those with 0.36 liter or less displacement.

tion hours (*hyojun sagyo jikan*) to purchasing pricing, which opened the way to a rationalized determination of pricing. In 1957, Toyota further changed its purchasing methodology from a three-month volume contract to a six-month unit pricing contract, thus alleviating the workload associated with frequent transactions while concentrating more on promoting subcontractors' long-term rationalization efforts. In regard to quality assurance, Toyota's inspection department in 1958 intensified its education program for subcontractors and later introduced a no-inspection system of incoming goods for those who had stabilized their manufacturing processes and achieved high quality levels.[28] Also in about 1958 the institution of "resident engineers" began with the Toyoda Machine Tools engineers regularly stationed at Toyota. They were not only in charge of maintaining the machine tools sold to Toyota but were also responsible for conveying detailed feedback from the customer to their own firm so that their products could be continuously improved (Toyota, 1978:208). The idea of resident engineers later became widespread in the Japanese automotive industry and helped enhance its competitiveness through the constant flow of interfirm information.[29]

Finally, the subcontractors' associations, or *kyoryokukai,* under the same prime contractor were organized or reorganized. In this regard, too, Toyota moved quickly.[30] The original purpose of its wartime *kyoryokukai* was promoting friendly communications (*shinboku*) among its members. The situation in the 1950s redirected this organization toward more functional goals. Systematic methods of reducing costs, improving technologies, and sharing information came to constitute the core of its activities. In 1952 Toyota and forty of its subcontractors voluntarily undertook the newly initiated inspection of enterprise *keiretsu* by the government's Small and Medium Enterprise Agency. By following the guidelines of this eleven-month inspection for good manufacturing and subcontracting practices, the subcontractors' performance improved significantly, and by the time eleven subcontractors had gone through the second inspection in 1954, they were found to have doubled their profitability and decreased their defect rates by 46 percent (Toyota, 1967:392–96).

Mitsubishi's Kawasaki factory—where buses, trucks, and high-speed diesel engines were manufactured—supported its subcontractors through technical assistance, machines on loan, and financing "in order to reconstruct subcontracting *keiretsu* that collapsed after the war." This effort materialized with the establishment in 1950 of the Fuso kyoryokukai, made up of twenty-four core machinery and

---

28. Toyota, 1967:395, 1987:305–8. This no-inspection system of incoming goods (or the system of "self-certified" subcontractors) was also adopted by electronics firms in the 1960s, as discussed in Chapter 4.

29. Chapter 4 discusses their functions in detail, based on my field research during the 1980s.

30. According to Chapter 2, Toyota's *kyoryokukai* (officially renamed the Kyohokai in 1943) was first organized in 1939, though the wartime Kyohokai consisted mainly of fairly small subcontractors in the Tokai region. Immediately after the war, subcontractors in the Kanto and Kansai regions—which were generally larger and had higher technical expertise—agreed to form their own regional organizations. In 1946, Toyota's Tokyo Kyohokai (renamed the Kanto Kyohokai in 1957) branched out from the original Kyohokai, the latter of which were now called the Tokai Kyohokai. In 1947 the Kansai Kyohokai was newly created, thus making the three Kyohokai based in three major regions (Toyota, 1967:254, 1978:150–51). When it is simply called the Kyohokai, it generally refers to a set of the three regional organizations.

metalwork subcontractors (Mitsubishi Heavy Industries, 1967a:96). Similarly, the Kashiwakai was formed in 1958 by Mitsubishi's sixty-seven subcontractors serving its Nagoya factory where miscellaneous motor vehicles and components were produced. This association organized activities for technical and quality improvements, rationalization, and cost reduction. Similar associations were formed by subcontractors in Kyoto, Mizushima, and Tokyo, where Mitsubishi's factories were located (Mitsubishi Heavy Industries, 1967b:217, 553, 597). Likewise, twenty of Toyo Kogyo's machinery and metalwork subcontractors established the Tokokai in 1952 (Toyo Kogyo, 1972:310), and Nippondenso's Denso kyoryokukai was founded in 1959 (Nippondenso, 1984:46). Nissan's Takarakai was also active in introducing mass production technologies between 1954 and 1958. Quality control methods— from statistical quality control (SQC) to total quality control (TQC)—were disseminated among its members in 1959–60. Further, cost reduction and value analysis (VA) techniques were promoted at all Takarakai member subcontractors in 1961–62. In fact, Nissan took the leadership in implementing these activities through its Takarakai and, as a result, achieved considerable cost reduction and improvement in the quality of its purchased components (Nissan, 1965:387).

The postwar institution of the *kyoryokukai* in the Japanese automotive industry thus began to produce impressive results for its constituent members during the 1950s. As assembler–subcontractor relations grew closer in the 1960s, these subcontractors' associations became even more important.

Similarities and Differences

The development of subcontracting institutions in the 1950s in the Japanese electrical and automotive industries marked, in part, the renaissance of the wartime subcontracting institutions. Both industries were responding to the rapid increase in demand, and both established closer purchaser–subcontractor relationships, on the surface at least. A significant difference, however, is that the postwar institutions developed spontaneously out of economic necessity, with little political pressure from the government. Moreover, when the differences in their actual functioning are more closely examined, apparent similarities in the resurgence of some of the institutions, such as *kyoryokukai*, may not look so alike. This can be seen particularly in the postwar automotive assemblers' assistance to their subcontractors, the rule setting of rational pricing, and the dissemination of advanced technologies through subcontractors' associations. Few of these activities were undertaken in wartime, partly because of the mismatch between government policy and the individual firms' needs and partly because of the devastation of the war. For the postwar subcontracting institutions, however, economic necessity replaced political coercion. Whereas aim and function had divorced under the wartime regime, they remarried in the postwar civil economy, bringing with them new economic functions in the subcontracting relations. In this regard, the rise of postwar subcontracting systems evolved quite differently from their wartime prototypes.

Moreover, certain interindustrial differences were evident in the 1950s. In electrical appliances, subcontracting was used mainly to expand capacity. In order to keep pace with the "electrification boom" and to increase market share in all the items that the electrical appliance firms produced, these firms sought to expand their manufacturing base through subcontracting. By contrast, the automotive sub-contracting systems developed more qualitatively, by building relationships, rather than quantitatively. Some rationalizing methodologies affecting pricing, ordering, and quality assurance emerged early on, and through the utilization of the *kyoryoku-kai* mechanisms, technical teaching was introduced. Whether these differences are circumstantial or intrinsic to the respective industries cannot be determined until we trace the developments in the industries after the 1960s.

Temporary Workers

The increased use of temporary workers in the 1950s, particularly after the Korean War and the 1955–56 economic boom, was a clear manifestation of a dualist strategy (Ministry of Labor, Labor Statistics and Research Bureau, 1953:100, 1957a:61–64; see also Ito, 1957:78, 220). In the wake of a sudden increase in demand combined with protection against future contraction, management exten-sively resorted to hiring temporary workers while maintaining a stable number of regular employees. According to the government's census of establishments, the number of temporary workers in all industries increased from more than 1 million in 1951—approximately 8 percent of all employees—to more than 1.4 million in 1955.[31] The government's Labor White Paper reports that temporary workers were hired, used, and fired, as a buffer against fluctuations in demand (Ministry of Labor, Labor Statistics and Research Bureau, 1956:142, 1958:20, 1959:72, 1960:41, 78). Table 3-9 shows the contrast between regular and temporary workers in all and selected industries from 1955 to 1959. In addition, Figure 3-1 reveals the shorter-term quarterly labor adjustments for four industries, between December 1956 and December 1957. The differing levels of the two categories of workers are, again, notable. Next, Table 3-10 shows how temporary workers were used, according to the size of the firm. The larger the establishment was, the more temporary workers it hired, and this gap between the large and small sectors widened toward the end of the 1950s.[32] Table 3-11 indicates, furthermore, that in certain industries (i.e., machinery, electrical, and transportation equipment industries) the greater propor-tion of temporary workers at large firms was even more prominent. The increased number of temporary workers in the electrical industry—a reflection of the "elec-trification" boom—is particularly noteworthy.

The golden age of dualism, however, did not last long. Unprecedented labor shortages, along with the high growth of the 1960s, not only narrowed interscale and regular-temporary workers' wage differentials but also virtually eliminated the feasibility of dualist strategies, at least in their original form. As we shall see in the

31. Ministry of Labor, Labor Statistics and Research Bureau (1953:50, 1956:140), *Rodo hakusho* (Labor white paper), for respective years. This figure of 8 percent in 1951 contrasts with 24.6 percent in 1934 (see Chapter 2).

32. In this connection, because of their high labor turnover and lower wages, "regular workers at small firms were virtually indistinguishable from temporary workers" (Labor Minister's Office, Labor Statistics and Research Bureau, 1957a:68).

TABLE 3-9. Percentage Increase of Regular and Temporary Workers in All and Selected Industries, 1955–59

Year	Percentage Increase of Regular Workers in All Industries	Industries			
		Manufacturing	Machinery	Electrical	Transportation Equipment
1955–56	3.2%	3.7%	5.2%	6.5%	3.8%
1956–57	3.3	4.4	5.2	10.3	4.7
1957–58	1.0	0.4	0.1	5.0	0.9
1958–59	4.3	6.1	5.6	17.4	6.0

Year	Percentage Increase of Temporary Workers in All Industries				
1955–56	43.0%	51.5%	118.7%	139.1%	62.0%
1956–57	10.0	14.7	8.2	22.2	29.6
1957–58	−6.0	−8.5	−15.7	8.9	−14.4
1958–59	31.5	38.5	51.8	62.4	12.5

Source: Labor Minister's Office, Labor Statistics and Research Bureau, 1958:107–8; Ministry of Labor, Labor Statistics and Research Bureau, 1959:74–75, 1960:79–80.

TABLE 3-10. Percentage of Temporary Workers in the Regular Work Force in Manufacturing Industries, 1956–59

(As of December of each year)

Year	No. of Employees per Establishment			
	Total	500 or more	100–499	30–99
1956	7.4%	8.4%	8.4%	4.7%
1957	6.4	9.3	7.1	2.0
1958	6.0	8.7	6.4	2.3
1959	7.7	11.9	7.4	2.5

Note: The issues of the Labor Ministry's White Papers for 1958, 1959, and 1960, on which this table is based, provides contradictory figures for 1956–58, and so the figures have been calculated from later editions, on the assumption that these errors were corrected.

Source: Labor Minister's Office, Labor Statistics and Research Bureau, 1958:110; Ministry of Labor, Labor Statistics and Research Bureau, 1959:76, 1960:81; *Rodo hakusho—Rodo keizai no bunseki* (Labor white paper: Analysis of labor economy). Original Source: Ministry of Labor, *Rodo ido chosa* (Survey on labor mobility), for respective years.

TABLE 3-11. Percentage of Temporary Workers in the Regular Work Force at Establishments with 500 or More Employees, 1956 and 1969

(As of December of each year)

Year	Manufacturing	Machinery	Electrical	Transportation Equipment
1956	8.4%	12.6%	14.9%	12.2%
1959	11.9	16.4	22.6	14.4

Source: Ministry of Labor, Labor Statistics and Research Bureau, 1960:41, *Rodo hakusho—Rodo keizai no bunseki* (Labor white paper: Analysis of labor economy). Original Source: Ministry of Labor, *Rodo ido chosa* (Survey on labor mobility), for respective years.

FIGURE 3-1. Employment Fluctuations of Regular and Temporary Workers in the Food, Machinery, Electrical Equipment, and Transportation Equipment Industries, 1956–57

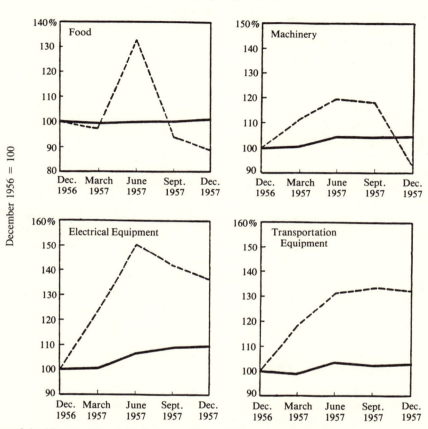

Source: Labor Minister's Office, Labor Statistics and Research Bureau, 1958:109. Original Source: Labor Minister's Office Labor Statistics and Research Bureau, 1958, *Rinjiko ni kansuru jicchi chosa* (Fieldwork survey of temporary workers).

next chapter, new subcontracting institutions, whose effects may be described as "revolutionary," appeared. The government's policies in regard to subcontracting in the dualist 1950s established a legal, political, and financial framework through which the subcontracting mechanisms were stabilized.

Government Policies

The resurgence of subcontracting in postwar Japan was supported mainly by the revival of a dualist infrastructure in the Japanese economy. With the coming of the economic boom, and where there was a growing disparity in wages and in union density between large and small firms, Japanese manufacturers revived the institution of subcontracting and hiring temporary workers. Characterized by unilateral price reduction and payment delays, subcontracting in Japan displayed little benevolence and goodwill. Except for some emerging practices in the automotive industry, there were as yet few signs of the collaborative manufacturing for which the Japanese system later became known. Although dualist contentions appear to be appropriate thus far, our observation suggests that cultural assumptions alone are insufficient to explain what happened.

For these new subcontracting mechanisms to be put into operation, the government had to become involved. Whereas during the war, the Japanese government encouraged subcontracting, now it discouraged the unfair practices accompanying it.

One characteristic of the government's postwar policies toward small businesses and subcontracting is pragmatism. Its problem-solving orientation and "follow-up" adaptation to change, as embodied in the increasingly specific laws passed, were a significant departure from the coercive (and failed) politics of the war years.

As early as August 1948, the Small and Medium Enterprise Agency (SMEA) was established as an independent organization within the framework of the Ministry of Commerce and Industry (the forerunner of the Ministry of International Trade and Industry, or MITI). SMEA was responsible for proposing and implementing small business policies and was "headed by a director-general capable of representing the interests of small businesses in government meetings and Diet sessions, with authority equivalent to that of a vice-minister."[33] The three policies for which SMEA was responsible in the 1950s were legislation prohibiting the discriminatory treatment of subcontractors, the promotion of cooperatives (*kyodo kumiai*), and the establishment of financing institutions for small businesses.[34]

Legislation Prohibiting Unfair Subcontracting Practices

The practice of withholding payments to subcontractors had become a major problem by the early 1950s; it was equivalent to using the subcontractors' capital without their consent while paying no interest to them. At that time, however, there was no legislation to control the practice. In response to pressures from small-business organizations,[35] the Fair Trade Commission (FTC) took action to regulate unfair subcontracting practices, including delayed payments. Drawing on Article 2, Clause 9, and Article 19 of the Antimonopoly Law, the FTC specified in the September 1953 announcement twelve types of "unfair trade practices," of which the tenth was concerned with subcontracting: "unduly unfavorable trading for the other party in the light of normal commercial practices, taking advantage of its own superior trading status to the other party." Unfortunately, however, the relevant

33. From the original 1947 proposal for the establishment of the SMEA by Ministry of Commerce and Industry, quoted in Japan External Trade Organization (JETRO), 1986:7.

34. In regard to the postwar government policies toward small firms, the time horizon has been freely extended beyond the 1950s, because their effects and consequences can be best assessed in their long-term development.

35. A wave of legislative support for small firms in the 1950s is largely due to their political pressure. See Appendix C.

regulation was not easily implemented; for example, it did not stipulate how many days' delay in payment after delivery constituted "unfair practice" or what measures would be taken against the insolvent prime contractor even if undue withholding of payment were established. These technical difficulties were resolved with the announcement in March 1954 of the Standards for the Recognition of Unfair Delay in the Payment of Subcontracting Charges (Shitauke daikin no futo na shiharai chien ni kansuru nintei kijun). But the lack of guidelines for its implementation still remained problematic, and the pressures from subcontractors and small-business organizations continued.[36] The fact that small businesses constituted a sizable electoral source for the Liberal Democratic party significantly affected (and to a great extent still do) government policies (see Friedman, 1988:166–67).

Defects in the earlier measures were largely corrected in the 1956 Law on the Prevention of Delay in the Payment of Subcontracting Charges and Related Matters (SMEA's official English translation of Shitauke daikin shiharai chien to boshi ho, or the Pay Delay Prevention Law). Along with clear legal definitions of the prime contractor and the subcontractor,[37] this law provided a legitimate framework through which the government—as represented by the FTC and SMEA, could intervene. The contents of this law can be summarized as follows:

First, a limit of sixty days after the receipt of the subcontracted item(s) is specified as the dividing line between fair and unfair practices, with the prime contractor required to pay subcontracting charges as soon as possible within this time (Article 2 of two added to the 1962 amendment). Second, the prime contractor is required to provide the subcontractor with documents stipulating the contents, charge(s), deadline(s), and payment method(s) of the order (Article 3). Third, certain practices are forbidden (*kinshi koi*) to the prime contractor (Article 4).[38] When the rules are broken, the director-general of SMEA, after an investigation, may require the FTC to take appropriate action (Article 6). Fourth, upon recognition of the prime contractor's violation of the law, the FTC will give the prime contractor recommendations (*kankoku*) for rectification (Article 7). If the prime contractor follows these recommendations, Articles 48, 49, 53 (Clause 3), and 54 of the

36. For an excellent account, written by FTC members, of the legislation prohibiting unfair practices in subcontracting, see Hasegawa & Ueki, 1978:13–18, on which this paragraph is based.

37. The prime contractor, or the "parent enterprise" (*oya jigyosha*), is defined in Article 2 as an enterprise with capital exceeding ¥10 million that subcontracts either manufacturing or repair to an individual or enterprise with capital of ¥10 million or less, the latter being defined as the subcontractor insofar as it receives subcontracts from the former (Hasegawa & Ueki, 1978:18, 251–52). The 1973 amendment of the law included an additional definition of the prime contractor as an enterprise with capital exceeding ¥100 million that subcontracts to an enterprise with capital of ¥100 million or less. As a result, those enterprises with capital over ¥10 million but less than ¥100 million came to be regarded as subcontractors when receiving subcontracts from a firm with capital exceeding ¥100 million and as prime contractors when subcontracting to those firms with ¥10 million yen or less (Hasegawa & Ueki, 1978:38, 251–52).

38. The forbidden practices (*kinshi koi*) are (1) unreasonable refusal of ordered items, (2) withholding payment after deadline, (3) demanding unfair discounts, (4) unfair return of items delivered, (5) unreasonable price bargaining, (6) forcing purchases, (7) acts of retaliation, (8) premature setoffs of costs for raw materials and others, and (9) payment in promissory notes that are difficult to negotiate. Item 2 is an alteration; Items 5, 6, and 7 are additions to the 1962 amendment; and Items 8 and 9 are additions to the 1965 amendment (Hasegawa & Ueki, 1978:252–53; SMEA, 1983:47).

Antimonopoly Law are not to be applied (Article 8). Fifth, if the prime contractor does not comply with the recommendations, its name and offenses will be made public as a social punishment, and the case will be judged according to the provisions of the unfair trade practices of the Antimonopoly Law (Article 7, Clauses 4 and 8). Sixth, the government's agents have the right to carry out examinations, including hearings (*hokoku choshu*) and on-the-spot inspections (*tachiiri kensa*) (Article 9). For this purpose, the prime contractor must prepare and preserve documents recording the contents, receipt, and payment of the subcontracted order (Article 5).

The law was by no means perfect, however, as it contained several loopholes. The weakness of the provision concerning recommendations was obvious. But the law's shortcomings were gradually rectified through a series of amendments in 1962, 1963, 1965, 1970, and 1973. For example, the 1962 amendment not only stipulated a pay deadline of sixty days after delivery as maximum, but it also introduced the requirement that a prime contractor not observing the deadline must pay interest (Article 2 of four). The interest rates were to be set by the FTC. They were originally set at ¥0.04 per day, which was changed in 1970 to 14.6 percent per year. Nevertheless, some prime contractors continued to ignore this provision, and so in the 1965 amendment, Article 7, Clause 1, was revised so that the FTC would make *kankoku,* or recommendations, ensuring and expediting the payment of interest. The 1965 amendment also added a preventive provision against "tunnel" firms (Article 2, Clause 5). A "tunnel" firm was usually a subsidiary or an affiliate with capital of under ¥10 million that had been increasingly used as a "surrogate contractor" by the real prime contractor in order to avoid such regulations. According to the new provision, "tunnel" firms were also prime contractors and thereby covered by the regulations (Hasegawa & Ueki, 1978:25, 256, 34, 254, 32, 50–53).

The success of these policies is better measured in their implementation than in the legislation itself. The FTC implements these regulations by investigating firms across the nation based on one of three forms.

Periodic investigations take place every year, covering a proportion of prime contractors in all industries. When the Pay Delay Prevention Law was enacted in 1956, the total number of prime contractors in the manufacturing industries was approximately 4,000, a number that jumped to more than 60,000 in the mid-1970s. The number of investigations conducted by the FTC in the mid-1970s was approximately 12,000. The SMEA also conducts periodic investigations, which steadily increased from around 10,000 in 1969 to 44,000 in 1981.[39] Putting these together, it is claimed that every prime contractor is investigated by the government every one to one and a half years (Hasegawa & Ueki, 1978:220–21).

Special investigations started in 1968 and have been conducted in selected industries each year in which there is a specific need (e.g., twelve industries, including textile wholesaling and machinery in 1970, shipbuilding and car sales and repair in 1976, and so on). Between 1968 and 1977, 15,388 establishments were the subject of special investigations.

---

39. Among those examined, 269 establishments in 1969 and 1,462 establishments in 1981 were further investigated on the spot (SMEA, 1982:109, 1983:48).

Investigations of subcontractors began in 1973 to complement the other two, which pertained mainly to prime contractors. Through these investigations, covering 25,156 subcontractors between 1973 and 1977, facts generally undetectable by surveying customers were revealed and used to rectify unfair transactions (Hasegawa & Ueki, 1978:220–23).

The second phase of more thorough inquiries of questionable prime contractors—including on-the-spot inspections[40]—is based on the results of these investigations, and appropriate action follows. Inspections may also be made, based on appeals from subcontractors and requests of the director-general of the SMEA. More recently, administrative guidance (*gyosei shido*), a milder version of the *kankoku* or recommendations, has been applied when the offenses are judged to be minor.[41] On average the second phase of inspections covered 10.1 percent of all the establishments surveyed in the FTC's periodic and special investigations between 1956 and 1977 (see Table 3-12 for a summary). Figure 3-2 diagrams the FTC's and SMEA's procedures for implementing the Pay Delay Prevention Law.

Although it is difficult to measure the effects of the government's intervention, we can assess them based on the payment of subcontracting charges. Figure 3-3 shows the withholding levels of subcontracting charges from 1961 to 1977. In 1962 the Pay Delay Prevention Law stipulated sixty days after delivery as the deadline for paying subcontractors and for beginning interest payments. Although the amendment was enacted in May 1962, its effect did not become apparent—in the decline in payment delays—until 1963–64. The *kankoku*, or recommendations, provision for expediting the payment of interest was included in 1965, and its effect is evident in a further decline in payment delays. It is also remarkable that although recessions are reflected in the graph (caused by the 1971 "Nixon shock," for example), there are no big deviations from this trend, perhaps because of the effects of the government's preventive *gyosei shido* or administrative guidance. Notifications (*tsutatsu*) in the name of the minister of the MITI and the chief commissioner of the FTC, for example, were sent to some one hundred federations of prime contractors and large firms, including the Japanese Chamber of Commerce. Each time it was feared that the burden of an expected recession would be shifted unduly to the subcontractors—such as the notifications in September 1971 after the "Nixon shock" and the shift to floating exchange rates; in February 1973 for the second shift to floating exchange rates; in November 1973 for the oil shock; and in September 1978 for the *endaka* or the sharp appreciation of the yen (Hasegawa & Ueki, 1978:263–71). In September 1986, the FTC sent more notifications to trade federations, including the Electronic Industries Association of Japan (EIAJ, or Denshi kogyokai), so as to prevent prime contractors from violating the Pay Delay Prevention Law in the event of further

40. In on-the-spot inspections, any reports regarding subcontracting and deemed relevant can be requested, and a wide range of documents, including account books, can be inspected (Hasegawa & Ueki, 1978:82, 254–55).

41. Administrative guidance (*gyosei shido*) is a nonlegally binding political means through which the Japanese government has increasingly been influencing the course of business and other activities to which the application of more coercive measures is seen as either inappropriate or unnecessary. Although this means has saved the government an enormous amount of administrative time and effort and has thus allowed quick adaptation to change, it also has saved the "face" of those guided—rather than ordered—to rectify certain practices "voluntarily."

TABLE 3-12. Periodic and Special Investigations of Subcontracting Relations by the Fair Trade Commission, 1956–77

Years	No. of Establishments Investigated on Documents (a)	No. of Establishments Inspected Further (2nd Phase) (b)	$\frac{b}{a} \times 100$ %	Inspected Cases				Completed Cases			
				Appeals from Subcontractors	Requests from SMEA's Director General	Others	Total	Recommendations	Administrative Guidance	Pass	Total
1956	304	61	20.0	20	0	—	81	0	19	46	65
1957	723	130	17.9	21	0	—	151	13	73	37	123
1958	769	161	20.9	21	0	—	182	5	110	39	154
1959	986	97	9.8	3	0	—	100	7	82	37	126
1960	1,214	105	8.6	5	0	—	110	0	38	20	58
1961	1,514	156	10.3	10	0	—	166	0	62	33	95
1962	1,803	261	14.4	33	0	—	294	12	149	35	196
1963	1,800	219	12.1	17	0	—	236	22	182	55	259
1964	2,004	218	10.8	17	14	—	249	14	180	104	298
1965	2,554	417	16.3	23	31	—	471	15	193	93	301
1966	3,631	541	14.8	15	19	—	575	14	299	111	424
1967	5,512	669	12.1	12	10	—	691	5	459	97	561
1968	6,030	414	6.8	7	0	—	421	9	416	171	596
1969	6,684	525	7.8	6	0	—	531	26	447	231	704
1970	7,214	430	5.9	5	2	—	437	52	354	80	486
1971	8,451	609	7.2	9	5	—	623	56	432	56	544
1972	8,751	690	7.8	2	0	2	692	41	485	99	625
1973	10,039	705	7.0	2	5	3	709	17	569	130	716
1974	10,045	736	7.3	5	18	1	749	4	542	296	842
1975	12,007	1,028	8.5	10	18	0	1,057	6	686	269	961
1976	12,171	1,220	10.0	15	59	0	1,253	12	906	255	1,173
1977	12,315	1,391	11.3	38	59	0	1,488	15	1,097	191	1,303
Total	116,521	11,983	10.1	296	181	6	11,266	345	7,780	2,485	10,610

Source: Hasegawa & Ueki, 1978:222.

74

FIGURE 3-2. Procedures for Implementing the Law on the Prevention of Delay in Payment of Subcontracting Charges and Related Matters

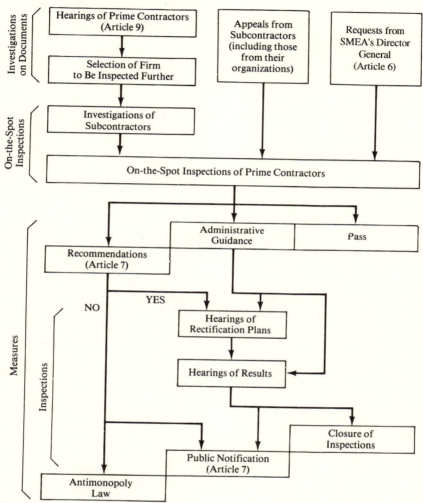

Source: Hasegawa & Ueki, 1978:81.

endaka. In response, nine core member firms, including Fuji Electric of the EIAJ, prepared a manual of preventive disciplinary guidelines and distributed it to its members. At Fuji Electric, central purchasing managers from its headquarters were dispatched to ten of its domestic plants, to give seminars to plant purchasing managers, teaching them how not to violate the law.[42] Taking this into account, we could assume that the shape of the graph in Figure 3-3 would have been quite different—and more detrimental to the subcontractors—had the legislation never been introduced.

42. Based on my interview with T. Imai, purchasing manager, control section, Purchasing Department, Fuji Electric Headquarters, April 3, 1986.

FIGURE 3-3. Payment Delays in Subcontracting Charges, 1961–77

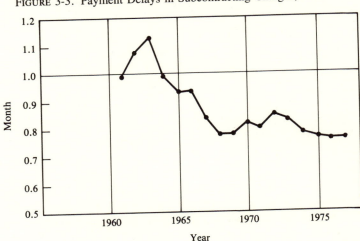

Source: Hasegawa & Ueki, 1978:240. Original Source: Fair Trade Commission, *Nenji hokoku* (Annual reports), for respective years.

Another effect is related to reputation. Although the limitations of the law's coercive power have been a constant target for criticism, it cannot be denied that the article specifying the public announcement of law violators has played an important role in discouraging large, established firms from resorting to unfair practices, as they are as much concerned with their own reputation and social image as they are with their profitability.[43]

We can, therefore, conclude that the government's policies to protect small subcontractors significantly contributed to the continuation of a system that might have been eliminated—or at least greatly altered—under more laissez-faire arrangements.[44]

Cooperatives

The second postwar government policy concerning small businesses was the promotion of cooperatives (*kyodo kumiai*), the result of which turned out to be somewhat

43. In my fieldwork in Japan in 1983, 1984 and 1986, many purchasing managers of large manufacturers mentioned that the last thing they wanted was the disclosure of their illegal action to the public because its damage to the firm's reputation would be pervasive (based on my interviews in the purchasing departments at Pioneer Electronic's headquarters and its Ohmori, Kawagoe, Shizuoka, and Tokorozawa plants, December 24, 26, and 27, 1983 and January 7 and 10, 1984; Fuji Electric's headquarters and its Tokyo plant, March 6 and April 3, 1986; Hitachi's Taga, Tokai, and Sawa plants, March 28, 1986).

44. In the high-growth 1960s, SMEA changed its policymaking orientation toward promotion rather than protection. Today, both protection and promotion are major features of SMEA's policies. But the protection side of it does not mean that SMEA's intention is to protect firms or sectors that cannot survive on their own. Rather, it is to help firms that suffer from unfair treatment or a categorical decline in business owing to circumstantial or structural conditions. Put differently, SMEA's concern is to cultivate the socioeconomic environment for healthy competition rather than simply helping out the weak. According to a SMEA official: "We don't say a word about those losing the-survival-of-the-fittest race as long as they comply with the rules" (based on my interview with H. Harada, assistant planning manager, subcontracting enterprise section, Planning Department, SMEA, MITI, March 14, 1986).

different from its original purpose. These cooperatives developed along the lines of a larger formal government policy in the late 1950s: the dissolution of dualism or, if not that, at least the removal of unfair socioeconomic conditions for small businesses.[45] In order to achieve this goal, an organization of small businesses was established with legislative backing.

As early as November 1946, the Law on Commercial and Industrial Cooperatives (Shoko kyodo kumiai ho) was enacted, replacing its predecessor (Shoko kumiai ho) passed in March 1943 in the midst of World War II. But the main function of the immediate postwar cooperatives was still the distribution of rationed materials. Accordingly, when rationing was discontinued, the cooperatives formed under this law became dysfunctional.[46]

In July 1949, when the effects of the Dodge Plan were beginning to be felt, the Law on Cooperatives of Small and Medium Enterprises and Other Parties (Chusho kigyo to kyodo kumiai ho) was enacted,[47] and the 1946 Law on Commercial and Industrial Cooperatives was abolished. The rationale behind the new legislation was fourfold. First, the solidarity of small businesses as organized into cooperatives was expected to enhance their otherwise weak bargaining power vis-à-vis other entities, including large firms and wholesalers. Second, it was hoped that cooperatives would facilitate the introduction of new machinery, facilities, and technologies to small businesses through collective purchase and utilization. Third, it was hoped that new sources of loans would be tapped as the cooperatives became better

45. The famous 1957 Economic White Paper referred to the Japanese economy as dual structured (*niju kozo*) and emphasized the need for government policies geared toward its dissolution. Following this line, SMEA confirmed its support for the organization of small businesses:

> It can be said that in securing the foundation for the progressive modernization of small businesses, the starting point of our policy should often be as follows: to achieve managerial economies of scale and rationalization, which otherwise would be difficult for individual firms by themselves, by establishing strong solidaristic organizations of small businesses, and to stabilize their performance by avoiding excess competition arising from the *shiwayose* (shifting instability to the margins) of the dual economy. (SMEA, 1959:10)

That the baseline of SMEA's policy has remained the same can be seen in the following remark in the Small and Medium Enterprise White Paper twenty-four years later:

> In general, small businesses have weaker business resources compared with those of large firms and, in many cases, find it difficult to cope with changes in economic environments individually. Therefore, it is extremely effective to respond to such problems through cooperation and organization beyond the constraints of individual firms. The significance of cooperation and organization for small businesses is to remove disadvantages arising from the lack of capital, labor, and informational resources or from trading conditions due to small size and to enhance competitiveness while improving their economic status by the merit of their organization. (SMEA, 1983:127)

46. Kato, 1960:277. The origins of Japanese cooperatives date back to the early Meiji period. Recognizing the merit of the then-emerging cooperatives, the Meiji government gave them a legislative framework with the enactment of the 1900 Law on Industrial Cooperatives (Sangyo kumiai ho). At that time, cooperatives were primarily concerned with agriculture. Later, with the development of commerce and manufacturing industry, the 1925 Law on Manufacturing Industrial Cooperatives (Kogyo kumiai ho) and the 1932 Law on Commerce Cooperatives (Shogyo kumiai ho) were enacted to reinforce the existing legislation. The wartime government policy toward cooperatives culminated in the 1943 Law on Commerce and Industrial Cooperatives (Shoko kumiai ho) which was geared to war needs. For a succinct history of prewar Japanese cooperatives, see SMEA, 1950:244–45.

47. This law covered four types: common facility cooperatives (the majority), credit cooperatives, federations of cooperatives, and business cooperatives. The 1957 amendment of the law added mutual fire relief cooperatives and small common facility cooperatives (Kato, 1960:276).

security risks. Fourth, cooperatives would function as an administrative agent for government policies that had been relatively ineffective without such entities (SMEA, 1950:242–43).

With particular emphasis on the first political factor, the law provided a range of support to enable small businesses to become independent, for example, exemption from application of the Antimonopoly Law so as to promote collective production and marketing; the preclusion of large firms from membership (the previous cooperatives had included large firms as members); the abolition of the government's approval and oversight (except for credit cooperatives); freedom of entrance and exit, election, and recall of officials by cooperative members; prohibition of nonmember officials; limitations on nonmembers' use of facilities; and assurance of autonomy.[48]

It was largely an accident of history, however, that the implementation of the law coincided with the progress of the Dodge Plan. The new cooperatives turned out to be a blessing for small businesses hard pressed for money. They learned that by establishing cooperatives, they could obtain access to loans not available otherwise. As the recession deepened, the number of new cooperatives, hastily set up by those desperate for financing, shot up, increasing twenty-seven-fold in less than a year: from 461 in October 1949 to 4,924 in March 1950 and then to 12,308 in July 1950. Part of the increase up until March 1950 was the "carryovers" reorganized under new legislation. These were those cooperatives forced by law to decide by the end of February 1950 whether to dissolve or continue, and they had chosen the latter option. But 7,384 cooperatives established after March—which constituted 60 percent of the total in July—were mostly new start-ups in dire need of money (SMEA, 1950:246–52). The effect of the March 1950 act, the Credit Issue of the Banks and Others (Ginko to no saiken hakko ni kansuru horitsu)—which dramatically enlarged

---

48. SMEA, 1950:246. These "revolutionary" provisions soon receded, however, through the subsequent amendments of the Law on Cooperatives of Small and Medium Enterprises and Other Parties.

The 1951 amendment gave government administrative organs the authority to inspect (*kensa*) and direct (*shiji*) cooperatives when the latter's management, finance, and business were recognized as unlawful. It also required permission from government administrative organs to convene a general assembly. The 1952 amendment allowed up to one-third of the officials to be nonmembers and gave government administrative organs the right to order (*meirei*), rather than simply direct, the cooperatives, as necessary. Moreover, the 1955 amendment turned out to be "reactionary," in that it not only required the government's permission to establish and change the cooperatives articles but also awarded the government's administrative organs the right to dissolve them. In addition, it allowed nomination and recommendation mechanisms for electing officials and simplified procedures for exercising the right of directing. Further, it legalized the establishment of the Central Society of National Small and Medium Enterprise Cooperatives and Others (Zenkoku chusho kigyo to kyodo kumiai chuokai, or Chuokai for short), which was a centralized organ to disseminate nationwide the government's policies regarding cooperatives. Finally, the 1957 amendment included the reorganized commercial and industrial cooperatives under the Chuokai, while giving common facility cooperatives and other small cooperatives the formal right of collective bargaining and arbitration organs (Kato, 1960:283–295).

Thus, the original progressive measures concerning cooperatives, which had been enacted in the revolutionary atmosphere of the immediate postwar period, reached a new equilibrium toward the end of the 1950s, in parallel, perhaps, with concomitant decline in labor movements.

It is not surprising in the context of this and the 1949–50 recession that the postwar Japanese cooperatives eventually turned out to be predominantly oriented toward financial, rather than political, activities.

the financing capacity of the Central Bank for Commercial and Industrial Cooperatives (Shoko kumiai chuo kinko), a financial institution primarily serving small-business cooperatives—fueled this boom of cooperative start-ups (SMEA, 1950:252; Kato, 1960:279). Thus, the emergence of postwar Japanese cooperatives was marked by a specific motive for organizing: money. By 1960 they were widely called "borrowing money" cooperatives (*kane kari kumiai*). Surprisingly, however, more than half of them in the late 1950s were said to be "dormant," and only one-third were undertaking any sort of collective operations.[49] This suggests that insofar as their financial needs were or were not met, the cooperatives' members were not concerned with more "intrinsic" activities. Furthermore, according to a 1958 survey by the Economic Bureau of the Tokyo metropolitan government, the majority of common facility cooperatives did not even have "common facilities," in the sense of sharing machines and technologies. At best, they shared only meeting rooms.[50]

Extending the time horizon a little, then, it is possible to see the major activities that these cooperatives emphasized, as reported by the cooperatives' members, in Table 3-13. Whereas joint purchases—the single largest item in 1958—slightly declined over twenty years, loans showed a steady increase to more than 50 percent. Together, handling and guaranteeing loans represented 76.5 percent of the cooperatives' activities for 1978. Also impressive is the jump in information sharing, signifying the greater importance of the "software" side of cooperative activities (as

49. Kato, 1960:276–77. Of the 12,308 cooperatives existing in July 1950, 9,559 (or 77.7 percent) were common facility cooperatives (*jigyo kyodo kumiai*), and they have continued to constitute the great majority of postwar Japanese cooperatives until today (see Figure 3-4). Therefore, our examination in this subsection is primarily concerned with this type of cooperative.

There are many types of cooperatives in Japan. In response to the vast variety of needs and peculiarities of small businesses, SMEA has, over time, orchestrated a series of fine-tuned legislation concerning cooperatives. In 1983 there were eight major cooperative-related laws and twenty-five types of cooperatives. Among the most important are the aforementioned 1949 Law on Cooperatives of Small and Medium Enterprises and Other Parties, covering six types of cooperatives (common facility cooperatives, small common facility cooperatives, mutual fire relief cooperatives, credit cooperatives, federations of cooperatives, and business cooperatives); the 1957 Law on the Organization of Small-Business Associations, covering two types (commercial and industrial cooperatives and federations of commercial and industrial cooperatives); the 1957 Law on the Optimization of Activities in Business Concerning Environmental Sanitation, covering three types; the 1962 Law on the Shopping District Promotion Cooperatives, covering two types; and the 1967 Law on the Organization of Small-Business Associations, covering one type of joint business cooperative. Restricting the parameters to those covered by the first two laws, the number of cooperatives was 52,276 in March 1982, of which 44,109 (or 84.4 percent) were common facility cooperatives (SMEA, 1983:29).

50. Tokyo Metropolitan Government, Economic Bureau, 1958, *Jigyo kyodo kumiai jittai chosa shukei hokokusho* (Report of the data collection on the actual conditions of common facility cooperatives), quoted in Kato, 1960:280. It is not easy to assess the extent to which the amendments of the Law on Cooperatives of Small and Medium Enterprises and Other Parties affected the fate of the cooperatives. Inasmuch as their autonomy was reduced by the amendments, there must have been few incentives left for cooperative members to be active politically. And this must have certainly affected the way in which many of the cooperatives became "dormant." But the fact that the cooperatives survived and followed financial activities suggests that the negative influence of legislative amendments should not be exaggerated.

After the 1960s, the cooperatives were progressively used as a base for government-backed industrial parks in many strategic areas of Japan, and this new move transformed the cooperatives' uncertain status in the 1950s.

TABLE 3-13. Major Activities[a] of Common Facility Cooperatives, 1958–78

Year	Joint Purchases (of Raw Materials)	Loans	Loan Guarantees	Education and Information Sharing	Joint Sales
1958	55.7%	38.7%	22.2%	28.5%	32.1%
1963	41.0	39.5	18.9	24.2	18.5
1966	43.5	42.3	19.0	25.1	22.4
1975	33.0	45.4	N.A.[b]	34.4[c]	N.A.[b]
1978	46.9	51.2	25.3	53.6[c]	22.3

[a] Major activities are those constantly appearing in the top five in each year's survey. Activity items omitted more than twice in the surveys are excluded. Owing to multiple replies, the total exceeds 100.

[b] Not available.

[c] Refers to information collection and sharing separate from education and training.

Source: Kato, 1960:278; SMEA, 1966:562, 1976:303, 1979:281. Original Sources: SMEA, 1958, 1963, 1966, 1978, *Jigyo kyodo kumiai jittai chosa* (Survey on the actual conditions of common facility cooperatives) and 1975, *Kumiai no kyodoka, shisutemuka ni kansuru jittai chosa* (Survey on actual conditions concerning collaboration and systematization of cooperatives).

opposed to simple sharing "hardware" facilities, as originally envisaged by the policymakers). Joint sales declined.

It is clear that despite the government's political orientation at the start, the postwar Japanese cooperatives took a purely economic direction. The predominant and increasing share of financing arrangements supports this fact. Joint purchase, which signifies a collective effort to buy materials and facilities cheaply, is another economic indicator. On the other hand, joint sales—perhaps the closest indicator of their "solidarity" if the government's original purpose is accepted—fell over time. Another indicator of solidarity is "price agreements," which were recorded at 27.5 percent in the 1958 survey but which disappeared in subsequent surveys. All these indicators suggest that the outcomes of the government's policy were quite different from its original intentions.

Thus, the mixed results of the government's policy are evident. Its "failure"— as seen in the gap between its original aim and the result—is in part due to the mismatch between the political visions of the policymakers and the economic needs of the recipients. Moreover, inconsistency in the government's support for the cooperatives' political independence—as seen in the frequent legislative amendments—also must have affected their development.

There was also another important structural factor unforeseeable at the outset of the institution: The high-growth 1960s substantially redefined subcontracting relations, with the increase of contract assembly and systems-components manufacture, as opposed to the traditional simple-process subcontracting (e.g., machining, sheet metals). In order to ensure quality, the prime contractors offered extensive technical training to their subcontractors, and inasmuch as the subcontractors came to be under the direct technical control of their major customers, they no longer needed "extracurricular" organizations such as cooperatives. Furthermore, when a flood of information about new technologies and methodologies came directly from their customers—frequently through the *kyoryokukai,* or subcontractors' associations— the subcontractors no longer needed an extra, and often less useful, framework.

FIGURE 3-4. Trend in the Number of Small Business Cooperatives, 1960–80

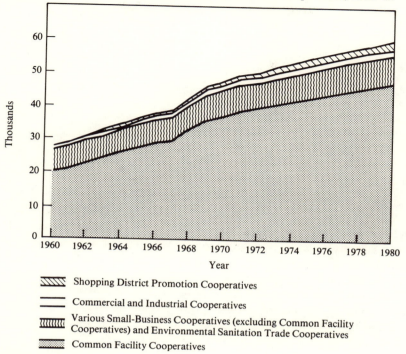

Shopping District Promotion Cooperatives

Commercial and Industrial Cooperatives

Various Small-Business Cooperatives (excluding Common Facility Cooperatives) and Environmental Sanitation Trade Cooperatives

Common Facility Cooperatives

Source: SMEA, 1983:127.

Although technical improvements were thus being made elsewhere, cooperatives became important for purely economic reasons, particularly because without equity relationships, subcontractors received little financial support from their customers. Indeed, this explains why financing continued to increase as one of the cooperatives' major activities.[51] In this respect, then, the government's policy can be described as a "success" in that it provided small businesses with an unexpectedly useful means for collective financing.[52] Accordingly, it is not difficult to see why cooperatives have continued to prosper in number, if not in collective activity. Figure 3-4 shows the long-term trend in the number of postwar Japanese cooperatives of small businesses.

Next, Table 3-14 provides data on the cooperatives' organization density be-

51. In this connection, a 1975 SMEA survey shows that cooperatives comprising subcontractors were, on average, more active in loans (76.5 percent as opposed to 45.4 percent). See SMEA, 1975, *Kumiai no kyodoka, shisutemuka ni kansuru jittai chosa* (Survey on actual conditions concerning collaboration and systematization of cooperatives), quoted in SMEA, 1976:303. We can reasonably infer from this that the many subcontractors unable to receive financial help from their customers established and/or joined cooperatives in order to tap their financial sources.

52. The institution of cooperatives was conveniently used by the national and local governments from the 1960s onward as a legal framework for establishing new industrial parks in strategic regions. This fact also intensified the cooperatives' financial function.

TABLE 3-14. Density[a] of Common Facility Cooperatives in
Manufacturing Industries, 1957–76

1957	42.6%
1962	37.8
1974	37.0
1976	37.9

[a]Density is the percentage of the common facility cooperatives' member firms in the total number of small and medium firms.

Source: SMEA, 1963:216, 1975:209, 1979:281. Original Sources: For 1974, SMEA/MITI, 1974, *Chiiki mondai jittai chosa* (Survey on the actual conditions of regional problems). For 1976, SMEA/MITI, 1976, *Kogyo jittai kihon chosa* (Basic survey of the actual conditions of industry).

tween 1957 and 1976. The decrease between 1957 and 1962 can be explained by the fact that other types of cooperatives emerged during this period, such as reorganized commercial and industrial cooperatives or newly created environmental sanitation trade cooperatives. In the meantime the memberships of common facility cooperatives stagnated, and some of the members presumably transferred to these new entities.[53] Taking this into account, it can be said that the density of cooperatives (as represented by common facility cooperatives) remained constant for two decades. The data once again indicate that many small businesses found cooperatives to be useful and have continued to participate in them.[54]

Small-Business Financing

With the systematization of small-business financing mechanisms in the 1950s, the Japanese government completed the trilogy of its small-business policies. The small firms, which prospered in the confusion of the immediate postwar period, gradually receded from the economic scene and were seriously hit by the effects of the Dodge Plan. At that time, there were three financial institutions specializing in small-business financing: the Central Bank for Commercial and Industrial Cooperatives, mutual loan firms, and credit cooperatives. Compared with ordinary financial institutions, however, their loan operations were quite restricted and could not meet the demand (JETRO, 1986:8). Seeing the problem and pressured by small-business organizations,[55] the government embarked on passing legislation for the financial support of small firms.

53. SMEA, 1963:216. SMEA estimated this indirectly, based on the 1962 density figure of commercial and industrial cooperative member firms, 30.8 percent, which is quite large for a relatively new entity restarted five years before. As cooperative memberships can be plural, however, one cannot precisely determine the levels of overall cooperative memberships single-handedly.

54. Appendix D briefly describes the Japanese cooperatives I visited in the 1980s.

55. In this connection, consider the following:

Postwar small firm leverage was enhanced by the creation of national coalitions of small enterprises such as the Small and Medium Business Federation [*sic*] (Chuseiren), headed by extremely powerful industrialists possessing "old-school" links to the LDP [Liberal Democratic party] leadership. Perhaps the best example was during the 1950s, a period of terrific legislative support for small firms, when Chuseiren was headed by Ayukawa [*sic*], the former president of Nissan and the darling of the old anti-*zaibatsu* militarists. What the

In June 1949, the People's Finance Corporation (Kokumin kin'yu koko) was established in accordance with the People's Finance Corporation Law. The corporation is a government agency, the successor to the prewar People's Bank and Pension Bank, and it lends to private individuals, usually the heads of family business operations, who have difficulty borrowing for business purposes from ordinary banks. Its resources comprise the capital subscription of and loans from the national government (Committee of Inquiry on Small Firms, 1971:399–400).

In June 1951 the Mutual Bank Law was enacted, which upgraded the existing mutual loan firms to mutual banks (*sogo ginko*) and credit depositories (*shin'yo kinko*) with the authority to receive deposits and savings by installments and to make loans and discount bills, in addition to their normal financing of small businesses. But these organizations are subject to certain ceilings in their lending, and the opening and operation were restricted to their respective regions.[56]

In June of the same year, the Credit Union Law was also passed, giving the existing credit cooperatives the opportunity to reorganize into credit unions (*shin'yo kumiai*). Credit unions can lend only to their members, and the loans they made must be used within their regions. Those not willing to reorganize remained credit cooperatives under the 1949 Law on Cooperatives of Small and Medium Enterprise and Other Parties (JETRO, 1986:8). Mutual banks, credit depositories, credit unions, credit cooperatives, and other ordinary commercial banks constitute the "private sector" of financial institutions geared to small-business financing, usually on a regional basis.

In response to the small sector's further growth after the Korean War boom, the Small Business Finance Corporation (Chusho kigyo kin'yu koko) was founded in 1953, which is wholly supported by the government and serves small and medium firms nationwide with term and installment loans for periods of one to five years. It is not permitted to receive deposits. The amount of each loan is limited so that many small businesses will benefit (Committee of Inquiry on Small Firms, 1971:399; JETRO, 1986:9).

The Central Bank for Commercial and Industrial Cooperatives (Shoko kumiai chuo kinko, or Shoko chukin for short) has been in operation since 1938. Its deposits and loans are restricted to member cooperatives and also their constituent members. The national government is authorized to intervene extensively in the bank's operations, including the appointment of its officers. The bank gives its member organizations five- to twenty-year term loans, overdrafts, and discounts on bills. A loan limit per borrower is fixed for each fiscal year.[57]

Chuseiren was able to do was hire influential conservative spokesmen to plead their case with the government, especially . . . with respect to the problem of investment capital for smaller operators. (Friedman, 1986, chap. 4, pp. 89–90).

For more information on the postwar small business movements, see Appendix C.

56. In 1968, however, this stipulation of regional restrictions was abolished. Within the interest rate ceilings set by the authorities, the Mutual Loans and Savings Banks Association fixes voluntary maximum rates according to the amount of the loan (Committee of Inquiry on Small Firms, 1971:398).

57. Committee of Inquiry on Small Firms, 1971:399; JETRO, 1986:9. Of the three government-affiliated financial institutions for small firms, the Central Bank for Commercial and Industrial Cooperatives has a mixed ownership, whereas the People's Finance Corporation and the Small-Business Finance Corporation are wholly publicly owned.

By 1953, therefore, all three "public-sector" financial institutions for small businesses were functioning nationwide, in a coordinated and complementary manner: the People's Finance Corporation serving very small business entities, the Small Business Finance Corporation attending to small and medium enterprises, and the Central Bank for Commercial and Industrial Cooperatives financing its member organizations. All are supervised by the Ministry of Finance, which also regulates the operations of mutual banks, credit depositories, and credit unions. Credit cooperatives are supervised by the prefectural governments.[58]

In 1955 the Credit Guarantee Association was introduced and underwrote, through its branches nationwide, those small firms seeking credit from ordinary financial institutions. The Small Business Credit Insurance Corporation, a government financial agency, in turn automatically reinsures the debts guaranteed by the association, drawing on funds from government sources. It also supplies funds to the association, in the form of six-month loans, for meeting its guarantee obligations and two-year loans for operating capital (Committee of Inquiry on Small Firms, 1971:400; SMEA, 1983:68–69; JETRO, 1986:9).

Thus, by the mid-1950s the basic structure of the government-regulated small-business financing was complete, with its public sector operating nationwide and its private sector covering specific regions. This system predominated during the subsequent periods of high growth and beyond, being reinforced when necessary by additional special financing programs.

Figure 3-5 illustrates the mid-1960s outlays of these financial institutions. Not surprisingly, the dedicated relationship of special-purpose financial institutions with their customers stands out. Most of their loans are to small businesses. By contrast, a much smaller part of ordinary private banks' lending is for small-firm financing. The data in the figure do not show, however, each institution's relative importance in the total picture of small-firm financing. If loans by private commercial banks, for example, outweigh those by small-business financial institutions in absolute terms, the figure may be misleading. We should then look for other evidence of each institution's relative financing contribution. Table 3-15 gives the amount and relative proportion of various institutions' loans to small businesses outstanding at the end of 1969. The private small-firm financial institutions and commercial banks stand at the top, in both absolute and relative terms. By contrast, the role of public financial institutions is minor, although not insignificant. The distribution of financing by size of firm and financial institution, however, is different. That is, the smaller the firm is, the more it relies on small-business financial institutions, as shown in Figure 3-6, a breakdown of borrowing features by size of firm and type of financial institution. The smaller firms—most frequently start-ups—borrow a significant part of their funds from unofficial or informal sources, such as business acquaintances, moneylenders, relatives, and friends. Outweighing this, however, is their borrowing from small-firm financial institutions. Commercial city banks play only a minor part in their funding. As firms grow in size, they rely more on city banks and less on long-term credit and trust banks. This evidence indicates that

---

58. Committee of Inquiry on Small Firms, 1971: 399–400. The Central Bank for Commercial and Industrial Cooperatives is also supervised by the Ministry of International Trade and Industry, which, with the Ministry of Finance, substantially intervenes in the bank's business operations.

FIGURE 3-5. Outlays by Financial Institutions to Small and Large Firms, 1966

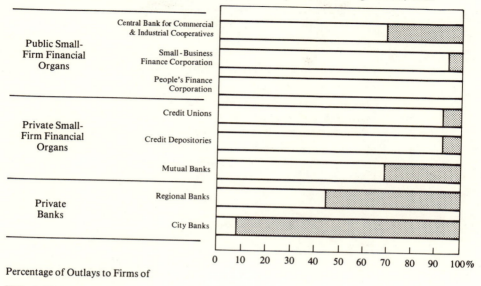

Percentage of Outlays to Firms of

☐ 0-299 Employees
▨ More Than 300 Employees

Source: Friedman, 1986, chap. 4, p. 92. Original Source: People's Finance Corporation, 1968:124, *Nohon no sho reisai kigyo* (Japanese small and very small enterprises).

ordinary commercial banks are not interested in funding smaller and presumably risky borrowers, which is where the small-firm financing institutions play an important supplementary role.

Furthermore, the role of these special-purpose financial institutions has, over time, become even more crucial to start-ups and smaller firms. Figure 3-7 shows the change between 1964 and 1982 in borrowing by nonbank financing, by size of firm—that is, the combination of loans from nonbank private and public small-firm financing institutions and other nonspecialized government sources as a proportion

TABLE 3-15. Outstanding Loans to Small Businesses by Financial Institutions, 1969

(¥360 = $1)

Institution	Millions of Yen	Percent
Public small-firm financial institutions[a]	¥2,353	9.4%
Private small-firm financial institutions[b]	10,788	43.1
Commercial banks	10,438	41.7
Other financial institutions	1,452	5.8
Total:	25,031	100.0

[a] Includes the Central Bank for Commercial and Industrial Cooperatives, the Small Business Finance Corporation, and the People's Finance Corporation.

[b] Includes the mutual banks, credit depositories, credit unions, and credit cooperatives.

Source: Committee of Inquiry on Small Firms, 1971:400.

FIGURE 3-6. Borrowing, by Size of Firm and by Financial Institution, 1957

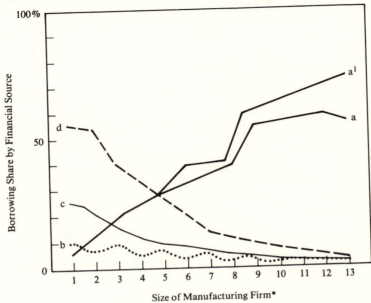

Note: * Size classifications are number of employees per firm: 1=1–9, 2=10–29, 3=30–49, 4=50–99, 5=100–199, 6=200–299, 7=300–499, 8=500–999, 9=1,000–1,999, 10=2,000–4,999, 11=5,000–9,999, 12=10,000 +.

    a: city banks.
    a[1]:a + long-term credit banks and trust banks
    b: business acquaintances
    c: b + moneylenders, relatives, and friends
    d: c + small-firm financial institutions

Source: Shinohara, 1968:53. Original Source: SMEA, 1957, *Chusho kigyo sogo kihon chosa* (Comprehensive basic survey of small and medium enterprises), quoted in Miyazawa, 1961:17.

of the total. The dependence of all sizes of firms on small-firm financial institutions and other government sources increased, but mostly for the smaller firms.

Appraisal of Government Policies

The empirical evidence we examined suggests that the current state of small Japanese firms would have been quite different if the government had not intervened, through an outpouring of legislation, to stop unfair subcontracting practices, promote cooperatives, and systematize small-firm financial institutions. Had more laissez-faire policies been pursued, or had more asymmetrical measures to the disadvantage of small entities been established, their very existence would have been at stake. Perhaps an industrial structure similar to the more mass production–oriented economies in which large firms predominate might have emerged in Japan. Large prime contractors could have squeezed out the last drops of blood from their subcontractors and jettisoned them when they were no longer needed. Legislation prohibiting the withholding of payments due and authorizing the continuous (and

FIGURE 3-7. Combined Loans from Nonbank Private and Public Small-Firm Financial Institutions and Other Government Sources

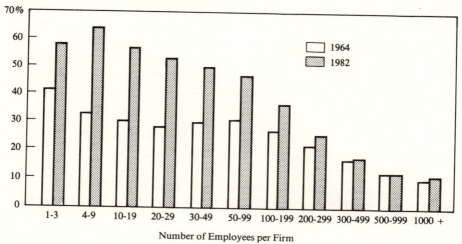

Source: Friedman 1986, chap. 4, p. 106. Original Sources: SMEA, 1968, *Chusho kigyo sogo kihon chosa* (Comprehensive basic survey of small and medium enterprises); SMEA/MITI, 1982, *Kogyo jittai kihon chosa hokoku sho* (Report of the basic survey of actual conditions of industries).

extensive) investigations by the FTC and SMEA must have considerably influenced the previously asymmetrical subcontracting relationships.

Cooperatives, though they developed haphazardly, provided an extremely convenient structure through which small firms could borrow funds with relative ease. Later, the cooperatives also served as a useful means for the government to implement the programs of industrial parks. Finally, an array of financial institutions specializing in small-firm financing encouraged start-ups and very small businesses. Indeed, all of these supportive measures have influenced the way that small firms and subcontractors developed as they did. Those who might have suffered the bitter effects of the laissez-faire market forces survived because of these measures.

The government's support does not, however, necessarily provide the conditions needed to perpetuate the system. On the contrary, it may offer a strong incentive for prime contractors to stop subcontracting altogether. As subcontracting procedures became more of a nuisance, owing to government intervention (and as the financial foundation of small firms became secure), it must theoretically have made more sense for prime contractors to revert to in-house production.[59] As the next chapter reveals, however, the large firms did not adopt this latter option. Instead, they further expanded their utilization of subcontracting, transforming its content into

59. In my field research a purchasing manager of an electronics prime contractor pointed out: "If there were no such thing as making and keeping documents of our subcontracting transactions for [the inspection by] the FTC, how much time could be saved! For this reason alone, we have to spend considerable labor hours and always have to worry about discrepancies in documents. We really want to get rid of this, but if our company's name were publicized for breaking the rule, my throat would be cut" (based on my interview with K. Yoshimura, purchasing manager, Production Control Department, Ohmori plant, Pioneer Electronic Corporation, May 15, 1986).

something new, which is precisely where it broke away from the traditional dualist framework.

What firm would decide to rely more on subcontracting when subcontracting itself had become more difficult? Why would a firm continue to use subcontractors when interscale wage differentials were narrowing, as they did in the high-growth 1960s owing to an unprecedented labor shortage? Unless there were reasons that made sufficient economic sense to them in the changed environment, the attachment of large firms to the institution of subcontracting would appear mysterious, if not foolhardy.

Summary and Conclusions

We examined the resurgence of subcontracting in Japanese manufacturing industries between 1945 and 1960 and found that the war-shattered institution of subcontracting revived in a new guise after the Korean War boom. Socioeconomic conditions (e.g., the widening disparity in wages and union status between large and small firms, increasing consumer purchasing power, undercapacity to meet demand) and technological factors (i.e., subcontractors' purchase of used equipment from large firms) prepared for and promoted this revival. But the harsher side of postwar subcontracting also became apparent, as exemplified by the prime contractors' beating down prices and withholding payments due. The subcontractors suffered from these unfair practices. Except for some pioneering efforts in the automotive industry, there were as yet few signs of collaborative manufacturing—let alone harmonious and trusting relationships—among Japanese traders during this period. This uneven coexistence is consistent with the claim that despite distinctive Japanese cultural values, neither benevolence nor goodwill accounted for the existence of Japanese subcontracting early in the postwar period. Owing to pressure from small-business organizations and in the interest of securing their political support, the government then intervened, with three types of policies: legislation against unfair subcontracting practices, the nurture of small-firm cooperatives, and the establishment of small-business financial organizations. Despite mixed results, these generally helped promote and stabilize postwar subcontracting systems in Japan.

These historical developments show that Japanese subcontracting is a complex evolutionary product, built on the interplay between historical events and the adaptations to them by human agents. For example, as a result of the Dodge Plan, the cooperatives quickly changed from a source of political support to a fund-gathering institution for small firms under financial pressure. Large Japanese manufacturers began to resort to using temporary workers and subcontractors in order to meet the burgeoning demand due to the Korean War, just after having suffered large-scale redundancies in the aftermath of the Dodge Plan. In the face of a succession of unexpected events, Japanese manufacturers used whatever means were available to them, constantly modifying, redeveloping, and transforming these means in order to adapt them to the changing situation. As we have seen, there were constraints as well as incentives, social, economic, and technological. As in the wartime period, however, it was the political factor that heavily influenced the history of Japanese subcontracting institutions. Legislation and other measures that the Japanese central government implemented to protect and promote small businesses after the 1950s established the legal framework within which certain rules of the game were imposed on all the players. No longer was subcontracting free trading in the marketplace, where the strong could easily defeat the weak. No longer were small businesses denied access to financial resources simply because of their size. No longer were they subject to the will of their customers and the market forces. Instead, small firms and subcontractors in Japan were stabilized with institutional backing.

It clearly would be difficult to try to explain the evolution of Japanese subcontracting from a single-faceted perspective. Surely, it was the development of dualism in the Japanese economy that created an infrastructure conducive to subcontracting. Surely, it was the Japanese with their particular cultural traits who developed and implemented these subcontracting practices. But neither Japanese culture nor even dualism alone is a sufficient explanation. The more comprehensive approach adopted in this study—taking into account a broad range of socioeconomic, technological, and political factors—seems to be a more powerful way to explain the *raison d'être* and current form of Japanese subcontracting.

4

The Transformation
of Japanese Subcontracting,
1960–1990

The three decades after 1960 were among the most outstanding in Japan's economic history, when its economy shifted from being second rate to becoming preeminent. In 1964 Japan joined the Organization for Economic Cooperation and Development (OECD), thereby signifying its status as a developed nation; by 1970 its gross national product (GNP) was second only to that of the United States in the free world; and by 1986 Japan's GNP per capita surpassed that of the United States. During these decades, subcontracting in Japan flourished, despite receding dualistic indicators, while shifting from instrumental use to collaborative manufacturing.

The Recession of Dualism

The previous two chapters demonstrated that aside from political influence, little in the development of Japanese subcontracting institutions until around 1960 departed from the traditional dualist framework. Since the 1960s, however, certain events have broken this barrier.

To recap Chapter 1, a dualist framework is characterized by a disparity in wage levels between the core and peripheral sectors of the economy, its divisive effects on the working class, the eventual decline of the peripheral sector, and the use of subcontractors as a buffer against fluctuations.[1] We shall use this framework to examine empirical evidence for the period from 1960 to 1990. The institution of subcontracting emerged in Japan when demand coincided with widening interscale wage differentials and also, in the postwar period, when the gap in the unionization of the large- and small-producer sectors was growing. Both during and after the war, the national government intervened to promote, or remove unfair practices from, existing subcontracting institutions.

What happened after the 1960s? Aside from the surge in demand, which was intrinsic to the continuing growth of the economy, were there still widening in-

---

1. The first and fourth points were made by both the liberal and the radical schools of dualism, and the second and third, mainly by the radical dualists.

FIGURE 4-1. Interscale Wage Differentials[a] in Manufacturing Industries, 1958–83

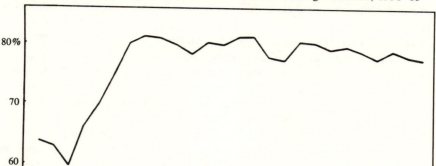

[a]Refers to percentage of average regular salary in cash for males at firms with 10 to 99 employees, as opposed to the same at firms with 1,000 or more employees (=100).

Source: SMEA, 1985b:23. Original Source: Ministry of Labor, *Basic Statistical Research on Wage Structure.*

terscale wage differentials and unionization gaps, providing a socioeconomic infrastructure conducive to subcontracting?

First, we shall review the long-term trend of interscale wage differentials between 1958 and 1983 in Japanese manufacturing industries, as shown in Figure 4-1. The disparity among interscale wages shrank by 20 percent within four years between 1960 and 1964, coinciding with the unprecedented labor shortages, which raised the starting wages at small firms even higher than those at large firms. The smaller wage differentials, now comparable to those of the United States, remained fairly constant through the 1980s (Friedman, 1988:139, 151). Thus at a macro level, this indicator of cheap labor in small firms (and cheap labor was what attracted the large firms to this secondary sector, by way of subcontracting) suddenly receded, if not disappearing. One could argue, however, that such macro-level data are misleading because they do not adjust for differences in labor composition, gender, age, length of service, and the like among workers in different sectors of the economy. What we must do, then, is to make an "apples-to-apples" comparison.

Ono (1973) produced interesting data concerning this issue. After weighting interscale differences in labor composition, gender, age, and length of service based on national statistics, he concluded that in 1966 the face-value wage differentials of 80.0 and 77.5 percent for establishments with 30 to 99 and 10 to 29 employees (as opposed to those with 500 or more employees, as 100 percent) turned out in fact to be 90.1 and 88.5 percent, respectively.[2] His findings thus suggest that the corrected

2. Ono, 1973:198. That these weighted statistics have since remained stable is pointed out by Smitka (1991:100). Adjusting variance in education, gender, and length of service, he claims that "[i]n 1981, the wages of 'standardized' workers in firms with 10–99 employees were 90% or more of those paid by firms with over 1,000 workers until age 44, and wages for young workers were actually higher than those paid by large firms."

wage differentials in the 1960s were smaller than their face values. Although this does not allow for the fact that the composition of labor was still not the same across different sectors of the economy by scale (including differences in access to non-monetary benefits), Ono's research results reinforce the view that the large firms' incentives for relying on small subcontracting firms solely because of their low wages were no longer as strong after the mid-1960s, at least at the macro level.[3]

What about the second factor, the divisive effects of dualism on the working class, as claimed by the radical school of dualism (Edwards, 1979)? Though there may not be a universally accepted way to measure them, the degree of unionization and, in particular, its interscale distribution do reflect the general balance of power between management and labor. If management attempts to weaken and divide the labor force and is successful, the result will be seen in declining union density—defined as the percentage of union members in the total population of employees. The last chapter demonstrated that there was a drop in union density overall, as well as a growing gap in union density between small and large firms during the 1950s, leading to the resurgence of subcontracting in Japan. Table 4-1 shows the long-term trend of union density between 1960 and 1977. There is no indication that union density fell; instead the data show stability throughout this period.

More important, however, is the interscale distribution of unionization. Between 1948 and 1956, union membership declined by half at firms with fewer than one thousand employees, whereas it doubled at firms with more than one thousand (see Table 3-4). This difference was a direct outcome of the 1949–50 recession induced by the Dodge Plan and was subsequently exploited by large Japanese manufacturers that turned to extensive nonunion subcontracting toward the end of the 1950s. Were there similar developments after the 1960s? Table 4-2 shows the distribution of union members for 1956, 1966, and 1976. The distribution of union memberships by firm size remained remarkably stable over the two decades. Unlike the 1950s, there was no indication in the 1960s and 1970s of unionization's being skewed toward the large sector. Thus, two important "dualist" catalyses for subcontracting apparently collapsed, or at least receded, in Japan after the 1960s.

This brings us to the third contention of dualism. If dualist assumptions regarding the correlation between interscale wage and unionization differences and the degree of reliance on subcontracting were right, we should see a decline in, or even the disappearance of, subcontracting institutions during this less dualistic period. Exposed to head-on competition with large firms, furthermore, small firms would eventually be forced out of business. This would sound plausible if we accepted that

---

3. This is not to argue, however, that large firms no longer tried to take advantage of interscale wage differentials, which at any rate continued to exist, albeit on a narrowing scale. In those segments of industry in which labor-intensive tasks accounted for a considerable amount of the work, the quest for relatively inexpensive labor continued. In electronics, for example, tasks that could not be easily automated or were too cumbersome to do so (e.g., simple manual tasks such as wiring, "preforming," and soldering) continued to be subcontracted out. Large-scale conversion of the formerly agricultural areas such as Tohoku and Shinshu after the mid-1960s produced a large pool of unskilled labor. Taking advantage of this new socioeconomic condition, many electronics firms—prime contractors and sub-contractors alike—established branch assembly factories in these areas. Around them mushroomed second-tier subcontractors. For more discussion on this, see Chapter 5.

TABLE 4-1. Union Density, 1960–77
(As of June each year)

Year	Percent
1960	32.2%
1961	34.5
1962	34.7
1963	34.7
1964	35.0
1965	34.8
1966	34.2
1967	34.1
1968	34.4
1969	35.2
1970	35.4
1971	34.8
1972	34.3
1973	33.1
1974	33.9
1975	34.4
1976	33.7
1977	33.2

Source: Labor Minister's Office, Statistics and Information Bureau, 1978:31.

the Japanese government's increasing intervention to prohibit unfair subcontracting practices made it even more difficult for prime contractors to subcontract out.

First, we shall consider the normative decline of the small sector itself, as attributed by the radical school of dualism to the large and small firms' differing access to new technologies and new markets (Edwards, 1979:77, 84).

Japan's technological progress, such as the microelectronics revolution, was especially striking after 1960. In barely two decades, the principal electronic building block shifted from vacuum tubes to transistors to integrated circuits (ICs) to large-scale integrated circuits (LSIs) to very large-scale integrated circuits (VLSIs). Each time there was a microelectronics innovation, the existing products and processes became obsolete. Furthermore, the microelectronics revolution spilled over from the electronics industry to other industries, as seen in such microelectronic applications as computerized ticketing, "smart" cars, and factory automation.

TABLE 4-2. Distribution of Union Members in All Industries, 1956, 1966, and 1976

Size of Firm[a]	1956		1966		1976	
1,000 or more	2,093,725	(33.0%)	3,477,677	(33.7)	4,188,813	(33.9%)
500–999	1,097,545	(17.3)	1,747,090	(16.9)	2,001,714	(16.2)
100–499	2,297,413	(36.2)	3,726,788	(36.2)	4,467,285	(36.1)
99 or less	861,674	(13.6)	1,356,565	(13.2)	1,716,476	(13.9)
Total:	6,350,357	(100.0)[b]	10,308,120	(100.0)	12,374,288	(100.0)[b]

[a]Number of union members per *tan'i kumiai* (union organization, corresponding roughly to an establishment).

[b]Because of rounding off, the percentage figures for 1956 and 1976 do not add up to 100.

Source: Labor Minister's Office, Statistics and Information Bureau, 1978:70–71.

FIGURE 4-2. Output of Japanese Manufacturing Industry by Size of Firm, 1954–81

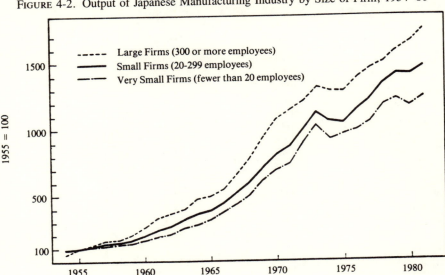

Source: SMEA, 1983:95. Original Sources: Ministry of International Trade and Industry (MITI), *Kogyo tokei hyo* (Statistics on industries); Bank of Japan, *Oroshiuri bukka shisu* (Index of wholesale prices).

This spillover ties in with the dualists' claim about the eventual decline of the peripheral sector when the "core firms" take over new markets and new industries. This claim is based on the assumption that even though technological innovation might take place both in large and small firms, it can be profitably exploited only by firms large enough to produce and sell for the national market, leaving no uncontested markets for potential competitors.[4] If the dualists are right, the core sector of the economy should expand at the expense of the peripheral sector, especially when "new markets and new industries" are constantly being created, in an age of rapid technological progress. The high-growth Japanese economy of the 1960s seems to fit this case perfectly, and it allows us to test this contention.

Figure 4-2 shows trends in the Japanese manufacturing industry output by size of firm between 1954 and 1981. There is no indication of the small sector's decline, let alone its disappearance, throughout the period. Its output was slightly more affected by the two oil shocks in the 1970s than was that of the large sector, but each time a quick recovery compensated for the brief decline. At any rate, there is no sign of support for the radical dualist view of a peripheral decline due to the core firms' dominance.

Figure 4-3 indicates the trend in added value of the small sector during the two decades from 1962 to 1982. Despite the economic fluctuations and radical technological innovations that took place during the period, the share of the small firms' added value remained stable, around 30 to 36 percent of the national aggregate.[5]

4. Edwards, 1979:77, 84. Note that mass-production and mass-marketing principles underlie this assumption.
5. Looking at the question from a different standpoint, these data also suggest that the "reversal of roles" between the hitherto-dominant large firms and the emerging, flexibly specialized small firms, as

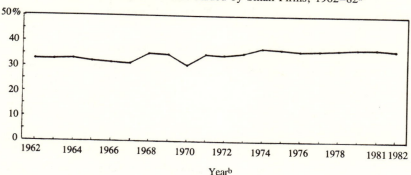

FIGURE 4-3. Share of Value Added by Small Firms, 1962–82[a]

[a]Small firms refer to firms with 20 to 299 employees.
[b]The year 1980 is missing in the source.

Source: SMEA, 1985a:97. Original Source: Ministry of International Trade and Industry (MITI), *Kogyo tokei hyo: Kigyo hen* (Statistics on industries: Enterprise edition).

Another indicator of the small sector's importance is the percentage of its employees in the total working population. National statistics indicate that for two decades after 1960 the share of small firms' employees in the manufacturing sector remained steady at about three-fourths.[6]

Thus, contrary to dualist predictions, the small sector not only survived but also secured its steady share of employment of the Japanese working population after 1960. This indicates that the technological innovations during this period did not mean that "new markets and new industries" were the exclusive province of large firms; small firms continued to prosper as well.

What about subcontracting? Did it decline? Did it stabilize? Or did its use increase? Given the receding dualistic indicators just considered, one might assume that it declined, within the dualist framework at least, even if the small sector itself remained stable.

Table 4-3 provides evidence, however, that the number and proportion of small firms that subcontracted steadily increased between 1966 and 1981 in Japanese manufacturing industries. Table 4-4 shows the proportion of small firms that made more than 80 percent of their output through subcontracting in 1976 and 1981.

Finally, Figure 4-4 shows the Japanese motor vehicle assemblers' increasing dependence on "outsourcing" from 1961 to 1986. Evident is the consistently high growth of outsourcing rates throughout the 1970s; even the two oil shocks in 1973–74 and 1979 had scarcely any effect on the trend. The 1973–74 oil shock entailed the first drop since 1955 in motor vehicle production output, by 7.5 percent.

claimed by Piore and Sabel (1984:206), has not taken place, insofar as the Japanese economy in this period is concerned.

6. SMEA, 1985a:97, Figure 1-1-2. Small firms in manufacturing industries refer to establishments with fewer than three hundred employees, an official definition of *chusho kigyo* by the Japanese government. *Chusho kigyo* literally means small and medium enterprises. For brevity, however, this study uses the terms small firms or small businesses for *chusho kigyo* unless otherwise specified.

TABLE 4-3. Number and Percentage of Small Manufacturing Firms That Subcontract, 1966–81

Year	Manufacturing		Machinery		Electrical		Transportation Equipment	
1966	299,577	(53.3%)	24,811	(70.7%)	11,422	(81.4%)	8,685	(67.1%)
1971	355,228	(58.7)	28,710	(75.9)	13,705	(79.0)	17,396	(77.9)
1976	373,439	(60.7)	42,977	(82.7)	19,520	(82.3)	15,086	(86.2)
1981	465,354	(65.5)	52,395	(84.1)	27,261	(85.3)	18,792	(87.7)

Source: SMEA, 1983:159.

In regard to the fourth contention of dualism, recall that both the liberal and the radical schools of dualism stressed the benefits to primary firms from using subcontracting to adjust to fluctuations in demand (Berger & Piore, 1980; Fujita, 1965). According to these schools' explanation, subcontractors are employed specifically because contract work may be reduced or eliminated in the face of recession, thereby maintaining a steady workload for the primary firm and its employees. Had their contention been right, the Japanese motor vehicle assemblers would have lowered their outsourcing in proportion to the lower output in 1973–74. In so doing they would have protected themselves in the way that the dualists had predicted. But Figure 4-4 reveals no significant decrease in outsourcing over this period. The drop of slightly over 1 percent in outsourcing between 1975 and 1976 is only a fraction of the earlier 7.5 percent decrease in total output. The fluctuation adjustment thesis of dualism is thus not sustained, according to these data.

Figure 4-4 does not cover subcontractors below the first tier, however, and so it does not show whether the effects of the oil shocks in the 1970s were absorbed by lower-tier subcontractors rather than the first-tier suppliers represented in the figure. Some anecdotal studies appear to support this reasoning, albeit using extremely small samples sizes (Ohshima, 1980:231–33), but national statistics on employment levels by size of establishment in the transportation equipment industries (Figure 4-5) do not support this assumption. Between 1970 and 1984, employment levels at establishments of different sizes remained stable, and so it is puzzling that the empirical evidence is not consistent with the traditional dualist claim.

The institution of temporary workers, which had played such an important role in Japanese labor markets since the 1920s, also noticeably shrank after the mid-1960s. Unprecedented labor shortages in the 1960s made it difficult to secure new workers and forced many manufacturers to "internalize" their existing tempo-

TABLE 4-4. Percentage of Small Manufacturing Firms Whose Dependence on Subcontracting Exceeded 80 Percent of Their Output, 1976 and 1981

Year	Manufacturing	Machinery	Electrical	Transportation Equipment
1976	49.3%	66.0%	70.7%	76.2%
1981	54.0	70.6	75.6	78.7

Source: Adapted from SMEA, 1983:163.

FIGURE 4-4. Outsourcing Percentage: Ten Major Japanese Motor Vehicle Assemblers, 1961–86

Year

Sources: Compiled from Ministry of Finance, 1961–86, *Yuka shoken hokokusho* (Report on securities), for Toyota, Nissan, Mazda, Honda, Suzuki, Isuzu, Fuji Heavy Industries, Daihatsu, Hino, and Nissan Diesel. Because Mitsubishi Motors was not a publicly quoted company until 1988, its outsourcing figures for this period are not available.

rary workers by upgrading them to "regular" status.[7] National statistics show that the percentage of temporary workers in manufacturing industries fell from 7.7 to 4.5 percent between 1959 and 1965.[8] At the firm level, these changes were more dramatic. At Toyota, for example, the percentage of temporary workers in its total work force dropped from 42.6 percent in 1961 to less than 5 percent in the first half of the 1970s (Table 4-5). At Toshiba, the peak of 33 percent in 1960 dropped similarly, to less than 1 percent in the 1970s (Table 4-6).

Including seasonal or part-time workers and temporary workers, the proportion of all marginal workers at Toyota and Toshiba decreased to a very low level, ranging from less than 1 percent to just a few percentage points after the 1970s. This indicates that although the buffer function of marginal workers may not have been eliminated, the degree to which they contributed to that function significantly declined after the mid-1960s, owing to the effects of change in the labor market. Taking into account all the foregoing, then, one may wonder why large Japanese firms continued to resort to—and even increased their dependence on—subcontracting for a few decades after 1960.

7. Ministry of Labor, 1965:90–91. In 1963, for example, this "upgrading" rate was 30.8 percent of temporary workers for all industries. At Toyota, the percentage escalated from 4.7 (1959) to 10 (1960) to 15 (1961) to 50 (1964) (Yamashita, 1980:152).

8. Ministry of Labor, 1959:74–75, 1960:79–80; 1966:98–99. The internalization of temporary workers through upgrading largely disappeared in the recession of the 1970s but intermittently resurfaced during the 1980s, reflecting periodic booms. At Toyota, for example, the temporary worker "upgrading" system revived in 1985 and 1988 (*Nihon Keizai Shinbun,* September 13, 1988).

FIGURE 4-5. Employment Levels by Size of Establishment in the Transportation Equipment
Industries, 1970, 1975, 1980, 1984

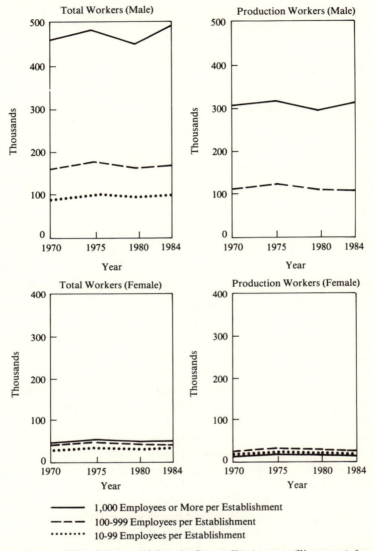

Source: Labor Minister's Office, Statistics and Information Bureau, *Chingin sensasu* (Wage census), for each year.

Producers' Strategies and the Market

Japan's domestic market after 1960 has three main producer-driven characteristics:
rapid and continuous growth, heavy competition, and product proliferation. The
first, rapid and continuous growth of the market, can be seen in the dissemination
patterns of consumer products. Figure 4-6 shows the dissemination rates of selected

TABLE 4-5. Temporary and Seasonal Workers at Toyota, 1946–79

Year[a]	Total Work Force	Temporary Workers	Seasonal Workers	All Marginal Workers
1946	6,463			
1947	6,345			
1948	6,481			
1949	7,457			
1950	5,398			
1951	5,315			
1952	5,228			
1953	5,291			
1954	5,249			
1955	5,162			
1956	5,061			
1957	5,904	5.9%		5.9%
1958	6,050	12.1		12.1
1959	7,210	12.2		12.2
1960	9,720	21.9		21.9
1961	11,963	42.6		42.6
1962	13,442	30.2		30.2
1963	15,999	26.5		26.5
1964	20,938	16.0	0.7%	16.7
1965	22,595	10.8	3.7	14.5
1966	25,580	11.9	1.1	14.0
1967	30,380	11.2	1.4	12.6
1968	34,078	7.9	2.6	10.3
1969	36,689	6.1	3.7	9.8
1970	40,365	5.0	2.8	7.8
1971	40,918	3.4	5.1	8.5
1972	41,256	1.2	1.6	2.8
1973	42,892	2.2	1.5	3.7
1974	44,880	1.9		1.9
1975	44,584	b		
1976	44,474			
1977	44,798			
1978	45,203			
1979	45,233			

[a] As of August for 1946–49, May for 1950, September for 1951, November for 1952–74, and June for 1975–79.
[b] Between 1975 and 1979, Toyota stopped employing temporary and seasonal workers (*Chunichi Shinbun*, June 9, 1979, quoted in Fujita, 1980:131).
Source: Adapted from Yamashita, 1980:148–49. Original Sources: Toyota, 1958:663, 1968:804; Ministry of Finance, *Yuka shoken hokokusho: Toyota* (Report on securities: Toyota), 1961–79.

consumer durables in 1957 and 1963. Substantial increases in ownership, some of them enormous, are noteworthy, such as the jump from less than 10 percent to more than 90 percent within six years for television sets.

Figures 4-7 and 4-8 offer similar data up to 1976 and 1982, respectively. The bold line in Figure 4-8 indicates a strong upward trend in real disposal income, an important condition for the continued dissemination of consumer products.

Consistent with this trend, new motor vehicle registrations in Japan jumped from 408,000 in 1960 to 6.7 million in 1988, and motor vehicle production (in units)

TABLE 4-6. Temporary and Part-Time Workers at Toshiba, 1958–83

(As of March of each year)

Year	Total Work Force	Temporary Workers	Part-Time Workers	All Marginal Workers
1958	36,413	24%		24.0%
1959	39,726	29		29.0
1960	48,906	33		33.0
1961	54,902	31		31.0
1962	62,817	31		31.0
1963	62,010	17		17.0
1964	60,271	10		10.0
1965	61,730	4.9		4.9
1966	59,211	1.8	0.8%	2.6
1967	62,672	6.0	3.9	9.9
1968	68,521	4.5	5.8	10.3
1969	72,140	3.7	4.6	8.3
1970	77,615	3.0	5.8	8.8
1971	74,711	0.4	1.0	1.4
1972	71,966	0.6	1.4	2.0
1973	74,800	2.2	3.6	5.8
1974	74,002	0.3	3.1	3.4
1975	68,030	—[a]	0.4	0.4
1976	66,755	—	0.3	0.3
1977	64,781	—	0.8	0.8
1978	64,237	—	0.3	0.3
1979	63,235	—	0.7	0.7
1980	64,508	—		
1981	65,305	0.1	2.2	2.3
1982	66,679	0.2	2.6	2.8
1983	67,387	—	2.5	2.5

[a] Indicates less than 0.1 percent.

Source: Andrew Gordon, *The Evolution of Labor Relations in Japan: Heavy Industry, 1853–1955* (Cambridge, MA: Council on East Asian Studies, Harvard University, 1985), p. 406. Reprinted here with the publisher's permission. Original Source: Personnel section, Toshiba.

climbed from 482,000 in 1960 to 12.7 million in 1988, compound annual growth rates of 10.5 percent and 12.4 percent, respectively (Cusumano, 1985:387, 392; *Ward's Automotive Yearbook 1989*:106–7).

Second, fierce domestic market competition among a considerable number of producers for the same or similar products was characteristic of the Japanese market for this period. In 1965, for example, there were twelve four-wheel motor vehicle producers. Two decades later, there were eleven, each trying to wrest away a little more market share from its competitors, with a similar range of product segments.[9] The national government's failure to rationalize the excessively competitive structure of motor vehicle manufacture in the late 1960s is well documented (Ito, 1987:18–21; Friedman, 1988:204–5). In this case, the motor vehicle assemblers'

9. Smitka, 1989:1. Market share–driven, "wide-range product line" strategies are distinctive characteristics of many Japanese producers.

FIGURE 4-6. Dissemination Rates of Selected Consumer Durables, 1957 and 1963

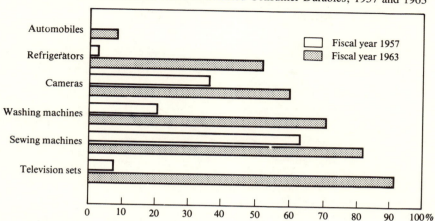

Source: Japan Development Bank, 1964:60. Original Source: Economic Planning Agency (EPA), *Shohisha doko yosoku chosa* (Survey of future consumer trends).

attempt to compete in the same or overlapping market segments resulted in the overturning of government policy and stronger global competitors.

In electronics, the situation was similar. The competition in color television sets is a case in point: Table 4-7 shows the number of new and discontinued color television models by twelve producers in the early 1970s. Twelve electronics manufacturers introduced 487 new models of color television sets while discontinuing 387 models, all within three years (1972–74). This foreshadows the third characteristic of the market: product proliferation.

FIGURE 4-7. Dissemination Rates of Selected Consumer Durables, 1958–76

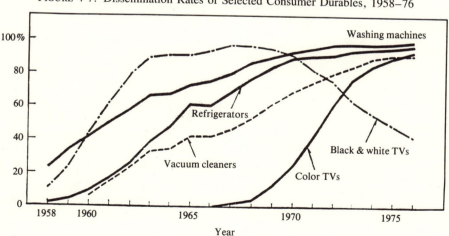

Source: Nakamura, Takafusa, 1981:94. Original Sources: Economic Planning Agency (EPA), *Shohisha doko chosa* (Survey of consumer trends), various years.

FIGURE 4-8. Dissemination Rates of Selected Consumer Durables and Disposable Real Income, 1970–82

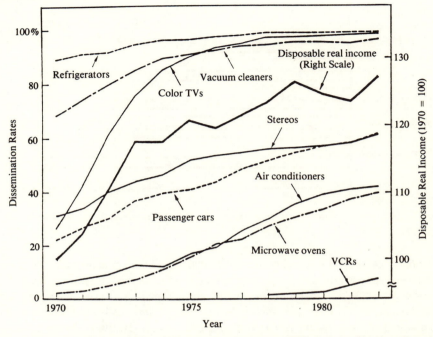

Source: SMEA, 1984:68. Original Sources: Economic Planning Agency (EPA), *Shohisha doko chosa* (Survey of consumer trends), various years; Prime Minister's Office, *Kakei chosa* (Survey of housekeeping) and *Shohisha bukka shisu* (Consumer price index), various years.

TABLE 4-7. Numbers of New and Discontinued Color Television Models by Twelve Japanese Producers, 1972–74

Producer	No. of New Models				No. of Discontinued Models	
	1972	1973	1974	1972–74	1974	1972–74
Toshiba	39	38	10	87	16	71
Matsushita Electric	36	24	13	73	14	64
Sanyo	30	14	8	52	12	41
Hitachi	19	19	10	48	12	38
Mitsubishi Electric	21	13	9	43	4	28
Sharp	14	15	12	41	0	29
General	11	13	7	31	8	29
Sony	6	13	9	28	2	17
Shin Nichi Den	10	11	4	25	6	25
Victor of Japan	14	9	0	23	2	14
Nippon Columbia	12	6	1	19	0	19
Fuji	8	6	3	17	4	12
Total:	220	181	86	487	80	387

Source: Suitsu, 1979:81. Original Source: *Nihon Keizai Shinbun* (Japan Economic Journal), January 14, 1975.

In the postwar growth period, many Japanese producers assumed the U.S. model of mass production was applicable to their own domestic market. Accordingly, in the late 1950s, many hastily introduced mass production technologies, such as transfer machines, in an effort to outpace the competition (Iwakoshi, 1968:83–84). Ironically, however, partly due to the effects of strong competition by many producers in overlapping market segments, no "typical" mass markets developed in Japan. As the data indicate, "congested" competition among many producers, constantly replacing existing product lines with many more new ones, persisted, in both electronics and motor vehicles. Compounding the problem was the pattern of annual model changes (or "face-lifts") and short product cycles that became apparent by the late 1950s. Annual model changes became common for electrical appliances,[10] and annual face-lifts and four- to five-year model cycles were established for automobiles.[11] Numerous new products were created by both industries.

Accelerating product proliferation coupled with short product cycles complicated manufacturing. In 1967, for example, Toyota produced 670,000 motor vehicles based on thirty-three different "platforms," or 20,300 units per platform.[12] In contrast, in 1965 GM's Chevrolet Division produced 1.65 million Impala, Bel Air, and Biscayne models, all on the same platform, or 1.65 million units per platform (Gunnel, 1982:155). Which was better suited to typical mass production methods with a combination of special-purpose, product-specific machines and semiskilled labor is obvious. Over time, moreover, manufacturing became even more complex. For example, the Toyota Corolla's variations based on options of engine, transmission, various appointments, and color jumped from a mere 72 in 1966 to 5,200 in 1987.[13] At Nissan the situation was similar, as shown in Figure 4-9.

To cope with the increasing manufacturing complexity, Japanese producers began to use, from the 1960s onward, a distinctive strategy to delegate the assembly of finished products and the subassembly or manufacture of systems components to major subcontractors. Over time, many parts of the assembly and subassembly lines

10. In this connection, it is worth referring to the origins of "annual model changes" in Japanese manufacturing, although the evidence is, surprisingly, scarce. Some evidence suggests that it became fairly common to see annual model changes in Japanese electrical appliances toward the end of the 1950s. For example, although Hitachi supplied refrigerators (whose manufacture had in fact been banned until the end of the war, as they were considered a "luxury") in large quantities for the Occupation forces between 1946 and 1951, there was only one model (200-liter capacity, 200 kilograms), unchanged throughout the period. In 1952 Hitachi introduced three new small refrigerators (capacities of 95, 130, and 200 liters), which tapped a latent domestic market, immediately gaining the producer a market share of 57.4 percent that year. In 1954, in response to the rising demand, a factory dedicated to manufacturing Hitachi refrigerators was constructed, and in the meantime the product variety increased. By 1958 the practice of annual model changes, with improved functions, specifications, and design, became established (Hitachi, 1960:342–43; Okamoto, 1979a:216–17).

11. Car model cycles in Japan have been "short" from the early 1960s through to the present. According to Fujimoto (1989:85), the average interval of major model changes (covering approximately seventy models) for all Japanese car producers was 4.9 years from 1960 to 1987. The comparable figure for 1980 to 1987 was also 4.9 years.

12. Calculated from Toyota, 1967:756–62. The *platform* is defined here as the wheelbase.

13. Toyota, 1967:660, and my interview with K. Kamei, manager, administration staff, Administration Department, July 6, 1987. The latter figure is not theoretical possibilities but those variations actually produced.

FIGURE 4-9. Proliferation of Models and Body Styles at Nissan, 1965–85

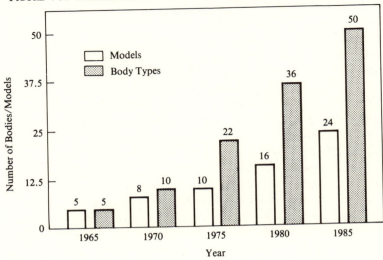

Source: Tidd, 1989:12.

at prime contractors were moved intact from major producers to their affiliated firms and subcontractors newly converted into contract assemblers and subsystems manufacturers.

The practice of contract assembly itself was not entirely a new one, however. In the late 1940s when Toyota had a capacity problem, part of its assembly of one passenger car model was contracted out to Kanto Electric Motor Manufacturing (later Kanto Auto Works) for "short-term capacity adjustment reasons" (Toyota, 1967:357). However, its contract assembly after the 1960s was far more strategic and was systematically executed; Table 4-8 shows Toyota's contract assembly "empire" as of 1987.

After three decades of evolution, Toyota motor vehicles in the late 1980s were thus assembled by Toyota itself and eight other contract assemblers. The general principle of this division of labor was that the main firm assembled volume products and strategically important "high-tech" models (e.g., the Toyota Soarer, a "high-tech" luxury 2 + 2 coupe), and the contract assemblers were responsible for relatively small-volume products and special-purpose motor vehicles. Specialization in a relatively narrow product range (e.g., trucks, multipurpose utility vehicles) and operational flexibility within that range (e.g., a high degree of "mix loading") were important requirements for contract assemblers. Table 4-9 shows the percentage of Hino Motors' contract assembly for Toyota. Hino Motors, an assembler of medium-to-large trucks and buses of its own and 11.3 percent owned by Toyota as of 1986, thus contributed significantly to Toyota's "full-product-line" strategy, by specializing in building Toyota-badge "light pickups" and "small-volume versions" of one of its passenger car models. Over time Nissan also developed a similar system of contract assembly. For example, after decades of experience in contract assembly,

TABLE 4-8. Toyota's Contract Assembly, 1987

	Assemblers[a]								
	TMC	TAL	TAB	KAW	Cen	HNM	Dai	AAB	GAB
Cars (incl. vans)									
Century				C					
Crown	C[b]sh[c]			Csvw					
Mark II	Cshvw			Csh					
Chaser				C					
Cresta				C					
Camry	C								
Vista	C								
Corona	Cscl		Csvwr5		Cs				
Carina	Ch		Cs		Cvwr5				
Celica	C								
Soarer	C								
Supra	C								
Corolla	Cscw2	Cl		Csc			Csvw		
Sprinter		Cl		Csc					
Tercel/Corsa	C35					C345			
Caribu	C								
Starlet		C							
Publica P/U		C							
MR2					C				
Minivans									
Hi Ace			C						
Town/Master Ace			C				C		
Lite Ace			C						
Trucks									
Dyna 2t	F		CB					CB	CB
Toyo Ace 1.5t	F		CB					CB	
Hi Ace	F		CB					CB	
Town/Lite Ace	F		CB						
Hi Lux	Cpm				Cp				
Land Cruiser	F							CB	
Big Truck	F		CB						
Blizzard							C		
Stout	F								CB
Coaster	F							CB	

[a] TMC: Toyota Motor Corp., TAL: Toyoda Automatic Loom Works, TAB: Toyota Auto Body, KAW: Kanto Auto Works, Cen: Central Car, HNM: Hino Motors, Dai: Daihatsu Motors, AAB: Arakawa Auto Body; GAB: Gifu Auto Body.

[b] C: Complete Assembly, F: Final Assembly, CB: Cab Assembly.

[c] s: sedan, h: hardtop, c: coupe, v: van, w: station wagon, l: liftback, p: pickup, m: multipurpose, 345: no. of doors, r: rear wheel drive.

Source: Data provided by Toyota Motor Corporation, 1987.

TABLE 4-9. Percentage of Contract Assembly for Toyota of
Hino Motors' Total Output, 1966–87

1966	14.8%
1967	13.3
1968	14.6
1969	17.5
1970	18.6
1971	20.8
1972	19.0
1973	17.6
1974	19.1
1975	22.7
1976	27.2
1977	31.5
1978	26.4
1979	24.3
1980	26.5
1981	26.2
1982	35.8
1983	40.9
1984	42.8
1985	40.5
1986	43.5
1987	35.8

Source: Data from Hino Motors, 1988.

Nissan Shatai, a subsidiary of Nissan, became an exclusive manufacturer (and designer) of the Nissan sports car line, the "Z" series.[14]

The manufacture of systems components was also increasingly delegated to subcontractors, and Table 4-10 shows five examples of automotive components subassembly lines transferred during the 1960s from Toyota to its subcontractors according to their specialties.

New arrangements of contract-assembly and systems-components "oursourcing" greatly relieved assemblers from having to manage the increasingly complex operational and administrative tasks concomitant with rapid growth and product proliferation. The assemblers now could focus their internal resources more on strategic activities, including product development, process innovation, and state-of-the-art manufacturing. This transfer of various production and, in part, development activities to external organizations shortened overall lead times and product cycles while not only maintaining but also expanding product lineups, which helped the primary producers adjust to shifting demands and get ahead of the competition.[15]

In electronics, too, similar developments began in the 1960s. In order to manage

14. Based on my interview with N. Yamamoto, vice-president and plant manager, Nissan Shatai, February 3, 1984; Cusumano, 1985:253, 256.

15. Based on my interviews with S. Ijichi, manager, administration staff, Purchasing Administration Department, Toyota Motor Corporation Headquarters, May 27, 1986; T. Maeda, general manager, Corporate Planning Office, Nissan Motor Company Headquarters, December 1, 1986.

TABLE 4-10. Transfer in the 1960s of Toyota's Automotive Components Subassembly Lines to Its Subcontractors

Year	Subcontractor	Subassembly Item
1964	Aichi Kogyo	Torque converters
1964	Chuo Seiki	Wheels
1964	Aisan Kogyo	Engine valves
1965	Aishin Seiki	Driving parts
1968	Hosei Brake	Brakes

Source: Society for Promotion of the Machinery Industry, Economic Research Institute, 1980:141. Original Source: *Nihon Keizai Shinbun* (Japan Economic Journal).

the increasing complexity of manufacturing accompanying the rapid proliferation of products in the 1960s the major electronics firms began to build up an external base of contract assembly and subsystems manufacture. Many of the subcontracting firms that were originally responsible for discrete treatment (e.g., machining, casting, forging, stamping, sheet metals, plating, painting, heat treatment, woodwork) were, over time, strategically converted into subsystems manufacturers and contract assemblers, according to their respective specialities. Similar—but not precisely equal—to the case for motor vehicles, the general rule was that whereas the principal firm concentrated its resources on strategically important products and processes (e.g., color television sets in the 1960s, video cassette recorders in the late 1970s), the assembly of more mature products (or "dry" [*kareta*] products in the industry's terminology, such as television sets, in the 1980s), the supply of small-batch items and the manufacture of subsystems were largely delegated to subcontractors.[16] Because electronic products require less capital-intensive facilities than motor vehicles do, "finished-products" subcontracting in electronics tended to be more widespread than in motor vehicles.[17] As in motor vehicles, the diffusion of various production and (to a lesser extent but still significant) development activities to subcontractors enabled the manufacturers to shorten overall lead times while maintaining a "full-product-line" strategy.

The evolution of this form of electronics subcontracting from the 1960s onward is illustrated in Table 4-11. An overall tendency toward greater responsibilities for the subcontractors, in the form of a shift from simple processes to more complicated assembly tasks can be seen in the quarter-century after 1965. This evolution of subcontracting is further illustrated in Figure 4-10, which depicts the chronological transition of the subcontracting job content at a subcontractor of Fuji Electric's

16. Based on my interviews with Mieno, manager, General Affairs Department, and Sakurabayashi, plant manager, Pioneer Electric's Kawagoe plant, December 22 and 27, 1983; K. Ohshita, manager, Production Department, Washing Machine Division, Matsushita Electric Industrial's Shizuoka plant, January 10, 1984; Horiuchi, manager, Production System Department, Oki Electric's Takasaki plant, January 26, 1984; K. Ono, executive managing director, Fuji Electric Headquarters, February 18, 1986; and N. Hattori, senior adviser, NEC Headquarters, March 12, 1986.

17. In 1968, for example, 36.9 percent (in terms of value) of the work subcontracted purchased by large electronics firms was devoted to "finished products." The comparable figure for motor vehicles was 18.9 percent. See SMEA (1968), *Shitauke kigyo kozo chosa* (Survey of subcontracting enterprise structure), quoted in Kiyonari, 1970:170.

TABLE 4-11. Breakdown of Subcontracting Content at Fuji
Electric's Tokyo Plant, 1965–90

(Percentage/value based)

Year	Processes[a]	Subassembly[b]	Finished Products Assembly
1965[c]	45.0%	28.0%	27.0%
1974	23.7	31.6	44.7
1980	19.0	40.5	40.5
1985	18.3	33.7	48.1
1990[d]	15.0	34.5	50.5

[a]Machining, stamping, sheet metals, and surface treatment (e.g., painting, plating).

[b]Mainly, electrical boards subassembly.

[c]Figures for this year are estimates.

[d]Projected.

Source: Adapted from data provided in 1986 by the subcontracting section, Purchasing Department, Fuji Electric's Tokyo plant.

Tokyo plant. Started in 1954 as a stamping parts specialist, this subcontractor gradually widened its range of skills and in 1966 began the subassembly of printed circuit boards (PCBs) at the request of Fuji Electric. Then from 1978 it further diversified into the complete assembly of protective relay systems, peripherals for electronic control systems, and telecommunication products, all at Fuji's request. Through this evolutionary process, this subcontractor was transformed from a mere

FIGURE 4-10. Transition of Subcontracting Work at a Subcontractor of Fuji Electric's Tokyo Plant, 1954–83

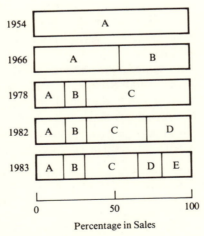

A: Stamping Parts   B: PCB[a] Assembly   C: Protection Relays
D: Electronic Control Peripherals
E: Telecommunication Equipment
[a]Printed circuit board.

Source: Ikeda, 1986b.

TABLE 4-12. Transition of Subcontracting, Number of First-Tier Subcontractors, and Number of Products at Fuji Electric's Tokyo Plant, 1974–90

Year	Subcontracting Rate[a]	No. of First-Tier Subcontractors	Total No. of Products
1974	49%	93	1,300[b]
1980	61	96	1,800[b]
1985	60	71	2,000
1990[c]	65	60	2,300

[a] Measured by task hours.

[b] Estimates.

[c] Figures for this year are projected.

Source: Data collected in 1986 from the subcontracting section, Purchasing Department, Fuji Electric's Tokyo plant.

stamping parts processor to a fairly comprehensive manufacturer assembling one hundred finished products consisting of ten thousand components.[18]

Table 4-12 shows the changes in subcontracting rate, number of first-tier subcontractors, and total number of products at Fuji Electric's Tokyo plant between 1974 and 1990. The data reveal an increasing reliance on subcontracting and a decreasing number of "select" first-tier subcontractors, each managing a steadily growing number of products.

Another important development of the new system was the delegation to subcontractors of not only assembly tasks but also testing, parts procurement, and design functions, as seen in Table 4-13 and Figure 4-11. Table 4-13 shows the distribution of design and assembly functions of measurement control products between Fuji Electric's Tokyo plant and its subcontractors. Whereas 88.8 percent of the assembly of 419 Fuji Electric measurement control products was outsourced in 1986, 13.6 percent of the Fuji products concerned were also designed by subcontractors. Figure 4-11 shows further breakdowns of these data according to subcontractor, grade, number of models, and delegated functions of design, parts procurement, assembly, and testing. The extensive delegation of assembly, testing, and parts procurement to subcontractors is apparent. Also, "grade-A" subcontractors were engaged in more comprehensive roles than "grade-B" subcontractors were.

There were similar developments at many other Japanese electronics firms. For example, Toshiba's Mie motor and transformer plant selected 20 subcontractors out of 120 and in 1967 converted them into systems-components manufacturers. Similarly, in the late 1960s Hitachi's Taga and Tokai plants converted many of their simple process and parts subcontractors into contract assemblers of radios and electrical motors (*Nikkan Kogyo Shinbun*, March 27, 1968, July 8, 1968, March 17, 1969). Mitsubishi Electric's Kyoto and Kamakura plants also adopted the same

18. Ikeda, 1986b:37. In 1986, 10 percent of this subcontractor's stock was owned by Enzan Fuji, a subsidiary of Fuji Electric (based on my interview with T. Ohyama, manager, subcontracting section, Purchasing Department, Fuji Electric's Tokyo plant, April 3, 1986). Smitka (1991:40–41) recites a good story about an automotive supplier that, at the request of its customer, Mitsubishi Motors, experienced an evolutionary process similar to the one described here.

TABLE 4-13. Distribution of Design and Assembly Functions of Measurement Control Products[a] Between Fuji Electric's Tokyo Plant and Its Subcontractors, 1985

Division of Labor	Design Model Nos.		Assembly Model Nos.	
In-house	362	(86.4%)	47	(11.2%)
Subcontracting	57	(13.6)	372	(88.8)
Total:	419	(100.0)	419	(100.0)

[a]In 1985, Fuji Electric's Tokyo plant had three product groups: measurement controls, data-processing systems, and power electronic systems. The total number of the models produced was approximately 2,000, of which 419 were measurement control products, considered as "dry" (*kareta*) items using conventional technologies.

Source: Data collected in 1986 from the subcontracting section, Purchasing Department, Fuji Electric's Tokyo plant.

subcontracting strategy in this period (Ichikawa, 1968:141). On the basis of this and other anecdotal evidence that indicates the same or a similar evolution, Fuji Electric's subcontractors seem fairly typical.

The evolution of Japanese subcontracting can be further reinforced with national statistics. Table 4-14 shows the chronological change in the top three subcontracting functions from the standpoint of the prime contractors in the machinery industry for 1934, 1950, and 1968. Although the subcontracting patterns did not substantially change between the prewar and immediate postwar periods, they did between 1950 and 1968. Subcontracting job functions shifted at the national level from simple discrete processes to more complex undertakings such as finished products and pressed components manufacture. Figure 4-12 further demonstrates this shift in subcontracting tasks between 1962 and 1972, from the subcontractors' standpoint. The general trend of simple processes being progressively replaced by semifinished and finished products assembly is thus confirmed from the standpoints of both customers and subcontractors.

An important outcome of this structural change was the emergence of multi-skilled subcontractors who took advantage of this increasing multifunctional tech-

TABLE 4-14. Change in Top Three Subcontracting Functions[a] in the Machinery Industry, 1934, 1950, and 1968

Year	No. 1		No. 2		No. 3
1934	Machining	(30.0%)	Forging	(27.3%)	Sheet metal (5.2%)
1950	Machining	(31.8%)	Forging	(17.9%)	Sheet metal (9.2%)
1968[b]	Finished products	(23.0%)	Pressed components	(22.8%)	Machining (21.3%)

[a] Value based, from the standpoint of prime contractors.

[b] Sample size: 634 manufacturers, including those in the automotive, automotive components, consumer electronics, electronic parts, and machine tool industries.

Sources: SMEA, 1950:103–6; Kiyonari, 1970:170; Original Sources: Survey by Ministry of Commerce and Industry (MCI) in 1934; Research Association of National Economy (Kokumin Keizai Kenkyu Kyokai) (1950), *Kikai kigu kogyo gaichu jyokyo chosa* (Survey of subcontracting conditions in the machinery and equipment industry); SMEA (1968), *Shitauke kigyo kozo chosa* (Survey of subcontracting enterprise structure).

FIGURE 4-11. Breakdown of Subcontracted Measurement Control Products at Fuji Electric's Tokyo Plant, 1985

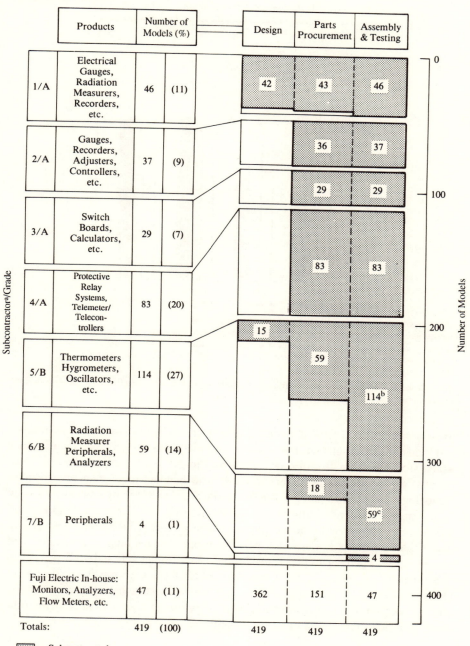

= Subcontracted

Source: Data from Fuji Electric's Tokyo plant in 1986.

FIGURE 4-12. Transition of Subcontractors' Work, 1962–72

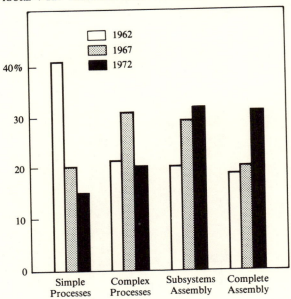

Simple processes: single discrete processes such as grinding or polishing.
Complex processes: multiple processes such as grinding and polishing combined.
Subsystems assembly: assembly of subsystems or systems components consisting of multiple processes.
Complete assembly: assembly of complete products that can be sold in the final product market.

Source: Ikeda, 1975:84. Original Source: SMEA, 1972, *Chusho kigyo choki doko chosa* (Long-term trend of small and medium enterprises).

nological expertise to serve their customers. A survey by the Ministry of Commerce and Industry (MCI) showed, for example, that in 1934 a mere 6.2 percent of value-added subcontracting from prime contractors in the machinery industry was accounted for by multiskilled subcontractors who handled more than two separate technologies (e.g., machining and heat treatment).[19] In 1968, by contrast, a survey by the Japan Metal Press Industry Association showed that 91.8 percent of first- and second-tier subcontractors in the stamping components industry were engaged in multiskilled operations (i.e., 51.8 percent in press, machining, die making, and assembly; 23.5 percent in press, machining, and die making; and 16.5 percent in press, machining, and assembly); whereas only 8.1 percent were engaged in press alone.[20] This ties in with the issue of the new subcontracting system's benefits, which appeared after the 1960s not only for prime contractors but also for subcontractors who acquired a diversity of skills.

19. Calculated from a survey of subcontracting conducted by MCI and quoted in SMEA, 1950:104. Incidentally, "assembly" subcontracting was categorically nonexistent insofar as this survey was concerned.

20. Nishida, 1975:4, quoted in Suitsu, 1979:103. Because of rounding off, the percentage figures do not add up to 100.

The Resurgence of the *Keiretsu*

By design, contract assembly and systems-components subassembly are apt to lead to asset-specific contractual relations because (1) the combination of the technologies is specific to the customer and (2) their manufacturing complexity requires a set of investments not readily applicable (without substantial alterations) to other contracts (as opposed to simple discrete treatment that can be handled by general-purpose technology).

Despite government protection and a multitude of small subcontracting firms in Japan, such firms' financial and technological resources in the late 1950s and the early 1960s were usually insufficient to prepare for the enhanced responsibilities that awaited them. Due partly to a producer strategy to get around this problem and partly to the fear of the impending liberalization of foreign investment in Japan (which eventually took place from the mid-1960s to the early 1970s) (Kiyonari, 1970:178–79; Nissan, 1983:105–7), large Japanese manufacturers began to invest seriously in their subcontractors from the late 1950s onward. Depending on the needs and the availability of resources, this investment ranged from creating 100 percent–owned subsidiaries to creating partially owned "related firms," to simply providing loans or loan guarantees. But the purpose was clear: to increase the large manufacturers' control over some of their major subcontractors—financially, managerially, and technologically—in order to ensure that they could produce the same quality products as could the in-house operation.

Table 4-15 shows the increase of large Japanese manufacturers' investments in

TABLE 4-15. Investment Trends of Large Japanese Electrical and Automotive Manufacturers in Related Firms,[a] 1956–63

(In millions of yen)

Manufacturer	A 1956		1960		B 1963		B/A
Electrical							
Hitachi	2,022	(21)[b]	6,969	(41)	18,785	(74)	9.3
Matsushita	1,356	(70)	4,073	(182)	12,200	(274)	9.0
Tokyo Shibaura	607	(16)	3,431	(45)	8,669	(50)	14.3
Fuji Electric	467	(6)	2,378	(10)	4,014	(10)	8.6
Mitsubishi Electric	114	(6)	749	(13)	2,401	(21)	21.1
Automotive							
Toyota	706	(13)	4,948	(16)	9,893	(19)	14.0
Nissan	394	(22)	1,120	(24)	4,406	(27)	11.2
Isuzu	311	(29)	1,214	(61)	2,780	(70)	8.9
Hino Diesel	379	(15)	659	(17)	1,157	(17)	3.1

[a] Before the 1977 revision of the Rules of Financial Statements (Zaimu shohyo kisoku), *related firms* were defined as those that were more than 10 percent owned by, and affiliated through business relationships with, the parent firm (Sato, 1988:180).

[b] Numbers in parentheses are related firms.

Source: Ikeda, 1968:127. Original Sources: Ministry of Finance, *Yuka shoken hokokusho* (Report on securities), for each firm for each year.

TABLE 4-16. Percentage of Large Japanese Manufacturers Having Capital and Managerial Relationships with Subcontractors, 1950 and 1968

( ) = sample size

Loan/Guarantees	Capital Relationship	Managers on Loan	Capital Loan Guarantees
1950[a]			
Transportation equipment	1.7%	5.7%	13.0%
Electrical	0.7	8.8	15.8
Machinery total	2.0	7.3	13.7
1968			
Automotive (11)	36.4	54.5	90.1
Consumer electrical (57)	28.1	28.1	57.9
Machinery total (634)	18.7	18.8	63.9

[a] Sample size unspecified.

Sources: SMEA, 1950:112; Kiyonari, 1970:180. Original Sources: Research Association of National Economy (Kokumin keizai kenkyu kyokai) (1950), *Kikai kigu kogyo gaichu jyokyo chosa* (Survey of subcontracting conditions in the machinery and equipment industry); SMEA (1968), *Shitauke kigyo kozo chosa* (Survey of subcontracting enterprise structure).

"related firms" in the electrical and automotive industries between 1956 and 1963. Although the data do not specify the kinds of businesses that the related firms engaged in and therefore do include those engaged in activities other than strictly manufacturing, a trend toward the resurgence of the *keiretsu* is apparent.

Table 4-16 further confirms this trend at the national level, of large Japanese manufacturers' increasing control over their subcontractors through capital and managerial assistance between 1950 and 1968. There are noteworthy differences between 1950 and 1968. For this period, the increase in percentage of large manufacturers that had capital relationships with, and provided capital or "managerial" loans to, subcontractors was in the order of threefold to fortyfold. Also noteworthy is the fact that although in 1950 there were no significant differences among the transportation equipment, electrical, and machinery industries as a whole, there were in 1968. Automotive and consumer electrical manufacturers, both typical "assemblers," made in 1968 greater capital and managerial commitments to their subcontractors than the machinery industry's average. Using these data and those from Table 4-14 (which shows the move in the machinery industry in subcontracting content from discrete treatment to finished products for the same period), we can conclude that a shift toward greater responsibilities for subcontractors was in large part supported by the large Japanese manufacturers' strategic financial and managerial support.

In general, the division of labor between *keiretsu* firms and nonaffiliates was that the former took responsibility for technically advanced, proprietary products, and the latter were usually in charge of simpler products and processes. But the differences were not always so distinct and were often further blurred by intermediate arrangements such as "weak" (e.g., a single digit as opposed to 100 percent) ownership by the parent firm. Patterns of "cross" ownerships by "competing" parent firms, a common practice in the automotive industry, also complicated the classifications,[21] and *keiretsu* firms were not exclusively "captive" entities.[22]

The Advantages of Subcontracting and the Emergence of Collaborative Manufacturing

Many subcontractors welcomed the new subcontracting system, for it had three advantages: more stable contractual relations, more opportunities for technological learning, and improved growth prospects.

First, whether or not customer and subcontractor had a financial and managerial relationship (and only a few subcontractors actually did), the emergence of contract assembly and subsystems manufacture tended to stabilize contractual relations because of the greater asset specificity. The reason was that because the assembly lines were moved from customer to subcontractor, it made little economic sense to discharge the subcontractor in a recession. According to a purchasing manager of a large Japanese electronics firm, "Considering the extent to which we have transferred [the assembly of] those items [we used to make in-house] to our subcontractors and the fact that they cannot be made in-house any more, it is essential that we maintain them through ups and downs."[23] The greater confidence that some contract assemblers had in the stability of their position is evident in the following comments by a Japanese subcontractor: "Our customers can subcontract simple components or simple treatment to anybody. This weakens our bargaining position. But assembly work makes us stronger, because they can't let just anybody do that."[24]

Second, it was in the customers' best interest that their products assembled by subcontractors did not lose competitiveness through poor manufacturing operations. Along with assembly lines, the "composite" know-how that contributed to upgrading the subcontractors' conventional (and frequently deficient) skills was also transplanted through teaching.

In 1950, there were few reported cases of customers' commitments to upgrade their subcontractors' technical capabilities. Rather, the customers' principal interest

21. In 1986, for example, "cross" ownerships by "competing" parent firms at Akebono Brake were, in percentages, Bendix (15.1), Nissan (14.7), Toyota (14.5), Isuzu (5.9), Hino Motors (2.7), and Mitsubishi Motors (1.7). Similarly, those at Kayaba Kogyo were Toyota (11.0) and Nissan (9.2); those at Jidosha Kiki were Diesel Kiki (later Zexel) (34.9), Bendix (16.2), Isuzu (5.6), Toyota (1.6), and Nissan (1.5); and those at Ichiko Kogyo were Nissan (22.4), Toyota (8.6), Isuzu (4.0), and Daihatsu (3.7). (Toyo Keizai Shinposha, 1986a:588–91).

22. A general myth (especially outside Japan) is that Japanese *keiretsu* firms do business only with those in the same *keiretsu* group. This is mistaken. Even in the Toyota *keiretsu* group (recognized as among the tightest), 41.7 percent of its affiliated firms (defined here as those more than 20 percent owned by Toyota) sold 40 to 80 percent of their products to outsiders (calculated from Sato, 1988:121).

23. Based on my interview with T. Ohyama, manager, subcontracting section, Purchasing Department, Fuji Electric's Tokyo plant, April 3, 1986.

24. Based on my interview with the president of a first-tier Japanese electronics subcontractor in Ibaragi prefecture, in the spring of 1986.

was to use their subcontractors as a buffer (SMEA, 1950:113). Data from 1984 show how much this attitude has changed. Of the Japanese subcontractors surveyed by the Small and Medium Enterprise Agency, 53.3 percent reported that their main source of new technology was from their customers, and 52 percent of the customers stated that their technical support for subcontractors would be reinforced in the face of increasing competition and technological innovation (SMEA, 1985a:187–88). According to the proprietor of a Japanese subcontracting firm, "There are many things to be learned from our customers through continuing subcontracting. At small firms like us, our view tends to be narrow, owing to our limited resources. By accepting subcontracting jobs, we have many opportunities to see and learn the leading technologies and new market trends."[25]

Third, by becoming an essential part of the large firms' production forces and demonstrating more "composite" skills, this new breed of assembly subcontractor could expect reasonably long-term growth through continuing contracts and could better allocate their resources for the future. Unlike "floating" subcontractors (see Chapter 2) whose subsistence was subject chiefly to market forces, the new Japanese contract assemblers could foresee—to the extent made possible by their customers' "symbiotic" strategy—the future trends of their business and thus could prepare in advance.[26] In sum, the emergence of contract assembly and subsystems manufacture noticeably changed the logic of subcontracting relations toward "collaborative manufacturing."

Long-term Contractual Relations

Along with the development of new subcontracting patterns, long-term contractual relations proliferated, as measured by the spread of "basic contracts" for purchasing or parts transactions[27] between customer and subcontractor, usually extending to a full year and automatically renewed unless one or both of the parties requested otherwise. Table 4-17 shows the growth of basic purchasing contracts in the manufacturing industries in 1965 and 1970.

Although an overall increase is apparent, even between first-tier and second-tier

25. Based on my interview with the president of a Japanese electronics subcontractor, in the early summer of 1986.

26. Although many of the subcontractors that I interviewed in 1983, 1984, and 1986 thought it risky and even suicidal to try to market their own brand products, and thus try to compete head-on with their customers, they regarded the strategy to remain assembly subcontractors as viable only insofar as the customer's strategy would not change.

27. Entering into a business relationship through the basic contract itself is considered an expression, by both parties, of fairly long term commitments, particularly by the customer. This contract establishes basic rules between purchaser and supplier covering a range of items, including quality assurance, price determination and payment, order and delivery, proprietary rights, and materials supply.

The SMEA's administrative guidance, along with the introduction of the Small and Medium Enterprise Modernization Promotion Law (Chusho kigyo kindaika sokushin ho) in the late 1960s, also helped promote the dissemination of the basic contract (based on my interview with Prof. S. Sei, Kanto-Gakuin University, June 19, 1990).

TABLE 4-17. Dissemination of Basic Purchasing Contracts in Manufacturing Industries, 1965 and 1970

(Sample size = 2,564)

	1965	1970
Manufacturing total	64.8%	84.0%
P-1[a]	65.3	84.7
1-2[b]	52.4	72.5
Transportation equipment	69.0	84.1
Electrical equipment	69.2	84.1
Precision equipment	57.4	79.1

[a]Between prime contractor and first-tier subcontractor.

[b]Between first-tier subcontractor and second-tier subcontractor.

Source: Central Bank for Commercial and Industrial Cooperatives, Survey Department, 1971:68–69.

subcontractors, the dissemination rate increased by 38.4 percent, from approximately one-half to nearly three-quarters of the respondents. Between prime customers and first-tier subcontractors, the rate rose by 29.7 percent. In both the transportation and electrical equipment industries, the dissemination rate was higher than the manufacturing average in 1965, although the latter caught up by 1970. Regarding the "continuation" of contracts, 57.8 percent of Japanese subcontractors in the manufacturing industries stated in 1967 that their contracts with main customers were based on "continuing contractual relations alone," whereas a mere 6.5 percent responded that they had "no continuing contractual relations" (SMEA, 1967, quoted in Kiyonari, 1970, Table 2-3-47, p. 171).

This trend toward long-term contractual relations can be seen in specific firms also. Table 4-18 compares two electrical manufacturers in the early 1960s and the early 1980s in terms of years of business with their subcontractors. Even though the

TABLE 4-18. Years of Business with Subcontractors: Fuji Electric in 1983 Versus Matsushita Electric, circa 1961

Years of Business	No. of Subcontractors			
	Matsushita Electric (circa 1961)		Fuji Electric[a] (1983)	
21 or more	10	(1.8%)	164	(25.0%)
11–20	59	(10.3)	154	(23.5)
6–10	127	(22.2)	93	(14.2)
5 or fewer	329	(57.6)	146	(22.3)
Unknown	46	(8.1)	99	(15.1)
Total:	571	(100.0)	656	(100.0)[b]

[a]Excluding twenty-six subsidiaries and related firms.

[b]Because of rounding off, this percentage figure actually is 100.1.

Source: Based on data collected in 1986 from the Materials Control Department, Fuji Electric Headquarters. For Matsushita Electric, data from Suitsu, 1979:70. Original Source: Osaka Prefectural Research Institute of Commerce, Industry and Economy (1961b), *Shiryo* (Materials), no. 258, p. 10.

two sampled firms are different, these data at least indicate the tendency toward long-term, stable contractual relations over the two decades since 1960.

Furthermore, this change was not restricted to formal contracts. At more operational levels, various "protective" measures for "asset-specific" subcontractors were frequently taken, particularly during downturns, because often there were no longer duplicates elsewhere. Cutting off the subcontractors during a recession thus became almost synonymous with shutting down part of the customer's own internal operations. In many respects, asset-specific subcontractors assumed the attributes of "insiders" even when there were no equity relations.

During recession, it became a general practice for the large customers not only to give advance warning (up to several months) about the forthcoming reduction in subcontracting orders but also to help those subcontractors most likely to be severely affected to change their products and look elsewhere for business. The large customers also frequently helped the subcontractors find stopgaps (e.g., by finding other, less affected business entities to work with or even by sharing parts of the customers' own in-house operations not as affected by the recession), in order to keep the subcontractors' factories running (see Chapter 6).

The following remarks, made by purchasing managers of Japanese electronics and motor vehicle producers, are typical:

> Because many of our products are assembled by our subcontractors and because we no longer have the same facilities [for these products] in-house, they are as important as ourselves. In a recession, we give them warnings [of an expected reduction in orders] well in advance and try to help them find stopgaps if possible.[28]

> When we started making motor vehicles, there were few full-fledged components manufacturers in Japan from whom we could buy necessary components "off the shelf" to assemble. We had to make many components in-house. But over time the situation has changed. Especially after the 1960s, we began to rely on our suppliers' ability to design and produce automotive components for us. Today, we just give them basic ideas and specifications of the components we want for a specific car. Then they give us professional ideas and turn them into products. Our job is to maintain our ability to judge their technical capabilities and proposals and to demand corrections if necessary. We can't actually make many of the components in-house. We make only engines, transmissions, and some other important components, which is why our suppliers are so important to us. We'll do whatever we can to help them become competitive because it's good for us, too. By design, it is impossible to switch them around or fire them simply because of fluctuations in demand.[29]

These remarks point to some of the essential features of the new contractual relations that emerged in Japan between 1960 and 1990. Those subcontractors who may have previously been perceived as inconspicuous pillars of a dualist economy now found an enhanced *raison d'être* in a changing contractual framework. And

28. Based on my interview with Y. Watanabe, assistant manager, subcontracting section, Materials Department, Hitachi's Taga plant, Ibaragi, March 28, 1986.

29. Based on my interview with S. Ijichi, manager, administration staff, Purchasing Administration Department, Toyota Motor Corporation Headquarters, May 27, 1986.

such a new framework was characterized by tendencies toward long-term commitments between customer and subcontractor, commitments embodied in the spread of basic purchasing contracts and even customers' "protective" measures regarding the more asset-specific subcontractors.

The Emergence of Clustered Control

Chapter 2 showed that although the "tiered" structure of Japanese subcontracting had existed mainly to absorb economic shocks and provide cheap labor, it was the wartime government's intervention in the 1940s that introduced a systematic pyramidal structure based on the *keiretsu*. In the vertical "channelization" of various manufacturing entities, each *keiretsu* subcontractor was ordered to be as "dedicated" as possible to a designated customer.

As we have seen in this chapter, *keiretsu* subcontracting arrangements rebounded around 1960 as a result of the producers' strategy in a new, consumer demand–driven environment. Although the traditional Japanese structure of subcontracting before 1960 may not be called "fully arm's length" in the usual sense of the term (under one main company, such as General Motors, sit tens of thousands of "direct" subcontractors[30]), at least the ties between purchaser and seller were fairly loose and far-reaching due to the laissez-faire pressures of a domestic market in which many subcontractors were competing for short-term contracts. The large manufacturers' new strategies changed this, however. There were considerable changes starting in the 1960s that entailed the concentration of orders, intensified specialization, and increased dependence on specific customers.

Figure 4-13 shows these tendencies at the national level. In 1971, 27 percent of the subcontractors surveyed recognized that the orders previously scattered over several competitors were now concentrated on themselves, and 23.5 percent of them acknowledged that they had been instructed by their customers to specialize in specific products. At the same time, 19.2 percent were asked to increase their business dependence on their customers.

Figure 4-14 breaks down these data by tier. Whereas the customers' demand for specialized production was acknowledged by first-tier subcontractors twice as frequently, there are similar patterns in the concentration of orders and requests for increased business dependence on specific customers, for both first- and second-tier (and below) subcontractors. The reduction in and cutoff of orders due to these changes were recognized relatively more often by second-tier (and lower) subcontractors, but none of the "classical" dualist indictors showed more than 10 percent recognition; and in fact many registered below 5 percent, in contrast with the much stronger recognition of order concentration, specialized production, and increased customer dependence. This indicates that the changes in subcontracting

---

30. In 1987 General Motors had 12,000 "direct" materials suppliers and 25,000 "direct" service and nonproducts suppliers (based on my interviews with O. Pedersen, commodity manager, and C. Koo Yun, manager, Purchasing Activities, General Motors Headquarters, May 1, 1987).

FIGURE 4-13. Reorganization of Subcontracting, 1971
(Sample size=2,564)

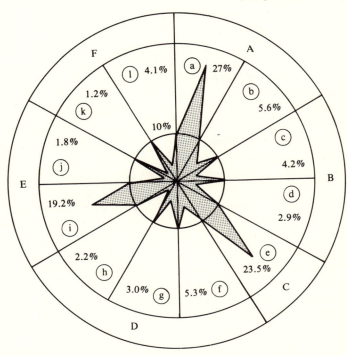

A: Concentrated Orders
B: Tier Mobility
C: Specialization
D: Group Activities
E: Change in Customer Dependence
F: Severance and Others

a: Previously dispersed orders now concentrated in respondent's firm.
b: Orders reduced owing to switches to in-house production or other subcontractors.
c: Elevated to a higher-tier subcontractor (e.g., from second to first tier).
d: Downgraded to a lower-tier subcontractor to serve another subcontractor in which orders are now concentrated.
e: Asked by customer to specialize in manufacturing specific products.
f: Collective order taking through cooperatives.
g: Asked by customer to cooperate with other subcontractors.
h: Asked by customer to merge with other subcontractors.
i: Asked by customer to increase sales dependence.
j: Asked by customer to decrease sales dependence.
k: Severed.
l: Others.

Source: Central Bank for Commercial and Industrial Cooperatives, 1971:39.

120

FIGURE 4-14. Reorganization of Subcontracting by Tier, 1971

(Sample size=2,564)

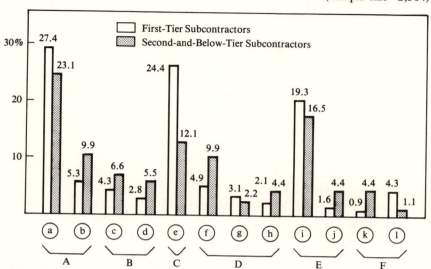

A: Concentrated Orders
B: Tier Mobility
C: Specialization
D: Group Activities
E: Change in Customer Dependence
F: Severance and Others

a: Previously dispersed orders now concentrated in respondent's firm.
b: Orders reduced owing to switches to in-house production or other subcontractors.
c: Elevated to a higher-tier subcontractor (e.g., from second to first tier).
d: Downgraded to a lower-tier subcontractor to serve another subcontractor in which orders are now concentrated.
e: Asked by customer to specialize in manufacturing specific products.
f: Collective order taking through cooperatives.
g: Asked by customer to cooperate with other subcontractors.
h: Asked by customer to merge with other subcontractors.
i: Asked by customer to increase sales dependence.
j: Asked by customer to decrease sales dependence.
k: Severed.
l: Others.

Source: Central Bank for Commercial and Industrial Cooperatives, 1971:43.

structure were not piecemeal but were systematic, extending to second-tier (and lower) subcontractors as important components of the entire production mechanism.[31]

These changes resulted in turning the traditional semi–arm's length or loosely tiered structure of subcontracting into a "tightly tiered" one, or what may be called

31. My field observations of approximately one hundred subcontractors in Japan from 1983 to 1989 support this argument. I found many second-tier subcontractors in Japan to be engaged not only in subsystems assembly but also in fairly complex contract assemblies of finished products requiring testing, packaging, and shipping on behalf of their customers. For a more detailed study with evidence, see Chapter 6.

a *clustered control* structure; that is, the firms at the top of this clustered control structure buy complete assemblies and systems components from a concentrated base (and therefore relatively limited number) of first-tier subcontractors, who buy specialized parts from a cluster of second-tier subcontractors, who buy discrete parts or labor from third-tier subcontractors, and so on. In this clustered structure, many subcontractors who used to supply directly to the top firm became second-tier subcontractors (to supply contract assemblers and subsystems manufacturers) within a designated "cluster."[32] As many first-tier subcontractors over time took over more comprehensive tasks from their customers, including testing, design, and parts procurement, they began to control their own subcontractors under their own regime. To reiterate the point already made, this system absolved those on top of the hierarchy from the increasingly complex controlling functions typical of external manufacturing organizations. Figure 4-15 illustrates the simplifying effect of this "clustered control" mechanism.[33]

Even though these developments took place in both the electronics and automotive industries, the clustered control model itself does not appear to be the exclusive province of Japanese producers. Having acknowledged the benefits of clustered control in an age of increasing product proliferation and shortened product cycles, many Western manufacturers began in the 1980s to reshuffle their purchasing structure in a direction similar to this model, with more responsibilities concentrated on a smaller number of first-tier systems-components suppliers who organize and control second-tier subcontractors within their own cluster. Figure 4-16 illustrates this at Daimler-Benz in 1988, although unlike Figure 4-15, this is a projection rather than a *fait accompli*.

Similarly, Ford, Renault, and BMW are some of the prominent Western automotive producers that pursued clustered control strategies of purchasing during the 1980s. For example, Ford U.S. shut down its in-house operations of wire harnesses assembly and "outsourced" them. In the latter half of the decade, moreover, Ford cut the total number of its twelve first-tier wire harness suppliers to four.[34] Renault also reduced the number of its components suppliers from sixteen hundred to six hundred by the end of the 1980s (Ikeda, 1986a:17). Although it did not make such a dramatic reduction in its twelve hundred materials suppliers, BMW also tried, based on a long-term corporate plan, to restructure its supply base, by making a number of its suppliers into "second-tier" entities.[35] These cases suggest a reform of purchasing organization that is influencing many of the world's producers today.

32. The newly established "subcontractor grading" system in the 1960s (to be discussed later) served as an objective yardstick for this change in status.

33. The conventional characterization of the Japanese industrial supply system as a pyramid is correct insofar as it describes the relationships between a single prime contractor and its subcontractors, but it is misleading if it is meant to imply a closed system. Taking into account the complex relationships among multiple prime contractors and cross-serving subcontractors, it is more accurate to describe the whole system as a series of pyramids overlapping one another, as do a range of mountains. Hence my own preferred term, the *Alps*. For more on the Alps structure of industrial sourcing, see Nishiguchi, 1987a.

34. Based on my interviews with M. Yamamoto, vice-president, K. Yoshinami, general manager, First Sales Department, American Yazaki Corporation, Michigan, March 16, 1987; L. Gene Stohler, vice-president, Sales and Marketing, ITT Automotive, Michigan, March 17, 1987.

35. Based on my interviews with W. Becker, director, Purchasing, and H. J. Preissler, general manager, International Purchasing, BMW Headquarters, Munich, September 12, 1988.

FIGURE 4-15. Clustered Control: Fuji Electric's Tokyo Plant, 1986

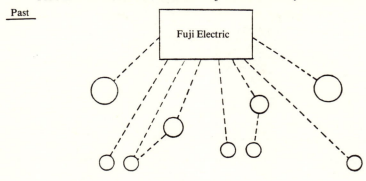

Past

Individual Relationships

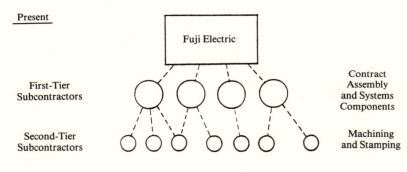

Present

First-Tier
Subcontractors

Second-Tier
Subcontractors

Contract
Assembly
and Systems
Components

Machining
and Stamping

Hierarchical Networking
Reduction in Direct Contacts
First Tiers Control Second Tiers
Externalizing "Dried-Out" Production

Source: Interviews at subcontracting control section, Materials Department, Fuji Electric's headquarters, and subcontracting section, Materials Department, Fuji Electric's Tokyo plant, April 3, 1986.

New Modes of Subcontracting[36]

Determining Price

An important outcome of the shift in industrial sourcing from discrete treatment to complete and subsystems assembly was that unlike the case of simple processing (e.g., machining, using a lathe or other general-purpose equipment), systems pricing could not be derived from market prices alone. Rather, the complexity and peculiarity of asset-specific contracts required substantial modifications of existing

36. This section, which describes the new modes of Japanese subcontracting relations for 1960 to 1990, draws heavily on my field interviews at many automotive and electronics firms, conducted between 1983 and 1989. Unless providing a specific source is deemed necessary, I shall not cite all the names of interviewees and their organizations, as this would create unnecessarily long footnotes. For a comprehensive list of my interviews, see Appendix A.

FIGURE 4-16. Changing Supplier Relations at Daimler-Benz, 1988

Before

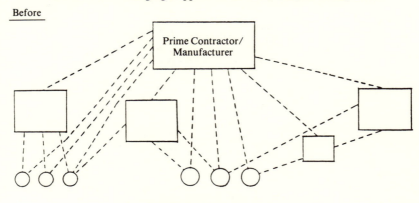

Suppliers and Subcontractors

After

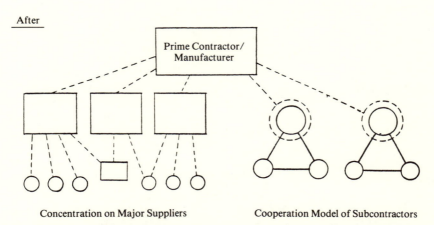

Concentration on Major Suppliers   Cooperation Model of Subcontractors

Source: Interviews at the Department of Materials Management, Procurement Logistics, Daimler-Benz AG, Stuttgart, September 14, 1988.

pricing mechanisms. It was no coincidence therefore, that value analysis (VA) techniques, originally developed by General Electric's purchasing department in 1947 and imported to Japan in the 1950s, came to be widely used in Japan to calculate costs from the 1960s onward, so that an increasingly complex cost structure could be decomposed into smaller parts and cost-sensitive elements could thus be identified item by item (Cusumano, 1985:258; Smitka, 1989:104).

For this purpose, customers frequently began to request detailed cost data from subcontractors, which opened the way to rational price determination on the basis of objective measurements. Rather than negotiating price downstream, prime contractors and subcontractors alike began to look at the possibility of reducing costs at the source by means of joint problem solving. The general tendency toward long-term contractual relations helped them cooperate. Prime contractors were able to demand subcontractors' continuous contribution to price reduction and product quality im-

TABLE 4-19. Price Determination Patterns in Manufacturing Industries, 1962–83

Year	Unilateral by Customer	By Customer, Based on Subcontractors' Quotations	Bilateral Agreements	Others
1962	23.4%	35.9%	31.9%	8.8%
1967	14.7	43.4	37.4	4.5
1972	12.2	36.3	45.8	5.7
1977	8.2	13.1	78.0	0.7
1983[a]	5.5	10.5	83.4	0.5

[a]Because of rounding off, the percentage figures for this year do not add up to 100.

Sources: Ikeda, 1975:82; Central Bank for Commercial and Industrial Cooperatives, Survey Department, 1977:36, 1983:37. Original Source: SMEA (1972), *Shitauke chusho kigyo choki doko chosa* (Survey on long-term trends of small and medium enterprises), quoted by Ikeda, 1975:82.

provement in exchange for long-term contractual relations. Subcontractors were thus provided with a strong motivation to invest and commit themselves to meeting these requirements. In the automotive industry in particular (because the impact of supplier input was stronger), purchaser–seller profit-sharing rules were developed on the basis of objective analytic value measurements.[37]

Over time, the traditional pattern of unilateral price determination by customers was gradually replaced by bilateral agreements. Table 4-19 shows national statistics on the chronological change in price determination patterns in Japanese manufacturing industries between 1962 and 1983. In 1962, nearly 60 percent of the subcontractors surveyed reported that prices were "unilaterally determined" by their customers. In sharp contrast, in 1983, 83.4 percent of the respondents used "bilateral price agreements." Along with this development, the basic orientation of price negotiations shifted from bargaining between unequal partners to joint problem solving, and the logic of contractual relations moved from exploitation to collaborative manufacturing.

From Unilateral Design to Bilateral Design

A logical continuum of this shift was the subcontractors' participation in bilateral cost reduction efforts by means of improved design.[38] In addition to the VA techniques used in reducing costs of ongoing components while maintaining or enhancing product quality, value engineering (VE) techniques came to be widely used at the design stage to lower the costs of new products. Japanese automotive producers led in this new move by adopting the "target cost" (or "cost-planning") method of new product development, which involved the components suppliers at an early stage.

37. Based on my interviews with M. Yamamoto, vice-president, and K. Yoshinami, general manager, First Sales Department, American Yazaki Corporation, Michigan, March 16, 1987.

38. It is widely recognized that although the extent to which costs can be reduced in manufacturing after the design is set is fairly limited, preproduction design changes are cheaper and can yield huge benefits. Many of my interviewees pointed this out.

The target cost method of product development works on market price–minus (rather than cost-plus) principles, as follows: First, the sale price of a new car model is determined, for example, X dollars, with Y profits and Z costs, and then the cost of each part is evaluated. Through this process, the cost for a console box, for example, is determined as C dollars, within which the required specifications for this part, such as performance, quality, durability, feel, and appearance, must be met. By jointly evaluating the various possibilities—keeping in view what the consumer needs and desires—in design, materials, surface treatment, mechanisms, manufacturing methods, and the like, the combined costs of the parts are reduced, step by step, toward the target cost while keeping constant the required specifications. VE techniques are particularly useful in this process. Proposals from the suppliers are encouraged because of their intimate professional knowledge of the part concerned. After Job 1 (i.e., the roll-off of a new car model), the design is continuously modified to lower costs even more. VA techniques are especially helpful at this stage.[39]

Along with the target cost method of new product development that emerged in Japan in the 1950s came "profit-sharing rules" for purchaser and supplier. If, for example, the price for an instrument cluster (in the dashboard) was agreed on as 120 points for the first car-model year, during which time 110 points, the target price for the second year, was in fact achieved by their "joint" efforts, then the assembler would pay the supplier 115 points, thus sharing the profit evenly. If, however, the cost was further reduced during that period, say, down to 108 points, then the balance would go to the supplier. In other words, the assembler did not ask for a cheaper price than the second-year target price. In the second year, the assembler paid either 109 points or 110 points net, and lower costs were continuously sought by encouraging more from the suppliers.[40] This rule setting was a significant departure from the traditional practice in which the suppliers' incentives for improvement were frequently negated by the purchaser's attempts to try to monopolize the benefits of its suppliers' new ideas.[41] In contrast, the new arrangements inspired

39. Based on my interviews with M. Nakao, manager, and H. Yamaguchi, assistant manager, Tokyo administration staff, Purchasing Administration Department, Toyota Motor Corporation, Tokyo branch, July 2, 1987.

40. Over time (particularly after the oil shocks in the 1970s), periodic purchasing price "rectification" (*kohshin*) in the language of Japanese manufacturing (especially in the automotive sector) became synonymous with automatic price reduction rather than increase (except for those occasions when the categorical cost increase of certain raw materials, say, oil, made this principle inoperative). This practice of periodic price rectification every six to twelve months became further formalized in the basic purchasing contract between customer and supplier, although the term *reduction* might not actually be used. In 1986, for example, Toyota's Basic Contract of Components Transactions (Buhin torihiki kihon keiyakusho) stipulated that "unless there are special circumstances, unit prices of supplied components will be rectified every six months." By the same token, such periodic price rectification came to be widely practiced among lower-tier subcontractors and stipulated in their basic contracts as well. The clause of this half-yearly price rectification can be found in the 1986 Basic Contract of Components Transactions of Kanto Auto Works, Toyota's first-tier contract assembler, and that of Anjo Electric, Nippondenso's first-tier and Toyota's second-tier subcontractor.

41. Although the traditional practice of monopolizing profits was largely replaced by profit-sharing arrangements in Japanese contractual relations after the 1960s, it persisted in other industrial societies. In the 1980s, for example, this practice was still so common among U.S. motor vehicle assemblers and

supplier entrepreneurship and led to a circle of purchaser–supplier competition and cooperation.[42]

As early as 1959, Toyota first applied the target cost method to the development of a new popular car model, the Publica, eventually marketed in 1961. A very competitive target cost (sale price of $1,000) was set, and VA/VE techniques were fully applied and shared between Toyota and its suppliers to achieve that goal. This action not only resulted in an overall cost reduction of 30 percent in three years but also made clear the importance of "cost planning" involving problem solving–oriented collaboration between assembler and supplier. In 1962, Toyota formally established the VA Proposal Institution and the Components Evaluation Meetings (Buhin kento kai) through which its suppliers' proposals for lowering costs (without compromising on quality) were strongly encouraged (Toyota, 1987:370–71).

Nissan, too, undertook similar developments. Building on the promising results of the 1964 "Value Sales" Conference, which yielded more than three hundred supplier VA proposals, leading to overall cost reductions of several tens of millions of yen per month, Nissan introduced the target cost method with the development of a new small car model, the Sunny (or the Sentra, as it is known in the United States), first marketed in 1966. From the early stages of product development, suppliers were called in to propose their own ideas for better design and lower cost. For example, instead of the "twisted" design of exhaust pipes (which was the result of designing them at the last minute after everything else under the body had been decided), a "straight" exhaust pipe from the engine to the rear end was proposed by a supplier and adopted. This simple design reduced weight, costs, and manufacturing complexity while increasing emission efficiency. Many similar supplier proposals were adopted, with the net result that the Sunny turned out to be among the most competitive in price, performance, and fuel consumption in its class.[43]

Likewise, Mazda extended its in-house VA/VE activities (respectively started in 1960 and 1962) to its suppliers from 1962 to 1964. In 1964, Mazda held a supplier VA presentation meeting and formally introduced the VA Proposal Institution. The latter established a fifty–fifty profit-sharing arrangement for joint value savings between Mazda and its suppliers. Furthermore, supplier performance in the VA

---

components suppliers that when newly opened Japanese assembly transplants in the United States asked for proposals from local suppliers, the latter reacted extremely cautiously, and many either rejected or asked for written agreements on proprietary knowledge, initially, at least. Similarly in Europe, the assemblers' tendency to take unilateral advantage of suppliers' designs and technologies was frequently reported in the 1980s (except for large suppliers such as Robert Bosch and Lucas, whose technological prowess and patents were more than enough to obviate the need for the assemblers' intervention) (based on my interviews with T. Shirokawa, vice-president and senior manager, Production Control; N. Morita, senior manager, Purchasing, Honda of America Manufacturing, Ohio, April 3, 1987; M. Miyamoto, manager, Purchasing, Mazda Manufacturing [USA], Michigan, February 11, 1988; R. Araki, general manager, Purchasing, Toyota Motor Manufacturing, U.S.A., Kentucky, March 10, 1989; W. Fritsch, managing director, Pebra GmbH Paulbraun, Saar, September 3, 1987; K. Schwarz, managing director, and K. Regitz, managing director, Columbus Neunkirchen Foundry GmbH, Saar, September 4, 1987).

42. This paragraph is based on my interviews with M. Yamamoto, vice-president, and K. Yoshinami, general manager, First Sales Department, American Yazaki Corporation, Michigan, March 16, 1987.

43. Based on my interview with K. Ishigaki, manufacturing manager, and M. Yokoyama, production control manager, Arvin Sango, Indiana, March 6, 1989; Nissan, 1975:60–61.

Proposal Institution became a criterion for deciding on future suppliers and the volume of their contract. VA/VE activities prospered at Mazda, with the emphasis increasingly on VE in new product development, eventually creating "functional VE teams" (according to component types), consisting of personnel from Mazda's planning, design, process, production, quality assurance, purchasing and its suppliers (Toyo Kogyo, 1972:419–20. Smitka [1991:38] reports similar trends at Mitsubishi Motors).

These early attempts (and successes) by automotive producers set the pattern for the application of VA/VE problem-solving techniques to, and purchase–seller collaboration in, product development, which later came to be adopted by many other firms in other industries as well.[44] By 1987, approximately 60 percent of subcontractors in the Japanese electronics, machinery, transportation equipment, and precision machinery industries were involved in the joint design of components they sold to their customers.[45]

Innovations Made by Suppliers[46]

As this practice of bilateral design spread, its impact on innovations, particularly supplier-driven innovations, became significant. The modularization of wire har-

---

44. The electronics industry is a case in point. In 1967, for example, Mitsubishi Electric's Kohriyama plant introduced the Vendor VE Proposal Institution, which required at least one proposal a month from a vendor, and established a fifty–fifty profit-sharing rule (*Nikkan Kogyo Shinbun*, February 6, 1967). Similarly in 1968, Hitachi's Hitachi plant introduced the VA Proposal Institution for its subcontractors and a fifty–fifty profit-sharing rule (*Nikkan Kogyo Shinbun*, July 31 & August 2, 1968). In both cases, the profit-sharing rules applied for a period of six months after a proposal was adopted, during which time the prime contractors did not ask for further purchase price reduction.

45. People's Finance Corporation, 1988:7. The same survey also found that many of those who were involved in design increased their sales even in the midst of the *endaka* (yen appreciation) recession of 1986, in contrast with those not involved in design who suffered a considerable decline in sales (p. 8).

46. This section is based on my interviews at the world's major wire harness suppliers: T. Takanaka, director and general manager, American Yazaki Corporation, El Paso Division, Texas, March 24, 1988; T. Ishihara, president, S. Yanagawa, general manager, Administration, Auto Partes Y Arneses De Mexico, Ciudad Juarez, March 24 & 25, 1988; T. Ohba, general plant manager, Auto Partes Y Arneses De Mexico, Ascencion, March 25, 1988; T. Fukui, vice-president, Sumitomo Electric Wiring Systems, Kentucky, October 26, 1988 & March 9, 1989; J. J. Martin, director, Materials Management, J. R. Anderson, purchasing manager, L. Wolfe, purchasing administrator, General Motors Packard Electric Division Headquarters, Ohio, April 30 & October 29, 1987; J. P. Walker, plant manager, B. Holloway, manager, Material Control, E. P. Castro, plant superintendent, General Motors Packard Electric Rio Bravo Electricos Planta IV, Ciudad Juarez, Mexico, March 22, 1988; A. Heymans, director general, J. Guidet, plant manager, C. Heymans, manager, Technical Services, J. Havaux, manager, Administration and Finance, Renault Industrie du Tournaisis, Belgium, September 7, 1987; P. Catlow, director and general manager, M. Bennett, operations director, R. J. Evans, chief buyer, M. Holland, manufacturing manager, Rists Headquarters & New Castle plant, England, August 27, 1987, September 4, 8, & 9, 1988; T. Jones, operations manager, C. Mann, module manager, A. Smith, production manager, Rists Ystradgynlais plant, Wales, September 8, 1988; N. Geisinger, general manager, Automotive Harnesses Manufacturing, J. Schmitt, manager, Systems Engineering, H. W. Schlamm, department manager, Electronics Development, Automobile Industry Department, P. G. Ranft, section manager, Retail Sales, Special Products, Cables & Wires Department, K. Enneper, line leader, composite technical, Automobile Industry Department, Kind, production manager, Cables & Wires, Reinshagen Headquarters & Wuppertal plant, Germany, September 15, 1988; V. Zinsser, director and works manager, Auto Accesso-

nesses is a case in point. Because of the greater number of electronics parts in a car, the number of electrical wires per vehicle also increased. In a typical passenger car, for example, the number of electrical wires for the dashboard alone doubled from 70 in 1973 to 140 in 1985.[47] For more luxurious models, the total number of electrical wires per vehicle was in the order of 1,000 for the Toyota Crown (not marketed in the United States) and 1,500 to 1,600 for the Toyota Soarer (Lexus SC300/400) in 1988.[48] This increased weight, bulk, and the manufacturing complexity of the wire harness assemblies while potentially compromising their reliability. The conventional one-big-unit design of wire harness assemblies was thus impractical. Seeing the problem (and opportunities), several Japanese wire harness suppliers proposed to divide the one big unit into blocks and connect them with small "junction boxes" in plastic housings. They further suggested incorporating microchips and microprocessors into these junction boxes, with the result that a new "intelligent" wire harness system came to replace the conventional, bulky wire assemblies. This new modular design radically reduced cost, weight, bulk, and manufacturing complexity while substantially enhancing reliability. More important, it helped accommodate frequent design changes throughout the model cycle of a given car. This point was crucial. As design improvements multiplied and as most of them entailed the wire harness, the modular design turned out to be a godsend, for only those modules of the wire harness affected by a design change needed to be modified. This enabled the continuous improvement of the design throughout the car's product life cycle. Thus, substantial cost reduction and a larger capability for design changes were not achieved through a single-minded devotion to economies of scale or downstream negotiations to reduce price; rather, they came from the suppliers' proposals at the source. The Japanese wire harness suppliers also profited by gaining advanced expertise in modular wire harness design, with the result that by 1987, Japan's top three automakers came to control 30 percent of the world's production. The effects of such supplier-driven innovations were thus more often of the "win–win" variety rather than the "I-win-you-lose" game between assembler and supplier.

Black Box Design

Over time, the shift from unilateral to bilateral design between customer and supplier led to the "black box" design concept. That is, the customer provides basic ideas and specifications of size and performance for a particular component, and the supplier attends to the details of the design, fully utilizing its expertise in its specialized area. This arrangement relieves the customer of part of the increasingly complex and expensive management of product development, and it also gives the supplier incentives to propose new ideas, invest, and expand its business.

Table 4-20 illustrates the different degrees of black box components develop-

ries Department, P. Wolfram, plant manager, wiring systems production, Auto Accessories Department, A. Schmitz, Customer Service, wiring systems production, Auto Accessories Department, Reinshagen Bochum-Linden and Bochum-Grumme plants, Germany, September 14 & 15, 1988.

47. Based on my interview with Prof. S. Sei, Kanto-Gakuin University, August 16, 1989.

48. Based on my interview with H. Ishikawa, senior engineer, production engineering section, Production Engineering Department, Sumitomo Wiring Systems Headquarters, September 8, 1988.

TABLE 4-20. Types of Automotive Components Development for a New Car Model: Japan, the United States, and Europe, 1987

( ) = sample size of car projects

Area		Detail-controlled by Assembler	Black Box	Suppliers' Proprietary
Japan	(12)	30%	62%	8%
United States	(6)	76	14	10
Europe	(9)	50	40	10

Source: Data from Clark, Fujimoto, & Dubinskas, 1987.

ment for Japanese, U.S., and European motor vehicle assemblers in 1987. Japanese automotive components development came to be characterized by a substantial reliance on black box design, in sharp contrast with the United States, where assemblers still detail-controlled three-fourths of components designs in 1987. Europe was in between.

Technologies Developed by Subcontractors

The foregoing evidence of enhanced subcontractor capabilities in Japan is further reinforced by the national statistics concerning the prevalence of self-developed technologies among subcontractors. Table 4-21 shows the percentages of subcontractors in Japanese manufacturing industries in 1983 that used self-developed technologies in process rationalization, new technologies, die making, machines, and patents and that also provided self-developed technologies to their customers. The range and degree of self-developed technologies used by Japanese subcontractors in the 1980s are impressive. The majority demonstrated their ability to rationalize processes on their own, and half also developed their own technologies and dies. Fully one-third of the subcontractors surveyed provided self-developed technologies to their customers. In all areas except die making in electronics, both automotive and electronics subcontractors overall demonstrated self-developing capabilities superior to the manufacturing average.

TABLE 4-21. Percentages of Subcontractors Using Self-developed Technologies and Providing Them to Customers in Manufacturing Industries, 1983

Self-developed Technologies in Use	Manufacturing[a]	Automotive	Electronics
Process rationalization	79.3	90.8	81.7
New technologies	52.8	63.9	56.8
Die making[b]	48.9	61.9	38.9
Machines	29.3	43.1	29.6
Patents	21.2	27.9	23.2
Provided technologies to customers	31.3	32.6	39.4

[a] Sample size = 1,592 subcontractors.

[b] Percentages of those using self-made dies among those whose processes included use of dies.

Source: Central Bank for Commercial and Industrial Cooperatives, Survey Department, 1983:61–68.

Resident Engineers

The tendencies toward collaborative design and production also led to the creation of a manpower institution that has come to play an important role in interfirm product development. Again, Japanese automotive producers pioneered in this area. Often at the request of customers or based on mutual agreement, the components suppliers formed engineer groups, in both development and manufacturing, regularly positioned at their customers' facilities (hence the term *resident engineers*).

In the product development phase, it has become common practice for major suppliers to send several "resident" design and/or product engineers to their customers for two to three years before Job 1.[49] They are made part of a project team consisting of the customer's planning, design, product, and process engineers (often reinforced with quality assurance and purchasing managers) and other suppliers' resident engineers. They collaborate to solve various design problems and to attain target costs. At this stage, the new model design-change proposals from the suppliers' "production" resident engineers (discussed later) are reevaluated and adopted as appropriate. The number of design changes and modifications tends to peak in this phase of new product development. Approximately one year before Job 1, production managers from the assembler and suppliers are called in to run pilot production. The "teething" problems of the new design are sorted out in this process. Frequently, second-tier subcontractors are also involved in this "debugging" process.[50] The final layouts and process technologies concerned are decided approximately six months before the launch of a new car model. As a result, there generally are relatively few design changes after Job 1.[51]

Compared with this process of new car development, the typical U.S. counterpart is organized radically differently, as reflected in design-change patterns. In the United States, design changes tend to skyrocket immediately after Job 1, during the first commercial production year of a new car model.[52] Then the design changes usually decline, but only slowly and never to the low level in Japan. In other words, the U.S. producer experiments with the reliability of its new car models in the field.

49. A developed derivative of this is the supplier's "dedicated team" of product development engineers always stationed at their customers' plants irrespective of product cycles. In Japan this practice was not unusual between assemblers and their "key" suppliers, and the team usually offered multidisciplinary expertise. In 1988, for example, Nisshin Kogyo, one of the world's largest automotive brake suppliers, had a product development team made up of six product and production engineers, one cost analysis engineer, one cost control manager, one accountant, and one salesman all regularly positioned at Honda's Research and Development Center. This team served as part of Honda itself and was heavily involved on a daily basis in the product development (and even research) of new Honda cars from the very beginning (i.e., three to four years before Job 1). With other customers, however, Nisshin Kogyo sent resident engineers only when asked (based on my interviews with T. Miyashita, manager, Total Quality Control and General Affairs, and S. Nezu, manager, Production Engineering and Investigation, Nisshin Kogyo, May 26, 1988).

50. Based on my interviews with M. Koitabashi, manager, production section, and H. Tsuda, manager, engineering section, Ishikawa Kogyo, July 4, 1986.

51. This paragraph is based on my interviews from 1986 to 1989 with the managers of many Japanese assemblers and suppliers. Although the details differ from company to company, the basic features of collaboration and scheduling of new product development are similar.

52. Based on my interviews with M. Yamamoto, vice-president, and K. Yoshinami, general manger, First Sales Department, American Yazaki Corporation, Michigan, March 16, 1987.

This in part reflects a different product development organization, in which the majority of the automotive components were still designed and detail-controlled by the assemblers in the late 1980s (Table 4-20), whereas the suppliers' tasks generally are restricted to producing as directed. Proposals from suppliers, let alone from resident engineers, have remained a rarity.[53]

After Job 1 in Japan, resident "design" engineers usually return to their home base after the project team has been disbanded, but resident "production" engineers remain in the customer's plant. Their main tasks are to observe how their components are being assembled into the car and to report back to their own firm any problems, including the customer's complaints, and also to suggest design changes for easier manufacture and cost reduction. They are in this sense customer-specific intelligence agents who serve as much for "preventive maintenance" purposes as for any *ex post facto* problems. The supplier then divides this information into three categories: (1) what has to be done immediately, (2) what would be better if adopted in the next model change, and (3) what should be discarded. The supplier's response is then communicated to the customer through its resident engineers. The latter's face-to-face contacts with the customer facilitate this communication. Another important job for the resident production engineers is obtaining information about the customer's long-term product strategy and reflecting this at an early stage in the supplier's next proposals for a new car model. Again, being on the spot is an advantage. Thus, in both development and production, the institution of resident engineers has an important role in promoting the benefits of bilateral design and collaborative manufacturing in the Japanese automotive industry.

Recognizing the advantage of this system, some Western firms have begun to introduce resident engineers in much the same manner as in Japan. In 1984, for example, Packard Electric, General Motor's in-house supplier of wire harnesses and electric connectors, received one of the lowest-quality ratings from New United Motor Manufacturing, Inc. (NUMMI), a Toyota–GM joint venture assembly plant in California, when Packard's first shipment was delivered. Rather than protesting NUMMI's decision, Packard managers came to see NUMMI managers for advice. After a series of talks, it was agreed that a long-standing Japanese supplier of wire harnesses to Toyota, and recently to NUMMI, would provide consultants to help Packard meet the customer's requirements. The consultants—six industrial engineers from the Japanese supplier—stayed at Packard for six months. Drawing on the principles of the Toyota production system (or more recently termed the "lean" production system by Womack, Jones, and Roos, 1990), they helped Packard reorganize its materials control, layouts, scheduling, quality control, and so on.

While the quality and productivity of Packard products rapidly improved, a

---

53. I (1988a, 1988b, 1988c, 1988d) discuss the problem of the traditional annual bidding system of the U.S. automotive industry, in which switches of suppliers merely because of price were so common that it institutionally prohibited suppliers from investing sufficiently and so resulted in poor product quality.

But my most recent field research (on automotive components development in Japan, the United States, and Europe) revealed that at the beginning of the 1990s, resident engineers were increasingly being used by advanced U.S. manufacturers, whereas many of the European automotive managers I interviewed had not even heard of them.

quality resident engineer (QRE) was also sent to NUMMI. He spent approximately 50 to 70 percent of his time at NUMMI and the remainder at Packard's Technical Center, following up on issues related to quality, cost savings, manufacturing, production control, and "pilot vehicle evaluation." This helped Packard by developing a firsthand, in-plant information source for its products.

As a result of these efforts, the quality of Packard products improved dramatically. Within eighteen months NUMMI was rating Packard as one of its best suppliers, its quality problem reports (QPRs) demonstrating the striking decline in Packard product defects: 102 in 1985, 47 in 1986, 10 in 1987, and 4 in 1988. According to a NUMMI quality control engineer who followed this development, "On balance the resident engineer was more important in improving Packard's performance than other 'joint teams' on a short-term basis." The case of Packard Electric has thus demonstrated that the resident engineer system can work in the United States, too.[54]

Grading

An important institution that was established during the 1960s among many Japanese manufacturers was *subcontractor grading*, in which the subcontractors' performance was continually evaluated by their customers in terms of product quality, price, delivery, engineering, and other areas. Each indicator of performance was scored, for example, 20 points each for quality, price, and delivery; 15 points for management competence and long-term business viability; and 10 points for other special factors. Each subcontractor was then graded according to the sum of these scores: grade A for those with a score of 80 to 100, B for 65 to 79, C for 50 to 64, D for 30 to 49, and E for less than 30.[55] In general, subcontractors were told their grades and were periodically given detailed scores (e.g., every three months, every half-year, every year, etc.), with indications of weak areas to be improved. Not infrequently, their customers extended technical help—and further financial and managerial support if deemed necessary—to those in trouble (see Chapter 6).

Grading and scoring methods and their contents differed from firm to firm, but the impact of grading on subcontractor prospects was consistent and clear. Those

54. This case history of Packard Electric is based on my interviews with K. Higashi, president, K. Kamiya, coordinator, General Affairs, D. Triantafyllos, manufacturing engineer, Quality Control Engineering, John F. Krafcik, former manufacturing engineer, Quality Control Engineering, New United Motor Manufacturing, California, February 4, July 20, & August 17, 1987; J. J. Martin, director, Materials Management, J. R. Anderson, purchasing manager, L. Wolfe, purchasing administrator, F. Gillett, cooperative involvement engineer, General Motors Packard Electric Division Headquarters, Ohio, April 30, October 29, 1987, and November 9, 1988; J. L. Williams, general manager, General Motors Packard Electric Mexican Operations, Texas, March 22, 1988; J. P. Walker, plant manager, B. Holloway, manager, Material Control, E. P. Castro, plant superintendent, General Motors Packard Electric Rio Bravo Electricos Planta IV, Ciudad Juarez, Mexico, March 22, 1988.

Reflecting the importance of this intercultural learning of the "best practice," there has emerged a body of literature that provides fascinating stories about NUMMI and Packard Electric. For example, see Krafcik, 1986; Nishiguchi, 1987b, 1989b, Walker, 1988; Gillett, 1992.

55. This example is taken from Fuji Electric's *Gaichusaki hyoka kijun* (Supplier assessment standards), 1986.

with better grades were given more responsibilities and long-term commitments from their customers, whereas those with poor grades were still given a chance to improve. If they did not improve after several periodic checks, however, they were either discharged or forced to become lower-tier subcontractors serving higher-tier subcontractors with better grades. This move toward clustered control (in the wake of the dispersion of contract assembly and systems-components manufacture) in the 1960s was thus supported by the application of systematic performance measurement programs to evaluate subcontractors' capabilities.

Some dramatic effects were reported. Three years after the introduction in 1965 of a subcontractor grading system and VA techniques, for example, Hitachi's Totsuka telecommunication equipment plant cut the number of its direct subcontractors by 57 percent (from 667 to 290), its own purchasing agent staff by 34 percent (from 125 to 83), delivery delays by 76 percent (from 19 to 4.5 percent of incoming goods), defects by 34 percent, and stocks by 88 percent, with overall savings of ¥300 million (*Nikkan Kogyo Shinbun*, April 18, 1968). Similar results were reported by other plants of Hitachi and its competitors that established subcontractor grading systems in the latter half of the 1960s: Hitachi's Hitachi, Kokubu, and Taga plants; Mitsubishi Electric's Kyoto and Kamakura plants; Fuji Electric's Kawasaki plants; and some of Toshiba's plants (*Nikkan Kogyo Shinbun*, December 7, 1965, January 8, 1968, April 2 & November 5, 1969, July 26, 1972; for Toshiba, see *Nihon Keizai Shinbun*, May 1 & June 21, 1967, quoted in Ichikawa, 1968:140–41).

One result of these systems was that they became closely linked with the subcontractors' quality assurance, eventually leading to the establishment of the "self-certified" subcontractor program. In this program, subcontractors, usually those with an A grade, were made wholly responsible for achieving a zero-defect rate for the components they supplied; their customers no longer inspected them. In 1967, for example, Fuji Electric's Kawasaki plant introduced a no-inspection system for its fifty machining subcontractors, to replace the traditional 100 percent receiving inspections and subsequent on-line inspections of supplied parts. Seeing the substantial variance of subcontractors' capabilities in achieving zero-defect quality assurance, however, in 1969 Fuji Electric further linked this program to its grading system and provided technical training focused on those with grades below B.[56]

The distribution of "self-certified" subcontractors can be seen in a 1974 survey by the Tokyo metropolitan government: 50 percent of the second-tier subcontractors in the electronics industry were self-certified, and 36.4 percent relied on their customers' inspection (Tokyo Metropolitan Government, 1974:77). By the mid-1970s the distribution of self-certified subcontractors was thus considerable even at the level of second-tier subcontractors.

Timely delivery was also an important factor in grading, and the "bonus–

---

56. *Nikkan Kogyo Shinbun*, November 5, 1969. By 1968, Fuji Electric had already formalized its no-inspection system as the "QR (quality and reliability) movement" at the corporate level and was actively promoting its dissemination to its subcontractors (*Nikkan Kogyo Shinbun*, May 3, 1970). Similarly in 1967, Hitachi's Tochigi plant introduced the "ZD (zero-defect) movement" to its subcontractors (*Nikkan Kogyo Shinbun*, January 10, 1968). In 1968 Mitsubishi Electric's Kamakura plant adopted a no-inspection system for approximately 150 computer parts for its six matching subcontractors (*Nikkan Kogyo Shinbun*, October 10, 1968).

TABLE 4-22. Change in Delivery Time-Units in Japanese Automotive and Electronics Industries, 1979–82[a]

Industry	Year	Monthly	Weekly	Daily	Hourly	Others
Automotive	1979	17.1%	11.2%	58.9%	10.5%	2.3%
	1982[b]	10.3	6.0	51.7	30.5	1.7
Electronics	1979	39.1	16.4	43.4	0.0	1.1
	1982	27.3	13.1	55.7	2.5	1.4

[a]The percentage of the subcontractors surveyed whose delivery time-units as demanded by their major customers fall into one of the categories listed.

[b]Because of rounding off, the percentage figures do not add up to 100.

Source: Central Bank for Commercial and Industrial Cooperatives, Survey Department, 1983:45.

penalty" system came to be widely practiced in this connection in both the electronics and automotive industries. As a result, subcontractors' average delivery delay over a specified period was constantly monitored, and accordingly, bonuses were awarded or penalties levied.[57] As customers increasingly demanded just-in-time (JIT) delivery, the bonus–penalty system became even more important, because the time unit of delivery scheduling was radically reduced from months to weeks to days to hours (see Chapter 7).

Table 4-22 shows this trend of shorter delivery time-units in the Japanese automotive and electronics industries between 1979 and 1982. Although the overall trend toward shorter delivery time-units is apparent for both industries, fully 30.5 percent of the automotive suppliers surveyed were delivering components hourly in 1982. This reflects the extent to which JIT deliveries were demanded by automotive producers, whose generally bulky components (compared with those in electronics) necessitated a stricter time schedule than did electronic components.

With the benefits of the subcontractor grading system and the self-certified subcontractor as practiced by Japanese producers being increasingly recognized internationally, a pattern of dispersion to other industrial societies was noted in the 1980s. The Q1 Program of the Ford Motor Company (United States), the After-Japan Programme of Ford Europe, the SPEAR (Supplier Performance Evaluation and Reporting), and the SAP (Supplier Assessment Program, a derivative of SPEAR, started in July 1987) of General Motors were some of the prominent examples.[58]

57. Based on my interviews with Irie, manager, Oikawa, assistant manager, Kobayashi, assistant manager, Hanta, staff, Outside Production Control, December 27, 1983, January 12 & 13, 1984, Pioneer's Kawagoe plant; N. Shishikura, manager, S. Kubota, staff, Outside Production Control, May 16, 1986, Pioneer's Kawagoe plant; *Nikkan Kogyo Shinbun,* August 2 & November 2, 1968.

58. Based on my interviews with C. G. Meyer, corporate strategy staff, Public Policy Issues, Ford Headquarters, September 15, 1986; O. Pedersen, commodity manager, C. Koo Yun, manager, Purchasing Activities, General Motors Headquarters, May 1 and 20, 1987. In the latter half of the 1980s, Ford's Q1 Program was used in all its worldwide assembly operations. In 1986, for example, Ford's Lio Ho assembly plant in Taiwan introduced the program, with the result that no local supplier was awarded the top grade, Q1, 41 percent were awarded grade A, 57 percent B, and 2 percent C (based on my interview with R. D. L. Lin, manager, Local Content and Supplier Development, Supply Operations, Ford Lio Ho Motor Company, Taiwan, July 9, 1987).

Having been influenced by Ford Europe's After-Japan Programme, moreover, Lucas CAV (a British supplier of automotive fuel injection systems, pumps, filters, etc.) introduced its own SQA (Supplier Quality Assurance) program in the first half of the 1980s. Lucas CAV's subcontractors were graded by the SQA as 1A, 1B, 2, 3, or 4 and were reevaluated every three months. Those who consistently received a grade of 1A were awarded self-certified status and usually received more orders, whereas those who consistently registered low grades were eventually discharged. Pricing mechanisms that had traditionally been handled by "nonengineering" staff were reevaluated by a team led by a new "purchasing engineering" manager, an engineer by profession, based in the purchasing department. On average, costs were reduced by 30 percent within less than a year through this program. This case of Lucas CAV thus demonstrates that the practices of grading and self-certified subcontractors can work in the United Kingdom, even between first-tier and second-tier subcontractors.[59]

An important effect of the foregoing change is that purchasing agents are no longer merely downstream price negotiators but are now evaluators of subcontractors' performance and coordinators of various intra- and interfirm functions. Whether or not purchasing agents are engineers by profession, sound technical knowledge has become one of their job requirements, so that they can judge their subcontractors' technical capabilities on their own. At Toyota, for example, all purchasing agents are technically trained so that whether or not they are engineers by profession they can evaluate subcontractors' technical competence and teach them the principles of the Toyota production system in the office and in the factory.[60] Even when the negotiations require professional engineers' participation, the purchasing agents' technical knowledge greatly enhances their coordinating roles in the negotiations.[61]

Summary and Conclusions

This chapter looked at the transformation of subcontracting in Japanese manufacturing industries between 1960 and 1990. Despite receding or stabilizing indicators of dualism (i.e., narrowing interscale wage differentials, stabilizing union density, and interscale distribution) and despite the radical dualists' predictions of the decline of small firms due to their lack of access to new technologies and new markets, small firms continued to keep pace with larger firms through the larger firms' commit-

59. Based on my interview with P. Hill, manager, Manufacturing Engineering Services, Lucas CAV's Finchley plant, London, March 11, 1985.

60. Based on my interviews with R. Araki, general manager, Purchasing, R. Shingo, executive coordinator, Purchasing, Toyota Motor Manufacturing, U.S.A., Inc., Headquarters and Assembly plant, Kentucky, February 8, 1988; Ohta, general manager, Koga, general manager, Hata, manager, Planning Office, OEM Sales Division, Pioneer Electronic Corporation Headquarters, Tokyo, June 25, 1986; Aiba, manager, Production Administration Department, N. Shishikura, manager, S. Kubota, staff, Outside Production Control, Pioneer Electronic's Kawagoe plant, Saitama, May 16, 1986.

61. I (1988a, 1988b, 1988c, 1988d) argued that the lack of technically trained purchasing agents was seriously hampering the effects of organizational reform on U.S. automotive components supply in the 1980s.

ments to subcontracting. In addition, compared with previous periods, the degree to which subcontractors and marginal workers were used as buffer agents (against fluctuations in demand) declined after the mid-1960s.

A major reason for the continued prosperity of subcontracting in Japanese manufacturing industries during this period was traced to a distinctive producer strategy to try to manage the demands of increasing product proliferation (due to rapid market expansion and competition among many producers in overlapping market segments) by outsourcing to subcontractors a substantial number of manufacturing functions. Over time, many of these subcontractors were converted from single discrete-process specialists (e.g., machining, sheet metals, surface treatment) to contract assemblers and systems-components manufacturers, who increasingly assumed responsibilities for designing, testing, and procuring parts for certain mature products. This arrangement allowed the primary producers to focus their internal resources on strategic activities, including state-of-the-art product development and process innovation. The delegation of production and development activities to external organizations shortened overall lead times and product cycles while allowing the product line to expand. Consequently, many producers could adjust more easily to shifting demands and improve their competitive position, and subcontractors had new opportunities to learn and develop the multifunctional technical expertise required for contract assembly and subsystems manufacture.

Asset-specific characteristics of contract assembly and systems-components manufacture contributed to stabilizing contractual relations, as exemplified by the distribution of "basic purchasing contracts," an expression of long-term contractual commitments, and protective measures taken by the primary producer in support of asset-specific subcontractors in recession (in the interest of preserving their irreplaceable assets). These provided continued growth prospects and incentives for the subcontractors to invest for the future. Along with the resurgence of the *keiretsu* (a phenomenon attributable partly to the need to compensate for the insufficient financial and technological base of the small subcontracting firms at the turn of the 1960s and partly to the fear of the impending liberalization of foreign investments in Japan, which eventually took place from the mid-1960s to the early 1970s), subcontractors were strategically reorganized into hierarchical "clusters" through the concentration of orders, intensified specialization, and increased dependence on particular customers (i.e., the clustered control model). This strategic reorganization resulted in turning the traditional semi–arm's length (or loosely tiered) structure into a clustered control (or tightly tiered) structure, in which controlling functions are systematically concentrated in a smaller number of first-tier subcontractors that control their own lower-tier subcontractors. This relieved those at the top of the hierarchy of the increasingly complex controlling functions typical of expanding external manufacturing organizations.

The shift in focus of subcontracting work from discrete treatments and simple processes to contract assembly and systems-components manufacture resulted in a series of institutional innovations in contractual relations. Pricing came to be jointly determined by the customer and the supplier, based on the objective value analysis (VA) method. Subcontractors also became more involved in design, in order to reduce costs further, using joint value engineering (VE) techniques.

In this area, Japanese automotive producers instituted the target cost or cost-planning method of product development and a profit-sharing system between assembler and supplier. Together, these innovations set the standard for the application of VA/VE problem-solving techniques and interfirm collaboration in product development in the automotive industry and in other manufacturing industries such as electronics. The new institutions of collaborative design and profit sharing inspired supplier-driven innovations (e.g., the modularization of wire harnesses) and established the black box design, in which suppliers assume critical responsibilities in drawing up the final design using their own expertise. Suppliers send resident engineers to work with key customers in design and production. They play innovative roles in promoting the benefits of collaborative design and manufacturing and in gathering information about their customers' long-term product strategies (which greatly assists the preparation of proposals for new products at an early stage). As a result of these developments, approximately 60 percent of subcontractors in the 1980s in Japan's electronics, transportation equipment, and precision machinery industries were involved in joint design projects with their customers. Furthermore, in the 1980s many subcontractors used self-developed technologies at their factories, and one-third of them provided these technologies to their customers.

As the importance of subcontractors thus grew, their performance was continually monitored and "graded" by customers, in such areas as product quality, price, delivery, and engineering. Those with consistently better grades were given more responsibilities and long-term commitments from their customers, whereas those with poor grades were still given a chance to improve—with their customer's help, if necessary. If they made no improvement after several periodic checks, however, they were either discharged or were forced to become lower-tier subcontractors serving higher-tier subcontractors with better grades, thereby still taking part in the clustered control structure. The subcontractor grading method structured subcontractor management and was used to promote quality assurance and just-in-time (JIT) delivery, in conjunction with the institution of self-certified subcontractors and the bonus–penalty system, respectively.[62] One effect of this change was that the main function of the customers' purchasing agents shifted from downstream price negotiation to the evaluation of the subcontractor's performance and the coordination of various intra- and interfirm functions.

With the economic and operational benefits of various institutional innovations of Japanese subcontracting being increasingly recognized internationally, there emerged a trend in the 1980s among many Western producers to "Japanize" their own practices, for example, resident engineers at Packard Electric; grading and self-certified subcontractors at Ford worldwide, General Motors, and Lucas CAV; and the clustered control structure at Daimler-Benz, Ford U.S., Renault, and BMW.

We thus can conclude that the distinctive Japanese producer strategy of delegating a substantial portion of manufacturing functions to subcontractors (a strategy that entailed various institutional innovations in Japanese subcontracting between

62. In 1974, for example, 50 percent of "second-tier" electronics subcontractors in Tokyo were found to be self-certified; that is, they were wholly responsible for quality self-inspection and zero-defect deliveries; in 1982, 31 percent of Japanese automotive components suppliers were found to be delivering hourly, and 52 percent daily.

1960 and 1990 and that in part were adopted by producers in other industrial societies in the 1980s) resulted in transforming the logic of subcontracting relations from exploitation to collaborative manufacturing. Consequently, both purchasers and suppliers benefited from the synergistic effects that accrued from joint problem solving and continuous improvement in price, product quality, delivery, design, and engineering.

In relation to traditional accounts, the evidence presented in this chapter has also made it clear that although conventional dualistic elements remain (e.g., narrowed but persistent interscale wage differentials), the continued evolution and prosperity of Japanese subcontracting between 1960 and 1990 cannot be comfortably accommodated within the traditional framework of dualism alone. Although it may have some overlapping elements, Japanese subcontracting does not seem to fit the framework of flexible specialization, which assumes a fairly dichotomous division, and a reversal of roles, between large and small firms. Although the notion of asset specificity has provided a useful analytical framework for the historical developments considered, it has also shown that an *ex ante* strategy produced *ex post* asset specificity, with the latter strongly influencing the subsequent patterns of obligational contracting. Finally, there is little direct evidence that the Japanese culture in itself can explain these subcontracting practices. Indeed, the diffusion of some of the new Japanese subcontracting practices across national boundaries has demonstrated their cross-cultural applicability.

II

THE CONTEMPORARY PRACTICE
OF SUBCONTRACTING

5

Asset Specificity Revisited

As described in the historical chapters, various developments in the Japanese econo-my resulted in the evolution of subcontracting from exploitative to collaborative manufacturing, which entailed asset-specific contractual relations as exemplified by the emergence of contract assemblers and systems-components producers.

This chapter looks at the issue of asset specificity based on my survey of electronics subcontracting in Japan and the United Kingdom, particularly rela-tionships between customer concentration and four types of asset specificity (i.e., physical, dedicated, human, and site). Although we shall touch on divergence by specialty (i.e., high-tech and assembly) and by tier (i.e., first tier and second tier), the main subject of this chapter is the greater asset specificity and customer con-centration of Japanese subcontractors compared with British subcontractors.

Contract Assembly

One of the most striking contrasts between Japan and the West in subcontracting organization in both motor vehicles and electronics is the large volume of contract-assembly and subassembly work in Japan, as opposed to the relative lack thereof in the United States and Europe. If subcontracting (excluding, in this case, the pur-chase of raw materials and services) were roughly divided into three classes—assembly or subassembly, components manufacture, and discrete treatment (e.g., plating, painting, machining)—assembly (or even subassembly) would be found to be relatively rare and often almost nonexistent in the United States and Europe. Although some cases of contract assembly can be found in the West,[1] they are exceptions and not comparable in scale and content to the highly systematic organi-

1. For example, the Renault Espace by Matra (based on my interview with T. Jones, operations manager, Rists Ystradgynlais plant, Wales, September 8, 1988), the BMW 3-Series Convertibles by a Bavarian contract assembler, the Opel Kadett cabriolet by Bertone (*Automotive News,* August 21, 1989), and a short series of Chrysler cars assembled by the American Motors Corporation (AMC) in the first part of 1987 before AMC was bought by Chrysler (*Wall Street Journal,* July 1, 1986; *New York Times,* March 10, 1987).

Although it is beyond the scope of this study, technically speaking, contract assembly can be distinguished further between contract assembly of a complete product (e.g., the Renault Espace as-sembled by Matra) and contract modification (e.g., the Opel Kadett cabriolet converted by Bertone). I am grateful to John F. Krafcik for pointing out this distinction (telephone and facsimile communications, November 13, 1989).

zation of contract assembly in Japan. These differences are the result of different producer strategies (as discussed in Chapter 4) and have a significant impact on subcontracting relations.

Contract assembly (or subassembly) consists of a combination of contract-specific technologies and customer-specific expertise. For example, a combination of special types of machines, tooling, and processes, often not readily applicable to other contracts, is required. In addition, end-product manufacturing for a specific customer requires the same level of specialized organizational input (e.g., regarding the division of labor, cycle times, degree of mix loading, and staff training) as does the customer's own in-house production. Furthermore, the longer the term of the contract or trading relationship is, the more likely the subcontractor will acquire customer-specific expertise. For example, a subcontractor might readily understand hidden codes and omissions in the customer's blueprints based on the subcontractor's own judgments derived from previous experiences with the customer and so not need further consultation.[2] In both visible and invisible aspects then, contract assembly (or subassembly) is usually more asset specific than is discrete treatment or standard-components manufacture. If this type of asset-specific subcontracting describes the main feature of transactions between traders, frequent switches of partners will be costly. Extensive arm's-length relationships may be shunned, and in the interest of preserving vested interests in the long run, the parties may even accept apparent short-term losses. Thus, what to subcontract defines the method. This is an important focus of this chapter.

Asset Specificity

As we pointed out in Chapter 1, Williamson (1985:30, 55, 83, 95, 96) maintains that asset specificity (defined as durable investments that are undertaken in support

2. It is widely recognized that Japanese automotive assemblers' blueprints for components, for example, are very sketchy compared with American blueprints, which detail not only the specifications of the components but also the production methods. This difference caused a problem when Japanese automotive transplants began operation in the United States in the 1980s, because local components suppliers often could not decode the hidden know-how behind the Japanese customers' drawings. This indicates the importance of accumulating, through continual contracts, customer-specific know-how in Japanese subcontracting relations, as opposed to the outcome of the traditional U.S. practice of annual bidding. Interestingly, however, adjustments have been made by both U.S. and Japanese assemblers. The Japanese automotive transplants have been trying to produce more unequivocal, detailed drawings for local suppliers, whereas U.S. assemblers have been trying to introduce the Japanese approach, including "sketchy" drawings, in a move toward single-sourcing, black box design, and long-term contracts, as exemplified by GM's Saturn project (based on my interviews with M. Yamamoto, vice-president, and K. Yoshinami, general manager of First Sales Department, American Yazaki Corporation, March 16, 1987; M. Miyamoto, purchasing manager, and T. Oka, leader, Production Procurement 1 Purchasing, Mazda Motor Manufacturing (USA) Corporation, March 23, 1987; A. Iwashita, president, Y. Hososaka, vice-president, and K. Sugiyama, manager of Engineering, Kantus Corporation, March 30, 1987; O. Pedersen, commodity manager, and C. Koo Yun, manager,Purchasing Activities, General Motors Headquarters, May 1, 1987).

From the standpoint of an institutional economist, Asanuma (1989) offers the notion of "relation-specific" skills accumulated by suppliers, which explains long-standing contractual relations. His distinction between *taiyozu* (drawings supplied) and *shoninzu* (drawings approved,) taken from the practice of the Japanese automotive industry, also is useful.

of particular transactions and that are not readily applicable to jobs for other customers) is critical to describing transactions, particularly in regard to what he calls "obligational contracting," or continued transactions in the middle of a spectrum extending from vertical integration to spot contracting. Asset specificity is further divided into physical, dedicated, human, and site, which are defined as follows:

Physical asset specificity refers to the mobile and physical features of assets such as specific dies, molds, and tooling for the manufacture of a contracted product.

Dedicated asset specificity represents a discrete and/or additional investment in generalized (as opposed to specific) production capacity in the expectation of making a significant sale of the product to a particular customer.

Human asset specificity arises in a learning-by-doing fashion through long-standing customer-specific operations.

Site asset specificity refers to the successive stages that are immobile and are located in close proximity to one another so as to economize on inventory and transportation expenses. The fact that the setup and/or relocation costs are great usually necessitates a bilateral exchange relationship between the parties for the useful life of the assets.

The Survey

Between 1983 and 1986 I conducted a comparative study of British and Japanese subcontracting in the electronics industry.[3] An important part of this research was systematically tracing the chain of subcontracting relations. In Japan, this usually entailed visiting distinctive layers of primary contractors, first-tier subcontractors, and second-tier subcontractors.[4] In Britain, by contrast, there was no distinctive layer of second-tier subcontractors; rather, many first-tier subcontractors mutually subcontracted a relatively minor part of their transactions. Thus their roles overlapped, and so many of my visits to British first-tier subcontractors automatically covered second-tier subcontractors, although I still treated them as first-tier subcontractors in this study. My research method was a combination of field visits, semistructured interviews of managers (i.e., presidents, purchasing, sales, accounting, personnel, and production managers), and questionnaire surveys (see Appendix B).

The electronics industry is in itself varied, with production ranging from sophisticated semiconductors to electrical appliances to standardized parts such as resistors. Depending on which segments are investigated and the research method employed, this variety can greatly increase complexity of an analysis without corresponding gains in understanding. In order to see differences within the same industry while maintaining a relatively simple research design, I chose two different groups of subcontractors: One specifically served those customers with high technological expertise in its subcontracting business, and the other had expertise in

3. The partial financial support of this survey of Nuffield College, Oxford University, is gratefully acknowledged.

4. Because my research focused on "interfirm" relations, third tiers, usually consisting of homeworkers, were not a direct concern.

TABLE 5-1. Breakdown of Electronics Manufacturers from U.K.–Japan Subcontracting Sample, 1983–86

( ) = sample size

Country	Category		Average No. of Employees per Establishment	Breakdown by Specialty: Average No. of Employees per Establishment		
Japan	Prime contractors	(6)	2,043			
	First-tier subcontractors	(36)	149	High-tech	(11)	109
				Assembly	(25)	166.6
	Second-tier subcontractors	(18)	30.8	High-tech	(6)	25.2
				Assembly	(12)	33.6
	Subcontractors total	(54)	109.6	High-tech	(17)	79.4
				Assembly	(37)	123.5
United Kingdom	Prime contractors	(2)	2,000			
	First-tier subcontractors	(13)	44.5	High-tech	(8)	35.3
				Assembly	(5)	59.2
Total:		(75)				

assembly or subassembly operations. I will call the former high-tech subcontractors (or specialists) and the latter, assembly subcontractors.

My study covered seventy-five establishments,[5] sixty Japanese and fifteen British. This disproportion (which reflected the difference in available opportunities to visit factories in the two countries) roughly corresponds to the difference in size of the electronics industry in the two countries.[6] Table 5-1 gives a breakdown of the establishments covered.

The sizes of prime contractors in the two countries were similar, though the Japanese first-tier subcontractors were, on average, three times larger than the British first-tier subcontractors. Japanese second-tier subcontractors, on the other hand, were about two-thirds the size of British first-tier subcontractors.

The products that the six Japanese prime contractors turned out ranged from consumer electronics (video cassette recorders, stereo equipment, washing machines, vacuum cleaners) to industrial electronics (control systems, testing equipment, breakers, motors, computers, information processors). One of the two British prime contractors that I investigated manufactured consumer electronics (television sets), and the other produced electronics equipment for defense applications.

5. This is the number of establishments whose data were, with a few exceptions, directly collected and used for this research. Of the seventy-five establishments, I actually visited sixty-three: forty-nine Japanese and fourteen British. I covered approximately one hundred establishments in the electronics industry in the two countries in my field research but had to discard some two dozen owing to the incompleteness of the data they provided.

The term *establishments* is used here because several plants of the same firm, all of which manufactured different products, warrant independent counting.

6. In 1985, for example, the total value of the combined markets of consumer electronics, telecommunications, data processing, and industrial electronics was £2,457 million for Japan, and the comparable figure for the United Kingdom was £240 million. Calculated from *Electronics Manufacture in Japan and South Korea* (1987), a report of a study tour sponsored by the Printed Circuit Association and the Department of Trade and Industry, quoted in Sako, 1988

The first-tier assembly subcontractors that I visited served the prime contractors that I surveyed, and the second-tier assembly subcontractors that I investigated served the first-tier assembly subcontractors that I covered. I selected the high-tech specialists from each country according to the following criteria:[7] They had to be involved in production processes for, or selling equipment to, customers whose technological prowess represented the state-of-the-art available in each country. This did not necessarily ensure that the subcontractors themselves were key decision-making participants in the industry, nor did it mean that their technology was indispensable to their customers. But I did assume that by comparing how subcontractors were involved in productive linkages with their customers, I would discover international differences. Using these assumptions, I chose high-tech subcontractors serving world-class electronics manufacturers in the defense and aircraft industries in the United Kingdom, through consultation with the Engineering Industries Association (EIA). In Japan, I selected subcontractors serving large semiconductor manufacturers, through advice from a consultant to the Tokyo Hachioji City Employment Policy Council. The British high-tech subcontractors were located in and around London, and their Japanese counterparts were on the western outskirts of Tokyo, clustered around the prime contractors' "development" factories and research centers. In both countries, I also visited "advanced" subcontractors or others recommended by advisers and included them in the survey.

Background

The general picture of Japanese high-tech subcontractors that came into view was that inside rather modest-looking, cramped factories were myriad examples of modern equipment, ranging from computer-aided design/computer-aided manufacturing (CAD/CAM) systems to computer(ized) numerical control (CNC) machines to laser milling machines to numerical control (NC) wire cutters. These factories were well lit, immaculate, and highly space efficient. Making full use of these facilities, many of them manufactured systems components or special-purpose production equipment. At the first tier, not a single one was solely a discrete treatment specialist. Some factories had a research and development (R&D) department where several highly educated engineers (often with master's degrees and doctorates) were developing new products and new processes on their own. On the shop floor, most of the workers were senior high school graduates and had been trained on the job to handle a variety of new machines. Only at the second-tier subcontractors did I observe narrow specialization in certain treatment and processes.

In Britain, the picture was grimmer. At many high-tech firms, the shop floors were ill lit, with relatively old-fashioned equipment (e.g., conventional lathes, milling machines) as if little had changed since the 1960s.[8] New technologies were encountered relatively infrequently: a single CNC machine on an entire shop floor,

---

7. Their subcontracting chains were traced down from the first-tier subcontractors. By chance, however, some of the first-tier high-tech subcontractors were found to share the same customers with the first-tier assembly subcontractors covered in this survey.

8. The MIT Commission on Industrial Productivity (1989, vol. 2, p. 92) shows that compared with other industrial countries, machine-tool age in the United Kingdom is largely dichotomous—either more than twenty years old or less than four years old.

for example. Most of the high-tech firms specialized in discrete treatment (e.g., precision machining) or "partial" prototype manufacture. At each firm, skills were generally hoarded, so that only a handful of persons (generally, a managing director who was also a craftsman and a few other skilled workers) operated the new machines. Other workers often were not even allowed to touch them.[9] The workers' education was usually the national minimum. A college education was a rare commodity, even among top managers, and R&D departments were rare. These observations came as a surprise to me, as all of the high-tech specialists that I visited were regular members of the EIA, an industrywide association of well-established firms.

In regard to assembly subcontracting, I found fewer differences between the two countries. In both Britain and Japan there was a less intimidating atmosphere on the shop floor, partly due to the diminutive size of the process: narrow belt conveyors, small desks, soldering irons, small partitioned containers for electronic parts, and testing equipment. Items were moved without the help of forklifts. Except for relatively large assembly subcontractors equipped with automatic parts insertion machines, the sole conspicuous capital-intensive machine, if present at all, was an automatic soldering vat. But even this looked like a weed among lilies compared with the forest of high-tech factories.

A closer look revealed some subtle differences between Japanese and British assembly subcontractors. In Japan, many contract assemblers not only completed finished products but also tested, packaged, stored, and shipped them on behalf of their customers. This was not even unusual for second-tier subcontractors. In Britain, however, subcontractors mainly subassembled printed circuit boards (PCBs) and no more. Indeed, the very existence of electronics assembly subcontractors was less common. An EIA list, for example, included only 18 electronics assembly subcontractors among 3,000 national members in 1984 (EIA, 1984:15, 60–62, 64). A British television set plant that I visited used only 3 PCB assembly subcontractors on a small scale, and all the color televisions were assembled in-house on eight long assembly lines crowded with female workers. In contrast, three Japanese prime contractors of comparable size manufacturing similar products had on average 20.33 full-fledged assembly subcontractors, of which approximately half assembled complete products for their customers.[10]

This description of subcontractors in the two countries suggests that there are some fundamental differences in the way that subcontractors are organized, what is expected from the subcontractors, and what the subcontractors do for their customers. My survey revealed the following general differences: In Britain, subcontractors were largely used on a short-term basis and were not expected to do any more than what the customer ordered. There were usually no institutional arrangements to connect customer and subcontractor other than basic agreements on price and speci-

---

9. Although I did not directly observe high-tech subcontractors outside Britain and Japan, skill hoarding appears to have been fairly widespread in some other European countries, notably in France (based on my interview on March 18, 1986, with Prof. M. Ikeda of Chuo University, who conducted fieldwork on high-tech subcontractors in Europe).

10. All three British PCB subcontractors mentioned were subassembling almost identical PCBs (i.e., those for monochrome television sets), whereas the Japanese subcontractors were assembling different products (e.g., car stereos, radio cassette players, transceivers) for the same customer with no or little overlapping among them in product reference numbers.

fications. Once the basic terms were fixed, trading continued until, as it often happened, one or two of the parties found a reason to discontinue it. There was neither prospect nor incentive for the progressive enrichment of the subcontractors' service to a particular customer in the long run. Rather, the subcontractors' job content tended to remain piecemeal and instrumental, for both high-tech and assembly subcontractors. High-tech firms in Britain seemed to be classified as such more on the basis of their customers than their own job content. Although the technical aptitude of some of the specialists was commendable, their equipment did not appear much different from that found at the second-tier Japanese subcontractors in the same high-tech business. The British firms' trade relations with their customers were erratic and reactive, not planned.[11]

By contrast, Japanese subcontracting mechanisms were quite different. High-tech subcontractors usually were assigned more integrated tasks, often including the development and manufacture of systems components or special-purpose complete equipment (e.g., wire-bonding machines, electron beam–drawing machines, supersonic cleaning machines). In fact, many of the high-tech subcontractors had originally specialized in discrete technologies. Over time, through interactions with their customers, they had found it so expedient to tap the "niche" opportunities overlooked by large firms (by enlarging and integrating their own specialist technologies) that they began—either at the request of their customers or on their own initiative—to make systems components and special-purpose complete equipment. Their strategy was that of product differentiation. Instead of directly competing with the large manufacturers, which had generally superior in-house technology in the same field and greater capital resources, some high-tech subcontractors began to specialize in producing smaller, inexpensive, special-purpose machines and systems components that the larger firms could not justify for reasons of economies of scale. The subcontractors then sold these products to large firms. Other subcontractors specialized in die, tool, and prototype manufacture and offered short lead times and flexibility. Their earlier service as subcontractors had given the small high-tech companies considerable knowledge about their customers and thus an ability to tap their latent needs. Radical innovations in the semiconductor industry also helped small high-tech specialists expand their own niches.[12]

---

11. This observation is reinforced by similar descriptions of British subcontractors by other studies. For example, see Sei, 1984:17–57.

12. This paragraph is based on a number of interviews I had in 1986 with the managers of Japanese high-tech subcontractors and a prime contractor located in Tokyo and Kanagawa prefecture: Masahiko Hiramoto, control manager, Micro Research Corporation, March 18, 1986; Ko Kikuchi, president, Kikuchi Seisakusho, March 18, 1986; Yasuyuki Harada, industrial machinery development manager, and Makoto Hasumi, general affairs manager, Pre-Tech, May 23, 1986; Kenji Ishida, managing director, Tomiji Hatakeyama, director and production manager, and Sachio Doi, control manager, Daiichi Seiki, May 23, 1986; Ikio Okazaki, president, Seigo Honmoku, director and sales manager, and Morio Hirano, general affairs and accounting manager, Elionix, May 24, 1986; Yasuo Seki, public affairs manager, JEOL, June 9, 1986; Junzo Tanaka, sales manager, Cho-onpa Kogyo, June 9, 1986; Katsuhito Nishimori, personnel manager, Tesec, June 9, 1986; Minoru Sumiyoshi, senior managing director, Sumiyoshi Seiki Seisakusho, June 12, 1986; Naoki Maruyama, president, Maruyama Seisakusho, June 27, 1986; Hiroshi Ohnishi, director, procurement and production control manager, Shinkawa, June 30, 1986; Reishiro Ide, president, Ide Seiki Seisakusho, June 30, 1986; Koichiro Hiruma, president, Technica, June 30, 1986; Ryuzo Kitagawa, president, Kitagawa Seisakusho, July 11, 1986; Tatsuro Ishii, president, Ishii Seiki Seisakusho, July 11, 1986.

TABLE 5-2. Number of Regular Customers[a] of Electronics Subcontractors in the United Kingdom and Japan, 1983–86

( ) = sample size

Country		No. of Customers	Breakdown by Specialty[b]		
Japan	(54)	10.13	High-tech	(17)	26.24
			Assembly	(37)	2.73
United Kingdom	(13)	29.96	High-tech	(8)	33.06
			Assembly	(5)	25.00

[a] Refers to those from whom orders were received over the last one year, approximately more than once in four months.

[b] High-tech subcontractors are those involved in production processes for, or selling equipment to, customers whose technological prowess represents the state of the art available in each country. Assembly subcontractors are those performing assembly or subassembly operations for their customers.

The situation for assembly subcontracting was similar. In the late 1950s, the majority of assembly jobs were still done by prime contractors on their own long assembly lines crowded with young female workers, a picture like that in Britain today. Japanese subcontractors at that time were just a collection of laborers providing temporary help. Over time, however, they were encouraged by their customers to do subassemblies and then complete assemblies. But this was not a one-way street. In the expectation of new opportunities, many assembly subcontractors took the initiative and created the capacity to take in more assembly jobs, by setting up new factories. Prime contractors responded by delegating mature or "dried out" products to assembly subcontractors while focusing their internal resources on developing new products and processes and manufacturing state-of-the-art products. Thus, a new division of labor evolved from the old and somewhat exploitative subcontracting mechanisms.[13]

Customer Base

Table 5-2 shows the number of electronics subcontractors' regular customers in Britain and Japan. On average, the British electronics subcontractors have three times as many regular customers as do their counterparts in Japan. More striking, however is the contrast between Japanese high-tech and assembly subcontractors: 26 as opposed to a mere 2.7 customers, a tenfold difference. By comparison, there is much less divergence in the number of regular customers of the two specialty groups of British subcontractors, indicating marked differences in the way that subcontracting is organized, not only between the two countries, but also between high-tech and assembly subcontractors in Japan.

Table 5-3 shows a breakdown of these data for Japan by tier and specialty. First-tier high-tech subcontractors in Japan have the widest customer base, some 40 firms, or nearly twelve times larger than the assembly subcontractors' customer base of 3.4 firms. At the second tier, however, there are only minor differences between high-tech and assembly subcontractors. This suggests that the Japanese

13. Based on my interviews with many managers of Hitachi, Fuji Electric, Pioneer Electronic, Oki Electric, NEC, Matsushita Electric, and their subcontractors, between 1983 and 1986.

TABLE 5-3. Number of Regular Customers[a] of Japanese Electronics Subcontractors by Tier and Specialty, 1983–86

( ) = sample size

No. of Customers by Tier			No. of Customers by Specialty		
First-tier subcontractors, total	(36)	14.42	High-tech	(11)	39.55
			Assembly	(25)	3.36
Second-tier subcontractors, total	(18)	1.55	High-tech	(6)	1.83
			Assembly	(12)	1.41

[a] Refers to those from whom orders were received over the last one year, approximately more than once in four months.

subcontracting system, which is customarily described as "closed," because subcontractors allegedly serve only a limited number of "parent firms," is more varied when examined segment by segment.

For the distribution of sales dependence on customers, consult Table 5-4, which gives the subcontractors' annual sales dependence on their top three customers. Japanese subcontractors depend on a single major customer for more than three-fourths of their sales, with the top three customers accounting for 92 percent of their total business. In contrast, British subcontractors apparently adhere to the principle of not putting all their eggs in one basket,[14] although nearly 60 percent of their sales are to their top three customers.

Table 5-5 gives the breakdown of these data. Dependence on a single customer is strongest in Japan at the second tier for both high-tech and assembly subcontractors. This reflects the fact that these firms are very small, with twenty-five to thirty-four employees on average (Table 5-1) and are deliberately located within twenty-nine to thirty-seven kilometers (Tables 5-13 and 5-14) of their largest customer. At the first tier, however, the high-tech specialists' dependence is more evenly spread out among their customers than is that of assembly subcontractors. In Britain, dependence on the top three customers is more evenly spread out for both high-tech and assembly subcontractors. Although we should be cautious about hastily drawing conclusions from this evidence alone (especially in view of the small British sample), it at least suggests some differences in the degree of customer dependence, not only between subcontractors in the two countries, but also among subcontractors in different tiers with different technical specialties in Japan.

Work Content

As discussed, contract assembly is widespread in Japan, and it is generally more asset specific than are other, simpler forms of subcontracting, such as discrete treatment. In this and the following sections we shall, first, determine the extent to which contract assembly is used relative to other forms of subcontracting and,

14. In my research, British subcontractors frequently referred to this policy and claimed that they did not want to have more than 30 percent of their sales with any single customer.

TABLE 5-4. British and Japanese Electronics Subcontractors' Percentage of Annual Sales to Top Three Customers, 1983–86

( ) = sample size

Country		No. 1	No. 2	No. 3	Total
Japan	(54)	77.66%	10.46%	3.55%	91.67%
United Kingdom	(13)	30.74	16.12	12.27	59.13

second, measure the degree of asset specificity in subcontracting relations among traders in different tiers with different specialties. In so doing, we may discover linkages between different patterns of customer and sales concentration and differences in degree of asset specificity.

For the purpose of this study, the work content of subcontracting in the electronics industry is divided into five categories, as follows:[15]

Complete assembly: The contract assembly of a complete product, consisting of more than twelve part numbers and/or six separate processes, often (but not necessarily) including testing, packaging, and shipping on behalf of the customer.

Subsystems assembly: The assembly of a subsystem (e.g., a PCB assembly) for a complete product, consisting of at least twelve part numbers and/or six separate processes.

Single components or simple subassembly: The manufacture of a nonstandard, customer-specific single component to be fitted into a subsystem of a complete product, or a simple subassembly consisting of fewer than twelve part numbers and/or six separate processes.

Discrete treatment: Miscellaneous discrete treatment using special technologies such as heat treatment, machining (e.g., milling, drilling, turning, boring, cutting, surface grinding, shaping, tapping, blanking), plating, sheet-metal work, press work, welding, forging, casting, or simple manual tasks.

Others: Miscellaneous other contracts of a unique kind, such as die/tool manufacture, prototypes, and repair.

Complete assembly requires the highest integration of contract-specific "physical" facilities, including dedicated assembly lines, tooling, and testing equipment (i.e., physical assets). If a significant amount of a product is sold to a particular customer, a discrete and/or additional investment in generalized (as contrasted with special-purpose) production capacity is likely (i.e., dedicated assets). Subsystems assembly ranks next to complete assembly in its physical and dedicated asset specificity, followed by single components manufacture or simple subassembly. In contrast, discrete treatment requires relatively few specific assets, as the technologies concerned are general purpose. Hence, discrete treatment subcontracting usually has a more generalized market, which requires more short-term trade relations.

15. Off-the-shelf, standardized components are excluded from this examination of subcontracting because they are, by definition, not asset specific and are better considered in a larger concept of purchasing.

TABLE 5-5. British and Japanese Electronics Subcontractors' Percentage of Annual Sales to Top Three Customers, by Tier and Specialty, 1983–86

( ) = sample size

Country		No. 1	No. 2	No. 3	Total
Japan					
High-tech total	(17)	65.40%	12.91%	5.26%	83.57%
Assembly total	(37)	83.29	9.33	2.76	95.38
First-tier total	(36)	72.37	11.39	4.15	87.91
High-tech	(11)	54.78	14.78	6.43	75.99
Assembly	(25)	80.11	9.90	3.15	93.16
Second-tier total	(18)	88.24	8.59	2.33	99.16
High-tech	(6)	84.88	9.48	3.12	97.48
Assembly	(12)	89.92	8.14	1.94	100.00
United Kingdom					
High-tech	(8)	31.20	18.00	14.00	63.20
Assembly	(5)	30.00	13.10	9.50	52.60

Other miscellaneous contracts of a unique kind are, by definition, the least asset specific.

As an illustration, Figure 5-1 shows a part-number breakdown of a vacuum cleaner marketed by a large Japanese electrical appliances firm in 1986. The unit is divided into seven blocks, each of which is subassembled by different firms. Of the total of 164 part numbers, the prime contractor manufactures only 16 motor parts in-house. Adding 3 other single components bought from two subcontractors, the prime contractor subassembles a motor unit in-house (Subsystem A). All other components are "outsourced" and subassembled by its subcontractors. For example, Subsystem B (38 part numbers) is made by one subcontractor, and Simple Subassembly C (3 part numbers) is put together by another subcontractor. The shaping and plating of the metal parts in these units are also subcontracted (discrete treatment). Finally, a subcontractor (which also makes subsystems) assembles the final unit for the prime contractor (complete assembly). When there are changes in the design or a new model is to be introduced, prototypes are subcontracted to prototype specialists (others).

Just as the level of contract-specific investment differs in each of these work contents of subcontracting, so do contractual fees. In 1986, for example, the ratio of hourly contractual fees that a large consumer electronics firm paid to a complete contract assembler, a subsystems assembler, and a subcontractor of simple discrete treatment was 100 to 87 to 50.[16]

Table 5-6 compares these five categories of subcontracting in Japan and the United Kingdom. In Japan a highly asset-specific form of subcontracting (i.e., complete assembly and subsystems assembly) makes up nearly a half of both the P-1 and 1-2 groups. In contrast, in the British sample there is no complete assembly, and

16. Based on my interviews with a consumer electronics firm in the spring of 1986. For confidential reasons, neither the name of the firm nor more details on the contractual fees can be disclosed.

FIGURE 5-1. Part-Number Breakdown of a Japanese Vacuum Cleaner, 1986

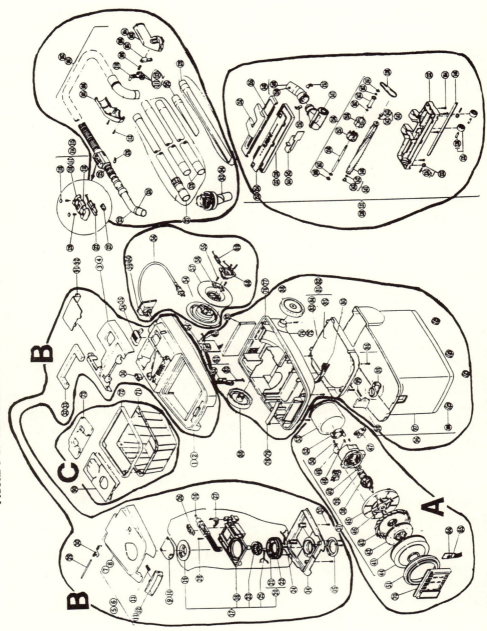

Source: Japanese electrical appliances plant visited in 1986.

TABLE 5-6. Percentage Breakdown[a] of Regular Electronics Subcontractors by Work Content and Tier: U.K.–Japan Comparison, 1983–86

( ) = sample size of customers

Country	Customer–Subcontractor		Complete Assembly	Subsystems Assembly	Single Components	Discrete Treatment	Other	Total
Japan	P-1[b]	(6)	15.9%	39.2%	33.9%	5.4%	5.7%	100.0%
	1-2[c]	(24)	1.7	41.3	13.0	39.3	4.8	100.0
United Kingdom	P-1[b]	(2)	—	15.3	26.2	46.5	8.0	100.0
	1-2[c]	(9)	—	2.0	34.0	61.0	3.0	100.0

[a] By the number of regular subcontractors with whom at least monthly orders have been regularly placed over the last one year.
[b] Prime contractors subcontracting to first-tier subcontractors.
[c] First-tier subcontractors subcontracting to second-tier subcontractors.

most of the subcontracting is for discrete treatment. Interestingly, in each country sample, the P-1 group shows higher asset-specific tendencies than does the 1-2 group. Table 5-7 is a breakdown of the 1-2 group in Table 5-6 by specialty. Patterns of high-tech subcontracting are similar in both countries except for the absence of subsystems assemblers in the United Kingdom. By contrast, patterns of assembly subcontracting are drastically different between the two countries. In Japan, 63 percent of the 1-2 assembly group is devoted to complete and subsystem assemblies, whereas in Britain, 83 percent is for discrete treatment.

Measuring Physical and Dedicated Asset Specificity

The physical and dedicated asset specificity factor can be calculated for each group in the following way: First, each of the five work contents of subcontracting in a customer–subcontractor group is scored, with 5 points for complete assembly, 4 for subsystems assembly, 3 for single components, 2 for discrete treatment, and 1 for others. Second, the scores are added, with the sum being the physical and dedicated asset specificity factor for that group. If the work content of a customer–subcontrac-

TABLE 5-7. Percentage Breakdown[a] of Electronics Subcontractors by Work Content and Specialty: U.K.–Japan Comparison, 1983–86

( ) = sample size of customers

Country	Customer–Subcontractor		Complete Assembly	Subsystems Assembly	Single Components	Discrete Treatment	Other	Total
Japan	1-2[b]							
	High-tech	(5)	—	19.9%	21.3%	55.2%	3.7%	100.0%
	Assembly	(19)	3.2	59.9	5.7	25.5	5.7	100.0
United Kingdom	1-2[b]							
	High-tech	(6)	—	—	38.64	57.95	3.41	100.0
	Assembly	(3)	—	16.7	—	83.3	—	100.0

[a] By the number of regular subcontractors with whom at least monthly orders have been regularly placed over the last one year.
[b] First-tier subcontractors subcontracting to second-tier subcontractors.

TABLE 5-8. Comparison of Physical and Dedicated Asset Specificity: Japanese and British Electronics Subcontracting, 1983–86

( ) = sample size of customers

Country	Customer–Subcontractor		Asset Specificity Factor[a]	Breakdown by Specialty		
Japan	P-1	(6)	354.5			
	1-2	(24)	296.1	High-tech	(5)	257.6
				Assembly	(19)	329.4
United Kingdom	P-1	(2)	248.8			
	1-2	(9)	235.0	High-tech	(6)	235.2
				Assembly	(3)	233.4

[a]Ranges from 500 to 100. The higher the score is, the more physical and dedicated asset specific the subcontracting relation will be.

tor group is 100 percent complete assembly, the physical and dedicated asset specificity factor will score a full 500 points. If the work content is 100 percent others, it will score a minimum of 100 points.[17] Table 5-8 shows the calculation of physical and dedicated asset specificity factors. Again, there are differences between the two countries' samples in regard to physical and dedicated asset specificity. In Britain, asset specificity is generally lower than it is in Japan, and there are no significant differences in the degree of asset specificity between the P-1 and 1-2 groups or between the high-tech and assembly subcontracting in the 1-2 group. In short, the subcontracting relations in the British sample are fairly homogeneous in this regard, irrespective of tier and specificity. In contrast, physical and dedicated asset specificity varies widely in Japan by tier and specialty, with the P-1 group more asset specific than the 1-2 group. Within the 1-2 group, assembly subcontracting shows more asset specificity (close to the level of the Japanese P-1 group) than does high-tech subcontracting (which is close to the level of the British P-1 group).

Table 5-9 ranks these data. In comparable electronics firms, the Japanese physical and dedicated asset specificity indices range between 71 and 52, whereas the British counterparts are between 48 and 47. The lowest Japanese figure, 52, for the 1-2 high-tech group is still higher than the highest British figure, 48, for the P-1 group.

Human Asset Specificity

Human asset specificity can be ideally measured by the number of hours that the subcontractor spends on management, engineering, and operation for each customer. But because such data are not available, a proxy can be obtained by dividing the number of the subcontractor's employees by the number of its regular customers. Table 5-10 shows a breakdown of human asset specificity thus calculated at Japanese and British electronics subcontractors, by tier and specialty, and Table 5-11 ranks human asset specificity, based on Table 5-10.

17. A nonzero minimum is reasonable because in any trade relation, it is impossible for there to be absolutely no degree (i.e., zero points) of physical and dedicated assets applied to a contract even if the work content itself is of the most generalized kind.

TABLE 5-9. Ranking of Physical and Dedicated Asset Specificity: Japanese and British Electronics Subcontracting, 1983–86

( ) = sample size of customers

Ranking	Country	Customer–Subcontractor		Asset Specificity Factor	Index[a]
1	Japan	P-1	(6)	354.5	70.9
2	Japan	1-2 assembly	(19)	329.4	65.9
3	Japan	P-1 + 1-2 total	(30)	322.4	64.5
4	Japan	1-2 total	(24)	314.4	62.9
5	Japan	1-2 high-tech	(5)	257.6	51.5
6	U.K.	P-1	(2)	240.8	48.2
7	U.K.	P-1 + 1-2 total	(12)	235.7	47.1
8	U.K.	1-2 high-tech	(7)	235.2	47.0
9	U.K.	1-2 total	(10)	234.7	46.9
10	U.K.	1-2 assembly	(3)	233.4	46.7

[a]The full score of 500 for the asset specificity factor is indexed as 100.

In Japan, first-tier assembly subcontractors assign, on average, 50 workers to each customer. Second-tier assembly subcontractors assign 24 workers to each customer, and second-tier and first-tier high-tech subcontractors allocate 14 and 3 workers, respectively, to each customer. In contrast, British subcontractors assign much smaller numbers of workers, only 2 workers per customer. The highest British figure, 2.37, of first-tier assembly subcontractors is still lower than the lowest Japanese figure, 2.76, of first-tier high-tech subcontractors.

But these figures do not take into account the firm's size, and so Table 5-12 ranks the size-adjusted human asset specificity factor at British and Japanese electronics subcontractors. Japanese second-tier subcontractors' remarkably high human asset specificity is a direct reflection of their limited customer base. The Japanese assembly total of 36.6 percent contrasts with the Japanese high-tech total of a mere 3.8 percent. In total, nearly one-tenth of a Japanese subcontractor's work force is dedicated to one customer, whereas the comparable British figure is 3.4 percent. Japanese first-tier high-tech subcontractors have the lowest figure, 2.5 percent,

TABLE 5-10. Number of Electronics Subcontractors' Employees per Regular Customer[a]: Japan and the United Kingdom, 1983–86

( ) = sample size

Country	No. of Employees by Tier			No. of Employees by Specificity		
Japan	First- + second-tier total	(54)	10.82	High-tech total	(17)	3.03
				Assembly total	(37)	45.24
	First-tier total	(36)	10.33	High-tech	(11)	2.76
				Assembly	(25)	49.58
	Second-tier total	(18)	19.87	High-tech	(6)	13.77
				Assembly	(12)	23.83
United Kingdom	First-tier total	(13)	1.49	High-tech	(8)	1.07
				Assembly	(5)	2.37

[a]Calculated from Tables 5-1, 5-2, and 5-3.

TABLE 5-11. Ranking of Unadjusted Human Asset Specificity: Japanese and British
Electronics Subcontracting, 1983–86

( ) = sample size

Ranking	Country	Category		No. of Subcontractors' Employees per Regular Customer
1	Japan	First-tier assembly	(25)	49.58
2	Japan	Assembly total	(37)	45.24
3	Japan	Second-tier assembly	(12)	23.83
4	Japan	Second-tier total	(18)	19.87
5	Japan	Second-tier high-tech	(6)	13.77
6	Japan	First- + second-tier total	(54)	10.82
7	Japan	First-tier total	(36)	10.33
8	Japan	High-tech total	(17)	3.03
9	Japan	First-tier high-tech	(11)	2.76
10	United Kingdom	First-tier assembly	(5)	2.37
11	United Kingdom	First-tier total	(13)	1.49
12	United Kingdom	First-tier high-tech	(8)	1.07

reflecting their wide customer base. In sum, the Japanese subcontractors in this
sample are nearly three times more human asset specific than are the British subcontractors.

Site Asset Specificity

According to Williamson, the more site asset specificity (i.e., successive stations
located in close proximity in order to economize on inventory and transportation
expenses) there is, the less likely the parties concerned are to violate a bilateral

TABLE 5-12. Ranking of Size-adjusted Human Asset Specificity: Japanese and British
Electronics Subcontracting, 1983–86

( ) = sample size

Ranking	Country	Category		Size-adjusted Human Asset Specificity Index[a]
1	Japan	Second-tier assembly	(12)	70.9
2	Japan	Second-tier total	(18)	64.5
3	Japan	Second-tier high-tech	(6)	54.6
4	Japan	Assembly total	(37)	36.6
5	Japan	First-tier assembly	(25)	29.8
6	Japan	First- + second-tier total	(54)	9.9
7	Japan	First-tier total	(36)	6.9
8	United Kingdom	First-tier assembly	(5)	4.0
9	Japan	High-tech total	(17)	3.8
10	United Kingdom	First-tier total	(13)	3.4
11	United Kingdom	First-tier high-tech	(8)	3.0
12	Japan	First-tier high-tech	(11)	2.5

[a] Calculated from Tables 5-1 and 5-11 as the percentage of a subcontractor's employees per regular customer of the total
work force, with 100 points being the maximum.

TABLE 5-13. Distance[a] Between Electronics Subcontractors and Their Major Customers in Japan and the United Kingdom 1983–86

( ) = sample size

Country	Category			Breakdown by Specialty		
Japan	First- + second-tier total	(54)	77.90 km	High-tech total	(17)	43.04 km
				Assembly total	(37)	93.92
	First-tier total	(36)	100.98	High-tech	(11)	46.4
				Assembly	(25)	125.0
	Second-tier total	(18)	31.74	High-tech	(6)	36.88
				Assembly	(12)	29.17
United Kingdom	First-tier total	(13)	79.58	High-tech	(8)	91.2
				Assembly	(5)	61.0

[a]Kilometers between the subcontractor and the main goods-receiving point of its no. 1 customer in terms of sales.

exchange relationship during the useful life of the assets, because the setup and/or relocation costs would be too great (Williamson, 1985:95). Put simply, the degree of geographical proximity between the plants largely determines their trade relations; hence, distance does matter.

Among Williamson's four asset specificities, site specificity appears to be the least difficult to measure. Table 5-13 shows the average number of kilometers between electronics subcontractors and their major customers in Britain and Japan. The apparent similarity between the Japanese and British aggregate figures should not be interpreted as showing no differences between the two countries' samples. In Japan the average distance of 125 kilometers (km) between first-tier assembly subcontractors and customers, which is the highest in the group, contrasts with 29.17 km, the lowest, between second-tier assembly subcontractors and customers, reflecting the labor market specificity in Japan. For more than a decade after the mid-1960s, many parts of Tohoku and Shinshu—formerly agricultural areas but now changing into semiindustrial–semiagricultural economies—produced a large pool of unskilled labor, especially female workers. Women constituted the major work force in electronics assembly factories that were established as "branch factories" (*bun kojo*) by urban prime contractors and subcontractors. The inconvenience arising from long distances was offset by the availability of an abundance of cheap labor, which was becoming a rare commodity in urban areas, owing to the rapid growth of the 1960s. Around these branch factories, second-tier subcontractors mushroomed. Seeing the opportunity, former farmers and those with miscellaneous trades (ranging from timber dealers to textile subcontractors) turned their sheds into workshops or set up prefabricated factories and recruited local women to subassemble electronics products. They acquired the necessary technology from their customers, normally located close by. From the beginning, second-tier subcontractors' dependence on a single local customer appears to have been high (based on my interviews; see footnote 13).

Figure 5-2 shows the geographical distribution of the first-tier assembly subcontractors for a Japanese consumer electronics plant based in Saitama prefecture (next to Tokyo) in 1986. Of the total of eleven assembly subcontractors, only two

FIGURE 5-2. Geographical Distribution of First-Tier Assembly Subcontractors of a Japanese Hi-Fi Equipment Plant, 1986

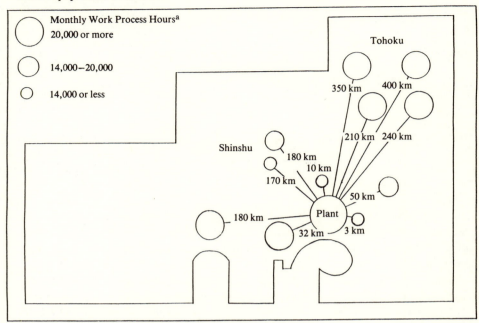

Monthly Work Process Hours[a]
20,000 or more

14,000–20,000

14,000 or less

Tohoku

350 km   400 km

210 km   240 km

Shinshu

180 km

170 km   10 km

180 km

50 km

Plant

32 km   3 km

[a]For confidential reasons, figures are altered.

Source: Japanese consumer electronics plant visited in 1986.

were within what may be called close proximity (less than 10 km), and their share of the total work process hours (as represented by the size of the circle) was not large. It is astonishing that two of the largest subcontractors were located 400 km and 350 km away, respectively.

The Japanese high-tech subcontractors in this sample had different origins, being either the evolutionary product of traditional specialist subcontractors or new ventures started by "dropout" engineers from large electronics firms who saw the opportunity to use their technical expertise to tap niche markets ignored by their former employers. They deliberately located near their customers (i.e., large firms' development plants and research institutions) on the outskirts of Tokyo, because their business (high-tech special-purpose devices, high-tech prototypes, etc.) necessitated frequent direct contacts. Around the first-tier high-tech specialists are clustered the second-tier high-tech subcontractors that specialize mainly in discrete treatment. The origins of these high-tech subcontractors thus explains their relatively close proximity to their customers (based on my interviews; see footnote 12).

In Britain, the differences within the sample were not as dramatic as they were in Japan. There was neither the mushrooming of assembly subcontractors in rural areas far away from their subcontractors nor the distinctive belt of high-tech specialists around their customers. Rather, as a reflection of the policy of concentrating on few

TABLE 5-14. Ranking of Site Asset Specificity: Japanese and British Electronics Subcontracting, 1983–86

( ) = sample size

Ranking	Country	Category		Kilometers from No. 1 Customer	Index[a]
1	Japan	Second-tier assembly	(12)	29.17	85.4
2	Japan	Second-tier total	(18)	31.74	84.1
3	Japan	Second-tier high-tech	(6)	36.88	81.6
4	Japan	High-tech total	(17)	43.04	78.5
5	Japan	First-tier high-tech	(11)	46.4	76.8
6	United Kingdom	First-tier assembly	(5)	61.0	69.5
7	Japan	First- + second-tier total	(54)	78.94	60.5
8	United Kingdom	First-tier total	(13)	79.58	60.2
9	United Kingdom	First-tier high-tech	(8)	91.2	54.5
10	Japan	Assembly total	(37)	93.92	53.0
11	Japan	First-tier total	(36)	100.98	49.5
12	Japan	First-tier assembly	(25)	125.0	37.5

[a]For comparison, zero distance (i.e., zero kilometers) is indexed as 100, and 200 kilometers (125 miles) or more is indexed as 0.

customers, their customer base often is scattered over a wider geographical area, and several high-tech subcontractors in fact operate nationwide.[18]

Table 5-14 is a rearrangement of Table 5-13 by means of ranking. Compared with physical, dedicated, and human asset specificities, these results are somewhat mixed. Japanese second-tier subcontractors are the most site asset specific, followed by Japanese first-tier high-tech subcontractors and British first-tier assembly subcontractors. On the other hand, Japanese first-tier assembly subcontractors are least site asset specific, which brings the Japanese assembly and first-tier totals below the level of the British first-tier total. In sum, then, because of the historical and labor market specificity of Japanese subcontractor development, site specificity diverges considerably by tier and specialty.

Total Asset Specificity

Total asset specificity is the sum of the physical, dedicated, human, and site asset specificities. Calculating this figure is straightforward: Add the indices of the respective specificities to obtain total scores by nationality, tier, and specialty, and then compare the results with the data on customer concentration to see the linkages.

Table 5-15 summarizes the results ranked by total asset specificity. The Japanese second-tier assembly contractors show the highest total asset specificity and customer concentration in the group, and the British first-tier high-tech subcontractors

18. Based on my interviews with thirteen British subcontractors in 1984, 1985, and 1986. For example, the principal customer of one London-based firm specializing in precision machining for telecommunications applications was located in Scotland.

TABLE 5-15. Ranking of Total Asset Specificity and Customer Concentration: British and Japanese Electronics Subcontractors, 1983–86

( ) = sample size

Ranking	Country	Category		Total Asset Specificity[a]	Customer Concentration[b]
1	Japan	Second-tier assembly	(12)	288.1	100.00
2	Japan	Second-tier total	(18)	274.4	99.16
3	Japan	Second-tier high-tech	(6)	239.2	97.48
4	Japan	Assembly total	(37)	226.4	95.38
5	Japan	First-tier high-tech	(11)	221.1	75.99
6	Japan	First- + second-tier total	(54)	212.2	91.67
7	Japan	First-tier assembly	(25)	209.1	93.16
8	Japan	High-tech total	(17)	204.7	83.57
9	Japan	First-tier total	(36)	198.2	87.91
10	United Kingdom	First-tier assembly	(5)	169.9	52.60
11	United Kingdom	First-tier total	(13)	160.0	59.13
12	United Kingdom	First-tier high-tech	(8)	153.6	63.20

[a]Calculated by adding physical, dedicated, human, and site specificity indices (Tables 5-9, 5-12, and 5-14). For the physical and dedicated asset specificity of first-tier subcontractors in each country, the P-1 groups's index is uniformly applied, owing to the inseparability of data by specialty (Table 5-9). Physical and dedicated asset specificity indices in Table 5-9 are doubled to represent two separate asset specificities for calculation purposes. The maximum score of total asset specificity is 400.

[b]Total percentage of annual sales to top three customers (see Table 5-5).

show the lowest. Although there are some nonlinear relations at certain levels, the aggregate figures show a divergence between Japan and the United Kingdom and a correlation between total asset specificity and customer concentration.

Variations Within the Pattern

Subcontracting relations in the electronics industry in Japan, insofar as this sample is concerned, are characterized by higher asset specificity than they are in the United Kingdom. It would be wrong, however, to assume that all Japanese subcontracting relations are thus monolithically defined. To demonstrate the differences, this section looks at two plants of the same Japanese electronics firm. Each plant manufactures similar products: car stereos and radio cassette players in one plant and hi-fi equipment in the other. Each is located in the same Kanto area, fairly close to each other, and they even share some of their assembly subcontractors. But when the "audio recession" hit these two plants in the early 1980s, they behaved remarkably differently toward their subcontractors. One weathered the downturn without dropping any of its subcontractors, thus adopting a long-term perspective. In sharp contrast, the other radically reduced its subcontracting base to make up for short-term losses. When I revisited them three years later, there were significant differences in the two plants' performance and atmosphere. It is interesting to see how different strategies have produced different outcomes.

Background

The Japanese Stereo Company (JSC)[19] is a world-class manufacturer of stereo equipment and other consumer electronics products. Throughout the 1960s and the 1970s, decades of high economic growth and an audio boom, JSC enjoyed phenomenal growth. Its products are now recognized worldwide as being of excellent quality.

In the early 1980s JSC had four major plants, of which the Mori plant and the Egawa plant (pseudonyms) are of particular interest to us. The Mori plant is located in Tokyo and produces hi-fi equipment (e.g., amplifiers, tuners) and audio-visual systems (e.g., cable television systems). The Egawa plant is situated north of Tokyo and manufactures car stereos and radio cassette players. The sizes of the plants are comparable, and the manufacturing technologies that they use are similar. Like many other Japanese competitors, both plants had fairly extensive subcontracting networks, ranging from Tokyo to Tohoku. Contract assembly and subassembly constituted a major part of their subcontracting.

In 1981 the Mori plant had twelve assembly subcontractors, and the Egawa plant had eight. Of these, they shared two assembly subsidiaries 100 percent owned by JSC. In 1986, however, after the 1982 audio recession, Mori had only six assembly subcontractors, of which only three were the same as five years before. In contrast, Egawa still had its original eight. The two plants were still sharing the two assembly subsidiaries. What happened between 1981 and 1986?

Two Approaches

The autumn of 1981 was disastrous for the Japanese hi-fi equipment industry, which had enjoyed two decades of uninterrupted growth. For complex reasons, including a saturation of stereo sets and the rapid dissemination of video cassette recorders (VCRs), the demand for conventional hi-fi products suddenly dropped. The sales of the Japanese Stereo Company in the following year dropped by 16.5 percent and its net profit by 38.2 percent. The press proclaimed that the "star of a success story" had fallen.

Apart from purchasing raw materials and standard electronics parts, JSC did not have a central unit controlling companywide subcontracting relations. Thus, the treatment of subcontractors during the audio recession was largely left to each plant's discretion. At both the Mori and the Egawa plants, the managers in charge of subcontracting were quite influential in determining plantwide subcontracting relations. Occasionally, managers at higher levels intervened when changes in companywide strategy were expected to affect the plant's subcontracting relations. But usually the subcontracting managers' decisions were approved without much trouble.

One of the subcontracting managers at Mori was known for his "oppressive" attitude toward his subcontractors. It was he who had drastically slashed the number

19. Owing to the nature of the materials used and discussed in this section, I have used pseudonyms for the company and its two plants. I conducted extensive field research on this company and its subcontracting networks in 1983, 1984, and 1986.

of his subcontractors from twenty-seven to twelve in the aftermath of the 1979 oil crisis. It was he who did not hesitate to announce that he had devised some dirty tricks to "smash" his subcontractors in the interest of preserving his plant's operations. For him, subcontractors were used solely to protect regular workers in his plant in the face of fluctuations in demand.

By contrast, this manager's counterpart at Egawa was reputed to be a "prosubcontracting" manager. He viewed his subcontractors essentially as semipermanent members of his plant and tried to help them whenever they had problems, whether technical, financial, or personnel. About half his subcontractors had been serving the Egawa plant since its establishment in 1970, and the remainder had at least seven or eight years of contractual relations with the plant. Based on the plant's long-term plan to subcontract more assembly jobs while concentrating on development activities in-house, his predecessors and he had strategically expanded the plant's subcontracting capacity. In 1973, there were eight assembly lines in-house and fewer than ten assembly lines at subcontractors. In 1983, the figures were four and seventeen, respectively.

The contrast between the two managers' styles can be seen by judging the frequency of their employees' visits to the subcontractors. At Mori, subcontracting agents visited a subcontractor once a month at best; usually it was something like once in three months. Visits to second-tier subcontractors were exceptional and were made only in emergencies (e.g., quality problems). In contrast, their colleagues at Egawa paid at least one visit a week to each subcontractor to monitor its operations. If they encountered any problems, they immediately tried to solve them on the spot. Second-tier subcontractors (and even their home workers) were also frequently visited to ensure that their operations were in order. At regular intervals, selected workers from both first- and second-tier subcontractors were invited to the Egawa plant, where they were retrained to follow proper procedures in production operations and, upon their return to their plant, to teach what they had learned to their fellow workers. Although it was not compulsory, subcontractors were also asked to submit a business report every half-year so that their financial "health" could regularly be checked. When any trouble was found, it was the responsibility of the Egawa subcontracting agent in charge to help the subcontractor solve it. In particular, a tacit consensus developed over the years of working together that maintaining a minimum profit level of 5 to 6 percent was vital to a subcontractor's viability, but if a subcontractor were unable to maintain that level, Egawa's response was "problem-solving" oriented rather than "bargaining" oriented. It hardly ever accepted an automatic increase of contractual prices without thoroughly analyzing the reasons for squeezed profits. If the problem were associated with the inefficient use of resources, production engineers and other appropriate staff were sent to solve it. Subcontractors were grateful for such extended help.[20] With few exceptions, however, none of this help was offered by Mori's subcontracting agents to their subcontractors.

20. Based on my interviews with Egawa's purchasing managers and their subcontractors in 1983, 1984, and 1986.

Myopia

Paradoxically, the Mori plant regarded the audio recession as a golden opportunity to rationalize its subcontracting base. For years, owing to neglect and a laissez-faire attitude, Mori's subcontractors had been in a state of chaos. On average, their productivity and quality levels were lower than those serving other JSC plants. Delays in production and delivery were not unusual, and as the recession deepened, idle capacity at Mori itself was becoming a problem. Thus, after obtaining internal approval, the subcontracting manager at Mori embarked on a radical rationalization plan concerning his subcontractors.

In January 1982 he called in three subcontractors on different occasions and announced that because of difficulties in the business environment, their contracts would be terminated as of April. Two of the three subcontractors had been entirely dependent on the Mori plant for several years. At the Mori plant's request, two years before this, one of the two subcontractors had opened a new factory equipped with semiautomated assembly lines dedicated to JSC products. Not surprisingly, it was this subcontractor that fought back most fiercely. Internal documents from the Mori plant, which were made available to me, recorded the negotiations that followed.

According to the documents, five meetings were held between the two parties between January 20 and February 22, 1982, before a final agreement was reached. The president of the subcontracting plant blamed the Mori plant for causing the impending bankruptcy of his firm. Based on a decade (since 1972) of commitments that he had made to Mori as a single customer, he demanded various forms of compensation. First, he requested a minimum of two months' extension of his contracts. (A partial one-month extension was eventually granted.) Second, he asked for compensation for the dramatic decline in orders during the three months between January and March. Third, he demanded compensation for the cost (in terminal bonuses) of firing many of his employees. Fourth, he requested similar compensation for payments that he felt he would have to make upon discharging most of his own subcontractors. Fifth, he asked for compensation to write off his new factory, a factory that had been constructed only two years before at the request of the Mori plant and that, owing to its high asset specificity, could not be used for other purposes. The Mori plant agreed to pay approximately a quarter of the compensation the subcontractor demanded.[21]

In the same way, the other two subcontractors of the Mori plant were discharged, and the remaining nine subcontractors suffered a dramatic decline in orders from Mori. After this incident, the subcontractors tried to shift their ties to other customers as much as possible. By 1986 when the audio recession had ended, the Mori plant was left with only six assembly subcontractors, of which only three were "carryovers" from 1981. Internal documents show that the subcontracting manager at Mori was clearly aware that if demand returned to prerecession levels, there would be a capacity shortage of 38 percent in one product range and 14 percent in the other. But he chose myopic solutions. There is no question that Mori's short-run

21. This subcontractor survived the recession by completely withdrawing its business from JSC and finding other customers in different segments of the electronics industry.

operating losses in the early 1982 crisis were thus minimized because of this radical "rationalization" of its subcontracting base. But when the economy picked up and a new audio-visual boom arrived, the Mori plant simply could not meet the demand. It was extremely difficult to find additional assembly contractors that could be relied on without months of teaching and training. Furthermore, it was impossible to find a subcontractor who would risk investing in such expensive facilities as semiauto-mated assembly lines dedicated to JSC, while similar lines had had to be written off a little earlier. Compounding this situation, there were severe quality problems due to the overwhelming production imposed on Mori's remaining subcontractors. In mid-1986 when I revisited the Mori plant, this subcontracting manager had been replaced.

Symbiosis

If the case of Mori was typical of an "exploitative" strategy to satisfy only its own short-term needs in a crisis, Egawa's behavior during the same recession was a good example of a "symbiotic" strategy based on long-term calculations.

Like Mori, the Egawa plant faced a critical juncture when the recession deep-ened in early 1982. About one hundred part-time workers directly employed by the plant were due to be laid off by the spring. But it became clear that more fundamen-tal solutions would be necessary if the plant were to operate without running into the red. Among the measures proposed at management meetings was the curtailment and selective discharge of subcontractors. The manager in charge of the sub-contracting section strongly opposed this idea, however. His opposition was based on a long-term calculation that once let go, it would be extremely costly to recon-struct, when necessary, the same collection of knowledge and expertise that his subcontractors had accumulated through years of contractual experience with the plant. According to this manager's computation, a selective discharge of 50 percent of his subcontractors might slash Egawa's operating losses by 20 to 25 percent in the short run. But when demand resumed, there would be not only a 30 percent shortage of capacity but also a requirement for an additional 720 man hours of new sub-contractor training, assuming he could find any. He further argued that the type and quality of investments that his subcontractors had made for JSC were such that if discharged, the subcontractors would certainly demand compensation for conver-sion or write-off. In either case it would be very expensive. He added that the ability of his subcontractors, with flexibility and a ready willingness, to respond to Egawa's requirements (especially for high quality and low costs) was such that once severed it would take years to restore. Finally, he proposed that in view of the situation he would nevertheless have to curtail the amount of orders to his sub-contractors, but without firing them. He would try to attain an *ex ante* consensus regarding the levels of output reduction between Egawa's production department and his subcontractors on the understanding that the reduction be distributed as evenly as possible among the parties concerned within feasible operating limits. After several interdepartmental meetings, the manager's proposal was accepted.

Following this, he and the presidents of his subcontracting firms held a series of meetings over several months in early 1982. The purposes of the meetings were to explain the problems that JSC had in facing up to the recession and to obtain the subcontractors' understanding of why orders had to be reduced, while at the same time assuring them that the remaining orders would be distributed as evenly as possible among the Egawa plant and its subcontractors. The subcontractors reacted favorably. No subcontractor had reason to challenge the logic underlying such an approach. My visits to Egawa's subcontractors later confirmed their reactions in favor of this approach. According to a senior manager of one subcontractor: "It was a tough time. Everybody was reducing capacity. But JSC treated us well. They warned us in advance. And they tried to give us small orders even if they had nothing to make on their assembly lines. Other customers weren't like that."

All of this is not to say that everything went smoothly. For example, a sub-contractor in Fukushima, whose sales to Egawa were four-fifth of its output, was badly hit, with the amount of its business with Egawa cut by 86 percent in the first half of 1982. Small orders that were carved out of Egawa's diminishing output and allocated to this firm did not help much. As a matter of necessity, this subcontractor immediately diversified into other segments of the electronics industry that were not hit by the audio recession. Two years later, when I visited this firm, it was assembling computers, monitors, printers, keyboards, calculators, radio cassette players, and the like. Its tie with Egawa, though maintained, never returned to its prerecession level. But its attitude toward Egawa was by no means negative. According to a senior managing director (*senmu*) of this subcontractor: "They taught us that no single product lasts, and so we diversified. We are much stronger now. But I could see how much effort they made to maintain us. Whenever Egawa needs us, we want to cooperate as much as we can."

When the recession was over, Egawa's subcontracting ties were tighter, and Egawa was able to handle the 30 percent increase in car stereo production for three years after 1982 without capacity problems. Subcontractors were eager to invest on their own initiative. JSC's internal audit shows that the quality and productivity levels of Egawa's subcontractors were consistently maintained as "high" to "best" within its companywide subcontracting networks. Thus, the "symbiosis" strategy so tenaciously maintained throughout a difficult period by the subcontracting manager at Egawa paid off.

Discussion

The striking contrast between different subcontracting strategies at two plants of a single Japanese electronics firm demonstrates that subcontracting patterns can be vastly different even within the same firm. What are the implications of this finding for our study of subcontracting relations? The very fact that even within the same Japanese firm such different strategies were pursued with considerably different outcomes suggests that "national characteristics" in themselves may have little influence on the choice of a contractual relation. Rather, the differences observed in this section can be reduced to those in the strategic planning horizon: one to make up for short-term losses by sacrificing outsiders and the other to compensate for apparent short-term losses through collective accommodation, by distributing them evenly for shared, long-term gains.

The two cases further indicate that asset specificity is not the cause but the consequence of a strategy to maintain contractual relations in the interest of preserving long-term reciprocal benefits. In this respect, Williamson's argument that asset specificity accounts for the continuation of "obligational contracting" is reversed. One party had to have decided to invest in specific assets in the first place, and such a decision would not have been made without the expectation that the other party's strategy would ensure the viability of such an investment. Destroying such an expectation is costly, as can be seen in the fact that having caused the write-off of a subcontractor's dedicated factory equipped with dedicated new technologies, JSC's Mori plant found it impossible to find a substitute when the recession was over. This dilemma was caused by the inconsistency of Mori's strategy, which originally expected such an investment but later refused to be responsible for it. This case has shown that asset specificity followed strategy and that a break in the latter resulted in a break in the former.

Thus our analysis has restored the correct ordering of strategy and specific assets. In short, *ex post* observations à la Williamson have discovered their *ex ante* strategy.

Summary and Conclusions

This chapter looked at comparative data on electronics subcontracting in the United Kingdom and Japan and the intriguing case of two plants in the same Japanese electronics firm. Our examination has led to three conclusions. First, there appear to be structural differences in the organization of subcontracting between the British and Japanese samples, even in the same industry. Second, subcontracting relations may be largely determined by what is subcontracted, where the subcontracting firm is located, and how many human resources are committed. Third, asset specificity seems to be not the cause but the consequence of a strategy, and in this regard, variations exist even within the same firm.

Major findings from the measurement of asset specificities can be summarized as follows:

1. Customer concentration is stronger in the Japanese sample than in the British sample. More specifically, the Japanese second-tier subcontractors show the highest customer concentration, irrespective of specialty, followed by the Japanese first-tier "assembly" subcontractors, whereas the Japanese first-tier "high-tech" subcontractors have a fairly extensive and level customer base, regardless of specialty.

2. Contract assembly and subassembly (characterized by heavy physical and dedicated asset specificity) constitute a major part of Japanese subcontracting, whereas discrete treatment and single components manufacture (characterized by light physical and dedicated asset specificity) are a predominant part of British subcontracting. Indices reveal that on the whole contractual relations are more physical and dedicated asset specific in Japan than in Britain.

3. The samples from both countries disclose that the higher the tier of sub-

contracting is, the more physical and dedicated asset specific the contracting relations will be. Intertier divergence, however, is much stronger in Japan than in the United Kingdom.

4. Although divergence by specialty was identified in the samples for both countries, there are also significant international differences. Between first-tier and second-tier assembly subcontractors, contract subassembly is still important in Japan, whereas discrete treatment predominates in Britain. Between first-tier and second-tier high-tech subcontractors, discrete treatment and single components manufacture prevail in both countries. In Japan, however, one-fifth of the subcontracting work is still performed by sub-systems assembly firms, whereas there are no such firms in Britain.

5. In regard to physical and dedicated asset specificity, Japanese subcontracting relations are far more varied by tier and specialty than are their British counterparts, with the latter showing remarkable homogeneity.

6. Overall, Japanese subcontractors are three times as human asset specific as are the British subcontractors in this sample. More specifically, Japanese second-tier subcontractors show the highest human asset specificity, followed (by a considerable margin) by Japanese first-tier subcontractors. In contrast, British subcontractors show the lowest human asset specificity and are homogeneous in this regard, too.

7. In terms of site asset specificity, British and Japanese subcontractors are very close at the aggregate level. When examined more closely, however, Japanese second-tier subcontractors show the highest site specificity, followed by a mix of Anglo-Japanese subcontractors. Interestingly, Japanese first-tier assembly subcontractors are the least site specific, reflecting their historical development and the specific characteristics of local labor markets in Japan.

8. Finally, a general correlation between total asset specificity (i.e., the sum of the physical, dedicated, human, and site asset specificity indices) and customer concentration was discovered. The highest total asset specificity and customer concentration of the Japanese second-tier subcontractors were contrasted with the lowest of the British subcontractors. The aggregate national figures revealed a noticeable difference between Japan and Britain in this respect.

These findings constitute a significant departure from conventional speculations based on macrolevel statistics, anecdotal evidence, and impressionistic observations. We compared different patterns of subcontracting in the same industry for the two countries' samples with numbers and indices. We redefined hitherto-obscure elements that tended to be attributed to differences in culture and found that the framework of asset specificity, if applied in an explicitly measurable manner, as we did, is useful for the type of data presented. Moreover, the methodology that we adopted enabled us to "operationalize" the concepts proposed by Williamson. It is from this empirical basis that our analysis of "obligational contracting" has been advanced.

The final portion of this chapter looked at the different subcontracting strategies of two plants of the same Japanese electronics firm. Despite similarities in products and location—as well as their common ownership—they behaved quite differently toward their subcontractors during a recession. Of the two distinctive strategies that they followed, one considered only the prime contractor and was designed to make up for short-term losses at the cost of the subcontractor, and the other, to compensate apparent short-term losses through interfirm collaborative efforts for shared long-term gains. The latter was the more successful.

What are the implications of this finding for our study of subcontracting relations? The fact that even within the same Japanese firm such different strategies were pursued, with considerably different outcomes, indicates that national characteristics can in themselves have very little influence on the choice of one contractual relation over another.

The results outlined in the latter part of the chapter are consistent with the claim that asset specificity is not the cause but the consequence of a particular strategy. In this context, Williamson's argument that asset specificity explains the continuation of obligational contracting is reversed. In contrast, our examination has clarified the relationship between—and restored the correct order of—*ex ante* strategy and *ex post* asset specificity. But a strategy that points to asset-specific contractual relations cannot by itself guarantee that it will work. For the relations between two firms to be viable, there must be interfirm relational mechanisms that enable them to function.

6

Bargaining
or Problem Solving?

Chapter 5 concluded that subcontracting relations in a sample of electronics producers from Japan were on the whole more asset specific than were those in a comparable sample from the United Kingdom and that strategy probably matters in determining the degree of asset specificity. This chapter qualitatively reinforces the findings of the last chapter.

Perception of Customers

We discovered in Chapter 5 that there is a link between total asset specificity and customer concentration. In this section we amplify this conclusion by comparing how customers are perceived by subcontractors in the United Kingdom and Japan and by examining the sources of these different perceptions.

Table 6-1 summarizes the findings from my survey of British–Japanese electronics subcontractors' perceptions of their customers between 1983 and 1986.[1] The most interesting difference is that 73 percent of the Japanese respondents regarded their customers as "demanding" or "strict," compared with only 31 percent of the British respondents. Not surprisingly, further explanations by the respondents made clear that Japanese customers demanded extremely high quality, low cost, and on-time delivery from their subcontractors, while the British customers were not so concerned with these criteria. Although I did not collect comprehensive data on product quality, anecdotal evidence from my interviews illustrates the degrees of difference between the two countries. In Britain, an electrical appliances firm found acceptable a failure rate of up to 20 percent in the field (i.e., once the consumers took the appliances home). Hence, nobody questioned reject rates of 6 to 15 percent

1. High-tech and assembly subcontractors who were separately treated in the last chapter are combined here. All the British and 90 percent of Japanese respondents covered in this survey are first-tier subcontractors, and 10 percent of Japanese respondents are second-tier subcontractors. In the interviews, I asked all of them to make three favorable and three critical comments about their customers. Although not all respondents observed the rule, this method of "semi-open-response" questioning helped me organize their replies. I then grouped their comments from a substantial part of the interview in various ways until I obtained a satisfactory classification scheme. I analyzed the results by using the method of "grounded coding" as explained, for example, by White and Trevor (1983:156).

TABLE 6-1. British and Japanese Electronics Subcontractors'
Perception of Their Customers, 1983–86

( ) = sample size

Perception[a]	United Kingdom (13)	Japan (40)
Good customers	23.1%	27.5%
Good support	15.4	35.0
Long-term oriented	7.7	17.5
Demanding, strict	30.8	72.5
Erratic trading	69.2	37.5
Monitored	15.4	42.5

[a]Respondents were asked to make three favorable and three critical comments about their customers. The following are the most frequently made.

Source: My interviews conducted from 1983 to 1986.

for PCB assemblies delivered to this firm from an assembly subcontractor. The latter in fact blamed bad components, and not their operations, for the high failure rates. Apparently, the appliances firm accepted this reasoning. By contrast, in Japan, a failure rate of more than 1 percent under first-year warranty coverage was considered "disgraceful," and a 0.04 percent "service call rate" (not necessarily a failure) in the field had been achieved by the best producer of comparable products. Moreover, many Japanese producers were no longer so concerned about failure rates of finished products as about those of the systems components from which they were made. At this level, twenty to thirty defects per million (or 0.002 to 0.003 percent) in the field were typical of the best producers. According to my survey, the worst performer was still in the range of an impressive 109 to 804 defects per million (or 0.0109 to 0.0804 percent) for the fiscal year 1986.[2] These figures certainly confirm Japanese prime contractors' frequent remark: "We accept no defects." And they mean it.[3]

More important, cross-country differences in the perception of customers as being "demanding" and "strict" were regarded in the interviews as radically different trade practices between the two countries. Japanese customers assumed that their subcontractors would automatically and continuously improve quality and reduce cost. If the subcontractors did not, many customers tried to discover the reasons for the problems and push the subcontractors to solve them at the source. This usually meant exhaustive data collection from subcontractors, data analysis, and recommendations. If the process were judged to be insufficient or the problems were identified as more serious than expected, on-site inspections and rigorous

2. I collected these data in my field research in Britain and Japan between 1985 and 1986. My more recent research on automotive components development documented that in 1990 the best defect figures being achieved by some Japanese suppliers were in the order of five to ten per million for systems components.

3. In support of these findings, national data (SMEA, 1986) also show that customers' demands for high quality (76.8 percent), quick delivery (72.0 percent), and low cost (70.7 percent) were felt most acutely by Japanese subcontractors (figures in parentheses indicate response rates). In contrast, factors related to "erratic trading" show much lower response rates: fewer orders because of customers' internalization of production (14.9 percent) and more orders because of customers' externalization of production (11.1 percent).

retraining of the subcontractors followed. This practice also explains the relatively higher perception of Japanese customers in Table 6-1 as "good customers" extending "good support," while the subcontractors themselves felt "monitored." With few exceptions, it was unusual for Japanese customers to fire or switch subcontractors without such methodical monitoring. In this respect, Japanese customers' approaches can be called *problem-solving oriented*.

The following are some illustrative remarks made by Japanese subcontractors:

> They don't really switch around subcontractors only for lower prices, because there can be other problems—technical problems, bad quality, delivery delays, and so on (a second-tier subcontractor).

> Several years ago, we felt we were losing to our competitors in this area. So we offered a less expensive contractual fee to Company A, our second biggest customer. I thought they'd accept it and increase our business. But they never said yes or no on the spot. Instead, they sent their staff, production engineers, and the like to our factory and thoroughly examined our operations. A few days later, they came back to me and said, "Don't be suicidal. You can't do that." Then they gave me detailed recommendations for improving our quality and productivity. We followed them, and several months later we managed to offer a lower price than we'd originally proposed. And this was done with increased profits! This time, they accepted. They taught us how to run our factory; I'm so grateful (a first-tier subcontractor).

These comments suggest that trade relations cannot be short term, as continual, mutual commitments are required. Furthermore, what Japanese customers were looking for was overall cost reduction, taking into account price, quality, delivery, and manufacturing technology, not just the face value of a contractual fee.

Here is what Japanese prime contractors had to say:

> We've hardly ever used on-the-spot subcontractors, except in an emergency. For years, we've been constantly assessing our subcontractors in terms of price, quality, delivery, and technical capability. We'd never switch them for reasons of price alone; that would be naive. If we'd done that, our overall cost structure would have been much higher.

> In our case, spot contracting is an exception. We rely on our customary subcontractors. They know our products and how to make them properly. They know how to solve technical problems without messing around. This is the result of many years of mutual experience. I cannot imagine new, on-the-spot subcontractors doing the same right away.

It is understandable why 18 percent of Japanese subcontractors stated (in Table 6-1) that their customers were "long-term oriented," whereas the comparable figure for Britain was only 8 percent.

In contrast, in the United Kingdom, cost increases over time were assumed to be natural and unavoidable, and so short-term "solutions" were used. Moreover, problems arising from subcontractors, such as requests for a price increase, tended to be interpreted as antagonistic power relations. When a subcontractor proposed a price increase, or there were any other problems regarding its performance, its customers usually bargained for a smaller increase or other forms of "compensation" while threatening to switch to a cheaper or better competitor. When this did not work, they frequently fired the subcontractor and resorted to substitutes, including in-house production. Throughout the negotiations, the customers generally showed little interest in joint efforts to reduce costs, nor were they interested in how the subcontractors were actually doing their work. Rather, British customers were apt to reach quick solutions through "in-the-office" negotiations. Such an approach may be called *bargaining oriented.*

The following comments made by British subcontractors are typical:

> All they [our customers] are concerned about is a cheap price. They are invariably trying to find cheaper subcontractors, and when they do, you are no longer there.

> Our customers send us blueprints and parts. We just assemble them and ship them back. With few exceptions, they never come around and see our factory. Price negotiations always take place in their office.

> The problem of manufacturing is shifted from our customers to us. How to make it cheaper is *our* problem. It's not easy. They just look at our offer prices. In order to survive, the only thing we can do is to decrease our wages.

Such different approaches in the United Kingdom and Japan relate to another important issue revealed in Table 6-1: "erratic trading."

The most common complaint by British subcontractors was the precariousness of their trade relations: New business often both started with and ended with a phone call.[4] With few exceptions, neither long-term production plans nor sufficient warning of reduction in business or severance was given in advance to subcontractors. It appeared that the use of subcontractors as a buffer against fluctuations in demand was stronger in Britain than in Japan. The following are examples of British subcontractors' feelings:

> We subcontractors are in a very, very vulnerable situation. They [our customers] just pick up the phone and say, "Cancel it all."

> The biggest blow we had recently was the case of Company X. For years, they were our biggest customer. They were responsible for one-third of our business. But one day they merged with Company Y. All new machines were there so they didn't need us any more. All of a sudden, we lost a business of £60,000 a year. They never told us in advance.

> Several years ago, we were suddenly fired by Company Z, our biggest and longest customer. We were obliged to become the master of our own destiny. Our business [with them] started again when the recession was over. But we never came back to the same relationship again. We don't want to.

> There were many cottage firms around here. But the recession forced many of them to go out of business. Large firms just got rid of them.

Because such precarious trade relations are not unusual, it is not surprising to see the following kind of reaction from British subcontractors:

> Our policy is not to do more than 30 percent of our business with any one customer, even if he asks us. You never know how long it would last.

---

4. Incidentally, this practice, so often encountered in the United Kingdom, is virtually nonexistent in Japan, insofar as my samples are concerned.

I don't want to put more than 30 percent of my eggs into one basket.[5]

No one of our customers takes up more than 20 percent of our total sales turnover. In this country, a business relationship is very loose. There's no such thing as a long-term commitment.

The situation is pretty "hand to mouth." We must find as many customers as possible, however small the contract. You can never rely on any one contract because it never lasts. [This firm went bankrupt one year after this interview.]

A significant proportion of the Japanese respondents also mentioned their "erratic trading" in Table 6-1, although less often than did the British. Their further explanations, however, revealed interesting qualitative differences in practice. That is, the precariousness of their trade situation was in fact not as harsh and dichotomous as in the United Kingdom but was "planned" and "coordinated." Japanese subcontractors were frequently warned about a reduction in business well in advance and were often even offered help from their customers to alleviate possible losses due to fewer orders. The following are comments by Japanese subcontractors:

Even if our customer decided to make parts in-house, it would inform us well in advance, so we could make preparations (a second-tier subcontractor).

Of course, coping with business fluctuations is our greatest headache. That's the same at our parent factory. But they never say, "Hey, there's no business for you beginning tomorrow." Instead, they warn us several months in advance. Usually, they ask us to change our components or to subassemble this and complete-assemble that. And they give us detailed instructions about what components to buy from whom and what we subcontract out to whom. All this is done to help us survive (a first-tier subcontractor).

This "protectionist" approach on the part of Japanese customers was confirmed by their own remarks, which revealed some methodical antirecession measures that attempt to maintain relationships instead of abruptly severing them:

Our approach [to our subcontractors] is: "We reduce our output by 30 percent. So you reduce yours by 30 percent, too. Let's rationalize together." Then, we assure them steady orders, if fewer when in recession, and based on this we ask them to reduce costs further. We do it together. We benefit from it together. Unless you undertake this [kind of collaborative undertaking], you'll never get your costs down in the long run and enhance your international competitiveness.

We regard our subcontractors as part of our enterprise group even if there's no equity relationship. Within the group we try to allocate the work load evenly. If a subcontractor's workload is down, we help him find a new job.

Recession doesn't make us shed them. Rather, we call them in, and together we try to think about how to get round the problem.

Even if we have to cut off our subcontractors, we don't do it harshly. Sometimes, we even ask other large firms to take care of them.

---

5. That British subcontractors were actually observing this self-protection rule is noted in the hard data presented in Chapter 5: On average a no. 1 customer accounted for 30.7 percent of their annual sales, in contrast with the comparable Japanese figure of 77.7 percent (Table 5-4).

The next comments reveal that the rationale behind these practices is not so much derived from Japanese customers' wholesale benevolence but from realistic long-term economic calculations, which also relate to the high degree of contract assembly and asset specificity in Japanese subcontracting relations:

> We are always trying to maintain coexistence and coprosperity with our subcontractors. It makes no sense to crush them anyway, because they are making our products.

> Essentially, we don't need them [our subcontractors] right now. But they have been making handsome investments for us. We can't just say good-bye. We have to think about ways to preserve this great asset so that we can make full use of it when business picks up again.

> If we cut out our subcontractors completely, they will never take us seriously if we approach them again. So we try to maintain our relationships by evenly reducing our own workload and theirs. If we approach them that way, they will understand and cooperate with us. Otherwise it's darn difficult to find other subcontractors [when business picks up] who can achieve the same quality standards.

With such a cooperative approach by the customers, it is not surprising that Japanese subcontractors responded in such a trusting manner. One subcontracting owner stated:

> At the moment, the business situation is no good. But within a year or so our parent firm will surely lay new rail tracks for us. We can say this from our past experience (a second-tier subcontractor).

These customer–subcontractor relations are not a natural product of Japanese culture but a strategic creation that has evolved over time from exploitative to symbiotic manufacturing. A high-ranking manager of a Japanese prime contractor pointed out:

> In the postwar period, it was very common for large firms to beat down subcontracting fees and to use subcontractors as a cushion against downturns. But during the high-growth period, we shifted our strategy in that we selected out good ones from bad ones and let them do more assembly jobs for us. So now we are symbiotic. Neither of us can exist without the other. We always say, "Become the world's no. 1 subcontractor. We'll always help you." This cannot be achieved by bashing them, cheapening them. We need them to be profitable. Otherwise, they'll never invest for us.

Finally, a senior manager of another prime contractor summarized the basic philosophy of the "win–win" game that permeates contemporary subcontracting practices in Japan:

> It's not that all is well if you alone are well. Without cooperation from your subcontractors, you'll all lose in the long run.

In sharp contrast, the philosophy underlying the British subcontracting practices can be called the "win–lose" principle. A purchasing manager of a British prime contractor concluded:

We don't really care what happens to subcontractors. We subcontract in order to protect our own work force. We use them as a buffer against fluctuations. And we try to subcontract unpleasant and messy jobs as well. How to survive is their business.

If this is the typical attitude of British prime contractors, it is not difficult to understand the British subcontractors' negative responses:

In this country, ties between customer and subcontractor are very, very weak unless you have large-batch, long-term contracts. And long-term contracts are a rare commodity. As a subcontractor, you are lucky if you can just make a good living.

Customers can do some dirty tricks. For instance, they all of a sudden make quality standards stricter when they want to get rid of us. Joint effort, eh? Nonsense.

How nice it would be if our customers came to us and asked for our help in design, manufacturing, and so on! But in this country, it never happens. They see us as a cheaper and dirtier version of their machines.

It is difficult to determine the extent to which these negative reactions were due to a long-term recession that the British economy had suffered since the mid-1970s. When I interviewed at these British firms, they were struggling. In a different time, their responses might not have been so negative.

At the same time, however, the Japanese respondents themselves were in a similar situation. I talked to most of them when the "semiconductor recession" had been substantially reducing their work load and at the same time the sharp appreciation of the yen was beginning to affect the Japanese economy as a whole. Some of the Japanese respondents' remarks indicate that they were not having an easy time, either. Yet the relatively positive reactions, from both Japanese prime contractors and subcontractors, suggest that they were reasonably confident about where they were heading. And it is not difficult to see that this confidence was based on the perceived benefits of long-term mutual commitments and joint problem solving between customer and subcontractor.

Continuous quality improvement and cost reduction at the source seem to be intrinsic to the mechanisms of Japanese subcontracting today. As some Japanese respondents have said, this helped them achieve continuous overall cost reduction, and almost endlessly so. The result was an array of defect-free, low-cost and ever-improving products that have continued to enhance their international competitiveness.

Thus the high degree of asset specificity and customer concentration in Japanese subcontracting, as indicated in the last chapter, is not a given but a result of continuous decision making by Japanese firms that see economic benefits in retaining and reinforcing the mechanisms of symbiotic subcontracting. Furthermore, we can infer from the outcomes of various adverse events in the world economy in the last two decades that the competitiveness of the Japanese economy has been sustained because the proper functioning of such mechanisms is not hampered by external forces alone, such as the oil shocks or the appreciation of the yen, as it is these contingencies with which the "problem solving" organization can so effectively cope. Frequently, if not invariably so, Japanese producers have demonstrated that these contingencies can be overcome in great part by continuously making better products with ever-fewer resources.[6]

In this sense, it would be reasonable to assume that the 1980s, during which time I conducted this study, may prove to be pivotal in indicating the future directions of not only the Japanese manufacturing industry but also the technoorganizational paths that industrial societies throughout the world could take. During this decade, Japan's gross national product (GNP) per capita surpassed that of the United States (*The Economist,* October 25–31, 1986). The average wage of Japanese factory workers almost reached parity with that of U.S. workers.[7] In many developed countries, the penetration of consumer products approached the saturation point (Piore & Sabel, 1984: 184). If the advantage of the Japanese manufacturing industry had been only cheap labor, or the "social dumping" of subcontractors in particular, and if its growth had been sustained only through large export markets that absorbed "cheap" Japanese goods, then its competitiveness would have been lost long ago to newly industrialized countries (NICs). Had the attractiveness of Japanese products been merely their low prices and energy-saving attributes, which undeniably increased their attractiveness during the oil shock–stricken 1970s, the sharp drop in oil prices and the rapid appreciation of the yen in the 1980s might have lowered their consumption. The reality is, however, that Japanese industry has proved itself viable in the long run by continuously producing large quantities of a large variety of high-quality products.

Subcontractor Improvement Programs

Based on the evidence presented in the last section, we have concluded that Japanese subcontracting relations are characterized by institutional attributes that promote continuous quality improvement and cost reduction through problem solving–oriented commitments by both customer and subcontractor. This conclusion will be reinforced by a brief case study of subcontractor improvement programs at Hitachi's Taga plant.[8]

---

6. This is not to say that the problem-solving organization is a panacea. Like all organizations, it has limits and is further circumscribed by larger developments in the international political–economic arena. For example, it can do little about embargoes or "voluntary" export restraints. Nor can it do much about the overall collapse of certain areas of industry whose competitiveness depends chiefly on cheap labor. But the point is that the effectiveness of the problem-solving organization is substantial, to the extent that the products' competitiveness can be maintained (or promoted) through the constantly enhanced, value-added, and increasingly efficient use of physical and human resources.

7. Recent data from the U.S. Department of Labor (1989:5) cite indices of hourly compensation costs for production workers in manufacturing as 100 for the United States and 95 for Japan, in contrast with the indices for such newly industrialized countries (NICs) as Singapore and Taiwan (19), Korea (18), and Hong Kong (17).

8. The following presentation is based on my interviews with, and data collected from, Hideo Ohshita, subcontracting manager, and Yoji Watanabe, assistant subcontracting manager, subcontracting section, Materials Department, Hitachi's Taga plant, March 28, 1986.

In 1986, the Taga plant was manufacturing home-use electrical appliances, small and medium-sized industrial motors, and information systems. Its materials department employed seventy-one people, of whom twenty-five were in the subcontracting section dealing with seventy subcontractors. Within the subcontracting section, there was a subcontractor *kaizen* (continuous improvement) team made up of six production engineers who regularly visited the subcontractors to monitor their performance, in collaboration with the subcontracting agents who constituted the remainder of the section. Among the other sections in the materials department was the value analysis (VA) section, consisting of six engineers who also closely worked with those in the subcontracting section in assessing and training the subcontractors. These people constituted the nucleus of subcontracting relations at Taga.

For years, the Taga plant has been implementing three main types of subcontractor improvement programs, quality assurance, subcontractors' study groups, and management guidance.[9]

Quality assurance has seven programs:

1. *Subcontractor quality assurance (QA) manual.* This manual is regularly revised by the subcontracting section in collaboration with Taga's inspection department. It is distributed to Taga's subcontractors and describes Hitachi's standard procedures of manufacturing and its quality standards.
2. *Certificates of approved inspectors.* Every three years, inspectors at the subcontracting firms are called in and tested so that their skill levels can be updated to Hitachi standards. For those who pass the tests, certificates are issued or renewed. For those who fail, retraining is provided until they do pass.
3. *Skill contest.* An annual dexterity contest of skilled workers from subcontractors as well as from Taga is held to encourage constructive competition among workers to manufacture defect-free products quickly and safely.
4. *Quality assurance inspection.* The quality assurance inspection is part of an overall annual inspection of subcontracting factories by a team of Taga staff made up of appropriate personnel from the subcontracting section, as well as quality inspectors and production engineers. Each subcontractor is graded. Poor performers are warned and given a grace period in which to improve. Taga extends various forms of technical assistance on a case-by-case basis.
5. *Quality awards.* The best performers in the quality assurance inspection are annually awarded prizes of quality excellence and are widely announced in trade journals, in-house magazines, and the like.
6. *Gleaning.* Gleaning refers to a biannual program focused on helping poor performers in the midterm. In contrast with the quality problem meetings (item 7), which are directed at special remedies, this program is for the overall improvement of poor performers' manufacturing capability, based on their past six-month record.
7. *Quality problem meetings.* Subcontractors who have had "serious" quality

---

9. As discussed in Chapter 4, its subcontractor grading system was introduced in the latter half of the 1960s.

problems in the past month are summoned to the monthly review meeting and asked to analyze the causes of their problems and to propose remedial measures that have been or will be taken.

In the second type of subcontractor improvement program, the so-called MST (minimum stock/standard time) study groups, consisting of five specialty groups (e.g., assembly, molded parts), the subcontractors are organized with the aim of sharing the just-in-time (JIT) operations (or MST in Hitachi's terminology) among them so that production flows between Taga and subcontractors can be linked to JIT in order to reduce operational costs (see Chapter 7). Production engineers from Taga are frequently sent to instruct these study groups.

Third, various kinds of assistance are extended directly to the management of subcontracting firms:

1. *Quality control (QC) seminars for subcontracting owners.* Taga provides a seminar series tailored to subcontracting owners or high-ranking managers, to ensure that they are well informed about the importance of QC. The seminars are based on the conviction that QC is not a mere shop-floor technique but part of an overall management philosophy (i.e., total QC or TQC) and that it can be meaningfully used only when the top managers of the subcontracting firms understand this and support its implementation.

2. *Analysis of monthly balance sheets.*[10] The principal subcontractors are asked to submit monthly balance sheets so that the management of each firm can be regularly checked. Taga offers poor performers advice, recommendations, and instructions, which often entails sending personnel from Taga to the subcontractor. High-ranking personnel such as directors are often sent for up to several years to help revitalize troubled firms that have equity ties to Hitachi.

3. *Subcontracting budget announcement meetings.* Every six months, the Taga plant's manager convenes a meeting with the subcontractors and presents them with a new budget disclosing planned allocations of subcontracting work for the next half–fiscal year.[11] Those subcontractors who have had outstanding performances in the past six to twelve months are given opportunities to discuss their achievements.

4. *Dispatch talks.* Department and section managers from Taga are often dispatched to various subcontractors' meetings to talk about low-cost and defect-free manufacturing management.

5. *Resident trainees.* Line leaders, inspectors, and engineers from the sub-

10. This practice of analyzing subcontractors' monthly balance sheets originated in July 1971 at Hitachi's Taga plant. Until then, many of its subcontractor's accounts had been settled only once or twice a year, supervised by certified accountants. Hitachi changed this custom so that its subcontractors' balance sheets could be monitored monthly. Seminars on making balance sheets were provided by Hitachi in mid-July followed by the dispatch to its subcontractors of a teaching team composed of Hitachi's purchasing and accounting personnel (*Nikkan Kogyo Shinbun*, July 15, 1971).

11. I observed this practice among Japanese electronics and automotive producers in my fieldwork from 1983 to 1989. In contrast, I did not observe these subcontracting budget announcement meetings in my research in Britain.

contracting firms are given opportunities to stay at Taga as "resident train-ees" for six to twelve months to learn various operational and engineering skills. Between 1981 and 1986, seventy people had completed this training program.

6. *Safety training.* Periodic training sessions on safety are provided for shop-floor workers and managers of subcontractors.

From sifting through these programs, we can see that Taga's commitment to its subcontractors was thorough and comprehensive. According to Taga's subcontractors, the programs were carried out in a rigorous and professional manner. Many of Hitachi's resources, from professional instructors to sophisticated training facilities, are used for reinforcing its own subcontracting base.[12] Furthermore, the rationale behind the programs was not to punish poor performers but to help them correct the problems at the source and to continue to enhance their performance. For this purpose, Taga did not hesitate to help educate its subcontractors' human resources from top management to engineers to inspectors to workers. Rather than trying to find quick substitutes, the programs were designed to change some of the poor performers into good ones.[13]

The Taga plant was interested in the long-term growth of its subcontractors, as can be seen in such practices as the analysis of subcontractors' monthly balance sheets and the subcontracting budget announcement meetings. But Taga's monitoring of its subcontractors is not restricted to these "official" programs. At the less official level, personnel from Taga's subcontracting section, occasionally accompanied by appropriate staff from other sections or departments, regularly visits the subcontractors (once a week to once a month, depending on priorities and necessities) to exchange information and monitor their operations. Irregularities are immediately reported, and remedial measures are taken. These frequent contacts enable Taga to obtain quick responses from subcontractors and minimize cross-purpose operations. Indeed, it is these unofficial, regular visits that provide the framework for the so-called official programs. Enforcement of the official programs alone might not be effective without such regular contacts.

To sum up, this case study demonstrates that Japanese subcontracting relations are characterized by an institutional design that aims at continuous quality improvement and cost reduction through problem solving–oriented commitments between customer and subcontractor at both official and unofficial levels.

British Subcontractors and Japanese Transplants in the United Kingdom

An interesting question concerning the effectiveness of a technoorganizational system is whether or not it can be transplanted to a radically different culture and/or

12. Based on my interviews with Yuzo Katogi, president, San-yu Seisakusho, April 24, 1986; Tetsunosuke Kurihara, secretary-general, Kuji Metalwork Cooperative, April 24, 1986.

13. But Taga did not endlessly help poor performers. Those who continually failed to meet the requirements were naturally screened out in the end.

socioeconomic environment. If the system recognizably loses its major advantages when it is transferred, we can argue that the advantages derive in large part from specific cultural values and customs shared by members of a particular society. If it does not, then we can maintain that the system is not culturally bound.

In this section, we present evidence on Japanese consumer electronics transplants in the United Kingdom and their local subcontractors that directly relates to this issue.[14]

For various geopolitical and marketing reasons, Japanese producers began to establish their own manufacturing facilities in Europe, particularly in the United Kingdom, during the 1970s. By March 1984, the number of Japanese transplants in Britain was thirty-two, employing a total of eight thousand people. Of these thirty-two, ten are consumer electronics transplants (Japan Institute of Labor, 1986: 171). Due to pressures for substantial local content, from early on these companies had to use many local parts and local subcontractors. The small production volume of the transplants and initial "debugging" problems inherent in a foreign environment did not allow them to achieve the same low costs as in Japan for a considerable number of years. The last thing they were willing to do, however, was to compromise on quality, a crucial factor that had promoted the competitiveness of Japanese products worldwide. From the very beginning, therefore, these transplants approached local subcontractors with the same "demanding" and "strict" standards as in their homeland.

For both the Japanese transplants and the local subcontractors, the first few months after operations began were trying. Gaps between the required quality standards and the actual output were phenomenal. For example, 30 percent of certain structural components of television sets supplied from a local subcontractor were rejected by a Japanese transplant because their quality was "substandard." Another transplant was shocked to discover that the integrated circuits (ICs) supplied by a European manufacturer had between three hundred and one thousand times more defects than did the best Japanese components. Even simple parts such as bolts and nuts were found to be irregular; for example, the head came off when tightened. Soon the managers of the Japanese transplants realized that in the United Kingdom the relevant unit of defect measurement was parts per hundred rather than per million. The quest for quality improvement began.

As in Japan, the approach that the managers of the Japanese transplants took was joint problem solving at the source. For example, instead of directly reproaching a poorly performing subcontractor, the engineers at one of the oldest transplants thoroughly tested and analyzed, with in-house testing equipment, the poor-quality components obtained from a local subcontractor. Based on the results, they called in the managers of the subcontracting firm and showed them the data analysis describing why their components failed and then recommended corrective measures. The Japanese managers even proposed to help solve the quality problem on site, because they believed that not everything could be communicated by paper or talks in the

14. This section is based on my interviews with Prof. Masayoshi Ikeda of Chuo University (March 18 and 19, 1985) and Prof. Shoichiro Sei of Kanto-Gakuin University (August 16, 1989). They independently conducted fieldwork on Japanese consumer electronics transplants in the United Kingdom in 1983 and 1984. I drew heavily on their materials, whose contribution is gratefully acknowledged.

office, especially in regard to manufacturing. With the agreement of the subcontractor, a team of Japanese production engineers visited the subcontracting factory, supervised the implementation of corrective measures, and stayed there until they saw satisfactory results.

Three other Japanese transplants of comparable products followed similar procedures. At one transplant, for example, there was a problem with the paint on plastic molded parts. The local subcontractor responsible for the bad paint claimed that it was a "design" problem with the parts themselves, not a paint problem. But the Japanese customer did not accept this claim, because the same parts of the same design had no such problem back in Japan. Instead of arguing further, the Japanese transplant called in specialist engineers from Japan and let them show the British subcontractor the right way to do it. The latter was more than convinced and tried to do the same.

As a result of these joint efforts, the Japanese consumer electronics transplants in the United Kingdom usually achieved, within a few years of start-up, an overall defect rate on incoming components of as low as 1 to 1.5 percent (but still substantially higher than in Japan), as opposed to the two-digit average at other British plants.

Responses from British subcontractors to the transplants varied. A negative outcome was usually the result for subcontractors who insisted that for years their products had been accepted by other non-Japanese customers with no problems and that the Japanese transplants were demanding hyperquality that was relevant only to spacecraft. For these subcontractors, the low defect rates (measured in parts per million [PPM]) that the Japanese managers were demanding was a symptom of "neurosis." These subcontractors, not surprisingly, stopped supplying the transplants. And indeed, twenty-six of thirty-four British television cabinet subcontractors, who initially served some of the old Japanese transplants but who did not react favorably to their strict standards of quality, either went bankrupt or had to change their business during a recession in the early 1980s.[15]

In contrast, those subcontractors who responded positively and improved product quality expanded their business not only with the Japanese transplants but also with other customers. One mechanical parts subcontractor, for example, doubled its sales within a few years in the midst of a recession in the early 1980s. Another structural parts subcontractor was able to open sales channels to Philips and other multinationals because of its continuous quality improvement and cost reduction, results that were widely appreciated by these new customers. The secret of this structural parts subcontractor's success was the implementation of techniques originally learned from a demanding Japanese customer. The managing director of this subcontractor was grateful to the managers of the Japanese customer who had insisted that value analysis (VA) techniques be applied to the subcontractor's cost calculation so that cost-sensitive elements could be identified and their effects

15. In this connection I quote from a similar study of Japanese participation in British industry: "[C]ertainly there have been cases of UK suppliers being unwilling to meet Japanese specifications for genuine economic reasons . . . [but] unwillingness is often a cloak for inability, complacency, laziness or ignorance, and the presence of Japanese affiliates in the UK is having a dramatic effect on some sections of UK industry" (Dunning, 1986:112).

mitigated, item by item. The Japanese managers requested cost data, for example, on parts that they were interested in buying from the subcontractor. After sifting through the data, they discovered many reasons why the subcontractor's offer price was so high. For instance, the subcontractor calculated the costs of certain raw materials 20 to 40 percent higher than that deemed to be appropriate. The cause was an excessively high scrap rate. Instead of arguing about the method of calculation, the Japanese managers proposed resolving the problem by reducing the scrap rate. This entailed a few days of classroom teaching on VA techniques and a few weeks of on-site training in manufacturing methods to "do it right the first time, every time." As a result, this subcontractor's average scrap rate was lowered from 30 or above to about 12 percent. Costs were thus minimized while quality improved. This incident demonstrated to the British subcontractor that the common belief that high quality means high costs is wrong; rather, the reverse is true.

Although we should not rely solely on anecdotal evidence, these examples nevertheless carry important messages. The problem-solving approach of Japanese prime contractors appears to be effective in the radically different cultural environment of Britain. They were able to maintain the same demanding and strict attitudes toward their British subcontractors regarding quality and cost. The Japanese transplants also seem to have extended as much help to local subcontractors as they do in their homeland to solve various operational problems.

The bottom line is clear: The Japanese transplants persuaded their British subcontractors that high quality and low cost were important strategic weapons for their mutual viability and that it was far wiser to try to tackle this problem by means of joint efforts than to do nothing but blame each other. That this was not mere propaganda has been verified by the observation of their aggressive attempts to ensure high quality and low cost through (1) demonstrations such as in-house analysis of poor-quality components, (2) recommendations and on-site supervision of remedial measures taken by the subcontractor, (3) demonstrations by Japanese engineers (who flew from Japan for this single purpose), (4) instruction in VA techniques, and (5) on-site training to reduce scrap.[16]

It is not surprising that the British subcontractors, possibly culture-shocked initially, began to understand the economic rationality of the demands and behavior of their Japanese customers. Step by step, as one good result led to another, they became convinced that what the Japanese customers were asking them to do would be beneficial to both of them. The fact that many of those subcontractors who dismissed the Japanese customers' demands as "neurotic" went bankrupt, whereas those who responded well and improved their product quality grew in the midst of a recession shows that the problem-solving organization of subcontracting that the Japanese had brought to the United Kingdom was a powerful paradigm.

In sum, then, we can conclude on the basis of the evidence presented in this section that the effectiveness of the problem-solving–oriented subcontracting organization—which leads to continuous quality improvement and cost reduction

---

16. Dunning (1986:103–39) reported similar findings from his research on the impact of Japanese transplants on British suppliers in the early 1980s. He also (1992) presents fascinating descriptive comparisons between American and Japanese manufacturing affiliates in the United Kingdom.

through collaboration between customer and subcontractor—is in itself neither a direct product of, nor restricted to, a specific culture. Rather, it happened to be invented and developed by the Japanese, through an evolutionary distillation from their past, and their ability to link and use efficiently various interfirm resources can also be adapted to other industrial societies.[17]

Sources of Entrepreneurship

We have suggested that the Japanese subcontracting organization is characterized by its problem-solving orientation and that its principles can succeed in other industrial societies if properly applied. We also demonstrated that the Japanese approach creates synergy effects through collaboration between customer and subcontractor. Our examination thus far has mainly concentrated on prime contractors' behavior and the rather passive, though often significant, reactions of subcontractors and their performance. But subcontractors, or more precisely the subcontracting business proprietors, do have a *raison d'être* independent of their ties with customers. This section focuses on Japanese subcontracting business proprietors and explores three aspects of their entrepreneurship: their career patterns, income, and job satisfaction.

Career Patterns

It is widely recognized that as in many other industrial societies, Japanese workers in small firms do not earn as much as those in large firms do (Friedman, 1988:139). However, it is not as well recognized that there is an institutional outlet for workers in small firms, especially in Japan: Frequently they become independent business proprietors operating their own subcontracting firms. In Japan, this appears to be a more common occurrence than in other industrial societies, owing to more opportunities arising from prevailing subcontracting practices in the economy and various government-backed institutions (e.g., cooperatives, small business financing organs), as we pointed out in Chapter 3.

The general career patterns of those entrepreneurs running subcontracting firms that I surveyed strongly support this view. A typical pattern is as follows: A man starts working for a manufacturing firm (typically a medium-sized one) after leaving senior high school (often a vocational senior high school).[18] He stays there for a considerable number of years until he accumulates enough knowledge and money to become independent. The decision to start his own firm depends on his ambition as well as other contingencies. Sometimes the firm he has been working for goes bankrupt, and he is forced to do something else. Either he finds a similar technical

17. I (1989b) provide more evidence concerning this issue of cross-cultural transference, drawing on original case studies of U.S. automotive firms' adoption of Japanese methodologies.

18. In my fieldwork covering fifty-four electronics subcontractors in Japan (Table 5-1), I found only one female proprietor of a high-tech firm, who took over that position after her husband's death. In many small "family" firms, however, the proprietors' wives are usually their "business partners' as well and actually work on site.

TABLE 6-2. Profiles of Average Proprietors of Assembly
Subcontracting Firms[a] in the Japanese Electronics Industry,
1986

	Years as Proprietor	Working Years Before Current Proprietorship	Age at Last Graduation
Age			
48.9	12.0	17.6	19.3

[a]Sample size: twenty-four firms, of which sixteen were first-tier and eight were second-tier subcontractors.

Source: My questionnaire survey in 1986 of thirty-seven electronics assembly subcontractors (of whom twenty-four completed the question on the proprietors' profiles).

job in another firm, or he becomes self-employed. Sometimes he takes over his father's firm. Table 6-2 shows profiles of average proprietors (and usually presidents) of the assembly subcontracting firms covered in my field research. The typical proprietor of an electronics assembly subcontracting firm (in this sample) is a middle-aged senior high school graduate who had 1.3 years of further education and 17.6 years of working experience before starting his own business at the age of 36.9.

Table 6-3 summarizes the career patterns of the subcontracting entrepreneurs before they became proprietors. With few exceptions (e.g., a long-distance truck driver, a policeman), the subcontracting proprietors had work experience in manufacturing before starting their own businesses. On average they had worked for 1.5 firms, one-fifth of which were large, established firms, the remainder being small to medium-sized ones. One-quarter of these entrepreneurs had worked up to a plant manager level in previous employment and a quarter had also been made redundant by previous employers. One-fifth took over their parents' firms. These two tables

TABLE 6-3. Career Patterns of Proprietors of Assembly
Subcontracting Firms in the Japanese Electronics Industry, 1986

Number of firms for which worked before starting own firm	1.5
Previous employment	
Manufacturing firms	83.3%
First-half quoted firms[a]	20.8
Self-owned firms	12.5
Experience as plant manager	25.0
Bankruptcy or redundancy as reason for leaving	25.0
Current proprietorship	
Taking over parent's firm	20.8%
Started after retirement	4.2

[a]Publicly quoted firms in the first section of the Tokyo Stock Exchange in 1986.

Source: My questionnaire survey in 1986 of thirty-seven electronics assembly subcontractors (of whom twenty-four completed the question on the proprietors' profiles).

indicate that the business proprietors of electronic assembly subcontracting firms used, consciously or unconsciously, their previous working experience in manufacturing as an institutional training ground before becoming independent.

Income

According to the traditional literature, the livelihood of subcontractors is generally depicted as "miserable." They are at the bottom of the manufacturing hierarchies, and all that they can do is follow their customers' instructions. Through this unequal exchange, any surplus value provided by subcontracting business proprietors is absorbed by superior capital, which in turn affects not only their income but also their workers' wages. To compensate, they work long hours—proprietors and workers alike. Subcontracting firms are, in a word, little dandelions to be run over by big corporate bulldozers. In short, they are victims in a capitalist society.[19]

My fieldwork revealed some counterevidence to this cliché. Despite the conventional images, a number of the Japanese subcontractors that I visited belied these stereotypes. Despite their modest remarks, many subcontracting business proprietors stood out as highly motivated individuals content with their lives and general circumstances. This was puzzling to me and in sharp contrast with the lifeless managers of large firms that I interviewed in the same survey. On one occasion, a shrewd subcontracting entrepreneur offered a clue: "Well, in this business, you can earn a great deal more than workers in large firms. They may have security but no great money. In my business I have less security but a lot of money. The more you work, the more you earn. The more clever you are, the more business you get. There's no limit. It's fascinating." He further mentioned that it was not unusual for somebody in his capacity to make ¥1 million to ¥2 million ($7,500 to $15,000) per month. This point is, curiously, ignored or given short shrift in the traditional literature.

In order to pursue this issue, I included these subcontractors' incomes in my questionnaire. For technical reasons, I have compared the annual incomes of first-tier electronics assembly subcontracting business owners with those of regular workers in manufacturing firms in the same age group. The reason is that the education background of the assembly subcontracting business owners in my survey was predominantly senior high school level and, in this regard, comparable to the majority of workers in manufacturing firms (in general), whereas high-tech subcontracting business owners' education varied from a graduate degree to a junior high school diploma, which made a meaningful comparison difficult. Table 6-4 shows the results.

On average, the first-tier electronics assembly subcontracting business pro-

---

19. Ito, 1957:53–55. Small subcontracting business proprietors are often depicted in the traditional Japanese radical literature as "victims" of the monopoly-capital system, and in this sense they are in the same boat as their own workers.

Using national data, however, Kiyonari (1980:107–9) counterargued that small firms' profits are, on average, greater than those of large firms and pointed out that the problem with small firms is not that their "surplus value" is exhaustively exploited by large firms through subcontracting but that there is far more variance in profits in the small sector than in the large sector, thus implying instability (but at the same time dynamism) in the former.

TABLE 6-4. Incomes of Proprietors of First-Tier Electronics Assembly Subcontracting Firms Versus Incomes of Workers in Manufacturing Firms in Japan, 1985

( ) = sample size

		Average Annual Income (¥)	Index	Age
Proprietors of subcontracting firms	(10)	11,350,000[a]	100	50.2[b]
Workers[c] in manufacturing firms	(233)	6,681,800[d]	58.9	50
Breakdown by size:				
1,000 employees or more		7,397,700[d]	65.2	50
Fewer than 1,000 employees		5,998,600[d]	52.9	50

[a] Total annual income between January and December 1985.

[b] Average age of subcontracting proprietors.

[c] Male, senior high school graduates.

[d] Total annual income between April 1984 and March 1985.

Source: My questionnaire survey of twenty-five first-tier electronics assembly subcontractors (of whom ten answered the question on their income) in Japan in 1986; Research Institute of Labor and Public Administration (Romu gyosei kenkyusho), 1985:10–11, 73–74. The latter provides precise data on the annual incomes and ages of its samples, in contrast with the *Wage Census* of the Ministry of Labor which gives data only on incomes for a particular month, usually June, and "age-band" groups (e.g., 50 to 54 years of age).

prietors earned 70 percent more than did regular workers in manufacturing firms of the same age and educational background.[20] Even compared with workers in large firms with more than one thousand employees, the subcontracting business owners earned 53 percent more. Further, compared with workers in small firms with fewer than one thousand employees, their income level was nearly double. Thus, although we must be cautious about drawing any definitive conclusions in view of the relatively small sample size, the high incomes of the independent business proprietors, as well as the lower wages in the small firms, probably are a strong incentive for workers in small firms to start their own firms (Kiyonari, 1980:89–90). Anecdotal evidence from my research helps illustrate.

At one subcontracting firm on the outskirts of Tokyo, I could not help but marvel at the view from the window of the president's second-floor office. His "stately" private residence was situated on the other side of the precincts. The president's private area consisted of a large Japanese garden with carp ponds, bamboo woods, and rocks, and a well-built residence with numerous Japanese-style rooms. In the garage were a white luxury sedan and an exotic sports car. On the *engawa* (Japanese veranda) facing the garden, an elderly gentleman (probably the president's father) in kimono was playing *go* alone. Serenity was everywhere on the other side, a stark contrast with the hurly-burly of the nearby factory.[21]

Another president of a Tokyo subcontracting firm confessed that he made "business trips" to Hawaii with his business friends three to four times a year. They played golf, ate, and drank together. In between they did talk about business. For

20. Although age and educational background were not adjusted and are therefore somewhat approximate, Kiyonari (1980:87–88) gives similar findings based on national data.

21. Based on my field observation of a Japanese subcontractor in the spring of 1986.

this pleasure alone he could not stop running his own firm, he said jokingly. In fact, many proprietors of the subcontracting firms that I visited were driving elegant "company" sedans for both private and business use. Thus, the perks were abundant, providing a strong material motive for starting one's own firm.

Job Satisfaction

If these monetary and fringe benefits are not unusual and if small business proprietors have considerable freedom to allocate resources in their firms, it is not surprising that their job satisfaction is high. For similar reasons, I compared assembly subcontracting business owners with workers in large electronics firms, as their educational backgrounds (i.e., high school graduates) were similar. Table 6-5 shows my findings.

Again, although we should be cautious about drawing any definitive conclusions from this small sample, it seems clear that self-employed entrepreneurs with similar educational backgrounds were more satisfied than were regular workers in large electronics firms. One-third of the entrepreneurs stated that they were very satisfied with their jobs; 45 percent were satisfied; only one out of five entrepreneurs was dissatisfied; and none was very dissatisfied. In contrast, more than one in three workers in large firms were dissatisfied or very dissatisfied.

Thus despite a presumably riskier operating base compared with that of large firms, the proprietors of Japanese assembly subcontracting firms seemed content with their work. This finding is all the more remarkable if one takes into account the fact that the samples were of only assembly subcontractors who were in general more directed by their customers' needs and desires, because of their work content, compared with high-tech subcontractors. This finding suggests the need for reconsidering the traditional view that small subcontractors are victims in a capitalist society in which their benefits are exclusively absorbed by large firms.

TABLE 6-5. Job Satisfaction of Proprietors of Assembly Subcontracting Firms Versus Workers for Large Manufacturers in the Japanese Electronics Industry, 1986

( ) = sample size

	Subcontracting Proprietors (29)	Workers in Large Firms (4,273)
Very satisfied	34.5%	14.3%
Satisfied	44.8	51.0
Dissatisfied	20.7	29.5
Very dissatisfied	0	4.2
Unknown	—	1.0
Total:	100.0	100.0

Source: My questionnaire in 1986 of thirty-seven electronics assembly subcontractors (of whom twenty-nine answered the question on job satisfaction); Federation of Electrical Machine Workers' Unions (Denki roren), 1975:134; *Chosa jiho* (Survey bulletin), no. 114.

Summary and Conclusions

In addition to the quantitative material of the last chapter, the more qualitative evidence presented in this chapter has confirmed the distinctiveness of Japanese subcontracting relations, as perceived by the subcontractors, compared with British practices in the same electronics industry.

The most important finding in this chapter is that Japanese subcontracting relations are characterized by institutional attributes that promote continuous quality improvement and cost reduction through problem-solving–oriented commitments by both customer and subcontractor. This contrasts with the bargaining orientation of British subcontracting relations, which often have adverse effects.

The results of this chapter confirm the claim that the main advantages of the Japanese subcontracting paradigm are the economic benefits derived from interfirm problem-solving mechanisms designed to ensure high-quality, low-cost products. The successful British subcontractors' acceptance of and commitment to the Japanese subcontracting system as implemented by Japanese transplants in the United Kingdom demonstrate that its principles are applicable to cultures outside Japan. The efficacy of this system may in large part be sustained by motivated and relatively well paid Japanese proprietors of subcontracting businesses.

Building on the findings of the last chapter, we can conclude that the different strategies of Japanese and British firms result in vastly different contractual relations, with the greatest divergence apparent in patterns of asset specificity and customer concentration in subcontracting relations.

7

Sources of Flexibility

The previous two chapters showed that a distinctive strategy of Japanese manufacturers has produced institutional arrangements that promote continuous quality improvement and cost reduction through problem solving–oriented commitments by customer and subcontractor and that this factor has significantly contributed to making obligational contracting function successfully.

This chapter completes Part II, on the contemporary practices of industrial sourcing, by comparing original data on the performance of automotive components suppliers in Japan, the United States, and Europe. This exercise will indicate that the traditional dualist framework must be reconsidered because its shortcomings are too readily apparent.

Traditional Framework

The liberal school of dualism argues that as a response to the rigidification of labor in the primary sector—because of union movements and the subsequent protective legislation—the managers of large firms in several industrial societies sought more flexible replacement in the secondary sector through various forms of *ad hoc* employment, including subcontracting. The prime contractors' increased use of subcontractors (or other forms of secondary labor) has contributed to its flexible operation. The underprivileged status of secondary economic agents—characterized by lower wages, legal loopholes based on small size, or a lack of union protection—subjected them to market forces that made many of them expendable. Risks are thus passed along to the secondary agents, who act as safety valves. Whenever adjustment problems arise, external entities can be discharged or switched at little of the expense normally associated with hiring and firing workers in the primary sector. Insofar as the economy's legal structure and general dualist structure sustain this mechanism, the greater use of subcontracting contributes to maintaining the prime contractors' flexibility in a world of flux and uncertainty (Berger & Piore, 1980). The radical school of dualism, on the other hand, sees an increasing tension in the labor control mechanisms in a capitalist society, the result of which, they argued, was to intensify the fracturing effects on the work force (Edwards, 1979).

The evidence presented in Appendix B, explaining why large Japanese firms use subcontracting firms, indicates, however, that the kind of flexibility that the liberal school of dualism emphasizes is not a primary factor. It also shows that dividing the work force by resorting to a secondary form of production, as the radical school of dualism stresses, obtained neither substantive support nor even recognition by the Japanese respondents that I questioned.

Thus there must be a discrepancy between the traditional dualist arguments and the current determinants of what is operative in subcontracting relations. At the very least, the dualists do not appreciate the important aspect of flexibility in productive linkages, preferring instead to focus on the expendability of external entities. But as the evidence in this chapter will demonstrate, it is even possible that contrary to traditional assumptions, the increased use of subcontracting under certain conditions may create even more rigidity than does flexibility. Flexibility is not automatically produced by contracting out; it may not come, however well the subcontractors meet the requirements prescribed in the dualist literature. One reason for this shortcoming in the traditional accounts can be traced to the ambiguity or confusion concerning the concept of flexibility.

Flexibility Revisited

During my fieldwork in the 1980s in Asia, North America, and Europe, it became clear that the principal focus of flexibility in contractual relations has been shifting from instrumental risk dispersion to collaborative manufacturing. Many managers of both large and small firms confirmed that such shifts in the final-product market and rapid technological development had greatly influenced their business. To a significant extent, they no longer saw exploitative subcontracting relations (as practiced in the old days) as viable. Instead, many argued that collaborative manufacturing, in which various players undertook new complementary roles, was now crucial to the manufacturers' survival, particularly in the motor vehicle industry.[1]

The "crash" of the U.S. automotive industry at the start of the 1980s was more than symptomatic of the fact that traditional mass production methodologies, pioneered in the United States, had become uncompetitive (Piore & Sabel: 1984). Its aftermath saw the U.S. motor vehicle assemblers shift, in principle, toward collaboration with the components suppliers[2] and away from a long tradition of antagonistic relationships in which they used to the full whatever market power they possessed.[3] Moreover, a series of new manufacturing methods, first employed in Japan and successful in enhancing operational flexibility, began to be widely disseminated in the United States. The just-in-time (JIT) methodology of manufacturing supply was introduced (see Nishiguchi, 1989b). Accommodation of diverse

1. Based on my field interviews between 1983 and 1992 of managers of automotive and electronics firms in Japan, Korea, Taiwan, the United States, Canada, Mexico, the United Kingdom, Germany, France, Italy, Spain, Belgium, and Sweden.

2. I use the words *assembler* and *supplier* in lieu of *prime contractor* and *subcontractor*. The former terms are commonly used in the world automotive industry today.

3. However, there persisted a recognizable organizational mismatch between aim and execution that led to several problems of dysfunction. For more discussion of this, see Nishiguchi, 1988a, 1988b, 1988c, and 1988d.

product mixes within individual production facilities came to be emphasized, in theory at least. Factors contributing to reducing lead times, cutting inventory levels, increasing delivery frequencies, and slashing changeover times were studied and implemented with varying degrees of success. Change also came directly from across the Pacific. To avoid the possibility of protectionism, and later taking advantage of the lower value of U.S. dollars versus the yen, many Japanese assemblers and components suppliers opened transplants in the United States, whose number had mushroomed to around two hundred by the end of the 1980s. The new wave swept across Europe, too, with European automotive firms also beginning to adopt a new approach to collaborative manufacturing.[4]

The new contractual relations arising from the changing environment vary in tone and detail, but their common features can be summarized as follows:

1. There is a consensus that flexibility at low cost is the key to competitiveness in today's manufacturing.[5]
2. In particular, the ability of suppliers, on the one hand, to actively develop and flexibly manufacture components rather than simply adopting a passive role and, on the other hand, to deliver them flexibly and "just in time" as required by customers, is becoming more important.
3. Unless suppliers can achieve "synchronized" manufacturing, not only between various stages of their own plants, but also with their customers' plants, the demand for flexible operations may create more problems than solutions.

4. My most recent study of automotive components development found that the concept and features of "lean" production, as promoted by Womack, Jones, and Roos (1990), were influencing even the most conservative European manufacturers at the turn of the 1990s. Ikeda (1984, 1986a) also reports early evidence of emerging new assembler–supplier relations in Europe in the 1980s.

5. Already there are many good empirical studies of the competitiveness of automobile manufacturers around the globe. David Friedman (1983), for example, demonstrated that Japanese assemblers have more product variants, body styles, and engine types for a given production volume than do their U.S. competitors. John Krafcik (1986, 1987, 1988a, 1988b; Krafcik & MacDuffie, 1989) produced a series of authoritative data on car assembly productivity. In 1989, for example, he found that Japanese manufacturers on average took 16.8 hours to assemble a car, whereas the comparative figures for the United States and Europe were 25.1 and 36.7 hours, respectively. Kim Clark and his associates (Clark, Chew, & Fujimoto, 1987; Clark & Fujimoto, 1987; Clark, Fujimoto, & Dubinskas, 1988) illustrated that it took Japanese assemblers 42.6 months to develop a new car, whereas the comparable lead times for U.S. and European assemblers were, respectively 61.9 and 62.6 months. J. D. Power and Associates (1986–89) demonstrated that Japanese cars had, respectively, 27 percent and 32 percent fewer defects (1987 figures) for the first three months of ownership than did U.S. and European cars marketed in the United States. The annual car repair–frequency record issue of *Consumer Reports* (April 1989) reported similar results based on their 562,000 U.S. samples over a five-year period. Finally, I (1989a) found clear correlations between a car's good reliability record and its slow rate of depreciation in the U.S. used car market for small four-door sedans.

With evidence of the competitiveness of assembled cars so abundant, there is a curious lack of similar data on automotive components manufacturers. This may well be due to the sheer variety of components (from bulbs to tires to engines to seats), as opposed to the simplicity of a single product like an automobile; the latter makes an apples-to-apples comparison easier. However, nobody would deny the importance of the relative competitiveness of components manufacturers, as their products account for roughly 50 to 80 percent of the manufacturing cost of motor vehicles around the world. This chapter adds to the discussion of competitiveness in today's manufacturing by providing comparative data on the flexible manufacturing capabilities of the world's automotive components firms.

Taking these factors into account, we can define flexibility, in connection with the emerging contractual relations and for the purpose of this study, as follows: *Flexibility* refers to the ability of the supplier (or subcontractor) to accommodate requirements from the prime contractor for increasing product mix and variants, design changes, quick and frequent deliveries, and the like without incurring prohibitive costs in their implementation. If a supplier is flexible in this sense, its status will be elevated from being a mere "shock absorber" (in the dualist sense) to an indispensable contributor to the prime contractor's production organization. If many suppliers can fulfill this new role, the competitiveness of the prime contractor and that of the industry as a whole will be substantially enhanced.

Types and Measurements of Flexibility

Although manufacturing flexibility can be attained at several levels—firm, plant, system, or machine—our concern here is with the components suppliers' flexibility at the plant level, because the main linkage between assembler and supplier is here (Tidd, 1989:11). The five kinds of plant-level flexibility are the following:[6]

1. The capability to accommodate a mix of products and variants, measured by the changeover time,[7] the changeover frequency, and the number of variants in a given set of manufacturing facilities.
2. The capability to accommodate design changes and new products, as measured by the lead times for a new set of fixtures and tooling, especially dies.
3. The capability to adjust to fluctuating product mixes without changing the size of the work force through its flexible interprocess mobilization, as measured, by proxy, by the number of job classifications and the multiskill levels of the workers.
4. The capability of achieving the foregoing requirements without resorting to production buffers (which increase storage costs and mask quality problems), as measured by inventory levels.
5. The capability of making quick and frequent deliveries to the customer, as measured by just-in-time (JIT) deliveries.

If there were significant differences in flexible capabilities among competitors, it would surely affect the overall performance of contractual relations.

The Survey

From 1987 to 1989, as part of a large project based at the Massachusetts Institute of Technology, I conducted focused field research at fifty-four automotive components

---

6. Parts of these classifications build on those given in Joseph Tidd's excellent work on assembly automation (1989:11). I have made additions and alterations in formulating these so as to apply them to automotive components suppliers. Moreover, I provide substantive quantitative evidence on manufacturing flexibility, a distinction that moves this work a step beyond Tidd's.

7. A reduction in changeover time decreases the size of economic orders, thus permitting the production of smaller batches (and hence greater variety within a given time) at a smaller cost.

TABLE 7-1. Breakdown of Fifty-four Automotive Components Plants Surveyed in Japan, the United States, and Europe, 1987–89

Components Produced	Nationality/Region[a]			
	Japan/Japan	Japan/U.S.	U.S./U.S.	Europe/Europe
Electrical/electronics[b]	7	3	4	7
Metal[c]	9	3	4	9
Composite[d]	1	1	1	1
Fabric assembly[e]	1	1	1	1
Total:	18	8	10	18

[a] Refers to nationality of plants in a region. For example, Japan/U.S. denotes Japanese-owned automotive components plants located in the United States.

[b] Wire harnesses, starters and alternators, relays, motors, and so on.

[c] Exhaust systems, brakes, pistons, cylinder heads, stampings, weld assemblies, and so on.

[d] Bumpers, instrumental panels, steering wheels, and so on.

[e] Seats and seat belts.

Source: My field research from 1987 to 1989.

plants: eighteen in Japan, eighteen in the United States, and eighteen in Europe.[8] I visited each plant, collected data on various indicators of flexibility, and (with few exceptions) observed each plant's shop-floor operations. Of the eighteen plants in the United States, eight were Japanese transplants. The mix of components the plants manufactured—electrical, forged, stamped, machined, cast, fabric-assembly, or composite components—was balanced so that each region had a comparable mix. This balance was important to making comparisons on a similar ground while covering a wide assortment of components—wire harnesses, alternators, exhaust systems, brakes, bumpers, and seats. The proportion of first-tier suppliers and second-tier subcontractors in each group is also reasonably representative.[9] Table 7-1 lists the plants surveyed according to specialty and region.

Although time-consuming, my method of collecting data firsthand, which was supplemented by observing the plant, usually in the company of production managers and/or engineers who answered my technical questions on the spot, turned out to be extremely useful, as I could immediately double-check apparent discrepancies, if

8. The MIT International Motor Vehicle Program (IMVP), in which I served as a full-time research fellow from September 1986 to December 1989, provided funds for this research. Prof. Daniel Roos, director, and Dr. James Womack, research director, supported my research and generously exempted me from many administrative tasks at IMVP so that I could write working papers and complete my study. Their support is gratefully acknowledged.

As in Chapter 5, which dealt with seventy-five electronics establishments out of a total of approximately one hundred covered, the total covered in this research was approximately seventy automotive components establishments. But only fifty-four plants provided complete data and manufactured products that allowed sufficient comparison of flexible manufacturing.

9. Inclusion of second-tier subcontractors in each regional group is seven (38.9 percent) for Japan, one (12.5 percent) for the Japanese transplants in the United States, one (10 percent) for the United States, and four (22 percent) for Europe (percentages in parentheses signify the second-tier subcontractors' share of each group). In view of the different "tiering" structures in respective regions (e.g., as quantitatively estimated by Lamming [1989:4–6] and Dodwell Marketing Consultants [1983:3]), the representation rate of second-tier subcontractors is appropriate.

any, between the data and my actual observation.[10] I could also question meanings often hidden behind numbers and clear up misunderstandings or misinterpretations due to circumstances or a lack of technical knowledge.

Product Mix and Variants

Given the great variety of automotive components, it makes little sense to compare the face-value number of product variants of different components. Even in the same product category, definitions of product variants differ from firm to firm, plant to plant. It is more important to assess the plant's ability to accommodate the product mix and variants by looking at specific indicators, such as changeover times and their frequency in a given time period. In this way, I could measure the relative flexibility of complex manufacturing operations even if there were some differences in the technical definition of product variants. Regardless of the kind of components, changeovers that involve die changes usually indicate major model switches. Therefore, I used the die-change time for a typical volume production item as an indicator of one aspect of flexibility.[11] Table 7-2 summarizes the results. Japan leads the group by a large margin. With only 7.9 minutes needed for a changeover, Japanese components suppliers can change dies fifteen to sixteen times in the time that it takes their U.S. and European competitors to change over just once.[12]

Table 7-3 shows the changeover frequency in these plants. Again, differences are impressive. Japanese suppliers change dies 7.5 times as often as European suppliers do.

Combining the results of Tables 7-2 and 7-3, we can make an interesting comparison by multiplying the die-change time in the plant in one region by its frequency and obtaining a total changeover time per day. In this way, the daily total changeover time for the plant in each region can be calculated as follows:

Japan/Japan:	7.9 minutes × 13.8 times = 109.02 minutes
Japan/U.S.:	21.4 minutes × 9.0 times = 192.60 minutes
U.S./U.S.:	114.3 minutes × 2.0 times = 228.60 minutes
Europe/Europe:	123.7 minutes × 1.83 times = 226.37 minutes

10. If no reasonable explanations could be provided for the discrepancy, the data and the plant were discarded from the sample. This in-plant "double-checking" method led me to conclude that although just-in-time (JIT) operations were frequently referred to and often beautifully explained by managers in their "in-the-office" presentations, their actual implementation dramatically differed from plant to plant and from region to region. This point will be discussed later using hard data.

11. To make the data comparable, the same types of components in different regional groups are matched, for example, composite bumper versus composite bumper, exhaust pipe versus exhaust pipe, wire harness connector versus wire harness connector.

12. The differences in changeover performance are not so much due to differences in the dies themselves as to their preparation in terms of, first, supportive fixtures and attachments to facilitate the swift removal and installation of dies and, second, the location of dies in the plant. It is common in Japanese plants for several dies that are frequently used to be placed right next to the line, ready to go. In contrast, it is not unusual in U.S. and European plants to find numerous dies stocked on huge, multi-layered shelves in the furthest corner of the site. This indicates that their intraplant transportation alone would take a lot of time (based on my plant observations of many assemblers and suppliers in Japan, the United States, and Europe, from 1985 to 1989).

TABLE 7-2. Die-Change Time at Automotive Components Plants in Japan, the United States, and Europe, 1987–89

( ) = sample size

Nationality/Region[a]		Die-Change Time (minutes)[b]	Index (Japan/Japan = 100)
Japan/Japan	(18)	7.9	100
Japan/U.S.	(8)	21.4	271
U.S./U.S.	(10)	114.3	1,447
Europe/Europe	(18)	123.7	1,566

[a]Nationality of plants in a region.

[b]For a major model switch on a volume production line where dies are changed at least once a week. Minor model switches that require changes of only peripheral jigs and fixtures are excluded.

Source: My field research from 1987 to 1989.

These figures indicate that Japanese components plants in Japan manufacture, on average, fourteen product variants per day (calculated as two shifts) on a given production line, spending 1.8 hours on the changeovers. Comparable figures for Japanese transplants in the United States are ten variants with 3.2 changeover hours and for Europe a mere two variants with 3.8 changeover hours. This suggests that if the European plants tried to produce fourteen variants per day, as do their competitors in Japan, they would have to spend more than 24 hours for the die change alone—clearly impossible! An alternative for the Europeans is to build up large buffer inventories from which variants may be shipped *prima facie* as flexibly as in Japan.

As noted, it is difficult to make direct comparisons of product variants across the board. But it is at least worth comparing "part number" variants or "references" of the same product between plants.[13] Table 7-4 looks at different production practices of alternator suppliers, one Japanese and the other American. Both firms are among the largest producers of alternators in the world, and their output volumes are comparable. However, their production strategies are quite different: The Japanese alternator plant runs far more product variants, 8.26 times as many, than does its U.S. competitor, even though both use two assembly lines. The number of variants per line in the Japanese plant is 95, as opposed to the U.S. plant's 11.5. The latter's maximum lot size is 3,000, and the comparable figure for the Japanese plant is only 60, or 40 percent less than the U.S. plant's minimum lot size of 100.

What is more striking and is not readily visible in Table 7-4 is the fact that the Japanese plant loses no time on changeovers. Each product on the line carries a small bar code label, and a bar code reader is located at the beginning of each production station, which feeds the information forward from the label. By the time an item reaches the next station, all the necessary changes in tooling and parts feeding have automatically been completed. Except in emergencies, the assembly line does not stop for changeovers, even for a second. In-process inventory takes up only 0.19 days of production. A product mix of up to 190 variants is thus managed in what may be called *fluid flexibility*.[14]

13. In my fieldwork I found that in referring to product variants, part numbers are frequently used in North America, whereas references or reference numbers are used in Europe.

14. Based on my field interviews and plant observations of a Japanese alternator plant in the summer of 1987.

TABLE 7-3. Die-Change Frequency at Automotive Components Plants in Japan, the United States, and Europe, 1987–89

( ) = sample size

Nationality/Region		No. of Die Changes[a] (daily)[b]	Index (Japan/Japan = 100)
Japan/Japan	(18)	13.8	100
Japan/U.S.	(8)	9.0	65.2
U.S./U.S.	(10)	2.0	14.5
Europe/Europe	(18)	1.83	13.3

[a] See Table 7-2; the average for the last week.

[b] Because 61 percent of the sample was operating on two shifts per day at the time of the survey, their two-shift figures are given. The figures from all other plants are adjusted to the two-shift level.

Source: My field research from 1987 to 1989.

A visit to the U.S. plant painted an entirely different picture. Here I found classic mass production mechanisms still at work. Dedicated machines continuously churn out identical components in impressive quantities. Everywhere there are heaps of in-process inventories. New technologies are present but apparently do not contribute to the flexible production at which they are supposed to excel. For example, ninety-two robots are used in the assembly area of this plant, but mainly to transfer in-process items from one station to another. Locating processes closer together and connecting them by angled rollers would do the same job more quickly and cheaply. In response to a customer's demand for JIT delivery, this plant turns out a few weeks' inventory of a required component in one lot from which very small quantities are shipped out daily. The plant's managers admit that their products have the highest production cost among their major competitors around the world. On leaving the site, I could not help feeling that there was no sense of flexible production in this plant.[15]

Design Changes and New Products

The ability to respond to design changes in existing products or to manufacture new models with quick modifications of existing equipment may be understood as an extension of the manufacturing flexibility just considered. But when one reaches the stage at which a major replacement of tooling, such as dies and molds, is necessary, the lead times for such equipment become crucial. Obviously, the longer the lead time is, the less flexibly a system can respond to design and model changes.

15. Based on my field interviews and plant observations of a U.S. alternator plant in the spring of 1987.
   There are good empirical studies that reveal similar contrasts. After comparing U.S. and Japanese flexible manufacturing systems (FMSs) in the machine tool and other related industries, Jaikumar (1986) found that unlike Japan, U.S. manufacturers were using FMSs most inflexibly. Similarly, Tidd (1989) found in his study of British–Japan assembly automation that the British firms were using sophisticated robots to assemble volume standardized products and that the remaining products, which consisted of numerous variants, were still assembled by hand. Tidd also discovered that Japanese competitors generally assembled entire product families on a single robotic assembly line.

TABLE 7-4. Product Variants at Two Alternator Plants in the United States and Japan, 1987

( ) = sample size

Nationality/Region		Basic Types	Variants[a]	No. of Assembly Lines	Lot Sizes	Variants per Line
Japan/Japan	(1)	3	190	2	1–60	95
U.S./U.S.	(1)	1	23	2	100–3,000	11.5

[a]Refers to part numbers actually produced on the assembly lines.

Source: My field research in the spring and summer of 1987.

In order to assess this component of flexible manufacturing, I compared the lead times for new dies at automotive components plants around the world. My findings are presented in Table 7-5. The U.S. and European suppliers wait, respectively, 3.1 times and 3.6 times longer than the Japanese suppliers do before new dies for new products are available at their plants. Put in another way, for every three new designs and/or new products the Japanese suppliers introduce, their U.S. and European competitors can barely introduce one. Who will win the race toward new product development is obvious.[16]

Manpower Flexibility

To be sure, the different levels of flexibility must be related to the ability of the work force to respond to various operational requirements. This can be considered at two levels: workplace (or the plant as a whole) and individual. At the workplace level, if workers can be flexibly moved among processes, stations, lines, and so forth, it will be easier to accommodate the fluctuating product mixes while maintaining the same overall manning levels. At the individual level, the more multiskilled the worker is, the easier the interprocess and interworkplace mobilization will be. If the job classification structure is such that each worker is tied to a narrowly defined job description not readily applicable to a different setting, the scope for mobilization

16. The differences in the lead times for dies are a reflection of different die development organizations around the globe. In Japan, several stages of die development and manufacture are "overlapped." In the United States and Europe, they are "sequenced." Clark and Fujimoto (1987:14–21) provide a good U.S.–Japan case study of different patterns of car body panel die making.

Recognizing the benefit of shorter lead times for die making, several U.S. and European manufacturers have begun to import dies from Japan. A European car assembler, for example, calculated that even including the long transportation time, Japanese sourcing was two times quicker than local sourcing (based on my interview with K. Tainaka, assistant manager, Honda Liaison Office, Honda of the U.K. Manufacturing, stationed at Cowley assembly plant, Austin Rover Group, Oxfordshire, August 25, 1987). For the same reason, another European car assembler switched all the body panel die sourcing of a car series to Japanese sourcing (based on my interviews with B. Bjorkman, director, Materials Management, and B. Andersson, manager, Purchasing Strategy and Development, SAAB-Scania, Trollhattan, Sweden, September 27 and 28, 1989).

TABLE 7-5. Lead Time for New Dies at Auto Components Plants in Japan, the United States, and Europe, 1987–89

( ) = sample size

Nationality/Region		Lead Time for New Dies (weeks)[a]	Index (Japan/Japan = 100)
Japan/Japan	(18)	11.1	100
Japan/U.S.	(8)	19.3	174
U.S./U.S.	(10)	34.5	311
Europe/Europe	(18)	40.0	360

[a]The average length of time from the release of an order to the delivery of the new production dies (as opposed to prototype dies) for a typical volume production item of the plant. If the plant has a die-making capability, it is used. If not, the lead time for subcontracted dies is employed. As in Table 7-2, the same types of components between different nationality/region groups are matched so as to make the data comparable (e.g., composite versus composite parts, pressed versus pressed parts).

Source: My field research from 1987 to 1989.

will be limited. Should there be labor agreements that prevent such mobilization, flexibility will be even more circumscribed. Conversely, if a worker's skill requirements are broader and there are few institutional barriers to interskill deployment, the human resource deployment flexibility will be considerable. Although in practice, a quantitative evaluation of all types of skills and multiskill levels is difficult, it is at least possible to compare formal job classification structures and the extent to which production workers carry out their usual operations in a given setting. As an approximate measurement, the latter can be represented by the extent of multimachine operations.

Job classifications are summarized in Table 7-6. In contrast with the U.S./U.S. group, in which the division of labor is rigid,[17] the Japanese plants, including those in the United States, have the simplest job classification structure, usually the direct production worker and one or two skilled trades; Europe sits in between. This suggests that there are significant structural barriers to the flexible deployment of labor in the United States, whereas there are few in Japanese-owned plants.[18]

What about multimachine operations? "Module building" (or where not applicable, parts subassembly) was used for comparison because it generally involves different types of operational skills and machines. Table 7-7 summarizes the results. A typical Japanese production worker in this sample, whose job description is the broadest, operates 7.4 machines to build a typical module. A worker in a Japanese transplant in the United States has 4.1 machines to look after. But the U.S. and European workers in this sample operate, respectively, 2.5 and 2.6 machines each, one-third the number for the Japanese workers.

More important, in Japan it is not only the number of machines but also the combination of jobs that makes the difference. In many cases, a worker undertakes a radically different combination of tasks in sequence: for example, bending, machin-

17. But not as extensive as in some of the traditional U.S. motor vehicle assembly plants.

18. In a boom period, it is not unusual at Japanese plants for white-collar workers and even managers to be called in to aid production on the line (based on my interviews with H. Mukai, Personnel Department, Hino Motors, Tokyo, March 25, 1986; M. Koitabashi, production manager, Gotenba plant, Ishikawa Kogyo, Shizuoka, July 4, 1986).

TABLE 7-6. Job Classifications of Blue-Collar Workers at Automotive Components Plants in Japan, the United States, and Europe, 1987–89

( ) = sample size

Nationality/Region		No. of Job Classifications[a]	Index (Japan/Japan = 100)
Japan/Japan	(18)	2.9	100
Japan/U.S.	(8)	3.4	117
U.S./U.S.	(10)	9.5	328
Europe/Europe	(18)	5.1	176

[a] Job classifications refer to those categorically not interchangeable in terms of the type and domain of skill requirements and promotion ladders, for example, skilled workers such as maintenance workers as opposed to unskilled assembly workers. This definition differs from grades, which are associated with pay scales within a job classification.

Source: My field research from 1987 to 1989.

ing, welding, and inspecting, and even plating and painting![19] This is related to the sequential arrangement of usually "autonomous" machines for one-piece-at-a-time production.[20] Worker training in many Japanese plants is rotated, so that within a few years a worker can master skills encompassing several product lines.[21] Furthermore, with few exceptions, Japanese workers are expected to do simple maintenance (and repair) of the machines they run. In one plant, there is even an intraplant maintenance training program in which selected production workers are sent to the maintenance department for one to twelve months to learn various maintenance skills.[22] These practices are rare in the United States and Europe, where production workers are usually assigned to a narrow range of repetitive tasks; in downturns, they are simply laid off. Maintenance is the exclusive domain of maintenance workers.

However, Japanese suppliers have been transferring the Japanese multimachine operation to the United States; American workers at Japanese transplants on average run 4.1 machines each, 1.64 times the traditional U.S. plant average. Asked about this, a Japanese production manager commented: "It's wrong to assume that U.S. workers don't accept the multimachine operation. They do. They welcome it, because it's far more interesting [than the single-machine operation]."[23] At another

19. Based on my interviews at Art Metal Manufacturing, Nagano, May 26, 1988; Nisshin Kogyo, Nagano, May 26, 1988; Koito Manufacturing, Shizuoka, June 3, 1988, Arvin Sango, Kentucky, March 6, 1989; Atsugi Motor Parts, Kanagawa, April 10, 1989.

20. Autonomous machines are those that automatically load and unload parts and check for abnormals in a process. For more technical details on this and the use of "U-shaped" production lines see Ikeda, Sei, and Nishiguchi, 1988. There is also a body of literature explaining how the "one-piece-at-a-time" production methodology backed up with "autonomous" equipment and flexible worker input has been developed to overcome the rigidities of traditional mass production methods, methods that had become increasingly dysfunctional with the fragmentation and volatility of the final product market. For example, see Toyota, 1967, 1987; Ohno, 1978, 1988; Monden, 1983, 1985.

21. Based on my interviews at Kanto Seat Manufacturing, Shizuoka, July 4, 1986; Art Metal Manufacturing, Nagano, May 26, 1988; Nisshin Kogyo, Nagano, May 26, 1988, Koito Manufacturing, Shizuoka, June 3, 1988.

22. Based on my interview at Hitachi's Sawa plant, Ibaragi (where electrical automotive components are produced), March 28, 1986.

23. Based on my interview with a Japanese manager (who asked for anonymity) of a Japanese supplier's transplant in the United States, October 1988.

TABLE 7-7. Multimachine Operations in Module Building at Automotive Components Plants in Japan, the United States, and Europe, 1987–89

( ) = sample size

Nationality/Region		No. of Machines per Worker[a]	Index
Japan/Japan	(18)	7.4	100
Japan/U.S.	(8)	4.1	55.4
U.S./U.S.	(10)	2.5	33.8
Europe/Europe	(18)	2.7	36.5

[a]The average number of machines attended by a production worker in module-building processes of a typical volume product.

Source: My field research from 1987 to 1989.

Japanese transplant of oil seals in the United States, 80 percent of the workers stated that they were happier with the multimachine operation than with the single-machine operation.[24] In one extreme case, Japanese management introduced conventional belt-conveyor lines of car heater assemblies to their U.S. transplant, assuming that this would be more acceptable to the American workers than multimachine operations. For training, some American managers and production leaders were sent to the mother plant in Japan. There they saw many flexible module-building lines that used multimachine operations. The first day, they saw a module-building line run by three operators; the next day, by four, and some days later, by five. Each time, each operator had a different combination and sequence of machines to work with. The American visitors were fascinated by the variety and proposed doing the same in the United States. Their suggestion was adopted. The belt-conveyor lines in the U.S. transplant were therefore replaced by one-man–multimachine flexible module lines, and the workers' morale and productivity increased.[25]

These cases illustrate that there are also qualitative differences in human resource flexibility relating to the different strategies of different producers in different regions. The extent of manpower flexibility in Japanese-owned plants perhaps goes significantly beyond the face value of the quantitative data regarding job classifications and the multimachine operation. This section has thus demonstrated that differing labor management practices are responsible for many of the differences seen in manufacturing flexibility around the world.

Inventory Levels

Is JIT Really JIT?

The just-in-time (JIT) system of manufacturing supply, developed by Toyota in the late 1940s, received much attention in the U.S. and European automotive industries

---

24. Field notes from Prof. Masayoshi Ikeda's interview made available to me: Minoru Kishibe, president, NOK, Inc., Georgia, March 29, 1988.

25. Based on my interview with Kentaro Arai, president, Calsonic Manufacturing Corporation, March 8, 1989.

during the 1980s. The essence of JIT is to provide only the necessary amount of the necessary items at the right time and place—no more, no less. This ultimately points to synchronized manufacturing, not only within each plant, but also between the assembly plants and their suppliers. If a supplier delivers components just in time to the assembler in small quantities out of its own buffer inventories, this may still be called JIT "delivery," but it only shifts the burden of maintaining inventory from the assembler to the supplier. The ultimate goal of true JIT "manufacturing" is to eliminate buffer stock on both sides.[26]

In the field, I was often struck by the remoteness of reality from the ideal of JIT manufacturing. Some European car assemblers claim that they have been doing JIT for more than ten years. But at the same time they contractually demand in their contracts that their suppliers carry buffer stock, or "stipulated inventory."[27] Some U.S. assemblers boast of running JIT operations on a par with Japan. Visits to their suppliers reveal, however, that supplies of a component as large as two weeks of production are hurriedly made in one lot, from which deliveries as small as ten pieces are sent daily to the assembler on a JIT basis.[28]

Managers of a European supplier are excited about their recent introduction of JIT, claiming that it eliminates wasteful documents and makes materials flow more smoothly. When asked about how JIT has reduced inventories and defects, though, the answer is often not at all. But they still call it JIT.[29]

My concern is not so much about their definition of JIT as that something is

---

26. There is a large body of literature on JIT manufacturing. Among the most influential contributors are Ohno, 1978, 1988; and Monden, 1983, 1985. The philosophy of JIT, as explained in simple words by the late Taiichi Ohno (the father of "lean" production), goes beyond the realm of manufacturing per se.

27. To look at this issue from a different angle, the fact that some assemblers have to "stipulate" inventory (normally ranging from several to a dozen days of production) indicates that they cannot provide level and/or realistic forecasts, owing to the lack of level and well-coordinated operations in their own plants. This suggests that no matter how "flexible" the suppliers are and whether or not the buffer inventory is stipulated, the suppliers must carry finished buffer inventory in order to cope with unpredictable orders from their customers. Furthermore, it is the assembler's buffer inventory of purchased components that really matters. If its production activity is level and reasonably synchronized with its suppliers', there will be little need for the assembler to carry more than a minimum stock of purchased components. In this regard, there are considerable variations among assemblers. A German supplier pointed out, for example, that although his company shipped the same range of brake components to various assemblers, the latter's stock levels of these components in the incoming goods area varied: a half-day of production at a U.S. transplant in Germany, two days at a German assembler, and two weeks at a British assembler (based on my interviews with B. Schmeling, managing director, and S. Vasilache, managing director, Bendix Deutchland GmbH, September 2, 1987). A comparable figure for comparable components for Japan was two hours just alongside (and not in an incoming goods area separated from) the assembly line (based on my interviews with Miura, Public Relations, Toyota's Tsutsumi plant, April 9, 1986; M. Shiozaki, deputy general manager, Publicity and Community Relations, Administration Department, Nissan's Zama plant, July 1, 1987; K. Miyaki, general manager, Honda's Sayama plant One, July 10, 1987). The implication is clear: Poor purchasing management can limit the supplier's attempts to implement JIT. Although the focus of this chapter is the assessment of suppliers' flexible capabilities, I am grateful to Prof. Michael Smitka and the chief executive officer of a U.S. supplier (the latter responded to my seminar presentation based on an earlier version of this chapter in the autumn of 1989) for their helpful suggestions that this point should be made here.

28. Based on my field interviews at and plant visits to European and U.S. automotive firms from 1987 to 1989.

29. Based on my interviews at and plant visits to an automotive components division of a French automotive manufacturer in the summer of 1988.

TABLE 7-8. Inventory levels at Auto Components Plants in Japan, the United States, and Europe, 1987–89

( ) = sample size

Nationality/Region	Inventory (days of production)		Total
	In-process[a]	Finished[b]	
Japan/Japan (18)	0.85	0.67	1.52
Japan/U.S. (8)	1.43	2.6	4.03
U.S./U.S. (10)	5.7	2.4	8.1
Europe/Europe (18)	6.1	10.2	16.3

[a] Unprocessed materials in the incoming goods area are not included.

[b] To make the data comparable, customers' "stipulated inventory" is not included. Nor is finished stock at "JIT depots" outside the components plant, due to technical problems in measurability.

Source: My field research from 1987 to 1989.

wrong here. With few exceptions, the so-called JIT system introduced in the United States and Europe does not synchronize manufacturing at the supplier's plant. In many cases, it creates more buffer stock than do the conventional methods it replaces. Some suppliers blame the JIT system itself. They argue that it is good only for the assemblers—at the expense of the suppliers. Looking at today's Japan, however, this does not necessarily hold.[30] It is the implementation that matters, not the abstract system.

Evidence

According to the data in Table 7-8, Japan again leads the group. With less than a day's supply in each of the in-process and finished inventories, its combined inventory level is only 1.52 days of production. The U.S. plants have a much higher in-process inventory level, which pushes up the combined total to 8.1 days. But they store only 2.4 days' finished inventory, 0.2 day less than the Japanese transplants do, whose total inventory level, though, is half that of the U.S./U.S. group. Europe lags behind; its finished inventory level of 10.2 days (fifteen times more than for Japan) pushes up the combined total to 16.3 days of production. The relative scale of inventory levels is shown in Table 7-9.

Creating Inflexibility

Two things should be noted. First, because samples containing customers' "stipulated inventory" were excluded from these data, the high levels of finished inventory are the suppliers' own creation. In this respect, Europe's performance, fifteen times worse than Japan, is "real." Second, by distinguishing in-process inventory

---

30. Shifting the burden of carrying buffer stock to suppliers in the implementation of JIT used to be quite common in Japan, too. In the 1970s this even became a hot issue for debate at the Diet (Monden, 1983:45–46, 1985:123–24). Over time, through joint problem-solving efforts between assembler and supplier, however, the existence of the buffer stock itself has been largely eliminated from their plants. The following data confirm this point.

TABLE 7-9. Relative Scale of Inventory Levels at Auto Components Plants in Japan, the United States, and Europe, 1987–89

( ) = sample size

Nationality/Region		Inventory Level		Total (Japan/Japan = 100)
		In-process	Finished	
Japan/Japan	(18)	100	100	100
Japan/U.S.	(8)	168	388	265
U.S./U.S.	(10)	671	358	533
Europe/Europe	(18)	718	1,522	1,072

Source: My field research from 1987 to 1989.

from finished inventory, the data clearly show a hitherto-ignored aspect that deserves comment. In the United States, it is the in-process stock that is problematic. In Europe, it is both: The high level of finished stock is problematic in addition to the high level of in-process stock. This finding adds to the general view that suppliers are unilaterally forced to maintain buffer inventories for JIT delivery. Customers may require a certain level of finished stock for quick delivery, but few customers would generally demand buffer "in-process" stock as a prerequisite.

This implies that something is wrong with the way that U.S. and European suppliers make their products. They do not make the right amount at the right time. Rather, as in the old days, they manufacture in large quantities in one lot and lavishly stock them between processes, and in Europe, in the shipping area, too. My observation of many U.S. and European plants, with large piles of in-process materials and rejects, reminded me of the cynical remark that Toyota purchasing managers make to wake up inefficient suppliers: "You aren't working in a warehouse, are you?"

The problem of carrying large stock is not restricted to the opportunity cost of capital or difficulties in tracing quality problems. It also relates to the accommodation of design changes. In a world of shorter product cycles and frequent design changes, carrying as little stock as possible is crucial. The more one relies on stock, the more difficult it will be to accommodate design changes. Whenever they occur, the firm must make time-consuming plans to use up existing stock (i.e., "buildouts"), modify it to new specifications, or jettison it. In any case, it is expensive. Usually, the purchasing contract requires the assemblers to bear the cost of materials already processed or purchased by suppliers for a contract. In the United States, there are numerous cases of costly design changes in which assemblers compensate for a few months' worth of stock carried by their suppliers. This discourages assemblers from going ahead with a design change even if they know it is essential to reducing costs, improving manufacturability, and getting ahead of the competition. If a supplier has a monopoly advantage, as is often the case for assemblers' in-house divisions, decisions are frequently made in the interest of using up existing stock and maintaining existing facilities unchanged, at the cost of competitiveness in the market.[31]

31. These practices were frequently mentioned in my interview with Yoshinari Fukuda, production manager, Hi-Lex Corporation, Michigan, March 26, 1987; L. Gene Stohler, vice-president, Sales and

If a supplier is lean in stock, it will fare better. The supplier may not only accept design changes more frequently but also may use this capability as a selling point. In pursuit of flexibility, assemblers are likely to increase the number of contracts with such a supplier.

Delivery Performance

JIT Delivery

Flexibility ties in with delivery, especially JIT delivery. If a supplier produces various components flexibly in the required small quantities without losing much changeover time and ships them as soon as they are made, it is truly synchronizing manufacturing with its customer. And the more "just in time" its operation is, the easier it will be to make frequent JIT deliveries. In fact, there are more incentives to do so.

Table 7-10 summarizes the findings from the study of JIT deliveries of "customer-specific" components to a major customer. Small and standard commodity items (e.g., screws, nuts, and bolts) are not included, as there are obvious disincentives to ship these items on a rigorously JIT basis. Although the term *JIT* is now commonly used around the globe, there are amazing differences in JIT delivery performance alone. In Japan, suppliers ship their products on a JIT basis twelve times as often per day as in Europe and five times as often as in the United States. Geographical approximation alone cannot be the primary advantage for more frequent delivery.[32] In the United States, suppliers deliver 2.4 times more often than in Europe. A new Japanese transplant in Europe (a case not included in these data) is already delivering three times a day, 4.5 times the European average, to its major customer.[33]

Quality of Components

A popular myth, still held by many, is that quality takes time; that quick manufacturing and delivery preclude high quality. Is this really so?

Table 7-11 shows the frequencies of auto components failures found in the field

Marketing, ITT Automotive, Inc., Michigan, March 17, 1987, and J. Brozovich, business market research manager, ITT Automotive, Inc., Michigan, April 28, 1987; M. Yamamoto, vice-president, and K. Yoshinami, general manager, First Sales Dept., American Yazaki Corporation, Michigan, March 24, 1987; T. Takanaka, director and general manager, American Yazaki Corporation, El Paso Division, Texas, March 24, 1988.

32. According to an American supplier: "For doing just-in-time delivery, North American distances are not a problem. It's just a matter of shipping one day earlier" (from my interview with John J. Martin, director, Materials Management, Packard Electric, Ohio, April 30, 1987). Also note that not all Japanese suppliers in Japan are located right next to their customers. For example, a Japanese supplier of brake systems in Saitama was making six JIT deliveries to Toyota City, more than 300 miles away, and four JIT deliveries to Hiroshima, more than 750 miles away (based on my interview with Isao Sasajima, assistant director, Iwatsuki plant, Akebono Brake Industry, April 14, 1989).

33. Based on field notes of Prof. Masayoshi Ikeda's interview at a Japanese automotive components supplier's transplant in Europe in the summer of 1988, made available to me.

TABLE 7-10. Number of JIT Deliveries per Day to a Major Customer, 1987–89

( ) = sample size

Nationality/Region		No. of Daily JIT Deliveries[a]	Index (Japan/Japan = 100)
Japan/Japan	(18)	7.9	100.0
U.S. and Japan/U.S.	(12)	1.59	20.1
Europe/Europe	(18)	0.67	8.5

[a] To make the data comparable, samples of only "direct" JIT deliveries of a typical single component or a typical single components system to a major plant of a major customer are represented. Deliveries to "JIT warehouses" or "JIT depots"—a common practice between U.S. assemblers and suppliers but less so elsewhere—are not included. To adjust the reduced sample size of the U.S./U.S. group, it is combined with Japanese transplants in the United States.

Source: My field research from 1987 to 1989.

after they have been installed in a car. Engines and transmissions, usually made by assemblers, were excluded. The evidence confirms the view that speed and quality are indeed correlated. In the field, European components are 2.6 times as defective as Japanese components, are stored in inventories 15 times as large, and are being delivered JIT with one-twelfth the frequency of components in Japan, as already noted. The United States does better, with 1.4 times as many defects, 3.6 times the finished stock, and one-fifth the delivery frequency, compared with Japan. These hard facts indicate that the differences in performance may not be ones of degree but of kind. One person's JIT plant can be another's warehouse.

The implication is clear: In today's world of rapid product cycles and frequent design changes, the mismatch between quick delivery requirements and traditional production for buffer inventory cannot be maintained without incurring detrimental costs to the long-term viability of manufacturers.

Summary and Conclusions

The quantitative data presented in this chapter strongly confirm that there are substantial differences in flexible manufacturing capabilities among automotive components producers in Japan, the United States, and Europe. In all types of manufacturing flexibility, Japanese firms have been found to excel, followed by their transplants in the United States. Compared with their U.S. and European competitors, Japanese producers accommodate far more production mixes and variants (through quicker and more frequent changeovers), respond most quickly to

TABLE 7-11. Automotive Components Failures, 1988

Region	Defects[a] per Car	Index
Japan	0.24	100
United States	0.329	137
Europe	0.621	259

[a] The number of components defects per car (excluding engines and transmissions) as "perceived" by consumers within three months after delivery of a new car. Data compiled by John F. Krafcik. Approximately half the European samples are German.

Source: J. D. Power & Associates, 1988.

design changes (due to a shorter lead time for new dies), better manage different production volumes (owing to flexible workers and interskill mobilization), carry the lowest inventory levels, and make the most frequent JIT deliveries, all while maintaining the highest quality. All this suggests that *ceteris paribus*, the benefits of using Japanese suppliers are considerable and may go recognizably beyond what liberal dualists envisaged in their formulation of flexibility arising from the instrumental use of subcontractors. In contrast, it is not unreasonable to assume that using U.S. and European suppliers, as they now stand, may add more operational rigidity than presumed flexibility to the effect of contractual relations. They accommodate far fewer product variants, design alterations, volume fluctuations, and JIT deliveries, while at the same time their inventory levels are higher and their product quality is lower.

What, then, are the implications of these findings for our study? It is clear from the very fact that there are such great differences in the various indicators of flexible production even in a similar mix of automotive components suppliers by nationality and region, that recourse to subcontracting can in itself be indeterminate in affecting changes in flexibility. The traditional dualist approach does not distinguish the benefits obtained from exploiting the subcontractors' disadvantageous attributes from their flexible manufacturing capabilities. Put differently, this approach does not appreciate the important fact that using subcontractors is one thing and whether or not their manufacturing operations are flexible is quite another. In the traditional paradigm, the disadvantaged status of secondary economic agents that conditioned their vulnerability was simply assumed to contribute to flexibility in favor of the prime contractor. However, apart from the first impressions created by their descriptive accounts of the relative ease of hiring and firing, the concept of flexibility itself has remained vague, and the typology and measurability of flexibility have remained untouched.

The types and measurements of manufacturing flexibility that we have discussed in this chapter have enabled us to compare different levels of flexible manufacturing by different producers across the board. By distinguishing five types of manufacturing flexibility and further establishing systematic methods to measure them, we have thus advanced the analysis beyond the traditional framework.

The important message of this chapter is that ultimately a prime contractor can have a flexible production system only if its suppliers are also flexible in their own internal operations. The data presented in this chapter have demonstrated how they can be flexible and that the Japanese-owned plants examined are.

Developing from the results of the previous historical and contemporary empirical chapters, we can then conclude that the Japanese subcontracting system has evolved into a distinctive mechanism in which the problem solving–oriented commitments by customer and subcontractor are reinforced from within, with the aid of institutional arrangements that promote continuous improvement in product quality, cost reduction, and manufacturing flexibility.

8

Conclusion

The principal objective of this book has been to examine the reasons for the persistence of subcontracting in industrial society. Our main conclusion is that subcontracting can best be explained as the evolutionary product of a complex historical interaction among socioeconomic, political, technological, and producer-level strategic factors. Economic dualism, political influence, culture, technology, or producer strategy alone were not found to be a sufficient explanation. Instead, the evidence presented in this study has demonstrated that each of these factors influenced the others at specific periods in history. This led to the emergence of subcontracting, which then evolved into a variety of subsequent forms. In an ever-changing socioeconomic environment, the result has been a series of new equilibria in contractor–subcontractor relations. In the case of Japan, the stage reached after nearly six decades of evolution is a new mode of contractual relations based on principles of problem solving–oriented collaborative manufacturing. This new form of contractual relations is supported by institutional arrangements that drive those concerned toward continuous improvement in product quality and cost reduction.

History

The fact that neither dualism nor subcontracting was an essential feature of the Japanese economy earlier in the twentieth century (discussed in Chapter 2) suggests the limitations inherent in the cultural thesis, as proposed by Dore (1987).[1] Likewise, the emergence of economic dualism in the 1920s (i.e., widening interscale wage differentials, the increased number of small firms) was not found sufficient, by itself, to explain the rise of subcontracting. Other technoinfrastructural factors (i.e., subcontractors in possession of lathes, the diffusion of electrical power, the expansion of national transportation and communication systems) were crucial to prepare for the forthcoming arrival of subcontracting practices. Ultimately it was the surge in demand for munitions between 1931 and 1945, together with government intervention, that structured and established the institution of subcontracting as an important component of the Japanese economy, despite the limited efficacy of subcontracting in the devastation of World War II (see Chapter 2).

1. Of course this does not dispute the outstanding range, detail, and quality of Professor Dore's work on Japan and the Japanese economy, which has opened the eyes of many students of Japan.

The postwar resurgence of subcontracting in Japan built on reemerging dualistic socioeconomic conditions of the 1950s (i.e., increasing interscale wage differentials plus the widening disparity between large and small firms with regard to the degree of their unionization). Also, subcontractors' technical capabilities were enhanced through their purchase of used equipment from large firms. But the harsher side of the postwar laissez-faire subcontracting also became apparent (i.e., large firms' forcing reductions in subcontractors' prices and withholding payments to them). In response to pressures from small-business organizations and in the interest of securing electoral support, the government intervened and introduced three "protective" measures for small businesses: legislation against unfair subcontracting practices, programs fostering small-firm cooperatives, and provisions to establish small-business financial organizations. Despite mixed results, these measures by and large offered a legal and institutional framework within which certain rules of the game were imposed on all players. With new access to financial resources and protection from unfair treatment, small businesses and subcontractors in Japan were thus stabilized by means of institutional support. These political measures also shaped the future course of subcontracting arrangements in Japan (see Chapter 3).

The high-growth economy, starting in the 1960s, transformed existing subcontracting institutions in many ways, despite receding (or stabilized) indicators of dualism (i.e., narrowing interscale wage differentials, stabilized union density, interscale distribution). In response to the greater demand for consumer products and seeing the great opportunity for growth, many producers rushed into the domestic markets with a "full-product-line" strategy. These markets became extremely congested, overlapped, and competitive. In the face of the increasing manufacturing complexity that resulted from this enormous product proliferation and in view of the usability of existing subcontracting networks, many producers over time strategically converted their existing "simple processing" subcontractors (in charge, e.g., of machining, sheet-metal stamping, or surface treatment) into contract assemblers and systems-components manufacturers. Besides manufacturing, these subcontractors were made responsible for the design, testing, and parts procurement for relatively mature products (e.g., television sets in the 1980s). This arrangement allowed prime contractors to focus their internal resources more on strategic activities, including state-of-the-art product development and process innovation. The simultaneous transfer of both production and development activities to external organizations shortened overall lead times and product cycles at the same time that product lines were being expanded. Prime contractors used this mechanism to adjust to the shifting demand and to get ahead of the competition, while subcontractors enjoyed the new opportunity to learn and develop the multifunctional technical expertise required for contract assembly and subsystems manufacture. In this way, symbiotic contractual relations were born (see Chapter 4).

The evolution of subcontracting in Japan after the 1960s thus provides evidence that belies the traditional framework of dualism and also, in part, that of flexible specialization. In short, the institutions of subcontracting in Japan not only continued but indeed prospered despite receding dualism and without either direct confrontation or a reversal in the dominant–subordinate relations between large and small firms. It is at this point that we looked at other explanatory factors: producer strategy and asset specificity.

An important finding from this examination was that it was producer strategy that converted subcontractors into highly asset-specific entities. The producers' strategic choices shifted the high-specificity assets to the subcontractors. Williamson's argument that asset specificity accounts for obligational contracting was found to be reversed. The results of our historical research (and a case study of two plants of a Japanese consumer electronics producer in Chapter 5) suggest that asset specificity is not the cause but the consequence of subcontracting strategy.

The shift in the content of subcontracting work from discrete treatment to subsystems manufacture and contract assembly entailed two important concomitants, one structural and the other institutional.

Structurally, subcontractors were reorganized over time into hierarchical "clusters," through a concentration of orders, intensified specialization, and increased dependence on particular customers. This resulted in turning the traditional semi—arm's length (or loosely tiered) structure of subcontracting into a clustered control (or a tightly tiered) structure, in which manufacturing control functions are systematically concentrated on select first-tier subcontractors who control their own lower-tier subcontractors under their own regime. This relieves those on top of the hierarchy of the increasingly complex control functions typical of external manufacturing organizations.

Institutionally, new interfirm practices were designed to ensure the continuous output of high-quality, low-cost products. These practices were based on problem-solving commitments by both customer and subcontractor. Examples include joint price determination based on objective value analysis (VA), joint design based on value engineering (VE), the target cost (or cost-planning) method of product development, profit-sharing rules, subcontractor proposals, black box design, resident engineers, subcontractor grading, quality assurance through self-certified subcontractors, and just-in-time (JIT) delivery circumscribed by bonus—penalty programs. Along with these institutional changes, the main purchasing function of the customer shifted from downstream price negotiation to the assessment of subcontractor performance and the coordination of various intra- and interfirm functions.

The most important outcome of this evolution of subcontracting in Japanese manufacturing was a transformation in the underlying logic of contractual relations. The basis for these relationships shifted from the notion of classical exploitation to a new view of collaborative manufacturing, in the sense that both purchasers and subcontractors came to benefit, under newly established rules, from the synergistic effects of bilateral problem solving.

Thus, the historical evidence presented and examined in Part I has not only provided a fairly extensive account of the evolution of subcontracting in Japan between 1900 and 1990—in light of the complex interactions among socioeconomic, political, technological and producer-strategic factors—but it has also made clear the shortcomings of traditional theories, which tend to focus on a relatively narrow range of immediate factors in an attempt to explain what are, in fact, a much broader set of issues.

Contemporary Practice

Building on these conclusions, Part II examined contemporary subcontracting practices through a series of more focused original research studies. These also showed the limitations of existing theories.[2]

Through both quantitative and qualitative analyses, our comparative study of electronics subcontracting in Japan and Britain concluded that different subcontracting strategies lead to divergent modes of contractual relations, even in the same industry (see Chapters 5 and 6). In the quantitative part of the research, asset specificity was the focus.

Despite the increasing popularity of the topic, few existing studies provide any direct means of measuring or comparing asset specificity. Given the centrality of the concept to these arguments, one of the major tasks of this book was to produce data on this question. I did this by developing an original methodology through which I could quantify by degree and then compare four types of asset specificity (physical, dedicated, human, and site). To demonstrate their use, I applied these measures to comparative data for British–Japanese electronics subcontracting. This work covered seventy-five manufacturing establishments in the two countries, divided by tier (prime contractors, first-tier subcontractors, and second-tier subcontractors) and by specialty (assembly and high-tech). This quantitative analysis was complemented by a case study of two plants from a Japanese consumer electronics firm.

These studies produced three conclusions. First, there are significant structural differences in subcontracting organization between the United Kingdom and Japan, even in the same industry. A focus on fewer customers by each subcontractor in Japan, compared with more customers per subcontractor in Britain, was seen to be a function of higher total asset specificity (the sum of the physical, dedicated, human, and site asset specificity indices) in Japan. Also, highly asset-specific subcontracting work in Japan (i.e., complete assembly and subsystems assembly) was con-

---

2. The results of a survey of forty large Japanese automotive and electronics manufacturers regarding the reasons for subcontracting (Appendix B) suggest that the reasons for subcontracting are more varied and gradational than the traditional accounts have contended. For one thing, "specialist technology" and "cheaper (*indirect*) control cost" (as opposed to cheaper direct labor cost) are the number one and number two reasons arguing against dualist reasons (i.e., interscale wage differentials, risk dispersion, buffer against fluctuations in demand, dividing up the work force); this indicates the limitations of the traditional dualist framework. For another, this finding reinforces the conclusion that the clustered control model of subcontracting is a direct result of the large manufacturers' strategy of delegating increasingly complex control functions to external production organizations through greater reliance on subcontractor specialization.

The survey also reveals a point that so far has been overlooked: The reasons for subcontracting differ substantially from industry to industry, due to the differences in the products. Automotive producers, whose products are complex and require a broad range of technical expertise, are principally concerned with the specialist technology of their subcontractors. In contrast, electronics manufacturers, whose products—especially consumer items—are generally simpler and require less technical expertise than do automobiles, generally look more for dualistic advantages (i.e., cheaper direct labor cost, the shock-absorber function) when subcontracting out the labor-intensive part of manufacturing processes. Finding this critical difference opens a new horizon in the dualism debate. Until now, the discussion has usually ignored the influence of the products themselves, and the manufacturing technologies, on the modes of production organization, including subcontracting.

trasted with the prevalence of low asset-specific subcontracting work in the United Kingdom (i.e., discrete treatment processes). Second, subcontracting relations are largely determined by producer strategies, concerning what to subcontract, where to locate, and how many people to commit. Third, asset specificity is not the cause but the consequence of the strategies, and in this regard, variations exist even within the same firm, as exemplified by two plants of a Japanese consumer electronics firm.[3]

The results of this empirical research on asset specificity reinforce the claim that different patterns of contractual relations are substantially defined by producer strategies. My original methodology, developed and applied in Chapter 5, produced a type of quantitative evidence that marks a new departure from the aggregate statistics, anecdotal evidence, and impressionistic observations of conventional studies.

From this quantitative empirical base, I examined qualitative data on electronics subcontractors' perceptions of their customers, in the United Kingdom and Japan. I discovered a sharp contrast in the subcontractors' perceptions of their customers. The British subcontractors most frequently commented on "erratic trading" relationships with their customers, whereas the Japanese subcontractors were most concerned with "being monitored" by their "demanding" and "strict" customers. Japanese subcontractors also noted their customers' readiness to help improve product quality and reduce costs. Subsequent case studies, of Hitachi's subcontractor improvement programs and of the interesting interactions between British subcontractors and their Japanese transplant customers in the United Kingdom, led to an important conclusion: Japanese subcontracting relations have institutional attributes that promote the continuous quality improvement and cost reduction through problem solving–oriented commitments by customer and subcontractor. This contrasts with the bargaining orientation of British subcontracting relations, which tends to produce adverse effects.

The results of our qualitative studies are consistent with the claim that the major advantages of the Japanese subcontracting paradigm lie chiefly in the economic benefits derived from interfirm problem-solving mechanisms designed to ensure high-quality, low-cost products. Successful British subcontractors' acceptance of and commitment to the Japanese subcontracting system, as implemented by Japanese transplants in Britain, have demonstrated that its principles are applicable to cultures outside Japan. A survey of career patterns, income, and job satisfaction for subcontracting business owners also suggested that the efficacy of this system may have been sustained in large part by the motivated and relatively high-income proprietors of subcontracting businesses in Japan.

Neither the cultural preference framework nor an account that depends on flexible specialization can fully explain the data presented in this book. The "Japanese"

3. Despite similarities in products and locations—let alone the same "national" culture—the two plants of this firm showed remarkably different behavior toward their subcontractors during recession. One plant, because its aim was to limit short-term losses, radically reduced its subcontracting base, including some highly asset-specific entities. The other plant persevered through the downturn without shedding any of its subcontractors, thus compensating apparent short-term losses through interfirm collaborative efforts, for long-term symbiotic gains. When the recession ended and a new economic boom arrived, the latter plant proved to be the more successful.

system of subcontracting was accepted by British subcontractors who by no means share common national characteristics with their Japanese transplant customers in the United Kingdom.[4] Instead, what they understood from the Japanese customers' persistent demands and support was that high quality and low cost were extremely important strategic weapons for both of them. It was far wiser to tackle this problem by means of joint efforts rather than to fall back on mutual recriminations. Many of the reluctant British subcontractors, who disregarded their Japanese customers' demands as neurotic, went bankrupt; those subcontractors who responded well and improved their quality grew in the midst of a recession. The problem-solving style of subcontracting that the Japanese had brought to Britain was a powerful and economically sound paradigm. It is also apparent that the cooperation between customer and subcontractor cannot be comfortably accommodated within the framework of flexible specialization. Flexible specialization assumes fairly dichotomous and exclusionary demarcations and a reversal of roles between large and small firms.

Finally, the shortcomings of the traditional dualist framework became clear from the original quantitative data on flexible manufacturing capabilities (see Chapter 7). These data derive from a comparable mix of fifty-four automotive components producers in Japan, the United States, and Europe. In all types of manufacturing flexibility, Japanese producers surpassed other global competitors by a considerable margin, followed by Japanese transplants in the United States and then American and European producers, in that order. Japanese suppliers accommodated a far greater production mix and more variants (through quicker and more frequent changeovers), responded most quickly to design changes (due to shorter lead times for new dies), managed different production volumes best (owing to flexible workers and interskill mobilization), carried the lowest inventory levels, and made the most frequent JIT deliveries, all while maintaining the best quality. Dualism proved inadequate in another way: Its proponents suggest that contracting out per se will result in flexibility for the prime contractor. Instead, I found that flexibility depends on the extent to which the subcontractors' manufacturing operations can flexibly satisfy the customers' needs.

The evidence urges a reconsideration of the traditional dualist approach. Dualism focuses on the benefits of exploiting subcontractors' disadvantageous attributes. It fails to distinguish, however, whether or not flexible manufacturing benefits are actually available. The important message here is that ultimately a customer can have a flexible production system only if its subcontractors also are flexible in their internal operations. In this respect, the symbiotic element in Japan's contractual relations is not incidental but, rather, is an essential part of the new system.

There are a variety of themes and results in both Part I, the historical section, and Part II, the contemporary section of this study. They can be synthesized in a single conclusion: The Japanese subcontracting system has undergone a long evolutionary process incorporating both dualistic and producer-level strategic elements.

---

4. Evidence of an international dissemination of Japanese subcontracting practices (e.g., subcontractor grading, self-certified subcontractors, clustered control, resident engineers) was also presented in Chapter 4.

The result is a distinctive mechanism in which the problem solving–oriented commitments by customer and subcontractor are reinforced from within by means of institutional arrangements that promote the continuous and flexible output of high-quality, low-cost products.

Having thus explained the transformation of subcontracting in Japan, further research is needed, particularly in the following four areas: first, an account of the evolution of subcontracting in other industrial societies, in both historical and contemporary contexts; second, a focused study of technology as the guiding principle for subcontracting relations;[5] third, an examination of subcontracting in manufacturing industries other than automotive and electronics; and fourth, an analysis of the emergence and development of subcontracting in the nonmanufacturing sectors (e.g., computer software, secretarial and other clerical services), whose importance is growing in many industrial societies. Clearly, much remains to be studied; this book is but a modest start.

5. Sabel (1989) provides an important analytical leverage in this direction.

Appendix A

List of Interviewees

This book owes a great deal of information and inspiration obtained during my field interviews. Although it was impossible to use all the information I gathered, I would like to list all the interviewees from fourteen countries with thanks for their time and cooperation. Organizations and job titles are those at the time the interviews were conducted. An overview of all 1,035 interviews* is presented below.

Notes:

1. All listings are alphabetical. Interviewees with an organizational affiliation are listed by organization within each category. Academic interviewees are listed by their last name.
2. Interview locations are not necessarily the same as the interviewees' organizations.
3. The total interview hours reflect time spent with individuals, with no adjustment for group (or otherwise overlapping) interviews.
4. Whenever possible, the job titles of the interviewees are taken from their English-language business cards or organizational charts.

*Group (or otherwise overlapping) interviews are not adjusted.

Interviews, 1983–89

Category	No. of Establishments	No. of Interviewees	Time Spent
1. National governments	7	8	11hrs 39min
2. Local authorities	10	21	37hrs 18min
3. Trade associations	11	24	38hrs 01min
4. Industrial cooperatives	7	20	42hrs 41min
5. Trade unions	4	8	11hrs 15min
6. Public research organizations	9	20	36hrs 37min
7. Prime contractors	71	251	566hrs 39min
8. Suppliers and subcontractors	172	320	909hrs 17min
9. Business consultants and private research organizations	27	31	72hrs 55min
10. Trading companies	3	5	10hrs 03min
11. Transportation companies	1	1	2hrs 00min
12. Car dealers	4	6	5hrs 50min
13. Banks and security companies	3	4	12hrs 35min
14. Journalists	8	10	19hrs 55min
15. Academic institutions	57[a]	84	391hrs 58min
Total:	394	813	2,168hrs 43min

[a]Counted by department, college, program, or research unit, whichever is deemed appropriate.

Organization	Position	Name	Date	Time
1. *National governments*				
Automotive Industry Authority of Australia (Melbourne)	Chief Executive & Associate Member	W. Scales	23/4/87	13:30–14:00 30min
			5/5/87	12:10–13:30 1h 20min
China National Automotive Industry Corporation (Beijing)	Director & Senior Engineer	Y. Zhou	17/9/86	15:40–16:10 30min
	Senior Engineer	C. L. Zhi	17/9/86	15:40/16:10 30min
Department of Industry, Technology & Commerce (Melbourne)	Executive Officer, Automotive Industry Council	G. Wall	7/3/88	12:00–14:00 2h
Department of Commerce (Washington, DC)	Director, Office of Automotive Industry Affairs	S. Keitz	10/5/89	20:00–21:45 1h 45min
Ministry of Economic Affairs (Taipei)	Chief, Transportation Section, First Div., Industrial Development Bureau	C. J. R. Ou	16/10/88	18:00–18:25 25min
Ministry of International Trade & Industry (Tokyo)	Assistant Planning Manager, Subcontracting Enterprise Section, Small & Medium Enterprise Agency	H. Harada	5/3/86	11:00–11:20 20min
			14/3/86	14:00–16:20 2h 20min
Ministry of Posts & Telecommunications (Tokyo)	Analyst, Tariff Regulatory Div., Telecommunications Bureau	K. Tomisawa	2/5/87	18:00–20:00 2h
2. *Local authorities*				
Aichi Prefecture (Aichi)	Manager, Labor Economic Investigation, Dept. of Labor	S. Chaya	31/1/86	10:00–13:00 3h
	Assistant Manager, Labor Economic Investigation, Dept. of Labor	K. Niwa	31/1/86	10:00–13:00
Flint–Genesee Corporation (Michigan)	Executive Director	A. Schifano	19/3/87	9:15–16:00 6h 45min
Ibaragi Prefecture (Ibaragi)	Director, Dept. of Labor	S. Hitomi	26/2/86	9:30–10:00 30min
	Manager, Business Promotion Section	N. Ishikawa	31/3/86	9:50–10:30 40min
	Assistant Manager, Business Promotion Section	J. Ishi	26/2/86	10:00–11:50 1h 50min

Organization	Position	Name	Date	Time
Ibaragi Prefectural Small-Business Promotion Corporation (Ibaragi)	Director, Small-Business Information Center	Y. Kumata	26/4/86	13:00–14:00 1h
	Assistant Manager, Subcontracting Promotion	K. Mizutani	26/4/86	13:00–14:20 1h 20min
Ministry of Industry, Trade & Technology, Ontario Government (Ontario)	Deputy Minister	P. Lavelle	9/12/86	14:30–15:10 40min
	Policy Adviser	M. Dube	9/12/86	14:00–15:10 1h 10min
Quebec Government (Quebec)	Industrial Adviser, Ministry of Industry and Commerce	S. E. Farah	14/9/86	18:00–18:40 40min
San Diego Economic Development Corporation (San Diego, California)	Vice-President	P. J. Devermann	23/3/88	9:27–10:25 1h 58min
Saarland Government (Saarland, Germany)	Minister of Economic Affairs	Hoffman[a]	31/8/87	11:30–14:00 2h 30min
	Director of Industrial Development, Ministry of Economic Affairs	Nierlich	31/8/87	11:30–14:00 2h 30min
	Minister of Federal and Special Affairs	Hahn	1/9/87	17:00–17:35 35min
	Personnel Director, Ministry of Federal and Special Affairs	C. Runge	1/9/87	17:00–17:35 35min
	Director, Ministry of Federal and Special Affairs	W. Weber	1/9/87	17:00–17:35 35min
Saarland Business Promotion & Development Corporation (Saarland, Germany)	Executive Director	A. Martens	31/8/87	9:30–11:30 2h
	Manager, Investment Promotion	F. Haase	31/8/87	12:00–14:00 2h
Tokyo Metropolitan Social Welfare Council (Tokyo)	Manager, Dept. of Local Welfare	I. Tsuda	21/12/83	14:00–16:00 2h
	Assistant Manager, Dept. of Local Welfare	C. Shishido	21/12/83	14:00–16:00 2h
3. *Trade associations*				
Automotive Parts Manufacturers' Association of Canada (Toronto)	President	O. V. Lonmo	8/5/87	15:05–16:00 55min
	Director of Business Affairs	H. Filger	8/5/87	16:00–19:00 3h

Organization	Position	Name	Date	Time
Deutsch–Japanische Gesellschaft in Saarbruecken (Saar, Germany)	Vice-President	M. Krischek	31/8/87	9:30–11:30 2h
Engineering Industries Association (London)	President	J. E. Bolton	29/3/85	15:45–16:45 1h
	Director-General	W. T. Williams	21/3/85	16:00–17:00 1h
	Trade Director	H. G. Keeling	21/3/85	16:00–17:00 1h
Federation of the Metal Trades Employers' Association in Saarland (Saar, Germany)	Chairman	H. Juette	4/9/87	16:00–17:40 1h 40min
Japan Automobile Manufacturers Association (Tokyo)	General Manager	K. Shinomiya	7/5/89	16:40–16:55 15min
	Associate Director, Planning and Research Dept.	T. Kagawa	1/12/86	11:00–12:40 1h 40min
			4/12/86	11:30–12:30 1h
			29/6/87	14:40–15:25 45min
	Manager, Planning and Research Dept.	I. Tanaka	1/12/86	11:00–12:40 1h 40min
	Assistant Manager, Planning and Research Dept.	H. Umemoto	29/6/87	14:40–15:25 45min
	Planning Staff, Planning and Research Dept.	M. Hoshino	1/12/86	11:00–12:40 1h 40min
			4/12/86	11:30–12:30 1h
			7/4/89	17:30–17:50 20min
Japan Auto Parts Industry Association (Tokyo)	Chairman	Y. Nobumoto	7/4/89	17:10–17:30 20min
	Executive Director	Y. Nakamura	7/4/89	16:55–17:10 15min
	Managing Director	A. Suzuki	7/4/89	12:20–13:30 1h 10min
	Manager, Overseas Dept.	A. Gyobu	7/4/89	10:00–10:20 14:00–14:30 50min
Japan External Trade Organization (Tokyo)	Planning & Information, Import Promotion & Cooperation Dept.	Y. Araki	15/7/87	10:30–12:00 1h 30min

Organization	Position	Name	Date	Time
Motor & Equipment Manufacturers Association (New Jersey)	President	W. Raftery	14/3/87	10:27–12:30 2h 3min
	Executive Vice-President	J. Conner	14/3/87	10:27–12:30 2h 3min
	Administrator, International Trade	J. Creamer	14/3/87	10:27–12:30 2h 3min
Motor Vehicle Manufacturers' Association (Toronto)	President	N. A. Clark	8/5/87	13:30–14:57 1h 27min
Society for Promotion of the Machinery Industry (Tokyo)	Assist. Director & Senior Researcher, Economic Research Institute	K. Shibata	20/11/87	18:00–20:00 2h
	Economist, Economic Research Institute	K. Ishiro	16/1/86	14:30–15:10 40min
			3/2/86	14:40–15:30 50min
Society of Motor Manufacturers & Trades (London)	Economist	C. Ford	15/3/85	18:20–21:30 3h 10min

4. *Industrial cooperatives*

Chigasaki Machinery & Metal Industrial Park Cooperative (Kanagawa)	Secretary-General	Y. Nakabayashi	28/11/86	9:45–12:00 2h 15min
Conference of the Small and Medium Industrial Park & Others (Ibaragi)	Director	S. Hitomi	26/2/86	9:30–10:00 30min
	Manager, Business Promotion Section	N. Ishikawa	31/3/86	9:50–10:30 40min
	Assistant Manager, Business Promotion Section	J. Ishi	26/2/86	10:00–11:50 1h 50min
Hitachi Metalwork Cooperative (Ibaragi)	Manager of a member firm, Kaiseisha	M. Mashiko	26/3/86	14:20–17:38 3h 18min
	Manager of a member firm, Kaiseisha	T. Sato	26/3/86	14:20–17:38 3h 18min
Kanazawa Machinery & Metal Industrial Park Cooperative (Kanagawa)	Director of a member firm, Kokan Kako	K. Maruyama	28/11/86	15:00–16:05 1h 5min
	Senior Managing Director of a member firm, Ohse Kogyo	H. Ohse	22/4/86	15:00–15:20 20min
	Managing Director of a member firm, Ohse Kogyo	S. Ohse	22/4/86	14:20–16:15 17:20–22:00 6h 35min

Organization	Position	Name	Date	Time
	Assistant Manager of a member firm, Ohse Kogyo	T. Yamazaki	22/4/86	19:00–20:00 1h
	President of a member firm, Yokohama Hi-Tech	K. Mashiko	28/11/86	16:10–16:30 20min
	Senior Researcher of a member firm, Yokohama Hi-Tech	Y. Ojima	28/11/86	16:10–18:35 2h 25min
	Managing Director of a member firm, Yokohama Kiko	T. Togoshi	28/11/86	13:30–15:00 1h 30min
	General Manager of a member firm, Yokohama Kiko	T. Hashiura	28/11/86	13:30–15:00 1h 30min
Kuji Metalwork Cooperative (Ibaragi)	President	Y. Katogi	24/4/86	14:00–15:20 1h 20min
	Secretary-General	T. Kurihara	24/4/86	10:10–15:40 5h 30min
Tama Industrial Cooperative (Tokyo)	Managing Director of a member firm, Daiichi Seiki	K. Ishida	23/5/86	13:10–15:00 1h 50min
	Director of a member firm, Daiichi Seiki	T. Hatakeyama	23/5/86	13:10–15:00 1h 50min
	Manager of a member firm, Daiichi Seiki	Y. Doi	23/5/86	14:20–15:00 40min
Tokyo Scale Industry Cooperative in Ibaragi Industrial Park (Ibaragi)	Secretary-General	Y. Nishiguchi	8/1/86	9:30–12:30 3h
5. *Trade unions*				
Pioneer Workers' Union (Tokyo)	President	Ogawa	22/12/83	9:15–10:35 1h 20min
Ohse Kogyo Workers' Union (Kanagawa)	President	H. Fujita	22/4/86	18:05–20:00 1h 55min
Federation of Electrical Machine Workers' Unions (Tokyo)	Executive, Committee Member, & Director, Industrial Dept.	T. Kawakami	16/1/86	15:50–16:50 1h
	Staff, Industrial Dept.	T. Kashiwagi	16/1/86	15:50–16:50 1h
	Staff, Wage Policy Dept.	N. Kato	16/1/86	15:50–16:50 1h
United Automobile Workers Union (Detroit)	Vice-President, Director, UAW–General Motors Department	D. F. Ephlin	4/5/87	19:10–19:30 20min

Organization	Position	Name	Date	Time
	Economist	C. Howes	1/5/87	14:15–16:35 2h 20min
	Research Associate	P. Unterwerger	1/5/87	14:15–16:35 2h 20min

6. *Public research organizations*

Organization	Position	Name	Date	Time
National Research Center for Science & Technology for Development (Beijing)	Council Member, Transportation Association	J. Luzhong	17/9/86	10:30–10:55 25min
Employment Promotion Corporation (Tokyo)	Senior Researcher, Research Institute of Employment and Occupations	T. Kudo	20/1/86	15:05–16:55 1h 50min
Institute for Economic Research (IFO) (Munich)	Senior Economist, Industry and Economic Structure Dept.	R. Hild	13/9/88	9:50–11:05 1h 15min
Institute for Social Scientific Research (ISF) (Munich)	Director	N. Altmann	11/9/88	17:15–20:45 3h
	Researcher	D. Sauer	13/9/88	11:30–15:00 3h 30min
	Researcher	K. Semlinger	13/9/88	11:30–12:50 1h 20min
Japan Institute of Labor (Tokyo)	Director, Research Dept.	O. Hirota	4/6/88	10:00–11:40 1h 40min
	Senior Research Associate & Lecturer at Yokohama National University	Y. Kuwahara	23/12/83	16:45–17:38 53min
	Research Associate, International Affairs Dept., & Lecturer at Saitama University	K. Hayashi	15/3/85	16:00–18:00 2h
	Planning Staff, Research Dept.	K. Nomura	5/2/88	13:00–15:00 2h
			4/6/88	10:00–11:40 1h 40min
Labor Research Council (Tokyo)	Executive Director	B. Watanabe	15/4/86	16:00–17:15 1h 15min
	General Secretary	T. Shiraishi	15/4/86	16:00–17:15 1h 15min
			16/4/86	16:20–17:00 40min
			18/4/86	15:00–16:00 1h
			28/4/86	16:30–17:20 50min
	Research Analyst	H. Nishimura	16/4/86	14:00–14:50 50min

Organization	Position	Name	Date	Time
Science Center (Berlin)	Researcher, International Institute for Comparative Social Research	U. Juergens	19/5/88	14:30–17:10 2h 40min
	Researcher, International Institute for Comparative Social Research	T. Malsch	19/5/88	14:30–16:20 1h 50min
Social Welfare Research Institute (Tokyo)	Research Associate	K. Hiraoka	4/12/83	18:00–20:00 2h
U.S. Congress (Washington, DC)	Program Manager, Industry, Technology & Employment, Office of Technology Assessment	A. Buyrn	28/3/89	15:20–16:10 50min
	Senior Associate, Office of Technology Assessment	K. Gillman	19/1/89	14:15–16:30 2h 15min
	Project Director & Senior Analyst, Office of Technology Assessment	J. F. Gorte	19/1/89	14:15–14:55 40min
	Policy Analyst	G. R. Morse	29/3/89	12:30–13:30 1h

7. *Prime contractors*

Organization	Position	Name	Date	Time
American Honda Motor Co., Inc. (Detroit)	Assistant Manager, Corporate Public Relations	S. Tanaka	22/7/87	11:30–13:00 1h 30min
Austin Rover Group, Cowley Assembly Plant (Cowley, UK)	Quality Manager	D. Taylor	25/8/87	9:55–11:05 1h 10min
	Production Manager	R. Russel	25/8/87	11:20–12:15 55min
Automobiles Peugeot Mulhouse Assembly Plant (France)	Director, Mulhouse Production Center	P. Ienne	5/9/88	8:40–15:03 6h 23min
	Manager, Production Coordination	M. Cabaton	5/9/88	8:40–15:03 6h 23min
	Manager, Press Shop and White Body Shop	J. C. Rousseau	5/9/88	9:10–11:18 2h 8min
BMW Headquarters (Munich)	Director, Purchasing	W. Becker	12/9/88	10:20–11:00 12:15–15:25 3h 50min
	General Manager, International Purchasing	H. J. Preissler	12/9/88	10:20–11:00 12:15–15:25 3h 50min
	Manager, Public Relations	W. Klaus	12/9/88	11:04–13:14 2h
Chrysler Corporation	Chief Engineer, Engineering Program	A. D. Bosley	5/5/87	12:20–12:50 30min

Organization	Position	Name	Date	Time
Headquarters (Detroit)	Planning Engineering Office			
Daimler-Benz Headquarters (Stuttgart)	Director, Materials Management	A. Daigger	14/9/88	9:35–13:00 3h 25min
	Manager, Materials Management/Procurement Logistics	R. Brulz	14/9/88	9:35–13:00 3h 25min
	Manager, Materials Management/Procurement Logistics	A. Boelstler	14/9/88	9:35–15:18 5h 43min
Diamond-Star Motors Headquarters & Assembly Plant (Indiana)	President and Chief Executive Officer	Y. Nakane	12/2/88	15:00–15:20 20min
	Executive Vice-President, Administration & Human Resources Secretary	K. Kawasoe	12/2/88	11:50–13:30 1h 40min
	Executive Assistant to President	W. Takayasu	12/2/88	11:50–13:30 1h 40min
	General Manager, Production Control and Systems	T. Ohta	12/2/88	14:55–15:27 32min
	Manager, General Affairs	T. Okubo	12/2/88	11:50–13:30 1h 40min 16:20–17:00 40min
	Manager, Production Purchasing	Y. Nakagawa	12/2/88	13:30–2:20 50min
	Coordinator, Final Assembly Manufacturing	T. Ando	12/2/88	15:27–16:20 53min
FIAT USA (New York)	Director, Corporate Communications	G. Ranieri	11/9/87	10:20–10:50 30min
Ford Motor Company Headquarters (Michigan)	Corporate Strategy Staff, Public Policy Issues	C. G. Meyer	15/9/86	18:30–20:00 1h 30min
Ford Lio Ho Motor Co. Lio Ho Assembly Plant (Chung-li, Taiwan)	Director, Manufacturing	D. A. Grenke	9/7/87	8:50–13:09 4h 19min
	Manager, Assembly Operations, Manufacturing Division	H. J. Liu	9/7/87	9:00–10:00 12:20–13:09 1h 49min
	Manager, Technical Service, Manufacturing Division	J. Guan	9/7/87	9:30–13:09 14:05–14:45 4h 19min
	Manager, Local Content & Supplier	R. D. L. Lin	9/7/87	13:09–14:03 54min

Organization	Position	Name	Date	Time
	Development, Supply Operations			
Fuji Electric, Headquarters (Tokyo)	Executive Managing Director	K. Ono	18/2/86	16:15–17:00 45min
			12/3/86	15:40–16:20 40min
	General Manager, Purchasing Dept.	A. Kubota	6/3/86	9:10–11:45 2h 35min
	Manager, Purchasing Control Sect., Purchasing Dept.	T. Imai	6/3/86	9:10–11:45 2h 35min
			3/4/86	17:20–20:00 2h 40min
	Manager, Personnel Dept.	S. Takahashi	11/3/86	9:00–10:45 1h 45min
Fuji Electric Tokyo Plant (Tokyo)	Manager, Subcontracting Sect., Purchasing Dept.	T. Ohyama	3/4/86	9:30–12:30 17:20–20:00 5h 40min
General Motors Corporation Headquarters (Detroit)	Director, Competitive Analysis	J. Trask	17/3/87	14:00–16:05 2h 5min
			27/4/87	12:00–13:40 1h 40min
			1/5/87	18:30–21:30 3h
	Director, Trade Analysis	G. Mustafa Mohatarem	17/3/87	14:00–16:05 2h 5min
	Senior Economist, Economic Analysis	F. I. Johnson	25/4/89	10:00–11:10 1h 10min
	Director	K. Izawa	17/3/87	14:00–16:37 2h 37min
	Project Manager	S. R. Brown	17/3/87	14:00–15:00 1h
	Manager, Asia Pacific	J. G. Pekarek	18/3/87	11:30–15:35 4h 5min
	Commodity Manager	O. Pedersen	1/5/87	9:00–12:05 3h 5min
			20/5/87	10:05–11:05 1h
	Purchasing Activities	C. Koo Yun	1/5/87	9:00–11:00 2h
GM Buick– Oldsmobile– Cadillac Group, Orion Assembly Plant (Michigan)	Purchasing Agent	J. Newlin	18/3/87	11:30–15:35 4h 5min
	Materials Management	T. Harris	18/3/87	13:35–15:35 2h
General Motors Overseas Corporation, Japan Branch (Tokyo)	Administrative Assistant, Planning & Liaison	C. Hirao	2/6/88	19:00–19:20 20min

Organization	Position	Name	Date	Time
Hino Motors Headquarters & Honsha Assembly Plant (Tokyo)	Chairman	S. Yamamoto	16/5/88	15:30–15:50 20min
	General Manager, Secretary Dept.	T. Yoshino	17/5/88	19:50–22:20 2h 30min
			24/5/88	12:00–13:10 1h 10min
	Manager, Public Relations	H. Nakamura	25/3/86	13:00–16:35 3h 35min
			24/5/88	9:30–13:10 3h 40min
	Assistant Manager, Public Relations	Y. Hara	24/5/88	9:30–13:10 3h 40min
	Personnel Dept.	H. Mukai	25/3/86	13:00–16:35 3h 35min
Hitachi Headquarters (Tokyo)	Building Facilities Dept., Central Sales Div.	Y. Takeuchi	6/3/86	16:00–16:40 40min
			20/3/86	14:10–16:25 2h 15min
	Control Group, Purchasing Div.	Y. Momiyama	6/3/86	16:00–16:40 40min
			20/3/86	14:00–16:25 2h 15min
Hitachi Taga Plant (Ibaragi)	Manager, Subcontracting Sect., Materials Dept.	H. Ohshita	28/3/86	10:15–12:50 2h 35min
	Assistant Manager, Subcontracting Sect., Materials Dept.	Y. Watanabe	28/3/86	10:15–12:50 2h 35min
Hitachi Tokai Plant (Ibaragi)	Manager, Subcontracting Sect., Materials Dept.	M. Tomita	28/3/86	13:30–15:50 2h 20min
Hitachi Sawa Plant (Ibaragi)	Manager, General Affairs Dept.	S. Ishiyama	26/3/86	10:00–13:30 3h 30min
	Engineer, Electronics Production	K. Horiuchi	26/3/86	10:00–12:00 2h
	Manager, Subcontracting Sect., Materials Dept.	R. Matsumura	28/3/86	15:55–17:00 1h 5min
Honda Motor Headquarters (Tokyo)	Senior Adviser	H. Sugiura	7/5/89	19:00–20:45 1h 45min
	Manager, International Planning Office	T. Takami	5/12/86	18:00–20:00 2h
			7/5/89	19:00–20:45 1h 45min
	Staff, Overseas Public Relations Dept.	R. Onodera	10/7/87	10:00–19:00 9h
Honda R & D Company, Tochigi R & D Center (Saitama)	Director & Deputy General Manager	H. Suzuki	5/12/86	13:15–16:55 3h 40min
	Chief Engineer & Deputy General Manager	T. Hatanaka	5/12/86	13:15–16:55 3h 40min

Organization	Position	Name	Date	Time
Honda R & D Company, Wako R & D Center (Saitama)	Deputy General Manager	N. Ishida	5/12/86	13:15–16:55 3h 40min
Honda Motor Sayama Assembly Plant (Saitama)	General Manager, Plant 1	K. Miyaki	10/7/87	13:20–17:35 5h 15min
	General Manager, Plant 2	K. Kasai	10/7/87	13:20–15:04 1h 44min
	Staff, General Affairs	Kawamura	10/7/87	16:30–17:20 50min
Honda of America Manufacturing Inc. Headquarters & Assembly Plant (Ohio)	Vice-President & Senior Manager, Production Control	T. Shirokawa	3/4/87	9:50–10:25 11:45–15:25 4h 15min
	Executive Vice-President	T. Amino	10/2/88	12:45–14:10 1h 25min
	Senior Manager, Purchasing	N. Morita	3/4/87	10:04–10:25 11:35–13:56 2h 42min
	Purchasing Manager	G. Berryman	20/10/88	18:20–18:50 40min
	Coordinator, Administration Dept.	K. Daiki	3/4/87	10:25–11:33 1h 8min
	Coordinator, Corporate Communications	Y. Harada	10/2/88	10:00–16:15 6h 15min
Honda of the U.K. Manufacturing (Swindon)	Manager & Senior Engineer	H. Onobe	25/8/87	15:38–16:34 56min
	Assistant Manager	K. Tainaka	25/8/87	9:55–15:38 5h 43min
Isuzu Motors Headquarters (Tokyo)	Manager, Purchasing Control Dept.	Y. Murayama	4/3/86	14:40–18:20 3h 40min
	General Manager, Training and Education Dept.	M. Yoda	17/3/86	13:00–15:00 2h
JEOL (Tokyo)	Acting Manager, Public Affairs Dept., General Affairs Div.	Y. Seki	9/6/86	9:55–11:50 1h 55min
Johnson & Johnson (New Jersey)	Vice-President, Purchasing	P. S. Boorujy	24/11/87	14:30–15:30 1h
Kia Motors Corporation Headquarters (Seoul)	Deputy Manager, Secretariat	Y. Lee	3/7/87	14:00–18:35 4h 35min
	Manager, Purchasing Planning Dept.	N. Cho	3/7/87	16:50–17:10 20min
	Staff, Purchasing Planning Dept.	Y. Park	3/7/87	15:55–17:10 1h 15min
Kia Motors Sohari Assembly Plant (Kyungki-do, Korea)	Manager, Body Welding Shop	H. Moon	3/7/87	17:20–18:35 1h 15min

Organization	Position	Name	Date	Time
LDC America (New Jersey)	Customs Sales Manager	K. Yamashita	27/12/86	14:00–16:30 2h 30min
Mazda Motor Corporation Headquarters & Honsha Assembly Plant (Hiroshima)	Director & Deputy General Manager, Technical Research Center	S. Mochizuki	3/12/86	13:00–17:00 4h
	Deputy Manager, Development Administration Div.	K. Suemori	3/12/86	13:00–17:00 4h
	Assistant Manager, Business Research Div.	T. Imai	3/12/86	13:00–17:00 4h
	Passenger Vehicle Product Planner, Office of Product Program Managers	K. Nobeoka	23/2/87	17:00–17:30 30min
			12/6/87	11:50–12:50 1h
			18/6/87	22:00–22:40 40min
	Manager, Production Planning Div.	S. Matsunami	7/7/87	11:00–12:10 1h 10min
	Assistant Project Manager, Product Planning & Development Div.	F. Inami	7/7/87	11:00–14:40 3h 40min
	Staff, Product Planning & Development Div.	Nakano	7/7/87	13:14–14:40 1h 26min
	Project General Manager, Value Auditing Group, Corporate Communication Div.	B. Suzuki	7/7/87	14:40–16:05 1h 25min
	Deputy General Manager, Education & Training Div.	T. Ogata	7/7/87	9:17–9:29 11:00–16:05 5h 17min
	Staff, Education & Training Div.	S. Kubo	7/7/87	9:17–11:00 1h 43min
Mazda Motor Manufacturing (USA) Corporation Headquarters & Assembly Plant (Michigan)	Executive Vice-President	M. Uchida	11/2/88	10:45–13:10 2h 25min 17:20–17:50 30min
	Manager, Purchasing	M. Miyamoto	23/3/87	10:15–14:10 3h 55min
			11/2/88	13:10–16:15 3h 5min
	Leader, Production Procurement 1, Purchasing	T. Oka	23/3/87	11:15–14:10 2h 55min
	Specialist, Process Engineering, Production Engineering	T. Yasuda	11/2/88	10:15–11:45 1h 30min

Organization	Position	Name	Date	Time
	Manager, Public Relations	N. A. Hennigar	11/2/88	10:00–13:00 3h
Mazda R & D of North America (Irvine, California)	President	H. Motoyoshi	11/5/89	10:40–11:20 40min
Mazda (North America) Inc. (Los Angeles)	Manager, Corporate Planning	N. Kondo	17/7/87	19:00–22:30 3h 30min
Matsushita Electric Shizuoka Plant (Shizuoka)	Manager, Production Dept., Washing Machine Division	K. Ohshita	10/1/84	15:15–16:00 45min
NEC Headquarters (Tokyo)	Senior Adviser	N. Hattori	12/3/86	13:00–15:00 2h
New United Motor Manufacturing (NUMMI) Headquarters & Assembly Plant (Fremont, California)	President	K. Higashi	4/5/87	15:30–15:45 15min
			20/7/87	8:45–9:55 1h 10min
	Coordinator, General Affairs	K. Kamiya	20/7/87	8:45–9:55 1h 10min
	former Manufacturing Engineer, Quality Control Engineering	J. F. Krafcik	4/2/87	15:08–16:48 1h 40min
	Manufacturing Engineer, Quality Control Engineering	D. Triantafyllos	17/8/87	17:30–18:10 40min
Nissan Motor Company Headquarters (Tokyo)	General Manager, Corporate Planning Office	T. Maeda	1/12/86	13:00–14:15 1h 15min
	Deputy General Manager, Corporate Planning Office	M. Asakura	1/12/86	13:00–14:15 1h 15min
	Manager, International Public Relations, International Div.	S. Sawada	2/7/87	16:55–17:15 20min
	Staff, International Public Relations, International Div.	M. Toba	2/7/87	14:10–18:30 4h 20min
Nissan Technical Center (Kanagawa)	Senior Project Designer, Development Planning Dept., Technological Strategy Planning Office	H. Takao	1/12/86	15:35–16:00 25min
	Staff, Development Planning Dept., Technological Strategy Planning Office	A. Arai	1/12/86	15:35–16:00 25min

Organization	Position	Name	Date	Time
	Senior Project Designer, Vehicle Planning Dept., Product Development Office	F. Yokoyama	1/12/86	15:35–16:00 17:30–19:00 1h 55min
	Senior Project Designer, Product Development Office	S. Sakai	1/12/86	15:35–16:00 17:30–20:30 3h 25min
	Staff, Computer-aided Engineering Section 1, Product Development Systems Dept.	T. Kishimoto	1/12/86	15:35–16:35 17:30–19:00 2h 30min
	Staff, Computer-aided Engineering Section 1, Product Development Systems Dept.	T. Ishimura	24/6/88	13:00–14:30 1h 30min
	Engineer, Body Design Control Sect., Body Design Dept.	T. Hagiwara	1/12/86	15:35–16:00 17:30–20:30 3h 25min
	Engineer, Brake System Design Sect., Chassis Design Dept.	K. Chiba	1/12/86	15:35–16:00 17:30–19:00 1h 55min
	Manager, Chassis Design Section 1, Chassis Design Dept.	I. Nakamura	1/12/86	15:35–16:00 17:30–19:00 1h 55min
	Design Engineer, Chassis Design Section 1, Chassis Design Dept.	H. Kan	1/12/86	15:35–16:00 17:30–19:00 1h 55min
	Senior Project Designer, Overseas Vehicle Design Dept.	T. Okamura	1/12/86	17:30–20:30 3h
	Engineer, Wind Tunnel	Wakamatsu	1/12/86	16:56–17:10 14min
	Engineer, Safety Experiment Sect.	Okamoto	1/12/86	17:10–17:30 20min
	Staff, Personnel Administration Sect., R & D Administration Dept.	K. Tokuoka	1/12/86	15:35–16:00 17:30–18:25 1h 20min
Nissan Motor Murayama Assembly Plant (Tokyo)	Manager, Accounting Sect., Administration Dept.	K. Ishida	27/3/86	10:00–12:22 2h 22min
	Staff, Accounting Sect., Administration Dept.	Kubo	27/3/86	10:00–12:22 2h 22min
	Manager, Machine Tool Control Sect.	Koinuma	27/3/86	10:00–12:22 2h 22min
Nissan Motor Oppama Assembly Plant (Kanagawa)	Manager, Production Control Sect.	K. Kigami	2/7/87	14:10–17:15 3h 5min
	Staff, Production Control Sect.	Y. Matsusaka	2/7/87	14:10–17:15 3h 5min

Organization	Position	Name	Date	Time
	Manager, P. R. Center	I. Ishii	2/7/87	14:10–17:15 3h 5min
Nissan Motor Zama Assembly Plant (Kanagawa)	Deputy General Manager, Publicity & Community Relations, Administration Dept.	M. Shiozaki	1/7/87	13:30–16:35 3h 5min
Nissan Motor Corporation in U.S.A. (Washington, DC)	Vice-President, External Relations	Y. Saegusa	4/5/87	19:30–21:00 1h 30min
Nissan Motor Manufacturing Corporation U.S.A. Headquarters & Assembly Plant (Tennessee)	Technical Services	S. Narita	30/3/87	18:30–2:10 3h 40min
	Purchasing Adviser, Technical Services	T. Kikuchi	30/3/87	18:30–2:10 3h 40min
			9/2/88	10:45–12:05 1h 20min
	Senior Adviser to President	S. Uchiyama	9/2/88	12:05–13:20 1h 15min
	Accounting, Technical Services	Y. Ikemoto	9/2/88	9:45–10:40 55min
	Director, Quality Assurances	K. Ichijo	9/2/88	12:05–13:20 1h 15min
	Personnel, Technical Services	M. Mori	9/2/88	9:30–13:20 3h 50min
Nissan Motor Manufacturing (UK) Ltd. Headquarters & Assembly Plant (Sunderland)	Deputy Managing Director	I. Gibson	28/8/87	13:10–14:20 1h 10min
	Senior Adviser to Managing Director	H. Moriyama	28/8/87	10:45–15:55 5h 10min
	Adviser to Director of Engineering	H. Suzuki	28/8/87	10:55–12:17 1h 22min
	Manager, Design	S. Miyajima	28/8/87	14:13–15:55 1h 42min
Nissan Shatai Headquarters & Assembly Plant (Kanagawa)	Vice-President & Plant Manager	N. Yamamoto	3/2/84	14:10–16:10 2h
Oki Electric Takasaki Plant (Gunma)	Manager, Automation & Troubleshooting Section	Okabe	26/1/84	13:52–14:26 34min
	Manager, Production System Dept.	Horiuchi	26/1/84	13:00–13:27 14:29–15:02 60 min
Pioneer Ansafone Manufacturing Corporation (Saitama)	International Business Dept.	M. Namakidani	15/1/84	15:05–15:35 30min
Pioneer Electronic Corporation	Personnel Manager, Personnel Div.	Abe	19/12/83	9:00–9:40 40min

Organization	Position	Name	Date	Time
Headquarters (Tokyo)	Manager, Employment Personnel Div.	Kataoka	20/12/83	17:45–18:15 30min
	Manager, Employment Personnel Div.	Miyazawa	14/5/86	10:25–12:35 2h 10min
	Staff, Employment Personnel Div.	Kawade	21/12/83	10:00–11:10 1h 10min
	Manager, Labor Relations Personnel Div.	Kudo	24/12/83	9:30–10:17 47min
	Assistant Manager, Labor Relations Personnel Div.	J. Nakamura	25/6/86	14:30–15:10 15:50–16:20 1h 10min
	Staff, Labor Relations Personnel Div.	Hori	9/1/84	15:10–16:20 1h 10min
	Staff, Overseas Personnel, Personnel Div.	Sueda	14/5/86	13:30–14:30 1h
			25/6/86	15:10–15:50 40min
	Manager, General Affairs, General Administration Div.	Sato	9/1/84	13:43–14:57 1h 14min
	Director & Manager, Audio Products Div. 1	Ichimura	23/12/83	9:30–10:30 1h
	Director & Manager, Audio Products Div. 2	Yanagisawa	14/12/84	9:50–10:10 20min
	Director & Manager, Production Coordination Div. & Procurement Control Div.	K. Kuroda	24/12/83	11:00–12:10 1h 10min
	Senior Assistant Manager, Production Coordination Div.	K. Ohnuma	14/5/86	14:35–17:05 2h 30min
	Manager, Production Coordination Div.	Nagashima	14/5/86	17:05–18:25 1h 20min
	Manager, Procurement Control Div.	Shimizu	24/12/83	14:00–14:35 35min
	Staff, Procurement Control Div.	S. Tanaka	24/12/83	14:00–14:35 35min
	Manager, Raw Material 2, Procurement Control Div.	Ohishi	24/12/83	15:40–16:10 30min
	Staff, Procurement Control Div.	K. Kida	24/12/83	15:40–16:10 30min
	Manager, General Audio Product Section, Marketing Coordination Dept., International Div.	Saito	29/12/83	10:35–11:00 25min

Organization	Position	Name	Date	Time
	Manager, Corporate Planning Div.	Ueno	11/1/84	10:35–12:15 1h 40min
	General Manager, OEM Sales Div.	Ohta	25/6/86	10:05–10:40 35min
	General Manager, OEM Sales Div.	Koga	25/6/86	10:05–10:40 13:00–14:35 2h 10min
	Manager, Planning Office, OEM Sales Div.	Hata	25/6/86	10:05–12:10 2h 5min
Pioneer Electronic Corporation Ohmori Plant (Tokyo)	Plant Manager	Tanaka	26/12/83	11:00–12:15 1h 5min
	Manager, Production & Subcontractors Control Production Dept. 1	Takahashi	26/12/83 15/2/84	9:40–11:00 1h 20min 13:20–13:50 30min
	Manager, Production Administration Dept.	Masamoto	26/12/83	12:50–13:35 45min
	Manager, General Affairs Dept.	Asano	26/12/83	13:36–16:00 2h 24min
	Manager, Production Control Dept.	Yoshimura	15/5/86	10:00–12:00 2h
Pioneer Electronic Corporation Kawagoe Plant (Saitama)	Plant Manager	Sakurabayashi	27/12/83	15:05–16:20 1h 15min
	Manager, General Affairs Dept.	Mieno	22/12/83	13:20–14:52 1h 32min
	Assistant Manager, General Affairs Dept.	Nishida	27/12/83	17:30–18:30 1h
	Staff, General Affairs Dept.	Kurokawa	16/5/86	10:30–12:00 19:00–19:50 2h 20min
	Manager, Outside Production Control	Irie	27/12/83	9:15–12:00 2h 45min
	Manager, Outside Production Control	N. Shishikura	16/5/86	10:30–12:00 17:00–19:00 3h 30min
	Assistant Manager, Outside Prod. Control	Oikawa	27/12/83	9:15–12:00 2h 45min
	Assistant Manager, Outside Prod. Control	Kobayashi	12/1/84 13/1/84	13:00–16:15 3h 15min 15:00–16:00 1h
	Staff, Outside Production Control	Hanta	27/12/83	9:15–12:00 2h 45min
	Staff, Outside Production Control	S. Kubota	16/5/86	10:30–12:00 12:45–19:00 7h 45min

Organization	Position	Name	Date	Time
	Manager, Production Administration Dept.	Yamashita	27/12/83	16:30–17:30 1h
	Manager, Production Administration Dept.	Aiba	16/5/86	17:45–18:40 55min
	Manager, Production Dept.	Murakami	27/12/83	14:40–15:00 20min
	Manager, Overseas Production, Production Dept.	Nose	27/12/83	13:00–14:05 1h 5min
	Assistant Manager, Unit Production Section, Production Dept.	Yanai	12/1/84	9:30–11:10 1h 40min
	Assistant Manager, Production Dept.	Sasazeki	12/1/84	11:15–12:05 50min
	Automation Center Production Dept.	Moriya	12/1/84	12:38–12:48 10min
Pioneer Electronic Corporation Shizuoka Plant (Shizuoka)	Plant Manager	Hibi	10/1/84	11:40–12:30 50min
	Manager, General Affairs, General Affairs Dept.	Kihara	10/1/84	13:20–14:40 1h 20min
	Manager, Production Dept. 2	Shiobara	10/1/84	16:30–17:20 50min
	Manager Overseas Production Section, Production Administration Dept.	M. Iiyama	10/1/84	10:25–11:40 1h 15min
	Manager, General Affairs, General Affairs Dept.	Hisakawa	10/1/84	9:15–9:57 42min
Pioneer Electronic Corporation Tokorozawa Plant (Saitama)	Plant Manager	Yanagi	7/1/84	11:10–11:38 28min
	Manager, General Affairs Dept.	Honda	7/1/84	9:35–11:05 1h 30min
	General Affairs	Ozawa	7/1/84	9:35–11:05 1h 30min 18:00–22:15 4h 15min
	Manager, Production Administration Dept.	Takeishi	7/1/84	13:45–15:15 1h 30min
	Manager, Production Control, Production Administration Dept.	Ohno	7/1/84	15:25–17:05 1h 40min
	Production Control, Production Administration Dept.	Akao	7/1/84	18:00–22:15 4h 15min
Pioneer Electronics Manufacturing	Production Engineer	K. Hayashi	13/12/84	14:00–17:30 2h 30min

Organization	Position	Name	Date	Time
N.V. Headquarters & Plant (Erpe, Belgium)				
Pioneer High Fidelity (G.B.) Ltd. Headquarters (Buckinghamshire, UK)	Managing Director	S. Ohnami	26/11/83	13:00–17:30 3h 30min
Pioneer High Fidelity (G.B.) Ltd. Headquarters (Middlesex, UK)	Managing Director	Minato	17/9/85	11:30–12:30 1h
	Manager, Sales & Marketing	Mori	17/9/85	14:18–16:00 1h 42min
			7/10/85	11:30–12:30 1h
	Overseas Marketing	Kubonoya	30/9/85	14:00–15:45 1h 45min
			9/10/85	10:15–11:00 45min
Saab-Scania Headquarters & Assembly Plant (Trollhattan, Sweden)	Director, Materials Management	B. Bjorkman	27/9/89	15:00–19:00 4h
	Manager, Purchasing Strategy & Development	B. Andersson	27/9/89	15:00–19:00 4h
			28/9/89	10:00–13:00 13:50–14:20 3h 30min
	Purchasing Manager, Body, Chassis & Power Train	B. Persson	28/9/89	10:00–13:00 13:50–14:20 3h 30min
	Purchasing Manager, Vehicle Components	P. O. Nyman	28/9/89	10:00–13:00 13:50–14:20 3h 30min
	Business Controller, Material	S. Larsson	28/9/89	10:00–13:00 13:50–14:20 3h 30min
	Manager, Body Equipment Design	G. Johansson	28/9/89	10:00–13:00 13:50–14:20 3h 30min
	Manager, Design Office, Safety Systems/ Instrument Panel	I. Eriksson	28/9/89	10:00–13:00 13:50–14:20 3h 30min
	Chief Engineer, Engine, Transmission & Climate System Design & Development	O. Granlund	28/9/89	10:00–13:00 13:50–14:20 3h 30min
	Manager, Marketing Support/Analysis After Sales	P. Malmstrom	27/9/89	17:00–17:30 30min
	Quality Manager, Central Quality	S. Wennerdal	27/9/89	17:30–18:15 45min

Organization	Position	Name	Date	Time
SONY Corporation Headquarters (Tokyo)	Personnel	Fujita	4/2/84	15:00–17:30 2h 30min
Thorn EMI Ferguson Gosport Plant (Hants, UK)	Manager, Management Services	R. N. Amey	11/4/84	16:33–17:55 1h 22min
	Engineer, Management Services	Hallet	11/4/84	16:33–17:55 1h 22min
Toyota Motor Corporation Headquarters (Aichi)	Assistant General Manager, Purchasing Administration Dept.	H. Ohashi	2/7/87	11:10–11:30 20min
	Manager, Administration Staff, Purchasing Administration Dept.	S. Ijichi	27/5/86	14:00–16:26 2h 26min
	Manager, Educational Planning Staff, Education & Training Dept.	K. Izuhara	30/5/86	10:00–11:30 1h 30min
	Assistant Manager, Product Services Staff, Overseas Planning Dept.	K. Ito	9/4/86	11:45–13:30 1h 45min
	Manager, Public Affairs Dept.	R. Muroya	6/7/87	12:20–16:40 4h 20min
	Staff, Public Afairs Dept.	Takenaka	6/7/87	14:00–16:40 2h 40min
Toyota Motor Corporation Tokyo Branch (Tokyo)	General Manager, Tokyo Research Dept.	M. Kiyomasu	5/5/87 15/7/87	20:00–21:30 1h 30min 12:30–13:40 1h 10min
	Business Environment Research Staff, Research Dept.	M. Nozaki	6/7/87	12:20–16:40 4h 20min
	Business Environment Research Staff, Research Dept.	M. Ohbu	7/4/89	17:50–18:10 20min
	Manager, Tokyo Administration Staff, Purchasing Administration Dept.	M. Nakao	2/7/87	10:40–12:15 1h 35min
	Assistant Manager, Tokyo Administration Staff, Purchasing Administration Dept.	H. Yamaguchi	2/7/87	10:40–11:55 1h 15min
	Operations Support Staff, Latin America & Caribbean Dept.	K. Tanabe	9/4/88	12:00–14:00 2h

Organization	Position	Name	Date	Time
Toyota Motor Corporation Kamigo Engine/Transmission Plant (Aichi)	Staff, Public Affairs Dept.	Miura	9/4/86	14:20–15:20 1h
Toyota Motor Corporation Takaoka Assembly Plant (Aichi)	Manager, Administration Staff, Administration Dept.	K. Kamei	6/7/87	14:00–16:40 2h 40min
	Assistant General Manager, Inspection Dept.	Y. Ogihara	6/7/87	14:45–15:12 27min
Toyota Motor Corporation Tsutsumi Assembly Plant (Aichi)	Staff, Public Affairs Dept.	Miura	9/4/86	15:30–16:40 1h 10min
Toyota Motor Corporate Services of North America (Michigan)	Group Manager, Purchasing	H. Kamimura	14/9/89	8:00–8:30 30min
Toyota Motor Corporation, U.S. Office (New York)	Assistant Manager	S. Goto	7/2/88	20:00–22:30 2h 30min
Toyota Motor Manufacturing, U.S.A., Inc., Headquarters & Assembly Plant (Kentucky)	Executive Vice-President & Chief Operating Officer	F. Cho	8/2/88	9:00–10:30 1h 30min
	General Manager, Purchasing	R. Araki	8/2/88 10/3/89	9:00–11:26 2h 26min 12:30–14:00 1h 30min
	Executive Coordinator, Purchasing	R. Shingo	8/2/88	9:00–13:00 4h
	Manager, General Affairs	K. Sato	8/2/88	8:30–9:00 30min
	Executive Coordinator	H. Haruna	10/3/89	15:25–16:30 1h 5min
	Assistant Manager, General Affairs	S. Tachihara	8/2/88	8:00–9:00 1h
	Legal Coordinator	N. Shimada	8/2/88	8:30–9:00 30min
	Executive Coordinator, Administration	H. Adachi	10/3/89	15:25–16:30 1h 5min
	Specialist	K. Sato	10/3/89	14:25–16:30 2h 5min
Toyota Motor Sales, USA, Inc. (Torrance, California)	President	Y. Togo	17/7/87	10:50–13:20 2h 30min
	Treasurer & Secretary	A. Kisaki	17/7/87	13:00–13:20 20min
	Senior Executive Coordinator	H. Yamada	17/7/87	10:50–16:00 5h 10min

Organization	Position	Name	Date	Time
Toyota Technical Center USA, Inc. (Gardena, California)	Executive Vice-President	K. Ito	17/7/87	13:30–15:15 1h 45min
	Director, Engineering	T. Taniguchi	17/7/87	13:30–15:15 1h 45min
	Manager, Engineering	Y. Nakagoshi	17/7/87	13:30–15:15 1h 45min

8. *Suppliers and subcontractors*

Organization	Position	Name	Date	Time
ACU/CAM Industries Inc. (Michigan)	President & Chairman	J. Mailey	19/3/87	14:00–15:30 1h 30min
	Executive Vice-President	J. Dodson	19/3/87	14:00–15:30 1h 30min
Aida Seisakusho (Kanagawa)	Director, Sales	S. Aida	28/11/86	10:45–12:00 1h 15min
Aisan Kogyo (Aichi)	Staff, Sales Planning Office	K. Yoneuchi	25/7/86	16:40–17:00 20min
Akebono Brake Industry Headquarters (Tokyo)	Senior Managing Director, General Manager, International Operations	S. Matsumura	5/5/87	17:00–18:00 1h
			17/9/87	18:30–23:30 5h
			7/5/89	21:40–23:25 1h 45min
			8/5/89	22:00–23:45 1h 45min
			10/5/89	21:20–24:00 2h 40min
	Director, International Operations	M. Miyazawa	14/4/89	10:10–16:20 17:00–20:30 9h 40min
Akebono Brake Industry Iwatsuki Plant (Saitama)	Managing Director & Plant Manager	T. Hashimoto	14/4/89	12:40–13:30 15:00–15:20 1h 10min
	Assistant Director, Iwatsuki Plant	I. Sasajima	14/4/89	11:45–15:20 3h 35min
Albecour (Montreal)	President	M. S. Schultz	5/2/87	10:30–12:30 13:30–14:30 3h
American Yazaki Corporation (Michigan)	Vice-President	M. Yamamoto	16/3/87	9:50–14:10 4h 20min
	General Manager, First Sales Dept.	K. Yoshinami	16/3/87	9:50–14:10 4h 20min
American Yazaki Corporation El Paso Division (El Paso, Texas)	Director & General Manager	T. Takanaka	24/3/88	9:00–18:50 9h 50min
	Controller, Accounting Dept.	S. Hoshino	24/3/88	8:30–9:00 30min
Ando Electrical (Tokyo)	Chairman	K. Ogata	18/2/86	9:30–11:00 1h 30min
			12/3/86	13:00–15:00 2h

Organization	Position	Name	Date	Time
Anjo Electric (Aichi)	Managing Director	M. Yamada	29/1/86	14:00–15:37 1h 37min
	Managing Director	H. Kakeno	29/1/86	14:00–14:56 56min
			28/5/86	14:25–16:40 2h 15min
			14/7/87	10:30–13:22 2h 52min
	Assistant General Manager, Production Control, Production Department	M. Ishikawa	14/7/87	10:30–13:22 2h 52min
	Manager, Administration Sect., General Affairs Dept.	M. Sakakibara	28/5/86	14:25–16:40 2h 15min
			30/5/86	13:40–18:10 4h 30min
			14/7/87	10:30–12:40 2h 10min
AP Technoglass (Ohio)	President	T. Kawauchi	10/2/88	15:30–16:15 45min
	Assistant Director, Sales	T. Takei	10/2/88	15:30–16:15 45min
Aquilla Plastics (Essex, UK)	General Sales Manager	M. S. L. Thomas	24/8/87	9:50–12:45 2h 55min
Art Metal Manufacturing (Nagano)	Executive Director	N. Kono	26/5/88	9:39–11:10 1h 31min
	General Manager, General Affairs	S. Izawa	26/5/88	9:30–11:10 1h 40min
	Manager, Personnel	N. Kanazawa	26/5/88	9:05–12:20 3h 15min
Arvin Sango (Indiana)	Manufacturing Manager	K. Ishigaki	6/3/89	11:35–15:40 4h 5min
	Production Control Manager	M. Yokoyama	6/3/89	11:35–15:40 4h 5min
Atsugi Motor Parts (Kanagawa)	General Manager, Product Management Group, Suspension Division	N. Sakamoto	10/4/89	13:34–17:34 4h
	Manager, Engineering Dept.	A. Yoshizawa	10/4/89	13:34–17:34 4h
	Administration Section, Overseas Operations Dept.	Y. Kai	10/4/89	17:40–18:10 30min
Automobile Peugeot Bart Components Plant (Montbeliard, France)	Director, Logistics Management	C. Dudouet	5/9/88	8:40–15:03 6h 23min
			6/9/88	8:40–14:45 6h 5min
	Production Manager	M. A. Gerin	5/9/88	15:23–18:28 3h 5min

Organization	Position	Name	Date	Time
	Manager, Bureau of Translation and Interpretation	B. Sementery	5/9/88	8:40–18:28 9h 48min
			6/9/88	9:00–17:45 8h 45min
Auto Partes Y Arneses De Mexico (Ciudad Juarez, Mexico)	Presidente	T. Ishihara	24/3/88	14:40–18:15 3h 35min
	Gerente Administrativo	S. Yanagawa	24/3/88	14:40–18:15 3h 35min
			25/3/88	9:20–19:30 10h 10min
Auto Partes Y Arneses De Mexico (Ascencion, Mexico)	Gerente de Planta	T. Ohba	25/3/88	11:55–16:05 4h 10min
Beard Bros. Engineering (London)	Director	G. K. Hake	13/3/85	16:49–18:00 1h 11min
Bendix Chassis & Brake Components Division (Michigan)	Account Representative	S. Masuzawa	16/3/87	15:30–16:30 1h
			18/3/87	17:30–22:30 5h
Bendix Deutschland GmbH (Saar, Germany)	Managing Director	B. Schmeling	2/9/87	14:05–18:15 4h 10min
	Managing Director	S. Vasilache	2/9/87	14:05–18:15 4h 10min
Bevende Moulds & Tools (London)	Managing Director	Ballard	20/3/85	10:18–11:25 1h 7min
	Director	George	20/3/85	10:18–11:25 1h 7min
BGM Engineering (Hampshire, UK)	Managing Director	McGrath	11/4/84	14:12–15:58 1h 46min
Bridgestone Headquarters (Tokyo)	Assistant Manager, Marketing Research Office	H. Shimamatsu	25/7/86	17:00–17:25 25min
	Planning Section, OE Sales Dept., Industrial Rubber Products Division	S. Fukaya	7/4/89	19:30–19:50 20min
Broomhill Electronics (London)	Director, Sales	Lynch	27/8/86	10:14–12:45 2h 31min
Calsonic Corporation Headquarters (Tokyo)	Senior Manager, Planning Dept.	M. Morita	13/4/89	10:30–17:30 7h
	General Manager, Chief Operating Officer for Export & Overseas Operations	A. Sato	13/4/89	10:30–13:30 3h
Calsonic Corporation	General Manager & Plant Manager	N. Komiya	13/4/89	15:35–17:30 1h 55min

Organization	Position	Name	Date	Time
Oppama Plant (Kanagawa)	Deputy Plant Manager	T. Okazaki	13/4/89	15:35–17:30 1h 55min
Calsonic Manufacturing Corporation (Tennessee)	President	K. Arai	8/3/89	11:00–13:20 2h 20min 14:40–15:20 40min
	Executive Vice-President & General Manager	M. Uchida	9/2/88 8/3/89	14:05–15:20 1h 15min 11:40–12:30 50min
	Vice-President, Purchasing	Y. Kato	9/2/88	16:45–17:20 35min
	Vice-President, Engineering Div.	K. Tachi	8/3/88	13:20–15:20 2h
	Director, Total Quality Control	W. A. Bohall	8/3/88	12:30–13:20 50min
	Design Assistant to Vice-President	H. Ochiai	9/2/88	15:20–17:20 2h
	Design Assistant to Vice-President	S. Kiuchi	27/3/88	9:00–11:30 2h 30min
	Assistant to Executive Vice-President	K. Yano	8/3/89	10:30–11:00 30min
Calsonic Yorozu Corporation (Tennessee)	President	K. Maruyama	8/3/89	16:15–16:50 35min
	Executive Vice-President & General Manager	T. Morino	8/3/89	16:15–18:35
Caltech Systems (London)	Managing Director	Caldicourt	22/3/85	10:16–12:06 1h 50min
Cho-onpa Kogyo/Ultrasonic Engineering Tokyo	Sales Manager	J. Tanaka	9/6/86	13:10–14:35 1h 25min
Circolec (Surrey, UK)	Managing Director	J. R. Bell	28/8/86	14:38–16:30 1h 52min
Colt Industries Holley Automotive Division (Michigan)	Vice-President, Sales & Marketing	E. P. Rowady	13/9/87	18:00–18:40 40min
Columbus Neunkirchen Foundry GmbH (Saar, Germany)	Managing Director	K. Schwarz	4/9/87	10:15–12:30 2h 15min
	Managing Director	K. Regitz	4/9/87	10:15–13:45 3h 30min
Cook & Perkins (London)	General Manager	F. Smith	19/3/85	9:50–11:15 1h 25min
Daiichi Seiki (Tokyo)	Managing Director	K. Ishida	23/5/86	13:10–15:00 1h 50min
	Director, Production Manager	T. Hatakeyama	23/5/86	13:10–15:00 1h 50min

Organization	Position	Name	Date	Time
	Manager, Control Dept.	Y. Doi	23/5/86	14:20–15:00 40min
Denki (Tijuana, Mexico)	President	U. Nogami	23/3/88	14:12–15:00 48min
	Vice-President	T. Nogami	23/3/88	14:12–15:00 48min
	Plant Manager	R. Delgato	23/3/88	14:12–15:00 48min
Diamond Denki (Osaka)	President	S. Ikenaga	7/4/89	19:10–19:30 20min
Diesel Kiki USA Co., Ltd. (Dallas, Texas)	President	T. Tani	25/3/87	11:00–16:15 5h 15min
	Assistant to Vice-President	M. Sekino	25/3/87	11:00–13:00 2h
Dowling and Fransen Engineers (Middlesex, UK)	Chairman	J. S. Dowling	19/3/85	14:40–16:25 1h 45min
	Managing Director	Ann[b]	19/3/85	14:40–16:25 1h 45min
ECIA Audincourt Plant (France)	Director, Audincourt Production Center	G. Grosjean	6/9/88	17:00–17:45 45min
	Production Manager	A. Tramaille	6/9/88	14:55–17:45 2h 50min
ECIA Beaulieu Plant (Valentigney, France)	Service Manager	R. Gauthier	6/9/88	8:40–14:45 6h 5min
	Director, Social Relations	B. Panchot	6/9/88	12:30–14:45 2h 15min
Elionix (Tokyo)	President	I. Okazaki	24/5/86	9:50–12:10 2h 20min
	Director & Deputy General Manager, Sales Dept.	S. Honme	24/5/86	10:50–12:10 1h 20min
	Manager, General Affairs & Accounting	M. Hirano	24/5/86	9:30–10:30 1h
Enzan Fuji (Yamanashi)	President	I. Nakano	3/4/86	14:00–16:20 2h 20min
Ernest F. Moy (London)	Managing Director	W. M. Weir	21/3/85	9:58–12:03 2h 5min
Fisher Group (Michigan)	Executive Vice-President, Strategic Planning	M. J. King	20/10/88	19:00–21:20 2h 20min
Ford Monroe Plant (Michigan)	Assistant Plant Manager	G. A. Cockerill	11/2/88	15:02–16:15 1h 13min
	Manager, Manufacturing Engineering	H. H. Seidel	11/2/88	15:02–16:15 1h 13min
Fukoku (Saitama)	Director	J. Kawamoto	1/6/87	11:30–12:00 30min
			11/6/87	18:00–21:00 3h

Organization	Position	Name	Date	Time
Fukunaga Denshi Kogyo (Tokyo)	President	Fukunaga	17/6/86	15:00–16:45 1h 45min
General Motors AC Spark Plug Division (Michigan)	Manufacturing Systems Engineer	S. McCan	21/4/87	10:15–11:20 1h 5min
			24/4/87	14:30–16:00 1h 30min
	Purchasing Agent	L. Baran	28/4/87	15:10–16:50 1h 40min
	Industry Analyst	M. Horton	2/10/87	10:30–11:00 30min
			20/8/87	15:50–16:30 40min
General Motors Delco Electronics Division (Indiana)	Manager, Purchasing	J. R. Stark	27/4/87	13:55–17:00 3h 5min
	Manager, Public Relations	M. Y. Grant	27/4/87	13:55–17:00 3h 5min
General Motors Delco Moraine Division (Ohio)	Supervisor Linings	B. T. Beck	16/11/87	10:00–11:15 1h 15min
			25/11/87	12:00–14:00 2h
			2/12/87	12:00–14:00 2h
General Motors Delco Remy Division (Indiana)	Plant Manager	D. M. Abel	27/4/87	7:45–10:10 2h 25min
	Production Control Plant 11	S. Smith	27/4/87	7:45–10:10 2h 25min
	Staff Assistant, Public Relations	M. Beach	27/4/87	7:45–11:25 3h 40min
	Director, Quality, Materials & Operation Support	W. L. Steinbrunner	27/4/87	10:20–11:25 1h 5min
	Divisional Coordinator, Production Readiness, Just-in-Time Manufacturing	J. A. Orbik	27/4/87	10:20–11:25 1h 5min
	Superintendent, Customer Service	S. D. Montgomery	27/4/87	10:20–11:25 1h 5min
General Motors Packard Electric Division (Ohio)	Director, Materials Management	J. J. Martin	30/4/87	8:20–13:20 5h
			29/10/87	10:45–11:10 25min
	Purchasing Manager	J. R. Anderson	30/4/87	8:20–13:20 5h
	Purchasing Administrator	L. Wolfe	30/4/87	9:26–14:28 5h 2min
	Cooperative Involvement Engineer	F. Gillett	9/11/88	10:20–11:40 1h 20min

Organization	Position	Name	Date	Time
General Motors Packard Electric Mexican Operations (El Paso, Texas)	General Manager	J. L. Williams	22/3/88	8:20–9:05 45min
General Motors Packard Electric Rio Bravo Electricos Planta IV (Ciudad Juarez, Mexico)	Plant Manager	J. P. Walker	22/3/88	8:20–15:20 7h
	Manager, Material Control	B. Holloway	22/3/88	9:35–12:10 2h 35min
	Plant Superintendent	E. P. Castro	22/3/88	9:35–12:10 2h 35min
GKN plc (Worcestershire, UK)	Head of Business & Economic Appraisal	I. M. Handley	19/9/86	14:00–15:00 1h
GKN Automotive Components (Michigan)	Manager, Investment Analysis	D. H. Norton	19/9/86	14:00–15:00 1h
GKN Technology (West Midlands, UK)	Director, Research & Development Resources	T. B. Smith	5/9/86	10:10–14:10 4h
	Manager, Technical Strategy	J. Pullen	5/9/86	12:40–14:10 1h 30min
	Head of Strategic Technologies	A. Millar	5/9/86	11:20–11:40 20min
	Group Head, Experimental Stress Analysis	G. Oakley	5/9/86	11:40–12:00 20min
	Project Engineer	T. Powell	5/9/86	12:00–12:20 20min
	Section Head, Composite Leaf Spring Development	L. T. Gobbon	5/9/86	12:20–12:40 20min
Halbergerhuette (Saar, Germany)	Managing Director, Automotive Casting	K. Westphal	31/8/87	15:14–17:20 2h 6min
	Director, Sales (Export)	J. Riedel	31/8/87	15:14–17:20 2h 6min
Hi-Lex Corporation (Michigan)	Production Manager	Y. Fukuda	26/3/87	13:45–16:30 2h 45min
Hitachi Automotive Products (USA), Inc. (Kentucky)	President	A. Okumura	27/10/88	9:20–17:27 8h 7min
	Vice-President & Corporate Secretary	A. Harada	27/10/88	13:30–17:27 3h 57min
	Dept. Manager, Localization Project Dept.	H. Ide	27/10/88	13:30–17:27 3h 57min
	Dept. Manager, Production Planning	S. Matsumoto	27/10/88	17:05–17:27 22min
	Manager, Production Dept.	I. Watanabe	27/10/88	9:35–11:07 1h 32min

Organization	Position	Name	Date	Time
	Treasury Dept. Manager, Accounting	M. Yamaoka	26/10/88	21:00–23:30 2h 30min
			27/10/88	9:20–17:27 8h 7min
Hitachi Shonan Electronics (Kanagawa)	Director	R. Kimura	12/2/86	16:00–20:00 4h
Horiuchi Seisakusho (Yamanashi)	President	M. Horiuchi	3/4/86	16:50–17:20 30min
Hydro-Quebec (Montreal)	Industrial Development, Senior Representative	L. G. Boucher	5/2/87	10:30–12:30 13:30–14:30 3h
Ide Seiki Seisakusho (Tokyo)	President	R. Ide	30/6/86	13:40–15:50 1h 10min
Ishii Seiki Seisakusho (Kanagawa)	President	T. Ishii	11/7/86	13:55–15:15 1h 20min
Ishijitsu Mekki Kogyosho (Aichi)	Director & Engineering Manager	M. Sugiyama	30/5/86	14:26–15:19 53min
Ishikawa Kogyo Gotenba Plant (Shizuoka)	Manager, Production Sect.	M. Koitabashi	4/7/86	12:54–15:20 2h 26min
	Manager, Engineering Sect.	H. Tsuda	4/7/86	12:54–15:20 2h 26min
ITT Automotive, Inc. (Michigan)	Vice-President, Sales & Marketing	L. Gene Stohler	17/3/87	10:40–11:15 35min
	Business Market Research Manager	J. Brozovich	28/4/87	11:30–12:30 1h
JE, Inc. (Michigan)	General Manager	A. Burnham	19/3/87	9:50–11:45 1h 55min
	Comptroller	M. Kirby	19/3/87	9:50–11:45 1h 55min
JIDECO of Bardstown (Kentucky)	President	M. Hirano	7/3/89	11:30–15:55 4h 25min
	Vice-President, Engineering	S. Ishihara	7/3/89	11:30–15:55 4h 25min
Jidosha Kiki Headquarters (Tokyo)	Managing Director, Overseas Division	T. Hayashida	7/4/89	18:10–18:30 20min
	Deputy Manager, Marketing Planning, & Sales	K. Hibiya	7/4/89	18:10–18:30 20min
Johnson Controls (Kentucky)	General Manager	D. Buchenberger	8/2/88	13:15–14:55 1h 40min
	Plant Engineer	R. C. Jaeger	8/2/88	13:15–14:55 1h 40min
	Toyota Project Manager	W. R. Peak	8/2/88	13:15–14:55 1h 40min

Organization	Position	Name	Date	Time
Kaiseisha (Ibaragi)	Manager, Car Electronics Dept.	M. Mashiko	26/3/86	14:20–17:38 3h 18min
	Manager, Purchasing Dept.	T. Sato	26/3/86	14:20–17:38 3h 18min
Kanagawa Kiko (Kanagawa)	President	H. Ishida	8/5/86	15:15–16:15 1h
Kanto Auto Works Headquarters & Assembly Plant (Kanagawa)	Manager, Purchasing Control Sect., Purchasing Dept.	K. Arakawa	24/6/86	16:25–18:10 1h 45min 18:40–21:20 2h 40min
	Staff, Purchasing Control Sect., Purchasing Dept.	M. Hakozaki	24/6/86	16:25–18:10 1h 45min 18:40–21:20 2h 40min
			4/7/86	15:40–17:25 1h 45min
	Manager, Technology Control Dept.	H. Sakurai	24/6/86	13:40–16:25 2h 45min 18:40–21:20 2h 40min
	Managing, Training & Education Dept.	H. Shoji	24/6/86	13:40–16:25 2h 45min
	Staff, Personnel Sect., Personnel Dept.	Y. Saito	24/6/86	13:40–16:25 2h 45min
Kanto Seat Manufacturing Gotenba Plant (Shizuoka)	Plant Manager	M. Hiramoto	4/7/86	9:50–12:03 2h 13min
Kantus Corporation (Tennessee)	President	A. Iwashita	30/3/87	10:30–17:30 7h
	Vice-President, Administration	Y. Hososaka	30/3/87	11:30–12:30 14:00–16:10 3h 10min
	Manager, Engineering	K. Sugiyama	30/3/87	9:00–10:20 1h 20min
Keisei Electronics (Kanagawa)	Senior Managing Director	I. Uraga	15/2/84	9:25–12:00 2h 35min
Kikuchi Seisakusho (Tokyo)	President	K. Kikuchi	18/3/86	13:00–16:20 3h 20min
Kitagawa Seisakusho (Kanagawa)	President	R. Kitagawa	11/7/86	10:10–12:00 1h 50min
Koito Manufacturing Haibara Plant (Shizuoka)	Deputy Plant Manager	H. Kodama	3/6/88	10:10–14:00 3h 50min
	Manager, Production Control	S. Arai	3/6/88	10:10–14:00 3h 50min
	Manager, Finance Dept.	K. Ishimoto	3/6/88	9:20–14:00 4h 40min

Organization	Position	Name	Date	Time
	Assistant Manager, Finance Dept.	S. Matsuura	3/6/88	9:20–14:00 4h 40min
Kokan Kako (Kanagawa)	Director, Marketing	K. Maruyama	28/11/86	15:00–16:05 1h 5min
Kondo Seiko (Aichi)	President	T. Kondo	30/5/86	16:00–17:50 1h 50min
Kuhn Werkzeug- und Maschienenbau GmbH (Saar, Germany)	Managing Director	A. Huber	2/9/87	9:00–13:30 4h 30min
Lewisham Engineering (London)	Managing Director	Johnson	12/3/85	14:49–17:02 2h 13min
Lucas CAV Finchley Plant (London)	Manager, Manufacturing Engineering Services	P. Hill	11/3/85	10:00–12:30 2h 30min
Lucas Electrical (Birmingham, UK)	Materials Manager, Starters & Alternators Div.	B. W. Russell	4/9/86	14:19–16:50 2h 31min
			27/8/87	10:15–14:10 3h 55min
	Assistant Manager, Purchasing, Starters & Alternators Div.	B. G. Carty	4/9/86	10:45–14:00 3h 15min
	Manager, Manufacturing Engineering, Starters & Alternators Div.	B. Lilly	4/9/86	14:19–16:50 2h 31min
			27/8/87	10:15–14:10 3h 55min
Lucas Electrical (West Midlands, UK)	Technical Manager, Starters & Alternators Div.	K. Beech	4/9/86	14:19–16:50 2h 31min
	Manager, Starters & Alternators Div.	Bunce	4/9/86	14:19–16:50 2h 31min
	Manager, Systems Development, Starters & Alternators Div.	I. Garth	27/8/87	10:15–14:10 3h 55min
	Manager & Facilitator, Starters & Alternators Div.	Hardy	4/9/86	14:19–16:50 2h 31min
Lucas Electrical Electronics & Systems (Oxfordshire, UK)	Manager, Product Marketing	H. Tulloch	4/9/86	10:14–14:00 3h 46min
Lucas Engineering & Systems (West Midlands, UK)	Engineering Manager	P. Johnson	27/8/87	10:15–14:10 3h 55min
	Technical Manager, Machine Systems	R. K. Davis	27/8/87	10:15–14:10 3h 55min

Organization	Position	Name	Date	Time
Lucas Girling Cwmbran Plant (Wales, UK)	Factory Manager	D. G. Bundred	26/8/87	10:45–15:06 4h 21min
Lucas Girling Pontypool Plant (Wales, UK)	Factory Manager	J. E. Gidney	26/8/87	10:45–16:30 5h 45min
	Programme Manager, European Car Brake Systems, U.K.	C. F. Thompson	26/8/87	10:45–16:30 5h 45min
	Programme Manager	D. Savage	26/8/87	10:45–13:25 15:52–16:30 3h 18min
	Technical Module Leader	N. Williams	26/8/87	13:15–15:06 1h 51min
	Manufacturing Manager	Michael	26/8/87	13:15–13:30 15min
Lucas Industries Lucas Services (Birmingham, UK)	Director & Group Controller	D. R. Shackley	26/8/87 27/8/87	10:45–16:30 5h 45min 10:15–17:10 6h 55min
Lucas Research Centre (West Midlands, UK)	Director	B. R. Jones	4/9/86	10:45–12:45 2h
	Commercial Controller	J. Skinner	4/9/86	10:14–14:00 3h 46min
	Public Relations Officer	B. T. Hill	4/9/86	10:14–14:00 3h 46min
Lynton Engineering (London)	Managing Director	Aranson	14/3/85	14:16–15:07 51min
Maruyama Seisakusho (Tokyo)	President	N. Maruyama	27/6/86	13:30–15:00 1h 30min
Matsuzaki Seiki (Fukushima)	President	Matsuzaki	13/1/84	10:00–10:30 30min
McGill Engineering (London)	Director	Cox	13/3/85	10:30–11:22 52min
Melborha Engineering (Herts., UK)	Managing Director	J. Taylor	14/3/85	10:54–12:20 1h 26min
Micro Research (Tokyo)	General Manager, Control Department	M. Hiramoto	18/3/86	9:30–11:25 1h 55min
Miharu Electric (Fukushima)	Managing Director & Plant Manager	T. Matsumaru	13/1/84	9:00–15:00 6h
Millipore (Massachusetts)	Director, Corporate Planning	E. Ward	8/8/89	10:05–11:00 55min
	Corporate Planning Analyst	R. B. Hawley	8/8/89	10:05–11:00 55min
Miyako Gomu (Tokyo)	President	Miyako	4/6/86 8/6/86	14:15–17:00 2h 45min 16:15–19:05 2h 50min

Organization	Position	Name	Date	Time
Miyachu Seiki (Chiba)	President	H. Kamata	6/2/84	9:20–12:45 3h 25min
	Managing Director	T. Toyao	6/2/84	9:20–12:45 3h 25min
MMC Services (Illinois)	Executive Vice-President & General Manager	M. Naito	12/2/88	14:20–15:27 1h 7min
Modine Manufacturing Company (Wisconsin)	Vice-President, Technical Services	Z. P. Saperstein	12/9/89	18:00–18:45 45min
Murray Productions (Middlesex, UK)	Director, Production	A. G. Bell	18/3/85	15:28–17:00 1h 32min
Nakamura Seiki (Tokyo)	President	S. Nakamura	27/6/86	15:45–17:10 1h 25min
New Atomic Brazing (Middlesex, UK)	Managing Director	M. R. Naylor	13/3/85	14:15–16:10 1h 55min
NHK International Corporation (Illinois)	President	H. Miyazaki	2/4/87	12:00–15:30 3h 30min
Nihon Tectron (Kanagawa)	President	I. Yanagida	31/1/84	15:30–16:00 30min
Nippondenso Headquarters (Aichi)	Director & General Manager, Corporate Planning Center	T. Iwaide	13/7/87	12:50–13:30 40min
			14/7/87	9:50–10:30 40min
	Assistant General Manager, Planning & Research, Corporate Planning Center	K. Furuta	13/7/87	12:50–17:25 4h 35min
			14/7/87	9:50–10:30 13:10–16:30 4h
	Assistant Manager, Planning & Research, Corporate Planning Center	T. Isogai	13/7/87	12:50–14:00 1h 10min
			14/7/87	9:50–13:56 4h 6min
	General Manager, Affiliated Companies Planning Center	S. Itaya	29/1/86	10:30–12:50 13:50–16:00 4h 30min
			29/5/86	10:10–10:20 16:20–16:45 35min
	Assistant Manager, Affiliated Companies Planning Center	T. Tsutsui	29/5/86	10:10–12:10 2h
	Staff, Affiliated Companies Planning Center	Y. Ito	29/5/86	10:10–13:00 2h 50min
			24/6/86	14:00–14:30 30min

Organization	Position	Name	Date	Time
	Assistant General Manager, Personnel Dept.	Y. Marumoto	29/5/86	13:00–14:35 15:20–16:20 2h 35min
Nippondenso Anjo Plant (Aichi)	General Manager, Administration Office	H. Takeuchi	13/7/87	14:22–14:52 30min
	Manager, Starter Production Sect. 4, Engine Electrical Products Mfg. Dept.	T. Takagi	13/7/87	14:25–16:55 2h 30min
	Manager, Alternator Production Sect., Engine Electrical Mfg. Dept.	Totsuku	13/7/87	15:38–16:55 1h 17min
Nippondenso Tokyo Office (Tokyo)	General Manager	T. Watanabe	7/4/89	18:50–19:10 20min
Nippondenso Manufacturing USA Inc. (Michigan)	Treasurer & Senior Manager	T. Doi	27/3/87	9:45–14:15 4h 30min
Nisshin Kogyo (Nagano)	Manager, Total Quality Control & General Affairs	T. Miyashita	26/5/88	13:35–17:20 3h 45min
	Manager, Production Engineering & Investigation	S. Nezu	26/5/88	13:35–17:20 3h 45min
North American Lighting Inc. (Illinois)	Vice-President	Y. Saegusa	24/3/87	11:40–17:30 5h 50min
Ohkuma Electronics (Fukushima)	President	Ohkuma	13/1/84	11:40–12:20 40min
Ohse Kogyo (Kanagawa)	Senior Managing Director	H. Ohse	22/4/86	15:00–15:20 20min
	Managing Director	S. Ohse	22/4/86	14:20–16:15 17:20–22:00 6h 35min
	Assistant Manager, General Afairs	T. Yamazaki	22/4/86	19:00–20:00 1h
Omega Dynamics (London)	Director	Parslow	22/3/85	14:30–15:50 1h 20min
Padmic Engineering (Middlesex, UK)	Managing Director	Jones	18/3/85	10:40–13:00 2h 20min
Paragon Engineering Group/London Foundries (London)	Group Managing Director	J. D. Crisfield	12/3/85	11:20–12:40 1h 20min

Organization	Position	Name	Date	Time
Parker Seal de Baja (Tijuana, Mexico)	General Manager	S. D. Barnes	23/3/88	15:12–16:10 58min
Paul Escare (London)	Director	Schreiber	14/3/85	15:50–17:00 1h 10min
	Works Manager	Duckewt	14/3/85	15:50–17:00 1h 10min
Pebra GmbH Paulbraun (Saar, Germany)	Managing Director	W. Fritsch	3/9/87	9:00–19:25 10h 25min
	Plant Manager	O. Schmid	3/9/87	9:40–11:20 1h 40min
Penstone (Michigan)	President	Y. Okada	11/2/88	13:10–14:30 1h 20min
	Executive Vice-President	T. Hiraoka	11/2/88	13:10–14:30 1h 20min
Pioneer Industrial Components (Ohio)	Vice-President, Marketing	T. Nakano	13/1/88	16:55–17:20 25min
	Manager, Sales & Marketing	T. Kasahara	28/10/88	9:45–13:00 3h 15min
Precision Machining Engineers (Middlesex, UK)	Managing Director	M. T. Craig	20/3/85	14:12–15:52 1h 40min
Press Kogyo (Kanagawa)	Managing Director	T. Toyota	7/4/89	18:30–18:50 20min
Press Service (Tokyo)	Staff, Sales	H. Takao	11/1/84	15:00–15:50 50min
Pre-Tech (Tokyo)	General Manager, Development & Technical Dept., Industrial Machinery Div.	Y. Harada	23/5/86	9:30–11:30 2h
	General Manager, General Affairs Dept.	M. Hasumi	23/5/86	9:55–11:30 1h 35min
R.C.S. Precision Tools (Essex, UK)	Managing Director	P. Emery	15/3/85	15:40–16:35 55min
Reinshagen Headquarters and Wuppertal Plant (Germany)	General Manager, Automotive Harnesses Manufacturing	N. Geisinger	15/9/88	9:15–16:50 7h 35min
	Manager, Systems Engineering	J. Schmitt	15/9/88	10:13–12:15 2h 2min
	Department Manager, Electronics Development, Automobile Industry Dept.	H. W. Schlamm	15/9/88	10:13–12:15 2h 2min
	Section Manager, Retail Sales, Special Products, Cables & Wires Dept.	P. G. Ranft	15/9/88	10:05–12:15 2h 10min

Organization	Position	Name	Date	Time
	Line Leader, Composite Technical, Automobile Industry Dept.	K. Enneper	15/9/88	10:05–12:15 2h 10min
	Production Manager, Cables & Wires	Kind	15/9/88	12:25–12:45 20min
Reinshagen Bochum-Linden & Bochum-Grumme Plants (Germany)	Director & Works Manager, Auto Accessories Dept.	V. Zinsser	15/9/88	13:20–16:50 3h 30min
	Plant Manager, Wiring Systems Production, Auto Accessories Dept.	P. Wolfram	15/9/88	13:20–16:50 3h 30min
	Customer Service, Wiring Systems Production, Auto Accessories Dept.	A. Schmitz	14/9/88 15/9/88	17:50–19:00 19:20–21:20 3h 10min 9:15–16:50 7h 35min
Renault Industrie du Tournaisis (Tournai, Belgium)	Director-General	A. Heymans	7/9/87	9:00–16:50 7h 50min
	Plant Manager	J. Guidet	7/9/87	9:57–16:50 6h 53min
	Manager, Technical Services	C. Heymans	7/9/87	9:57–16:50 6h 53min
	Manager, Administration & Finance	J. Havaux	7/9/87	9:10–10:00 50min
Richmond Research (London)	Managing Director	R. J. Peto	27/8/86 29/8/86	15:30–17:20 1h 50min 11:49–13:00 1h 11min
Rists Headquarters & Newcastle Plant (S. Ys., UK)	Director & General Manager	P. Catlow	9/9/88	12:00–15:10 3h 10min
	Operations Director	M. Bennett	8/9/88 9/9/88	19:00–22:00 3h 9:00–15:10 6h 10min
	Chief Buyer	R. J. Evans	27/8/87 4/9/88	10:15–14:10 3h 55min 10:20–10:40 20min
	Manufacturing Manager	M. Holland	9/9/88	9:00–12:00 3h
	Rover 800 Series Task Force Leader	Christopher	9/9/88	9:00–12:00 3h
	Module Manager	Steve	9/9/88	9:00–12:00 3h
	Manufacturing Manager	M. Beckwith	9/9/88	9:00–12:00 3h

Organization	Position	Name	Date	Time
Rists Ystradgynlais Plant (Wales, UK)	Operations Manager	T. Jones	8/9/88	9:10–10:07 12:30–16:00 4h 27min
	Module Manager	C. Mann	8/9/88	10:07–11:14 1h 7min
	Production Manager	A. Smith	8/9/88	11:14–16:00 4h 46min
SAF (France)	Director, Production	J. L. Mounier	7/9/88	9:55–16:00 6h 5min
	Plant Manager, Electrical Facilities	J. Hennegrave	7/9/88	9:55–16:00 6h 5min
San-yu Seisakusho (Ibaragi)	President	Y. Katogi	24/4/86	14:00–15:20 1h 20min
Schaeffler Waelzlager GmbH (Saar, Germany)	Purchasing Manager	B. Bauer	1/9/87	17:30–18:30 1h
Senbokuya Seisakusho (Kanagawa)	Managing Director	S. Takahashi	12/2/86	10:45–12:00 1h 15min
	Director, Marketing	T. Aoyama	12/2/86	9:20–13:00 3h 40min
SGF (Montreal)	Director, Analysis & Investment, Aluminium	M. Desmeules	5/2/87	10:30–12:30 13:30–14:30 3h
	Director, Development Projects	B. Hamel	5/2/87	10:30–12:30 13:30–14:30 3h
Shinkawa (Tokyo)	Director, Procurement & Production Control Div.	H. Ohnishi	30/6/86	13:20–17:20 4h
Shinko Denshi (Tokyo)	President	Y. Nishiguchi	4/6/88	18:00–20:30 2h 30min
Shinsei Kogyo (Aichi)	Managing Director & General Manager, Administration Dept. 2	H. Hayashi	14/7/87	14:15–16:05 1h 50min
	Assistant Manager, Administration Dept. 2	M. Yoshikawa	14/7/87	14:15–16:05 1h 50min
Showa Aluminum Corporation of America (Ohio)	Executive Vice-President	A. Furusawa	4/4/87	10:40–12:50 2h 10min
SK Electronics Kogyo (Fukushima)	Senior Managing Director	S. Takagi	12/1/84	17:05–19:05 2h
	Production Manager	S. Narita	12/1/84	17:05–19:05 2h
	Procurement Manager	Y. Kamiho	12/1/84	17:05–19:05 2h
Solent Electronics (Hants., UK)	Chairman	J. R. Machin	11/4/84	10:07–12:45 2h 38min
Solid Kogyo (Nagano)	President	Fukai	27/5/88	10:50–11:25 35min

Organization	Position	Name	Date	Time
Sumitomo Wiring Systems Headquarters (Mie)	Senior Engineer, Production Engineering Sect., Production Engineering Dept.	H. Ishikawa	8/9/88	11:14–16:00 4h 46min
Sumitomo Electric Wiring Systems (Kentucky)	Vice-President	T. Fukui	26/10/88	10:15–12:50 13:50–16:12 4h 57min
			9/3/89	11:05–13:50 14:50–16:00 3h 55min
	Director, Human Resources & External Affairs	L. W. Davis	26/10/88	10:45–14:30 3h 45min
	Production Manager	Matsunaga	9/3/89	13:50–14:50 1h
	Production Engineer	S. Constant	9/3/89	13:50–14:50 1h
	Personnel Manager	Richard	9/3/89	13:50–14:50 1h
Sumiyoshi Seiki Seisakusho (Tokyo)	Senior Managing Director	M. Sumiyoshi	12/6/86	10:25–12:10 1h 45min
Taiyo Kogyo Co., Ltd. (Tokyo)	Chairman	K. Sakai	1/4/87	16:00–17:00 1h
Tatekita Metal (Nagano)	Director & Plant Manager	K. Hashizume	27/5/88	12:50–14:16 1h 26min
Technica (Tokyo)	President	K. Hiruma	30/6/86	15:00–17:05 2h 5min
Telesis International (Aichi)	First-Class Architect	T. Ishikawa	19/6/89	19:00–20:30 1h 30min
TESEC Corporation (Tokyo)	Manager, Personnel Section, Administration Dept.	K. Nishimori	9/6/86	15:00–17:00 2h
Tokai Denso (Nagoya, Aichi)	President	H. Asai	30/1/86	9:35–12:00 2h 25min
	Senior Managing Director	Y. Suzuki	30/1/86	9:35–12:00 2h 25min
Tokai Metal (Tokyo)	Senior Consultant	Y. Tanaka	18/2/86	9:30–12:00 2h 30min
Tokyo Radiator Manufacturing (Tokyo)	Manager, Purchasing Dept.	Sasaki	30/4/86	13:00–14:00 14:15–16:45 3h 30min
Transcraft Fordertechnik (Saar, Germany)	Managing Director	H. Mang	1/9/87	18:30–19:00 30min
	Chief Engineer	J. Wietzel	1/9/87	19:00–19:45 45min
Trolitan Gebr. Meyer GmbH (Saar, Germany)	Managing Director	K. Meyer	1/9/87	10:10–13:50 3h 40min

Organization	Position	Name	Date	Time
United L-N Glass (Kentucky)	Vice-President & General Manager	D. E. Robinson	8/2/88	15:35–17:05 1h 30min
	Vice-President & Assistant General Manager	K. Sato	8/2/88	15:35–17:05 1h 30min
	Marketing Manager	T. Nakazawa	8/2/88	15:35–17:05 1h 30min
US Steel USX (Michigan)	Manager, Product Applications & International Automotive Sales	P. R. Mould	21/10/88	10:00–10:30 30min
Weyburn-Bartel (Surrey, UK)	General Operating Manager	M. Lee	11/3/85	15:19–17:30 2h 11min
	Sales Manager	W. Hambleton	11/3/85	15:19–17:30 2h 11min
Yanagisawa Koki (Nagano)	Vice-President	Yanagisawa	27/5/88	9:45–10:15 30min
Yokohama Hi-Tech (Kanagawa)	President	K. Mashiko	28/11/86	16:10–16:30 20min
	Senior Researcher	Y. Ojima	28/11/86	16:10–18:35 2h 25min
Yokohama Kiko (Kanagawa)	Managing Director, Planning & Purchasing Dept.	T. Togashi	28/11/86	13:30–15:00 1h 30min
	General Manager, Sales Dept.	T. Hashiura	28/11/86	13:30–15:00 1h 30min
Yoshida Kogyo (Nagano)	President	Y. Yoshida	27/5/88	15:00–17:30 2h 30min

9. *Business consultants and private research organizations*

Organization	Position	Name	Date	Time
Asahi Agency (Tokyo)	Principal Partner	A. Nagashima	23/3/88	9:27–9:47 20min
Bain & Co. (Massachusetts)	Consultant	S. Fukushima	10/5/88	11:40–14:00 2h 20min
Competitive Manufacturing Research (Texas)	President	J. F. Krafcik	13/7/89	11:45–12:30 45min
DesRosiers Automotive Research (Toronto)	President	D. DesRosiers	8/5/87	11:00–12:10 1h 10min
	Research Associate	A. King	8/5/87	11:00–12:10 1h 10min
Gendai Advanced Research Institute (Tokyo)	Senior Researcher, Market Research & Development Dept.	Y. Takayama	4/12/86	17:00–18:50
Industrial Technology Institute (Michigan)	Senior Researcher	M. Flynn	20/3/87	20:00–20:30 30min

Organization	Position	Name	Date	Time
Ingenieurbuero (Munich)	Managing Director	H. Meier	13/9/88	11:30–15:00 3h 30min
Institute for International Economic Studies (Tokyo)	Executive Researcher	N. Tani	9/4/86	18:30–20:10 1h 40min
	Executive Researcher	S. Ohtsuji	9/5/88	12:00–14:00 2h
International Design Experts (California)	Vice-President	J. A. Dubon	23/3/88	12:00–13:00 1h
Japan America Automotive Systems Inc. (Illinois)	President	A. Oshikawa	22/3/87	17:00–19:30 2h 30min
JEMCO (Tokyo)	Director	K. Ochiai	3/3/86	13:30–13:45 16:30–16:45 30min
	Director	K. Murata	3/3/86	13:30–16:30 3h
JMA Consultants (Tokyo)	Director, Engineering, Institute of Science & Technology	T. Sakura	16/2/84	14:00–16:04 2h 8min
Lang Marketing Resources Inc. (New Jersey)	President	J. A. Lang	14/3/87	10:27–12:30 2h 3min
Mars & Co. (Connecticut)	Analyst	Z. J. Fisher	1/3/89	10:00–11:40 1h 40min
	Analyst	C. E. Giblain	1/3/89	10:00–11:40 1h 40min
Mitsubishi Research Institute (Tokyo)	Analyst	A. Takeishi	10/12/89	16:15–17:25 1h 10min
Modern Economics Co. (Massachusetts)	Economic Analysis Consultant	R. C. Wood	20/2/88	20:00–23:00 3h
MUFF of Kunisawa (Tokyo)	President	M. Kunisawa	12/8/88	18:05–23:30 5h 25min
Multisystems (Massachusetts)	President	M. Flusberg	5/2/88	9:00–11:30 2h 30min
Nippon Enterprise Development Corporation (Tokyo)	Managing Director	M. Mizota	27/1/84	11:20–14:00 2h 40min
Nomura Research Institute (Tokyo)	Economist	M. Kichikawa	31/7/87	18:00–22:15 4h 15min
			18/6/88	18:00–23:30 5h 30min
			7/1/89	17:00–21:30 4h 30min

Organization	Position	Name	Date	Time
			9/6/89	18:00–22:20 4h 20min
Oakes Associates (California)	President	R. C. Oakes	17/3/87	14:00–14:30 30min
PADECO Co., Ltd. (Tokyo)	President	Y. Motomura	5/4/88	18:30–20:30 2h
P.D.S. International Ltd. (Tokyo)	President	A. Takayama	17/3/87	21:00–23:00 2h
PRIME (California)	President	I. Wachi	23/3/88	7:30–9:10 1h 40min
Ross Associates (California)	President	H. R. Ross	13/9/86	20:00–20:30 30min
SMC (Massachusetts)	President	R. J. Rosenberg	1/4/87	18:50–19:30 40min
Synergistic Systems (Florida)	President	L. Wintrode	5/2/88	9:00–11:30 2h 30min

10. *Trading companies*

Organization	Position	Name	Date	Time
Atisa & Associates (Tijuana, Mexico)	President	B. I. Sanders	23/3/88	13:15–14:05 50min
C. Itoh & Co. (Tokyo)	Managing Director, Corporate Planning Div.	Y. Nakayama	27/1/84	11:20–14:00 2h 40min
	General Manager, New Technology Dept.	K. Ohmura	27/1/84	11:20–14:00 2h 40min
	General Manager, Overseas Market Dept.	N. Suzuki	27/1/84	11:20–14:00 2h 40min
Mitsui & Co. (USA), Inc. (California)	Manager	M. Kaneko	23/3/88	10:27–11:40 1h 13min

11. *Transportation companies*

Organization	Position	Name	Date	Time
Sankyu Co., Ltd. (Tokyo)	Manager, Business Planning	N. Yamamoto	5/4/88	18:30–20:30 2h

12. *Car dealers*

Organization	Position	Name	Date	Time
Honda of Commonwealth (Massachusetts)	Sales Executive	G. A. Silverman	18/1/87	15:00–16:00 1h
	Sales Consultant	D. Iantosca	7/12/87	19:30–21:30 2h
Humphris Oxford Nissan (Oxford, UK)	Sales Executive	C. Theobald	1/9/86	14:00–14:30 30min
Lee Honda (Maine)	Sales Representative	K. R. Richardson	11/10/88	10:30–11:00 30min
Toyota of Boston (Massachusetts)	Sales Executive	S. M. Ayer	16/1/87	19:25–19:45 30min
	Sales Executive	S. Baker	5/10/87	18:00–19:20 1h 20min

Organization	Position	Name	Date	Time
13. *Banks and security companies*				
Salomon Brothers Asia Ltd. (Tokyo)	Auditor, Internal Audit	Y. Ohta	9/4/89	13:00–15:00 2h
Dai-ichi Kangyo Bank Chicago Branch (Chicago)	Vice-President, Corporate Finance	M. Murata	2/4/87	12:00–15:30 3h 30min
			14/10/87	15:20–17:00 1h 40min
			20/1/88	12:00–14:00 2h
Export–Import Bank of Japan (Tokyo)	Senior Economist, Research Institute of Overseas Investment	M. Ishii	13/10/89	15:45–17:30 1h 45min
	Economist, Research Institute of Overseas Investment	H. Takaoka	13/10/89	15:45–17:30 1h 45min
14. *Journalists*				
Asahi Shinbunsha (Tokyo)	Staff Writer, Asahi Weekly *AERA*	A. Tsuji	1/4/88	15:00–16:00 1h
			5/4/88	12:00–13:40 1h 40min
Automotive News, Tokyo Bureau (Tokyo)	Tokyo Bureau Chief	M. A. Maskery	14/4/89	17:00–20:30 3h 30min
Car Sensor (Tokyo)	Editor-in-Chief	T. Yoshihara	29/6/87	16:00–18:10 2h 10min
	Senior Editorial Coordinator	K. Horigome	29/6/87	16:00–18:10 2h 10min
	Editorial Director	K. Yamashita	29/6/87	16:00–17:30 1h 30min
NHK (Tokyo)	News Commentator	H. Oyama	15/7/87	14:30–15:30 1h
Nihon Keizai Shinbunsha (Tokyo)	Staff Writer, Business News Dept., Editorial Bureau	Y. Ohta	21/6/89	15:05–15:50 45min
Mainichi Shinbunsha (Tokyo)	Editor, *Ekonomisuto*	M. Sato	25/11/86	19:00–19:50 50min
			27/11/86	10:00–11:20 1h 20min
Nikkan Jidosha Shinbun (Tokyo)	Staff Writer	H. Nemoto	7/4/89	13:00–13:00 30min
Shogakukan (Tokyo)	Senior Editor, *Weekly Post Economics Today*	M. Suzuki	2/11/88	19:00–22:30 3h 30min

Organization	Position	Name	Date	Time

15. *Academic Institutions*

Note: Interviews, scheduled meetings, official supervisions (* supervisors have asterisks) and study
   sessions on topics related to this study. In alphabetical order by individuals' names.

Organization	Position	Name	Date	Time
MIT (Massachusetts)	Project Director, Program on Communications Policy	D. B. Allen	4/8/87	14:00–17:00 3h
Oregon State Univ.	Professor of Management, College of Business	M. Amano	8/3/89	12:30–13:20 50min
Wolverhampton Polytechnic (West Midlands, UK)	Lecturer, Government–Industry Relations	Appleton	6/12/85	12:00–17:30 5h 30min
Univ. of Sussex (Brighton, UK)	Researcher, Institute of Manpower Studies	J. Atkinson	2/12/85	14:30–15:50 1h 20min
Univ. of Sussex (Brighton, UK)	Research Fellow, Science Policy Research Unit	Y. Baba	3/9/86	17:00–21:00 4h
Univ. of Oxford (UK)	Faculty Fellow, Dean, & Lecturer in Industrial Sociology, Nuffield College	E. V. Batstone*	24/6/83	16:00–17:33 1h 33min
			24/10/83	10:30–11:38 1h 8min
			29/11/83	14:00–15:30 1h 30min
			2/7/84	16:15–18:08 1h 53min
			8/1/85	16:00–17:40 1h 40min
			23/5/85	11:30–13:05 1h 35min
			19/8/85	13:49–15:05 1h 16min
			27/8/85	13:43–15:05 1h 22min
			24/9/85	12:30–13:40 1h 10min
MIT (Massachusetts)	Ph.D. Candidate, Sloan School of Management	M. Bensaou	23/10/89	11:10–11:50 40min
			30/10/89	11:30–14:00 2h 30min
Stanford Univ. (California)	Visiting Professor, Graduate School of Business	H. C. de Bettignies	3/3/89	12:30–13:45 1h 15min
MIT (Massachusetts)	M.Sc. Student	A. Camuffo	7/11/89	12:00–14:05 2h 5min
Harvard Univ. (Massachusetts)	Professor, Graduate School of Business Administration	K. B. Clark	9/1/89	12:00–13:15 1h 15min
Univ. of Michigan	Professor, Dept. of Sociology	R. E. Cole	20/3/87	20:00–22:30 2h 30min

Organization	Position	Name	Date	Time
INSEAD (Fontainebleau)	Assoc. Professor, Business Policy	K. Cool	17/2/89	9:30–10:00 30min
MIT (Massachusetts)	Assist. Professor, Sloan School of Management	M. A. Cusumano	3/12/87	12:00–13:30 1h 30min
			1/4/88	12:45–14:25 1h 40min
			27/6/88	12:00–13:55 1h 55min
			24/10/88	12:45–14:00 1h 15min
INSEAD (Fontainebleau)	Assoc. Professor, Technology Management	A. De Meyer	16/2/89	14:30–15:30 1h
Technical Change Centre (London)	Professor & Assistant Director	R. P. Dore*	3/12/85	10:30–11:45 1h 15min
Univ. of London	Director, Center for Japanese & Comparative Industrial Research, Imperial College	R. P. Dore*	13/4/87	14:45–15:56 1h 11min
			30/5/87	10:00–11:55 1h 55min
			7/2/88	11:00–12:20 1h 20min
			17/3/88	11:00–15:50 4h 50min
			4/5/88	10:00–10:30 30min
			19/9/88	9:30–11:30 12:30–13:45 3h 15min
			24/9/88	13:06–13:26 20min
			17/5/89	15:00–16:40 1h 40min
			6/10/89	9:00–10:50 16:15–16:45 2h 20min
INSEAD (Fontainebleau)	Professor, Business Policy	Y. L. Doz	17/2/89	14:30–15:00 30min
Chuo Univ. (Tokyo)	Professor, Dept. of Economics	E. Eguchi	16/8/86	16:00–18:45 2h 45min
INSEAD (Fontainebleau)	Assoc. Professor, Production & Operations Management	K. Ferdows	16/2/89	16:00–16:45 45min
INSEAD (Fontainebleau)	Professor, Euro-Asia Centre	W. M. Fruin	29/9/89	14:30–16:00 1h 30min
Harvard Univ. (Massachusetts)	D.B.A. Candidate, Graduate School of Business Administration	T. Fujimoto	23/9/89	18:30–23:30 5h
Harvard Univ. (Massachusetts)	Assoc. Professor, Graduate School of Business Administration	D. A. Garvin	28/2/89	11:45–12:30 45min

Organization	Position	Name	Date	Time
Univ. of Oxford (UK)	Official Fellow, Sociology, Nuffield College	J. H. Goldthorpe*	5/11/82	14:00–15:10 1h 10min
			3/2/83	14:30–16:05 1h 35min
			10/3/83	16:15–17:38 1h 23min
			5/5/83	15:00–16:30 1h 30min
			15/6/83	9:30–11:10 1h 40min
			24/10/83	14:00–15:30 1h 30min
			28/11/83	14:05–15:18 1h 13min
			20/6/84	16:35–19:53 3h 18min
			17/12/84	15:23–16:10 47min
			21/12/84	15:45–18:00 2h 15min
			21/1/85	16:39–18:00 1h 21min
			23/5/85	16:41–17:45 1h 4min
			19/8/85	15:18–16:23 1h 5min
			27/8/85	15:07–16:25 1h 18min
			10/10/85	14:00–15:15 1h 15min
			20/12/85	15:00–16:30 1h 30min
			24/8/87	20:30–22:26 1h 56min
			10/9/88	11:15–12:56 1h 41min
Univ. of Oxford (UK)	Fellow, Oxford Centre for Management Studies	D. Gowler	1/11/82	17:00–17:40 40min
Harvard Univ. (Massachusetts)	Assist. Professor, Graduate School of Business Administration	O. Hauptman	27/2/89	13:00–13:45 45min
Chuo Univ. (Tokyo)	Professor of Business Management, Dept. of Commerce	M. Hayashi	7/8/86	16:00–19:30 3h 30min
Harvard Univ. (Massachusetts)	Professor, Graduate School of Business Administration	R. H. Hayes	27/2/89	11:00–11:45 45min
Harvard Univ. (Massachusetts)	Ph. D. Candidate, Dept. of Economics	S. Helper	7/11/86	15:00–17:00 2h
			13/3/87	14:00–15:55 1h 55min
			28/5/87	12:30–15:40 3h 10min
			29/7/87	10:30–12:00 1h 30min

Organization	Position	Name	Date	Time
MIT (Massachusetts)	Ph. D. Candidate, Dept. of Political Science	G. Herrigel	14/10/87	17:45–18:45 1h
			19/10/87	12:00–15:05 3h 5min
			29/10/87	11:00–13:00 2h
			6/11/87	13:30–15:00 1h 30min
			20/11/87	15:00–17:30 2h 30min
			7/12/87	12:00–14:05 2h 5min
Univ. of Tokyo	Professor, Dept. of Economics	T. Hyodo	25/1/84	11:20–13:20 2h
Hannam Univ. (Taejon, S. Korea)	Assoc. Professor, Business Administration	Y. S. Hyun	12/9/89	21:10–22:10 1h
Chuo Univ. (Tokyo)	Professor, Dept. of Economics	M. Ikeda	18/3/85	22:30–02:10 3h 40min
			19/3/85	22:17–24:25 2h 8min
			29/3/85	17:00–18:40 1h 40min
			7/4/86	11:30–13:00 1h 30min
			22/11/86	20:00–21:00 1h
			27/11/86	13:00–17:00 4h
			2/3/87	10:00–11:20 1h 20min
			10/3/87	9:30–10:30 1h
			17/3/87	18:00–19:30 1h 30min
			23/6/87	10:10–11:05 55min
			11/1/88	9:30–10:45 1h 15min
			19/1/88	10:00–11:30 1h 30min
			26/1/88	9:25–9:55 30min
			16/2/88	9:00–10:56 1h 56min
			8/3/88	10:38–11:46 1h 8min
			25/3/88	9:05–9:45 40min
			13/9/88	10:10–11:10 1h
			10/4/88	9:16–10:12 56min

Organization	Position	Name	Date	Time
			15/4/88	14:00–15:10 1h 10min
			4/5/88	10:35–11:45 1h 10min
			27/7/89	14:25–14:20 55min
Hosei Univ. (Tokyo)	Professor, Dept. of Sociology	T. Inagami	23/12/83	14:00–16:15 2h 15min
			2/2/84	21:05–22:10 1h 5min
			4/5/84	13:50–16:25 2h 35min
			7/3/86	18:00–23:00 5h
			12/6/86	14:00–15:00 1h
			16/6/86	15:00–15:50 50min
			14/8/86	11:40–13:55 2h 15min
			23/9/88	19:00–23:45 4h 45min
			30/9/89	19:30–22:30 3h
Chubu Univ. (Aichi)	Professor, Mechanical Engineering	Y. Ishihara	30/1/86	14:00–14:40 40min
Univ. of Tokyo	Assist. Professor, Dept. of Economics	M. Ito	26/11/86	11:00–12:15 1h 15min
Univ. of Kyoto	Assist. Professor, Research Institute of Economics	Ito	3/4/89	18:00–20:40 2h 40min
Harvard Univ. (Massachusetts)	Assoc. Professor, Graduate School of Business Administration	R. Jaikumar	28/2/89	11:00–11:45 45min
Univ. of Sussex (Sussex, UK)	Senior Research Fellow, Science Policy Research Unit	D. T. Jones	2/12/85	11:30–14:00 2h 30min
			3/9/86	11:30–15:00 3h 30min
INSEAD (Fontainebleau)	Professor, Organizational Behavior	A. Laurent	16/2/89	14:00–14:30 30min
Univ. of Rochester (New York)	Assist. Professor, Management & Operations Research	P. J. Lederer	29/7/88	13:30–14:55 1h 25min
Wolverhampton Polytechnic (West Midlands, UK)	Lecturer, Labour Management	Lewis	6/12/85	12:00–17:30 5h 30min
MIT (Massachusetts)	Assist. Professor, Sloan School of Management	R. M. Locke	9/1/89	9:00–10:00 1h
			25/2/89	15:00–16:10 1h 10min

Organization	Position	Name	Date	Time
			23/6/89	12:00–13:10 1h 10min
			23/10/89	13:20–14:00 40min
Univ. of Oxford (UK)	Professor, Economics, & Associate Member, Nuffield College	H. F. Lydall	11/6/85	16:00–17:10 1h 10min
Kansei Gakuin Univ. (Hyogo)	Lecturer, Dept. of Law	T. Kitayama	8/6/89	19:00–23:30 4h 30min
Hosei Univ. (Tokyo)	Professor, Dept. of Business Administration	T. Kiyonari	31/1/84	14:10–16:00 1h 50min
Univ. of Kyoto	Professor, Economic Research Institute	K. Koike	2/2/84	11:00–13:34 2h 34min
Brighton Polytechnic (E. Sussex)	Lecturer, Dept. of Business Studies	R. Lamming	3/9/86	11:30–15:00 3h 30min
			5/3/87	12:20–13:20 1h
			14/3/87	10:27–12:30 2h 3min
			14/4/89	15:30–16:40 1h 10min
MIT (Massachusetts)	NSF Fellow	B. Loyd	15/8/89	13:00–13:53 53min
MIT (Massachusetts)	Researcher, Center for Technology, Policy & Industrial Development	K. R. Magiawala	18/12/86	14:39–16:30 1h 51min
Univ. of California at San Diego	Professor, Economics, Graduate School of International Relations & Pacific Studies	J. McMillan	3/4/89	18:00–20:40 2h 40min
Aoyama Gakuin Univ. (Tokyo)	Professor, Department of Economics	T. Minato	3/6/89	15:30–17:15 1h 45min
Komazawa Univ. (Tokyo)	Assoc. Professor, Dept. of Economics	I. Mitsui	3/3/86	19:00–21:50 2h 50min
Univ. of London	Professor, London School of Economics & Political Science	M. Morishima	31/5/83	14:45–16:00 1h 15min
Univ. of Oxford (UK)	Fellow, Oxford Centre for Management Studies	J. E. Nahapiet*	21/10/82	16:00–17:23 1h 23min
			28/10/82	16:15–17:15 1h
			24/11/82	10:00–11:30 1h 30min
			7/12/82	9:00–10:15 1h 15min
Senshu Univ. (Tokyo)	Professor, Dept. of Economics	H. Nakamura	10/2/84	20:10–21:06 54min
Chubu Univ. (Aichi)	Professor, Electronics Engineering	K. Nishiguchi	28/5/86	19:00–21:00 2h

Organization	Position	Name	Date	Time
Kokushikan Univ. (Tokyo)	Professor, Dept. of Economics	N. Ohnishi	18/2/86	16:15–17:00 45min
Hosei Univ. (Tokyo)	Assoc. Professor, Dept. of Social Sciences	H. Ohyama	31/10/83	15:00–18:00 3h
Osaka City Univ. (Osaka)	Assoc. Professor, Institute of Economic Research	T. Ohshima	6/4/87	17:30–18:00 30min
			23/5/87	18:00–20:00 2h
MIT (Massachusetts)	Director, Center for Technology, Policy & Industrial Development	D. Roos	27/10/86	11:00–12:00 1h
			13/3/87	12:30–13:45 1h 15min
MIT (Massachusetts)	Assoc. Professor, Dept. of Political Science	C. F. Sabel	9/1/87	16:00–17:00 1h
			9/1/87	17:50–18:35 45min
			9/3/87	15:30–18:00 2h 30min
			13/3/87	16:00–18:15 2h 15min
			6/8/87	16:00–19:25 3h 25min
			14/10/87	17:10–18:45 1h 35min
			19/10/87	12:00–15:05 3h 5min
			29/10/87	11:00–13:00 2h
			6/11/87	13:30–15:00 1h 30min
			20/11/87	15:00–17:30 2h 30min
			7/12/87	12:00–14:05 2h 5min
			29/3/88	12:00–12:44 44min
			12/5/88	14:05–15:05 1h
			12/8/88	14:20–15:50 1h 30min
			23/2/89	15:00–16:50 1h 50min
			20/9/89	13:15–14:15 1h
			10/10/89	10:05–10:50 45min
			10/25/89	16:00–17:05 1h 5min
Univ. of London	Lecturer, London School of Economics & Political Science	M. Sako	13/12/88	18:30–19:30 1h

Organization	Position	Name	Date	Time
Kanto-Gakuin Univ. (Kanagawa)	Assoc. Professor, Dept. of Economics	S. Sei	27/11/86	13:00–17:00 4h
			22/3/87	19:30–20:30 1h
			23/3/87	18:30–20:00 1h 30min
			25/3/88	9:55–10:25 30min
			27/3/87	15:00–17:00 2h
			30/3/87	21:00–22:00 1h
			28/4/89	16:45–18:30 1h 45min
			12/6/89	13:20–14:23 1h 3min
			19/6/89	19:00–22:05 3h 5min
			16/8/89	16:00–18:50 2h 50min
Harvard Univ. (Massachusetts)	Professor, Graduate School of Business Administration	R. Shapiro	27/2/89	16:40–5:30 50min
Washington & Lee Univ. (Virginia)	Assist. Professor, Dept. of Economics	M. Smitka	18/4/87	12:00–13:30 1h 30min
			26/1/88	13:00–13:45 45min
			20/2/88	20:00–23:00 3h
			26/7/89	14:30–15:15 45min
			7/7/89	10:45–11:30 45min
			6/10/89	14:05–14:20 15min
			16/10/89	15:04–16:56 1h 52min
Univ. of Oxford (UK)	Fellow, Oxford Centre for Management Studies	R. G. Stewart	10/11/82	10:00–10:40 40min
Univ. of Cambridge (UK)	Professor, Economic History, Christ's College	B. Supple*	26/11/82	14:15–14:45 30min
			4/2/83	13:40–14:05 25min
			21/2/83	12:40–13:05 25min
			4/3/83	12:50–13:10 20min
			29/4/83	12:30–13:00 13:45–14:08 53min
			17/5/83	11:50–12:10 20min

Organization	Position	Name	Date	Time
			2/6/83	15:10–16:00 50min
Hosei Univ. (Tokyo)	Assoc. Professor, Law, Dept. of Sociology	Y. Suwa	8/2/84	14:30–16:20 1h 50min
Aichi Univ. (Aichi)	Assoc. Professor, Dept. of Economics	K. Takasu	31/1/86	13:30–15:30 2h
Univ. of Tokyo	Professor of Industrial Relations, Institute of Social Sciences	H. Totsuka	29/7/83	12:00–13:50 1h 50min
			10/8/83	12:30–14:30 2h
			5/1/84	11:00–14:00 3h
			9/2/84	16:30–20:00 3h 30min
			21/8/85	12:00–14:00 2h
			24/8/85	15:30–17:00 1h 30min
MIT (Massachusetts)	Assist. Professor, Sloan School of Management	M. J. Tyre	18/9/89	10:00–11:00 1h
Univ. of Kyoto	Assoc. Professor, Dept. of Economics	K. Ueda	22/3/85	19:00–19:30 30min
Keio Univ. (Tokyo)	Assoc. Professor, Dept. of Economics	Y. Watanabe	29/3/85	17:00–18:40 1h 40min
			1/12/85	20:00–22:30 2h 30min
			2/12/85	18:00–21:30 3h 30min
			5/12/85	19:00–22:00 3h
Meiji-Gakuin Univ. (Tokyo)	Assoc. Professor, Dept. of Economics	K. Watarai	16/2/84	21:00–21:47 47min
Harvard Univ. (Massachusetts)	Professor, Graduate School of Business Administration	S. C. Wheelwright	28/2/89	10:30–11:00 30min
MIT (Massachusetts)	Assoc. Professor, Sloan School of Management	D. E. Westney	23/11/88	14:00–14:35 35min
Harvard Univ. (Massachusetts)	Fellow, Program on U.S.–Japan Relations	H. Whittaker	5/1/89	12:30–14:45 2h 15min
MIT (Massachusetts)	Research Director, International Motor Vehicle Program	J. P. Womack	26/9/86	10:30–11:30 1h
			26/10/86	15:00–17:30 2h 30min
Univ. of London	Senior Lecturer, London School of Economics & Political Science	S. Wood	8/4/86	19:00–22:00 3h
			9/4/86	16:50–18:10 1h 20min
			16/9/87	18:00–21:30 3h 30min

Organization	Position	Name	Date	Time
Chubu Univ. (Aichi)	Dept. Head Professor, Dept. of Management & Information	T. Yamabe	31/1/86	17:30–19:00 1h 30min
Nagoya Univ. (Aichi)	Lecturer, Dept. of Economics	M. Yamada	15/3/89	11:50–13:50 2h
			3/6/89	15:30–17:15 1h 45min
Korea Advanced Institute of Group Science & Technology (Seoul)	Researcher, Techno-Economics Group	J. E. Yoon	10/12/87	16:30–19:00 2h 30min
Univ. of Venice (Italy)	Assoc. Professor, Business Administration Dept.	G. Volpato	7/11/89	12:00–14:05 2h 5min
MIT (Massachusetts)	Professor, Sloan School of Management	E. Von Hippel	14/12/87	14:00–15:00 1h

[a]Surnames alone indicate that given names or initials were not available.

[b]Given names alone indicate that surnames were not available.

APPENDIX B

Reasons for Subcontracting and Excerpts from Questions Asked

In order to test some of my conclusions, in 1986 I conducted a mail questionnaire survey of forty large Japanese automotive and electronics manufacturers. Because of my limited means, I could not put my ideas to a thorough test. The results of my survey are presented in this appendix, therefore, not so much to strengthen my claims but, rather, to add another stone to the mosaic of the empirical material presented in this study as well as to indicate directions for further inquiry.

Reasons for Subcontracting

In 1984 and 1986 I conducted exploratory and preliminary field research in Japan, interviewing purchasing managers of large automotive and electronics manufacturers. My principle purpose was to determine the purchasing managers' major preoccupations regarding subcontracting. My interview scheme at this stage was unstructured; I was trying to get the most from the interviewees, whom I asked to talk relatively freely in response to my questions. Among the many questions I asked was, "Why contract out?" The answers given differed in terminology, but they clustered around several key conceptual categories. Although there were recognizable overlaps, the reasons to subcontract fell into three broad categories: technological, economic, and operational (in the sense of protecting the stability and viability of internal operations and the work force, by externalizing riskier or more instrumental parts of operations).

I was struck by the fact that almost every interviewee mentioned the subcontractors' specialist technology as one of the key reasons for subcontracting. When I asked what they meant by specialist technology, their responses differed in nuance, but basically they relied on subcontractors because the latter possessed specific technical skills that were either not available in-house or, if available, difficult to manage. This reason was more frequently pointed out as important by motor vehicle than by electronics manufacturers. For example, a Toyota purchasing manager stated that Toyota must continuously rely on its suppliers on a long-term basis,

271

because the latter produced components that could not be made in-house.[1] By contrast, a number of purchasing managers in electronics firms played down the technological factor in subcontracting. A Hitachi purchasing manager at the Tokai plant, one of the world's leading video cassette recorder plants, commented that there was little that it could not make in-house. Further, he pointed out that one of the major reasons for subcontracting was the availability of cheap, nonunionized labor in the surrounding area of Ibaragi prefecture, where the plant was located.[2] This contrast indicates intriguing interindustrial differences in the reasons for subcontracting.

The second category, economic reasons for subcontracting, was also often mentioned and can be divided into two subcategories: direct labor cost and indirect control cost. Economizing on direct labor cost was generally understood as the exploitation of interscale wage differentials and was acknowledged as such by some managers. Subcontractors and temporary workers historically had been extensively used whenever there was both a surge in demand and substantial interscale wage differentials. Although dualism has receded in the Japanese economy since the mid-1960s and the primary producers' reliance on subcontractors for cheap labor alone has also declined, these practices have not entirely disappeared. Interestingly, however, there were also interindustrial differences in the responses regarding the respondents' perception of cheap labor cost as an incentive. Those in the electronics industry did not hesitate to acknowledge this factor in subcontracting firms as an incentive for their use. Conversely, those in the motor vehicle industry tended to deny that cheap labor was a major incentive, because the technological characteristics of many motor vehicle components, they claimed, made it impossible for certain subcontracting firms to participate, however cheaply these firms might bid.

By contrast, the second subcategory of indirect control cost (as opposed to direct labor cost) gained equal support from both automotive and electronics managers. Frequently, they claimed that the proliferation of product variety and the shorter product cycles made it difficult to manage production. Further, permitting subcontractors to specialize in a range of complete products and systems components and to control their own work force and their own lower-tier subcontractors, at their own risk and with their own responsibility, relieved the parent firm of much of its organizational burden.

The third category of subcontracting reasons is operational, in that subcontracting was used in order to protect the regularity of internal operations by dispersing the riskier parts of business elsewhere or by overtly using external production organizations as a buffer against fluctuations in demand. These reasons constitute a central part of the dualist contentions and therefore were closely followed in the interviews (Berger & Piore, 1980). But the emphasis that the field interviewees placed on these operational–dualistic reasons was relatively weak compared with the technological and economic reasons. This was particularly true of the motor vehicle assemblers. A purchasing manager at Isuzu stressed that in many cases it

1. Based on my interview with Shun'ichiro Ijichi, purchasing control manager, Toyota, May 27, 1986.

2. Based on my interview with Minoru Tomita, purchasing manager, Hitachi's Tokai plant, March 28, 1986.

was not feasible to use suppliers as a buffer or to switch them frequently, because the characteristics of contract-specific investments and the technical know-how concerned were such that neither intersupplier mobilization nor the internalization of resources would be possible without incurring prohibitive costs.[3] By contrast, again, the electronics manufacturers had different views. Admitting that the instrumental use of subcontractors to smooth fluctuations had become less important over time, many respondents from electronics firms nonetheless did not deny that "in certain segments of subcontracting" that were purely labor intensive, with few specific skills required, instrumental hiring and firing still were possible. Asking for anonymity, one purchasing manager furthermore commented that the purchasing managers would not overtly disclose this in more formal and authoritative surveys, such as MITI's, but in his opinion the "shock-absorber" function of subcontractors would continue to be vital as long as economic dualism in Japan did not entirely disappear. Again, there were noticeable differences between motor vehicles and electronics. Further, one might ask whether these operational–dualistic reasons were central and what their magnitude was relative to the other reasons.

Interestingly, not a single manager ever mentioned a contentious reason for subcontracting—dividing the work force against itself—as is claimed by the radical school of dualism (Edwards, 1979). Somewhat puzzled, I took the initiative in asking this question. With few exceptions, the interviewees had difficulty, initially at least, in understanding what I meant. I thus restated the question following Edwards's line of argument. Still there were moments of silence. Then I simplified the question into a long but single sentence: Would it be management's strategy to break up the broadly defined working class in Japanese society into two segments, by using cheaper and nonunionized workers outside the large firm and letting them compete head-to-head with more expensive, unionized workers within the firm, so that wages would be lowered overall and competitiveness would be achieved? Their answer was that that kind of problem setting did not apply to Japan because, in a sense, Japanese workers had already been divided as "ins and outs" even before large Japanese companies started to use subcontractors extensively. Then they would bring up further arguments, often ending by claiming that the origin of this division of workers could be traced back to the postwar turmoil of Japanese industrial relations, noting that this eventually rigidified the dual labor markets before subcontracting started to be used extensively in the late 1950s. It was fortunate that some of the senior managers that I interviewed in 1986 had witnessed in their younger years the rise of dual labor markets in postwar Japan and so had much to say about their firsthand observations, which were consistent with what we discussed in Chapter 3. In any event, they did not support Edwards's contention that breaking up the working class was a reason for subcontracting, an observation that my later mail questionnaire confirmed.[4]

3. Based on my interview with Yoshizo Murayama, purchasing manager, Isuzu, March 4, 1986.
4. The peculiar history of Japanese industrial relations is such that the dual labor markets, which originated in the 1920s, came to be institutionally rigidified along the lines of "enterprise unionism" in the immediate postwar period, before subcontracting practice became widespread in the late 1950s. This fact may have influenced the Japanese managers' perception of the question about a deliberate strategy to break up the work force. Because the work force had been divided so long ago and had been maintained with such consistency, the managers unquestionably accepted the division.

Had my research stopped here, it would have ended up producing yet another set of anecdotes and impressionistic conclusions. To substantiate my observations, I therefore had to do more systematic research.

Results of the Survey

My exploratory questionnaire about reasons for subcontracting as perceived by large Japanese motor vehicle and electronics manufacturers focused on testing dualist hypotheses in the contemporary context. This survey covered twenty automotive and twenty electronics/electrical firms, as shown in Table B-1.

I sent my questionnaire to the public relations office of each firm (a common initial contact in Japan) and asked that it be filled in by a senior manager of each firm's central purchasing department.[5] To those who did not respond quickly enough, I sent letters of reminder at regular intervals. Eventually, managers from nineteen automotive and twenty electronics firms responded, making a return rate of 97.5 percent.

The sample was selected according to two criteria: the size of the firm and the political influence of the firm, in the broad sense of affecting the general direction of the industry. I chose only the top large firms in each industry, because it is they that are influential in shaping, among other things, the prevailing subcontracting practices.

In motor vehicles, the choice was thirteen motor vehicle assemblers, including two motorcycle manufacturers. They constitute the major members of the Japan Automobile Manufacturers' Association (JAMA) and are considered key firms in the industry. Their strategies in regard to subcontracting substantially affect industrial order and practice. In addition, I selected three contract assemblers and the four largest automotive components firms (the latter being members of the Japan Auto Parts Industries Association, JAPIA), employing more than 5,000 people. In total, the sample firms had 370,000 employees, or 52 percent, of the workers in the automotive industry.

In electronics and electrical products, the choice was not as clear-cut as in motor vehicles, because there is no assembler equivalent in this industry. Selecting firms according to employment or sales size alone would mean ignoring political influence in favor of methodological simplicity. Concentrating on core members of trade organization also seemed problematic because unlike JAMA in motor vehicles, there was no single central trade association; instead there were several. Compounding the problem, these trade associations are relatively narrowly focused, such as electronics, semiconductors, telecommunication equipment, and heavy electrical equipment. There was a pragmatic solution to this methodological question, however. The membership of Denki roren or the Federation of Electrical Machine Workers' Unions, or "enterprise unions," was very broad in terms of the products

---

5. Multiple responses from each firm would have enabled me to collect enough data to represent overall company policy, as well as to minimize the effects of potential bias in the answers provided by only one respondent in a senior position from each firm. Owing to my limited means, however, it was impossible to do this. Thus the survey results should be interpreted with caution, and their implications should be regarded as exploratory.

TABLE B-1. The Twenty Automotive and Twenty Electronics/Electrical Firms in Japan Covered in the Survey, 1986

	Firms	No. of Employees[a]
Automotive		
Assemblers/members of JAMA[b]	1. Toyota	59,164
	2. Nissan	59,784
	3. Mazda	27,865
	4. Honda	27,897
	5. Mitsubishi Motors	24,682
	6. Suzuki	12,347
	7. Isuzu	16,093
	8. Fuji Heavy Industries	14,344
	9. Daihatsu	10,753
	10. Hino	8,271
	11. Nissan Diesel	6,420
	12. Yamaha	9,878
	13. Kawasaki Heavy Industries	22,880
	Subtotal:	300,378
Contract assemblers	14. Toyota Auto Body	7,157
	15. Nissan Shatai	7,100
	16. Kanto Auto Works	5,715
	Subtotal:	19,972
Components suppliers/members of JAPIA[c]	17. Nihon Radiator	5,015
	18. Aishin Seiki	8,772
	19. Nippondenso	32,466
	20. Toyoda Gosei	4,945
	Subtotal:	51,198
	Total:	371,548
Electronics/Electrical		
Denki Roren Chuto members[d]	1. Hitachi	80,084
	2. Matsushita Electric Industrial	39,980
	3. Toshiba	70,617
	4. Fujitsu	49,065
	5. Mitsubishi Electric	49,765
	6. NEC	37,855
	7. Sanyo Electric	20,907
	8. Fuji Electric	13,728
	9. Sharp	22,821
	10. Oki Electric	13,956
	11. Yasukawa Electric	4,427
	12. Meidensha	4,216
	13. Fujitsu General	2,872
	14. Nippon Columbia	2,606
	Subtotal:	412,899
Other Denki Roren members	15. Matsushita Electric Works	13,613
	16. Pioneer Electronic	7,440
	Subtotal:	21,053

(*continued*)

Table B-1. (*Continued*)

Automotive	Firms	No. of Employees[a]
Non-Denki Roren members	17. Sony	15,231
	18. Tokyo Sanyo Electric	14,706
	19. Victor Co. of Japan (JVC)	14,365
	20. Kyocera	12,704
	Subtotal:	57,006
	Total:	490,958

[a] As of January 1986, excluding those in subsidiaries.

[b] Japan Automobile Manufacturers' Association.

[c] Japan Auto Parts Industries Association.

[d] Central Disputes Committee of the Federation of Electrical Machine Workers' Unions.

Source: Toyo Keizai Shinposha, 1986a, 1986b, *Kaisha shikiho* (Quarterly reports of firms), vol. 1., and *Kaisha shikiho mijojogaisha-ban* (Quarterly reports of unquoted firms), vol. 1.

they made, ranging from consumer electronics to heavy electrical equipment. Denki roren's fourteen *chuto* (central disputes committee) members represented a kind of collective political influence in the electrical and electronics industries, similar to that of the motor vehicle assemblers. Thus, they were chosen. Two other Denki roren firms and four non–Denki roren manufacturers (including Sony and JVC), employing more than 5,000 people, were added to the sample. In total, this sample covered firms employing 490,000 people, or 39 percent, of the workers in the industry.

The questionnaire asked three things: First, did the firms subcontract according to the definition used in this book, that is, contracting that contributes to carrying out a major contract, in the form of parts fabrication, usually (but not necessarily) of the customer's design, in the form of contract assembly or subassembly, or in the form of providing capacity or labor for processes or other miscellaneous services? Second, what are the reasons for—and, third, the strategic importance of—contracting out?

To the first question, all the respondents answered that they did subcontract in this way. Regarding the second question, the respondents were asked to choose three answers in order of preference, out of six choices: specialist technology, cheaper control cost, wage differentials, risk dispersion, buffer against fluctuations, and division of the work force. In the compilation, 3 points were awarded to their first choice, 2 points to their second, and 1 point to their third, which were added up for the total score in each industry.

Definitions of each choice were provided in the questionnaire as follows:

Specialist technology: Relying on specific technical skills and expertise that are either not available internally or, if they are available, are too costly or difficult to manage in-house.

Cheaper control cost: Economizing on the indirect control cost of managing production, through the externalization of productive activities to subcontractors.

TABLE B-2. Reasons for Contracting Out: Large Japanese Automotive and
Electrical/Electronics Manufacturers, 1986

Category	Reasons	Total Score	Automotive	Electrical/Electronics
Technological	Specialist technology	80	47	33
Economic	Lower control costs	50	23	27
	Wage differentials	49	19	30
Operational	Risk dispersion	14	7	7
	Buffer against fluctuations	13	2	11
Others	Division of the work force	1	1	0

Source: 1986 mail questionnaire.

Wage differentials: Obtaining lower direct labor costs from subcontracting firms, thereby making it attractive to contract out, especially labor-intensive operations.

Risk dispersion: Handing over the riskier parts of operations to subcontractors, so as to protect the stability and viability of internal operations.

Buffer against fluctuations: Using subcontractors as "shock absorbers" in the face of fluctuations in demand.

Division of the work force: Breaking up the work force into two segments by using cheaper, nonunionized workers outside the firm and by letting them compete with more expensive, unionized workers within the firm, so as to reduce overall wages and increase labor competitiveness.

Table B-2 summarizes the answers to the question. Specialist technology was named as the most important reason for contracting out. Two economic reasons—lower indirect control costs and wage differentials (i.e., direct labor costs)—came second and third. But operational reasons—risk dispersion and shock-absorber functions—had relatively weak support.[6] Division of the work force against itself earned only one point. The overall results more or less corresponded to the findings from my preliminary fieldwork.[7]

The differences between the two industries that my earlier fieldwork revealed

6. Again, the term *operational* is used in the sense of protecting the stability and viability of in-house operations and work force, by peripheralizing riskier parts of operations, compared with more straightforward hard-cost considerations, which are termed *economic* in this survey. As stated earlier, however, there are recognized overlaps across these categories.

7. Some other national data show similar results. For example, 81.8 percent of automotive and 61.4 percent of electrical appliances prime contractors chose specialist technology; 18.2 and 40.0 percent of the respective respondents pointed out wage differentials; and 0 and 8.8 percent of them buffer against fluctuations. See SMEA (1968), *Shitauke kigyo kozo chosa* (Survey of subcontracting enterprise structure), quoted in Central Bank for Commercial and Industrial Cooperatives, Survey Department, 1971:19; and Ikeda, 1975:81.

Note also that 63.2 percent of the automotive subcontractors stated that their contractual relationship with their customers was on a continual basis only, whereas the comparable figure for electrical appliances subcontractors was 20.8 percent. See SMEA (1967), *Keiretsu shitauke kigyo chosa.* (Survey of *keiretsu* subcontracting enterprises), quoted in Kiyonari, 1970:171.

were apparent here as well. In electronics, technological reasons and each of the two economic reasons obtained similar scores. By contrast, in motor vehicles, the technological reason alone stands out, exceeding the total score of the two economic reasons. Subcontracting as a buffer function earned 11 points in electronics but only 2 in motor vehicles.

Finally, the respondents answered the third question, whether subcontracting is strategically important in the sense that the firm took it into account when planning its long-term goals and objectives, allocating its resources, and adopting courses of action to achieve these goals. Respectively, 63.2 and 50 percent of the automotive and the electronics/electrical respondents chose "very important"; 36.8 and 40 percent of them selected "important"; and 5 percent of the electronics/electrical respondents chose "unimportant." (The remaining 5 percent of the electronics/electrical respondents did not answer the question.) Thus, the great majority of the respondents considered subcontracting to be strategically important, the automotive respondents even more so than their electronics/electrical counterparts.

Discussion

Despite the limitations and exploratory nature of this survey, the results appear to be consistent in each category and suggest a reconsideration of the traditional arguments for subcontracting in three ways.

First, the reasons for subcontracting given in this survey appear to be more varied and "gradational" than those in most of the traditional accounts. This point was made in remarks added to the end of the questionnaire by several purchasing managers. For example, the manager of a diversified electronics manufacturer wrote:

> It is difficult to state a single sweeping reason for subcontracting. The reasons vary enormously from product to product, from process to process. The reason for subcontracting the manual subassembly of a PCB [printed circuit board] for a radio is entirely different from that for subcontracting the construction of special equipment for an atomic reactor.

Second and more important, the fact that specialist technology was perceived as the most important reason for subcontracting indicates the fallacy of dualists' simplistic exploitation thesis. The exploitation thesis holds that inherent inequalities in a dualistic industrial regime (inequalities, that is, between the core and the peripheral economies, in terms of access to technological, capital, and human resources) seriously restrict the courses of action that those in the periphery can take. The radical version of this position further argues that this mechanism leaves "no potential markets" to the periphery.[8] If this position were correct, reliance on the subcontractors' specialist technology would lead to a contradiction: that is, subcontractors are important because they have useful specialist technical skills, but there are no potential markets in which these skills can be used. Instead, the

8. Edwards, 1979:77. The limitations of this claim were pointed out earlier. Data from this survey also indicate that contemporary events contradict this contention.

overwhelming support for subcontractors as a source of specialist technology suggests that there exist real markets for subcontractors whose usefulness and marketability are not seriously affected by the alleged inequality of access to resources. Thus the subcontractors' *raison d'être* cannot be simply explained, as the dualists claim, in terms of their replaceability, that is, that they represent a flexible replacement for more rigid labor in the primary sector. The reason is that they may not, in fact, be readily replaceable (see Chapter 7).

Third, the survey results indicate that there may be interindustrial differences among the various reasons for subcontracting. This important question has hardly been addressed by the traditional literature, a curious omission. In manufacturing, the product to be made defines how it is manufactured. The way in which an electronic product, say a microphone, is made differs significantly from the way an automobile is built. The former is simple, the latter is much more complex.[9]

Even a relatively complex electronic product such as a video cassette recorder (VCR) appears to be simple compared with a passenger car in its manufacturing complexity and in the variety of components required.[10] Ignoring this important difference and reducing the arguments merely to transactions of intermediate goods or the replacement function of subcontractors or to general-purpose and special-purpose technologies indicate serious omissions.

If the foregoing is accepted, then, it is not difficult to see the shortcomings of the existing literature. To repeat, the type of product defines the production methods used, which in turn defines the modes of production organization, including subcontracting relations. In a dualistic environment, subcontractors are likely to be used instrumentally for simple, labor-intensive products like microphones, and cheap labor and buffer functions are likely to be sought. Conversely, for complex products requiring thousands of components and assembly operations, like automobiles, a symbiotic customer–subcontractor relationship is more likely to develop. In this case, what is sought is a variety of special technological expertise to complement a lack of, or perhaps an unwillingness to develop internally, such a capability in the primary producer, whereas cheap labor is considered secondary and the shock-absorber function is almost nonexistent, owing to the subcontractors' indispensability.

---

9. Constructing a microphone requires the assembly of only a few components: a case, wires, small metal and plastic parts, and a simple circuit board. The final assembly is relatively simple, usually needing manual operations such as soldering, putting parts together, and testing. Building an automobile is entirely different and far more complex. It requires the assembly of anywhere from 12,000 to 24,000 components (depending on the definition of a component)—electrical, forged, stamped, machined, and molded, and metal, glass, composite, rubber, ceramics, and so on—requiring complex, large-scale sites; numerous machines and robots; and thousands of different players cooperating with one another.

10. This is not to argue that a VCR, usually consisting of a thousand or so components, is not complex. The precision levels required in its mechanisms (especially the heads) are far stricter than in automotive engine parts. Rather, the point is that even a basic passenger car still has a higher degree of manufacturing complexity and a greater variety of components required than a VCR does. In today's automated manufacturing system, a VCR can be manufactured on an almost unmanned assembly line, extending barely over 30 meters long (based on my observation of Hitachi's Tokai plant, March 28, 1986). In contrast, even the most automated automotive assembly plant requires much greater human and physical input.

Although no definitive conclusion can be drawn from these survey data alone, they at least suggest that the differences in the overall manufacturing complexity of the products and the nature and variety of their components may partly explain the different patterns of the two industries. Although the purchasing managers from both industries responded readily to the three categories of reasons for subcontracting, the top three answers given by the electronics managers were difficult to distinguish, whereas the automotive managers' first choice, "specialist technology," could be clearly distinguished from the rest. This difference indicates another area of research that has been relatively ignored in the traditional literature, which tends to speculate, in too-generic terms, about the efficacy or dysfunctionality of industrial sourcing.

In addition to these three points, the fact that "lower control costs" was chosen as the second most important reason for subcontracting in the survey appears to support a point made in Chapter 4, that the emergence of a clustered control structure in Japanese contractual relations was a product of the large manufacturers' strategy to delegate increasingly complex control functions to external production organizations. The results of this survey indicate that Japanese purchasing managers in motor vehicles and electronics recognize the economic advantages of this control externalization strategy.

Excerpts from Questions Asked

From among the questions asked in the different steps of my field research, the following questions are those reported in this study. The numbering scheme I used indicates the chapters and/or tables where the responses to these questions are given. For example, when a question is numbered 5-2, it indicates that the responses are reported in Table 5-2. The two exceptions to this are questions B1 and B3, which are not found in any table but are discussed in Appendix B. Italicized terms have been defined in the chapters indicated.

Questions for Large Automotive and Electronics
Manufacturers in Japan (mail questionnaire):

B-1. Does your firm *subcontract* out for part or for all of its manufacturing processes?

(   ) Yes   (   ) No

B-2. What are the major *reasons for subcontracting*? Please choose three from the following six reasons and number them in the order of their importance.

(   ) Specialist technology   (   ) Buffer against fluctuations
(   ) Wage differentials   (   ) Cheaper control cost
(   ) Risk dispersion   (   ) Division of the work force

B-3. Is subcontracting out *strategically important* for your firm as a manufacturer?

Questions for Electronics Subcontractors in the United Kingdom and Japan (field interview):

5-1. What is the total number of employees at your establishment?

5-2. How many *regular customers* do you have?

5-4. What are the percentages of your annual sales that your no. 1 through no. 3 customers represent?

5-6. How many *regular subcontractors* do you have in charge of *complete assembly, subsystems assembly, single components, discrete treatment*, and *others*?

5-13. What is the distance between your establishment and a primary goods receiving point of your no. 1 customer (in terms of sales) in kilometers?

6-1. Please make three favorable and three critical comments about your customers.

Questions for Business Proprietors of Electronics Subcontracting Firms in Japan (field interview):

6-2. Please provide the following information:

Your age.
Years as proprietor of your firm.
Working years before current proprietorship.
Age at last graduation.

6-3. Please provide the following information:

No. of firms for which you worked before the current proprietorship.

Profiles of previous employment (check those appropriate):

( ) Manufacturing firms.
( ) Quoted firms in the first half of the Tokyo Stock Exchange.
( ) Self-owned firms.
( ) Experience as plant manager.
( ) Bankruptcy or redundancy.
( ) Others. Please briefly describe:

Profiles of current proprietorship (check those appropriate):

( ) Succeeding a parent, who established the firm.
( ) Started after retirement from a prior career.
( ) Others. Please briefly describe:

6-4. Which annual income group (in ￥ million) do you belong to?

( ) below 2   ( ) 2–3   ( ) 3–4   ( ) 4–5   ( ) 5–6   ( ) 6–7
( ) 7–8   ( ) 8–9   ( ) 9–10   ( ) 10–11   ( ) 11–12   ( ) 12–13
( ) 13–14   ( ) 14–15   ( ) 15–16   ( ) 16–17   ( ) 17–18   ( ) 18–19
( ) 19–20   ( ) 20–25   ( ) 25–30   ( ) over 30

6-5. How do you feel about your present job and responsibility?

(   ) Very satisfied   (   ) Satisfied
(   ) Dissatisfied   (   ) Very dissatisfied

Questions for Automotive Components Suppliers in Japan,
the United States, and Europe (field interview):

7-2. What is the die-change time for a typical volume production item in the plant (i.e., for a major model switch on a volume production line where dies are changed at least once a week, excluding minor model switches that require only changes of peripheral jigs and fixtures)?

7-3. How many times a day do you change dies on this production line (calculated as two shifts)?

7-4. Please provide the following information:

No. of basic types of alternators produced, no. of variants (i.e., part numbers) produced, no. of assembly lines, range of lot sizes.

7-5. What is the lead time from the release of an order to the delivery of new production dies (as opposed to prototype dies) for a typical production item in the plant? (If dies are made in-house, please use that figure. If not, please indicate the lead time for subcontracted dies.)

7-6. How many different *job classifications* are there for blue-collar workers in this plant?

7-7. What is the average number of machines attended by a production worker in module-building processes of a typical volume product in the plant?

7-8. What are the *in-process and finished inventory* levels, calculated as days of production?

7-10. How many JIT (just-in-time) deliveries of a typical single component, or a typical single component system, are made to a major plant of a major customer each day?

APPENDIX C

Postwar Small-Business Organizations

Even though the supreme commander for the Allied Powers (SCAP) did not approve of national organizations of small firms, many nonetheless were established in the immediate postwar period. The most noteworthy were the Conference of All Japanese Small and Medium Industries (Zen Nippon chusho kogyo kyogikai, or Zenchukyo) and the Japanese Small and Medium Enterprise Federation (Nippon chusho kigyo renmei, or Nicchuren) established in 1947 and 1948, respectively. The Dodge Plan further fueled the Japanese small-business movements, which created many more independent groups, including the Political Federation of Japanese Small and Medium Enterprises (Nippon chusho kigyo seiji renmei, or Chuseiren) founded in 1956 by Yoshisuke Aikawa, the former president of Nissan.

The Zenchukyo prepared its own draft of the Law on the Adjustments of Subcontracting Relations in 1950 and widely declared the need for correcting unfair subcontracting practices, including withholding payments. In 1954 the Socialist party took up this issue, and in July 1956, the Law on the Prevention of Delay in the Payment of Subcontracting Charges and Related Matters was passed. However, the organization was split in 1957 with the branching out and establishment of the Friendly Society of All Japanese Small and Medium Entrepreneurs (Zen Nippon chusho kigyoka doyukai), which diminished the power of the Zenchuko as a pressure group.

The Nicchuren was active as a de facto national center of small businesses until the 1950 Amendment of the Law on Cooperatives of Small and Medium Enterprises and Other Parties which established the government-backed institution of the Central Society of National Small and Medium Enterprise Cooperatives and Others (Zenkoku chusho kigyo to kyodo kumiai chukai, or Chuokai), thus replacing the position of the Nicchuren. Further, the Nicchuren lost its social footing with the enactment of the 1957 Law on the Organization of Small and Medium Enterprises (Chusho kigyo dantai soshiki ho) which renamed the Chuokai as the Central Society of National Small and Medium Enterprise Organizations (Zenkoku chusho kigyo dantai chukai, or Zenkoku chukai). The Zenkoku chukai received subsidies from the government and assumed the central responsibility for regulating small business cooperatives nationwide.

Similarly, the 1957 Law on the Organization of Small and Medium Enterprises was in part a product of fierce lobbying by the Chuseiren. This organization was at its political peak as a pressure group when the Diet passed the law. In 1958 Aikawa

went to see President Dwight Eisenhower and on his return implemented the
"Aikawa Plan" to save the Japanese cutlery industry in the face of rising U.S.
tariffs. In the same year Aikawa became the second president of the Zenkoku
chuokai. The Chuseiren, however, virtually disintegrated after its loss in the 1959
election of the House of the Councillors. In this election, all the candidates from the
Chuseiren, except for Aikawa and his son, were defeated. Moreover, many board
members were subsequently investigated on suspicion of violating the election law.
In the end the Aikawas resigned from the Diet, and the Chuseiren lost its support.
For a more detailed account of the postwar small-business movements, see Kato
(1960:296–302), on which this appendix is based.

APPENDIX D

Cooperatives

During my fieldwork in 1986, I visited six different types of common facility cooperatives and a federation of common facility cooperatives, all in different locations. The cooperatives were (1) the Kuji Metalwork Cooperative (Kuji tekko kyodo kumiai) (April 24, 1986), (2) the Hitachi Metalwork Cooperative (Hitachi tekko kyodo kumiai) (March 26, 1986), (3) the Tokyo Scale Industrial Cooperative (Tokyo hakari kogyo kyodo kumiai) located in Ibaragi Industrial Park (Ibaragi kogyo danchi) (January 8, 1986), (4) the Conference of the Small and Medium Industrial Parks and Others in Ibaragi prefecture (Ibaragiken chusho kigyo kojo danchi to kyogikai) (February 26 and March 31, 1986), (5) the Tama Industrial Cooperative (Tama kogyo kyodo kumiai) (May 23, 1986), (6) the Chigasaki Machinery and Metal Industrial Park Cooperative (Chigasaki kikai kinzoku kogyo danchi kyodo kumiai) (November 28, 1986), and (7) the Kanazawa Machinery and Metal Industrial Park Cooperative (Kanazawa kikai kinzoku danchi kyodo kumiai) (April 22 and November 28, 1986).

Of the seven, (4) was a federation of common facility cooperatives, including (1) and (3) as its federated members. Its central office was located in the business promotion section, Department of Labor, Ibaragi prefectural government.

Both (1) and (2) consisted of subcontractors dedicated to Hitachi, and (3) comprised small manufacturers of scales that had branched out from their Tokyo operations to Ibaragi prefecture. The Ibaragi prefectural government invited them to establish a new industrial park with its prefectural subsidies. Nos. (5) consisted of miscellaneous small manufacturers who had united in response to an invitation from the Tokyo metropolitan government, which provided subsidies for the establishment of an industrial park, and (6) and (7) were also set up on the basis of new industrial parks with invitations and subsidies from the Kanagawa prefectural government. The former consisted of a handful of small subcontractors in the electronics, automotive, and precision industries, whereas the latter was a huge cooperative of many medium-sized manufacturers.

Although the size, constitution, and characteristics of each cooperative differed, the majority were established for purely financial reasons. Individual firms needed money, and they were offered incentives from local governments. In order to benefit from these incentives, they had to set up cooperatives and go to new industrial parks. As soon as they settled down, they no longer needed one another. Although their geographical proximity to one another facilitated their occasional communication, in many cases it was not essential. Asked how many cooperative members there were and what they were doing, a managing director of a manufacturer of special-purpose precision machines for the semiconductor business bluntly said: "I don't know. We happen to be here together for the purpose of financing. There's absolutely no other connection. I don't know how many firms there are, and I don't care what they do" (based on my interview with Mr. K. Ishida, managing director, Daiichi Seiki, May 23, 1986).

One exception was the Kuji Metalwork Cooperative, which contains thirteen subcontractors, nearly all of them dedicated to, though not owned by, Hitachi. Four presidents of the thirteen firms were ex-Hitachi workers or managers. The division of labor among these subcontractors was such that none directly competed, but they did complement one another. When necessary, machines were temporarily lent to one another, and even *oen* or interfirm temporary loans of workers were made. When I visited this organization, the Japanese manufacturing industry in general was being seriously hit by *endaka,* or the yen appreciation that had curbed exports. At the end of my interview with the president of the cooperative, he confessed with a sigh that he and his colleagues were on their way to Hitachi's Taga plant, their primary customer, to plead for the maintenance of steady business. Unfortunately, I did not have the chance to hear about the results from him. But through my interviews with purchasing managers at the Taga plant one month earlier, I knew that Hitachi was in the process of rerationalizing its subcontracting operations. This case shows that cooperatives can be functional outside the sphere of financing if the interests of the cooperative members are close enough and the members are prepared to take collective action (based on my interviews at the Kuji Metalwork Cooperative, April 24, 1986; the Hitachi Taga plant, March 28, 1986).

Finally, I found the term *cooperative* to be virtually identical with *industrial park,* and vice versa, for all the cooperatives I visited (excluding the Federation of Common Facility Cooperatives, which was merely an office). This is a reflection of the emergence of industrial parks in the 1960s and their marriage to the existing institution of cooperatives as a result of national and local government policies.

BIBLIOGRAPHY

Amagai, Shogo.
    1982. *Nihon jidosha kogyo no shiteki tenkai* (Historical development of the Japanese automotive industry). Tokyo: Aki Shobo.

Arisawa, Hiromi, ed.
    1967. *Nihon sangyo hyakunen shi, jo* (A hundred-year history of Japanese industry, vol. 1). Tokyo: Nihon Keizai Shinbunsha.

Arrow, Kenneth J.
    1969. "The Organization of Economic Activity: Issues Pertinent to the Choice of Market Versus Nonmarket Allocation." In U.S. Congress, Joint Economic Committee, 1969:59–73.

Asanuma, Banri.
    1989. "Manufacturer–Supplier Relationships in Japan and the Concept of Relation-specific Skill." *Journal of the Japanese and International Economies* 3:1–30.

Automotive News.
    1989. August 21.

Averitt, R. T.
    1968. *The Dual Economy: The Dynamics of American Industry Structure.* New York: Norton.

Bakke, E. W., ed.
    1954. *Labor Mobility and Economic Opportunity.* Cambridge, MA: MIT Press.

Berger, Suzanne D., & Piore, Michael J.
    1980. *Dualism and Discontinuity in Industrial Societies.* Cambridge: Cambridge University Press.

Bureau of Social Affairs, Labor Section (Shakaikyoku rodobu).
    1935. *Rinji shokko oyobi ninpu ni kansuru chosa* (Survey of temporary workers and laborers). Quoted in Hazama, 1978:64.

Car Sensor.
    1989. March 3.

Central Bank for Commercial and Industrial Cooperatives, Survey Department (Shoko kumiai chuo kinko chosa bu).
    1971. *Shitauke chusho kogyo no jittai* (Actual conditions of subcontracting small and medium industries). Tokyo: Yaesu Shoko.
    1977. *Shitauke chusho kigyo no genkyo* (Current situations of subcontracting small and medium enterprises). Tokyo: Yaesu Shoko.
    1983. *Shitauke chusho kigyo no shin kyokumen* (New facets of subcontracting small and medium enterprises). Tokyo: Central Bank for Commercial and Industrial Cooperatives.

Chang, C. S.
    1981. *The Japanese Auto Industry and the U.S. Market.* New York: Praeger.

Chunichi Shinbun.
    1979. June 9. Quoted in Fujita, Eishi, 1980:131.

Chuo University, Economic Research Institute (Chuo daigaku keizai kenkyusho).
   1975.   *Sengo no Nihon keizai—Kodo seicho to sono hyoka* (Postwar Japanese econo-
           my: High growth and its evaluation). Tokyo: Chuo University Press.
   1976.   *Chusho kigyo no kaiso kozo—Hitachi seisakusho shitauke kigyo kozo no jittai
           bunseki* (The layered structure of small and medium enterprises: Analyses of the
           actual subcontracting structure of Hitachi). Tokyo: Chuo University Press.
Clark, Kim B., Chew, W. Bruce, & Fujimoto, Takahiro.
   1987.   "Product Development in the World Auto Industry: Strategy, Organization and
           Performance." Paper presented at the Brookings Microeconomics Conference,
           December.
Clark, Kim B., & Fujimoto, Takahiro.
   1987.   "Overlapping Problem Solving in Product Development." Working Paper 87-
           048, March, Harvard Business School.
   1988.   "The European Model of Product Development: Challenge and Opportunity."
           Policy Forum Paper, International Motor Vehicle Program, MIT, May.
Clark, Kim B., Fujimoto, Takahiro, & Dubinskas, Frank A.
   1987.   "Product Development in the U.S., Japanese & European Auto Companies." A
           collection of viewgraphs, Harvard Business School.
Clark, Rodney.
   1979.   *The Japanese Company*. New Haven, CT: Yale University Press.
Committee of Inquiry on Small Firms.
   1971.   *Small Firms*. Cmnd. 4811. London: Her Majesty's Stationery Office.
Consumer Reports.
   1989.   Annual Auto Issue: The 1989 Cars, April.
Cusumano, Michael A.
   1985.   *The Japanese Automobile Industry*. Cambridge, MA: Harvard University Press.
Dodwell Marketing Consultants.
   1983.   *The Structure of the Japanese Auto Parts Industry*. Tokyo: Dodwell Marketing
           Consultants.
Doeringer, Peter B., & Piore, Michael J.
   1971.   *Internal Labor Markets and Manpower Analysis*. Lexington, MA: Heath Lex-
           ington Books.
Dore, Ronald P.
   1987.   *Taking Japan Seriously*. Stanford, CA: Stanford University Press.
Dore, Ronald P., ed.
   1967.   *Aspects of Social Change in Modern Japan*. Princeton, NJ: Princeton University
           Press.
Dunning, John H.
   1986.   *Japanese Participation in British Industry*. London: Croom Helm.
   1993.   "The Governance of Japanese and U.S. Manufacturing Affiliates in the U.K.:
           Some Country Specific Differences." In Kogut, ed., 1993.
Economic Planning Agency (Keizai kikaku cho)
   1956.   *Keizai hakusho* (Economic white paper). Quoted in Ito, 1957:160.
   1957.   *Keizai hakusho* (Economic white paper). Quoted in SMEA, 1959:10.
Economics Today.
   1988.   Spring Issue. Tokyo: Shogakukan.
Economist, The.
   1986.   October 25–31.
Ekonomisuto.
   1984.   August 28.

Edwards, Richard C.
    1979.   *Contested Terrain.* New York: Basic Books.
Edwards, Richard C., Reich, Michael, & Gordon, David M., eds.
    1975.   *Labor Market Segmentation.* Lexington, MA: Heath Lexington Books.
Engineering Industries Association (EIA).
    1984.   *Engineering Buyer's Guide and Directory.* Todmorden, Lancs.: Northern Advertising Agency.
Employment Research Institute (Rodo jijo chosasho).
    1935.   *Rinjiko mondai no kenkyu* (A study of the problem of temporary workers). Quoted in Hazama, 1978:496–97.
Federation of Electrical Machine Workers' Unions (Denki roren).
    1975.   *Chosa jiho* (Survey bulletin), no. 114.
Foreign Press Center, Japan.
    1977.   *About Japan.* Series 2. Tokyo: Foreign Press Center.
Friedman, David.
    1983.   "Beyond the Age of Ford: The Strategic Basis of the Japanese Success in Automobiles." In Zysman & Tyson, eds., 1983:350–90.
    1986.   "The Misunderstood Miracle: Politics and the Development of a Hybrid Economy in Japan." Ph.D. dissertation, Political Science Department, MIT.
    1988.   *The Misunderstood Miracle: Industrial Development and Political Change in Japan.* Ithaca, NY: Cornell University Press.
Fujimoto, Takahiro.
    1989.   "Organizations for Effective Product Development: The Case of the Global Automotive Industry" (compact version). D.B.A. dissertation, Graduate School of Business Administration, Harvard University.
Fujita, Eishi.
    1980.   "Toyota shokuan kan'nai no rodo shijo—Toyota shokuan gyomu nenpo no kento o chushin ni" (The labor market within the jurisdiction of the Toyota Employment Security Office: A focused examination of the annual bulletin of the Toyota Employment Security Office). In Japan University of Social Welfare, Project Team on the Social and Economic Structure of Tokai Aichi, 1980:105–31.
Fujita, Keizo.
    1965.   *Nihon sangyo kozo to chusho kigyo* (Japanese industrial structure and small business). Tokyo: Iwanami Shoten.
Galbraith, John Kenneth.
    1972.   *The New Industrial State.* 2nd. ed. Harmondsworth: Penguin Books.
Garvin, David A.
    1983.   "Quality on the Line." *Harvard Business Review,* September–October, pp. 65–75.
Gillett, Frank E.
    1992.   "The Integrating Supplier: A Study of an Auto Industry Supplier's Relations Across Several Customers." M.S. thesis (draft), Political Science Department, MIT.
Gordon, Andrew.
    1985.   *The Evolution of Labor Relations in Japan: Heavy Industry, 1853–1955.* Cambridge, MA: Harvard University Press.
Gunnel, John A., ed.
    1982.   *Standard Catalog of American Cars 1946–1975.* Iola, WI: Krause Publications.

Harada, Shuichi.
    1928. *Labour Conditions in Japan.* Quoted in Orchard, 1930:344–45.
Harvard Business Review.
    1983. September–October.
    1986. November–December.
Hasegawa, H., & Ueki, K., eds.
    1978. *Jirei kaisetsu shitauke daikin shiharai chien to boshi ho* (Case explanation of the Law on the Prevention of Delay in the Payment of Subcontracting Charges and Related Matters). Tokyo: Kyoso mondai kenkyusho.
Hazama, Hiroshi.
    1978. *Nihon romu kanri shi kenkyu* (A study of Japanese labor control history). Tokyo: Ochanomizu Shobo.
Heiki Koku Kogyo Shinbun Shuppanbu (Journal of the arms and aircraft industries, publishing department).
    1943. *Taryo seisan kenkyu, jo* (A study of volume production, vol. 1). Tokyo: Heiki Koku Kogyo Shinbun Shuppanbu.
Hirschmeier, J., & Yui, T.
    1975. *The Development of Japanese Business 1600–1973.* London: Allen & Unwin.
Hitachi.
    1949. *Hitachi seisakusho shi* (History of Hitachi). Vol. 1. Tokyo: Hitachi.
    1960. *Hitachi seisakusho shi* (History of Hitachi). Vol. 2. Tokyo: Hitachi.
Hodson, Randy, & Kaufman, Robert L.
    1982. "Economic Dualism: A Critical Review." *American Sociological Review* 47:727–39.
Hoselitz, Bert F., ed.
    1968. *The Role of Small Industry in the Process of Economic Growth.* The Hague: Mouton.
Hosono, Koichi.
    1950. "Taihei yo senka ni okeru chusho kogyo no seibi" (The rationalization of small and medium industries during the Pacific War). In Yamanaka, ed., 1950.
Hyodo, Tsutomu.
    1971. *Nihon ni okeru roshi kankei no tenkai* (Development of labor–management relations in Japan). Tokyo: University of Tokyo Press.
Ichikawa, Hirokatsu.
    1968. "Shitauke keiretsu no shuyakuka to shitauke kanri no kyoka" (Concentration of subcontracting *keiretsu* and intensified subcontracting control). In Ichikawa, ed., 1968:137–51.
Ichikawa, Hirokatsu, ed.
    1968. *Gendai Nihon no chusho kigyo* (Small and medium enterprises in modern Japan). Tokyo: Shin Hyoron.
Ikeda, Masayoshi.
    1968. "Shitauke keiretsu saihensei no shinten" (The development of subcontracting *keiretsu* reform), sec. 1–2. In Ichikawa, ed., 1968:126–36.
    1975. "Sangyo no kaiso betsu kozo" (Stratified structure of industry). In Chuo University, Economic Research Institute, 1975:55–90.
    1984. "Sai hensei susumu ohshu no jidosha shitauke" (Progressive reorganization of European automotive subcontracting). *Ekonomisuto,* August 28, 1984.
    1986a. "Ohshu no jidosha buhin kogyo no genjo to kadai" (The current situation and issues of the European automotive components industry). *Jidosha kogyo* 20 (February):11–18.

1986b. "Shinai kigyo ni okeru ME-ka ni tomonau koyo, sagyo soshiki, seisan kanri no henka ni kansuru jittai chosa" (Survey of actual change in employment, work organization and production management due to microelectronics technologies in [Hachioji] City), March. Tokyo: Hachioji City Employment Policy Council.

Ikeda, Masayoshi, Sei, Shoichiro, & Nishiguchi, Toshihiro.
1988. "U-Line Auto Arts Production." Research Affiliates' Meeting Paper, International Motor Vehicle Program, MIT, October.

INSEAD Information.
1991. Summer.

InSite.
1988. Vol. 1, no. 4, April.

Isobe, Kiichi.
1942. "Chusho kikai kogyo no tosei soshiki" (Controlling organization of small and medium machinery industry). In *Jikyoku to chusho kigyo—Chusho kigyo tosei soshiki* (The situation and small and medium enterprises: Controlling organization of small and medium enterprises). Vol. 5. Tokyo: Yuhikaku.

Isuzu Motors.
1957. *Isuzu jidosha shi* (A history of Isuzu Motors). Tokyo: Isuzu Motors.

Ito, Motoshige.
1987. "Industrial Policy and Corporate Growth in the Automotive Industry: Japan's Postwar Experience" (preliminary draft), Department of Economics, University of Tokyo.

Ito, Taikichi.
1957. *Chusho kigyo ron* (On small and medium enterprises). Tokyo: Nihon Hyoronsha.

Iwakoshi, Tadahiro.
1968. *Jidosha kogyo ron* (On the automotive industry). Tokyo: University of Tokyo Press.

Jaikumar, Ramchandran.
1986. "Postindustrial Manufacturing." *Harvard Business Review*, November–December, pp. 69–76.

JAMA Forum, The.
1989. Vol. 7, no. 4, April. Tokyo: Japan Automobile Manufacturers Association.

Japan External Trade Organization (JETRO).
1986. *Japan's Postwar Small and Medium Enterprise Policy—For Promotion of Corporate Vitality.* Tokyo: JETRO.

Japan Development Bank.
1964. *Postwar Growth of the Japanese Economy.* Tokyo: Japan Development Bank.

Japan Institute of Labor (Nihon rodo kyokai).
1986. *Igirisu nikkei kigyo no rodo jijo* (Employment conditions of Japanese enterprises in the U.K.). Tokyo: Japan Institute of Labor.

Japan University of Social Welfare (Nihon fukushi daigaku), Project Team on the Social and Economic Structure of Tokai Aichi (Chiiki kozo kenkyukai).
1980. "Shiryo: Aichiken ni okeru jidosha oyobi do kanren sangyo no rodo shijo to Toyota jidosha kogyo no koyo kanri" (Materials: The labor markets in the motor vehicle and its related industries in Aichi prefecture and Toyota Motor Corporation's employment management). *Kenkyu kiyo* (Research bulletin of Japan University of Social Welfare) 45:75–169.

J. D. Power & Associates.
1986–89. *New Car Initial Quality Survey.* Agoura Hills, CA: J. D. Power & Associates.

Jidosha Kogyo (Automotive industry).
    1986. Vol. 20, no. 2, February. Tokyo: Japan Automobile Manufacturers Association.
    1988. Vol. 22, no. 7, July. Tokyo: Japan Automobile Manufacturers Association.
Kasai, K., Iwao, H., Kobayashi, Y., & Ito, T., eds.
    1960. *Koza chusho kigyo—dai 2 kan—Dokusen shihon to chusho kigyo* (Lectures on small and medium enterprises. Vol. 2: Monopoly capital and small and medium enterprises). Tokyo: Yuhikaku.

Kato, Seiichi.
    1960. "Chusho kigyo no kumiai seido to nin'i dantai" (Institutions of small and medium enterprise cooperatives and voluntary organizations). In Kasai et al., eds., 1960:273–302.

Kenney, Martin, & Florida, Richard.
    1988. "Beyond Mass Production: Production and the Labor Process in Japan." *Politics and Society* 16(1):121–58.

Kerr, Clark.
    1954. "The Balkanization of Labor Markets." In Bakke, ed., 1954.

Kiyonari, Tadao.
    1970. *Nihon chusho kigyo no kozo hendo* (Structural change of Japanese small and medium enterprises). Tokyo: Shin Hyoron.
    1980. *Chusho kigyo dokuhon* (Textbook of small and medium enterprises). Tokyo: Toyo Keizai Shinposha.

Kogut, Bruce, ed.
    1993. *Country Competitiveness: Technology and Organizing of Work.* New York: Oxford University Press.

Koike, Kazuo.
    1983. "Internal Labor Markets: Workers in Large Firms." In Shirai, ed., 1983:29–61.

Kojo kanri (Factory management).
    1984. Vol. 30, no. 7.

Komiyama, Takuji.
    1941. *Nihon chusho kogyo kenkyu* (A study on Japanese small- and medium-sized manufacturing industry). Tokyo: Chuo Koronsha.

Krafcik, John K.
    1986. "Learning from NUMMI." Research Affiliates' Meeting Paper, International Motor Vehicle Program, MIT, September.
    1988a. "Comparative Analysis of Performance Indicators at World Auto Assembly Plants." M.S. thesis, Sloan School of Management, MIT.
    1988b. "European Manufacturing Practice in a World Perspective." Policy Forum Paper, International Motor Vehicle Program, MIT, May.

Krafcik, John K., & MacDuffie, John Paul.
    1989. "Explaining High Performance Manufacturing: The International Automotive Assembly Plant Study." Policy Forum Paper, International Motor Vehicle Program, MIT, May.

Krafcik, John K., & Womack, James P.
    1987. "Comparative Manufacturing Practice: Imbalances and Implications." Policy Forum Paper, International Motor Vehicle Program, MIT, May.

Kumaki, K.
    1959. *Nihon no jidosha, Toyota jidosha: Nihon shuyo sangyo, jidosha hen* (The Japanese motor vehicle, Toyota Motor: Japanese major industries, the automotive industry). Tokyo: Tenbosha.

Labor Minister's Office, Labor Statistics and Research Bureau.
>1957a. *Rodo hakusho—Rodo keizai no bunseki* (Labor white paper: Analysis of labor economy). Tokyo: Labor Minister's Office.
>1957b. *Showa 31 nen rodo keizai no bunseki* (Analysis of 1956 labor economy). Tokyo: Labor Minister's Office.
>1958. *Rodo hakusho* (Labor white paper). Tokyo: Labor Minister's Office.

Labor Minister's Office, Statistics and Information Bureau.
>1970, 1975, 1980, 1984.
>>*Chingin sensasu* (The wage census). Tokyo: Labor Minister's Office.
>1978. *Rodo kumiai kihon chosa 30 nen shi* (A 30-year history of basic survey of labor unions). Tokyo: Labor Minister's Office.

Lamming, Richard.
>1989. "The International Automotive Components Industry: The Next 'Best Practice' for Suppliers." Policy Forum Paper, International Motor Vehicle Program, MIT, May.

Leibenstein, Harvey.
>1966. "Allocative Efficiency Versus X-Efficiency." *American Economic Review,* June.

Littler, Craig. R.
>1982. *The Development of the Labour Process in Capitalist Societies: A Comparative Study of the Transformation of Work Organization in Britain, Japan and the USA.* London: Heinemann.

Minato, Tetsuo.
>1986. "Nihongata shitauke shisutemu keisei katei" (Formation processes of Japanese-style subcontracting systems). In Society for the Promotion of the Machinery Industry, Economic Research Institute, 1986:45–68.

Ministry of Agriculture and Commerce.
>1903. *Shokko jijo* (Conditions of workers). Quoted in Sumiya, 1966:50; and Hazama, 1978:277.
>1908. *Kojo tokeihyo* (Statistics on factories). Quoted in Hazama, 1978:57.
>1920. *Kojo tokeihyo* (Statistics on factories). Quoted in Hyodo, 1971:418.

Ministry of Commerce and Industry.
>1930. *Kojo tokeihyo* (Statistics on factories). Quoted in Hazama, 1978:57; and Hyodo, 1971:418.
>1933. *Kojo tokeihyo* (Statistics on factories). Quoted in Minato, 1986:55.
>1940. "Kikai tekko seihin kogyo seibi yoko" (The rationalization outline of the machinery and iron and steel industries). Quoted in Minato, 1986:64–68.

Ministry of Commerce and Industry, Minister's Secretariat, Statistics Section (Shokosho daijin kanbo tokeika).
>1936. *Kikai kigu kogyo gaichu jokyo shirabe* (An inquiry into the subcontracting conditions of the machinery and equipment industry). Quoted in Fujita, Keizo, 1965:38.

Ministry of Finance.
>1955. *Yuka shoken hokokusho: Toyota* (Report on securities: Toyota).
>1957. *Yuka shoken hokokusho: Nissan* (Report on securities: Nissan).
>1961–86. *Yuka shoken hokokusho* (Report on securities), for Toyota, Nissan, Mazda (Toyo Kogyo until 1985), Honda, Suzuki, Isuzu, Fuji Heavy Industries, Daihatsu, Hino, and Nissan Diesel. Tokyo: Ministry of Finance, Printing Bureau.

Ministry of Internal Affairs, Bureau of Social Affairs (Naimusho shakaikyoku).
    1930. *Kojo kozan rodosha ido shirabe* (Survey of factory and mining workers' mobility). Quoted in Hyodo, 1971:406.
Ministry of Labor, Labor Statistics and Research Bureau.
    1948. *Rodo kumiai chosa hokoku* (Report on the survey of labor unions). Tokyo: Ministry of Labor.
    1953, 1956, 1959–60, 1965–66. *Rodo hakusho—Rodo keizai no bunseki* (Labor white paper: Analysis of labor economy). Tokyo: Ministry of Labor.
MIT Commission on Industrial Productivity.
    1989. *The Working Papers of the MIT Commission on Industrial Productivity*. Vol. 2. Cambridge, MA: MIT Press.
Mitsubishi Heavy Industries.
    1967a. *Mitsubishi Nihon jyukogyo kabushiki gaisha shi* (A history of Mitsubishi Japan Heavy Industries). Tokyo: Mitsubishi Heavy Industries.
    1967b. *Shin Mitsubishi jyukogyo kabushiki gaisha shi* (A history of New Mitsubishi Heavy Industries). Tokyo: Mitsubishi Heavy Industries.
Miyazawa, Ken'ichi.
    1961. *Shihon shuchu to niju kozo* (Capital concentration and dual structure). Quoted in Shinohara, 1968:53; originally in Nakamura, ed., 1961:17.
Monden, Yasuhiro.
    1983. *Toyota Production System: Practical Approach to Production Management*. Atlanta: Industrial Engineering and Management Press.
    1985. *Toyota shisutemu* (Toyota system). Tokyo: Kodansha.
Nakamura, Hideichiro, et al.
    1981. *Gendai chusho kigyo shi* (A contemporary history of small and medium enterprises). Tokyo: Nihon Keizai Shinbunsha.
Nakamura, Ichiro, ed.
    1961. *Shihon chikuseki to kin'yu kozo* (Capital accumulation and financing structure). Tokyo: Toyo Keizai.
Nakamura, S.
    1983. *Gendai jidosha kogyo ron: Gendai shihon shugi bunseki no hitokoma* (On the modern automotive industry: A passage in the analysis of modern capitalism). Tokyo: Yuhikaku.
Nakamura, Takafusa.
    1967. "Niju kozo no mebae" (The budding of dualism). In Arisawa, ed., 1967.
    1981. *The Postwar Japanese Economy: Its Development and Structure*. Tokyo: University of Tokyo Press.
    1983. *Economic Growth in Prewar Japan*. New Haven, CT: Yale University Press.
Nakamura, Tsutomu.
    1983. *Chushokigyo to daikigyo: Nihon no sangyo hatten to jun suichokuteki togo* (Small- and medium-sized firms and large firms: Japan's industrial development and quasi-vertical integration). Tokyo: Toyo Keizai Shinposha.
Nariai, Osamu.
    1977. "The Modernization of the Japanese Economy." In Foreign Press Center, Japan, 1977.
New York Times, The.
    1987. March 10.
Nihon Keizai Shinbun (Japan Economic Journal).
    1967. May 1 & June 21. Quoted in Ichikawa, 1968:140–41.
    1988. September 13.

Nikkan Kogyo Shinbun (Daily Industrial Journal).
 1940. May 12. Quoted in Fujita, Keizo, 1965:60–61.
 1965. December 7.
 1967. February 6.
 1968. January 8 & 10, March 27, April 18, July 8 & 31, August 2, October 10, & November 2.
 1969. March 17, April 2, & November 5.
 1970. May 3.
 1971. July 15.
 1972. July 26.
Nippondenso.
 1984. *Nippondenso 35 nen shi* (A thirty-five-year history of Nippondenso). Aichi: Nippondenso.
Nippon Sangyo Keizai (Japanese Industrial Economy).
 1943. July 8 & September 23. Quoted in Fujita, Keizo, 1965:186–87.
Nishida, Jiro.
 1975. "Fuka chusho kogyo no setsubi kindaika no eikyo—Sono 4, puresu kako kinzoku seizo gyo" (Influence of facilities modernization at small and medium enterprises in the [Osaka] prefecture, no. 4—The press process metal products industry). In Osaka Prefectural Research Institute of Commerce, Industry and Economy, 1975:4. Quoted in Suitsu, 1979:102–3.
Nishiguchi, Toshihiro.
 1987a. "Competing Systems of Automotive Components Supply: An Examination of the Japanese 'Clustered Control' Model and the 'Alps' Structure." Policy Forum Paper, International Motor Vehicle Program, MIT, May.
 1987b. "New Trends in American Auto Components Supply: Is Good Management Always Culturally Bound?" Research Affiliates' Meeting Paper, International Motor Vehicle Program, MIT, September.
 1988a. "Sangyo kokka Amerika no fukken o uranau: Biggu 3 wa jidosha shijo o dakkan dekiruka" (Foretelling the recovery of industrial America: Will the Big 3 retrieve the auto market?). *Economics Today,* Spring, pp. 110–19.
 1988b. "Problems with U.S. Automotive Components Supply." *InSite* 1 (April):10–20.
 1988c. "Reforming Automotive Purchasing Organization in North America: Lessons for Europe?" Policy Forum Paper, International Motor Vehicle Program, MIT, May.
 1988d. "Hokubei shijo ni okeru jidosha buhin kobai soshiki no henkaku" (Changing automotive purchasing organization in North America). *Jidosha kogyo* (The automotive industry) 22 (July):12–18.
 1989a. "Saishin Amerika U-car jijo" (The new market situation of used cars in America). *Car Sensor,* March 3, pp. 64–67.
 1989b. "Good Management Is Good Management: The Japanization of the U.S. Auto Industry." *The JAMA Forum* 7 (April):3–7.
 1989c. "Is JIT Really JIT?" Policy Forum Paper, International Motor Vehicle Program, MIT, May.
 1991. "Beyond the Honeymoon Effect." *INSEAD Information,* Summer, pp. 8–9.
Nissan Motor Company.
 1965. *Nissan jidosha 30 nen shi* (A thirty-year history of Nissan Motor). Yokohama: Nissan Motor Company.

1975.   *Nissan jidosha shashi: 1964–1973* (A history of Nissan Motor). Tokyo: Nissan
        Motor Company.

1983.   *21 seiki e no michi: Nissan jidosha 50 nen shi* (The road toward the 21st
        century: A fifty-year history of Nissan Motor). Tokyo: Nissan Motor Com-
        pany.

Ohkawa, Kazushi.

1956.   *Nihon keizai no seichoritsu* (Growth rates of the Japanese economy). Tokyo:
        Iwanami Shoten.

Ohno, Taiichi.

1978.   *Toyota seisan hoshiki—Datsu kibo no keiei o mezashite* (Toyota production
        system: Toward post–mass-scale management). Tokyo: Daiyamondosha.

1988.   *Toyota Production System: Beyond Large-Scale Production.* Cambridge, MA:
        Productivity Press.

Ohta, Yoichi.

1985.   "Intercompany Relationship in Japanese Industries." M. Litt. thesis, University
        of Oxford.

Okamoto, Yasuo.

1979a. *Hitachi to Matsushita* (Hitachi and Matsushita). Vol. 1. Tokyo: Chuo Koronsha.

1979b. *Hitachi to Matsushita* (Hitachi and Matsushita). Vol. 2. Tokyo: Chuo Koronsha.

Ono, Akira.

1973.   *Sengo Nihon no chingin kettei* (Wage determination in postwar Japan). Tokyo:
        Toyo Keizai Shinposha.

Orchard, John E.

1930.   *Japan's Economic Position.* New York: Whittlesey House.

Osaka Municipal University, Economic Research Institute (Osaka daigaku keizai kenkyusho).

1979.   *Chusho kigyo kenkyu: Choryu to tenbo* (Small-business studies: Schools and
        perspectives). Tokyo: Nichi Gai Associates.

Osaka Prefectural Research Institute of Commerce, Industry and Economy.

1961a. *Shiryo* (Materials). No. 248. Quoted in Suitsu, 1979:71, 73–74.

1961b. *Shiryo* (Materials). No. 258. Quoted in Suitsu, 1979:70, 77.

1975.   *Shiryo* (Materials). No. 604. Quoted in Suitsu, 1979:102–3.

Ohshima, Taku.

1980.   "Tei seicho no teichaku to jidosha meika no nai-gaisei seisaku no henbo"
        (Stabilization of low growth and change of automakers' make-or-buy strategy).
        In Sato, Yoshio, ed., 1980:205–39.

Oshiro, Taromaru.

1970.   *Nihon chusho kogyo shi ron* (On the history of small and medium industries).
        Tokyo: Nihon hyoronsha.

Osterman, Paul, ed.

1984.   *Internal Labor Markets.* Cambridge, MA: MIT Press.

People's Finance Corporation (Kokumin kin'yu koko).

1988.   *Chosa geppo* (Monthly survey bulletin), May.

Piore, Michael J.

1975.   "Notes for a Theory of Labor Market Stratification." In Edwards, R. C., Reich,
        M., & Gordon, D. M., eds., 1975:125–50.

Piore, Michael J., & Sabel, Charles F.

1984.   *The Second Industrial Divide: Possibilities for Prosperity.* New York: Basic
        Books.

Research Institute of Labor and Public Administration (Romu gyosei kenkyusho).
  1985. *Saishin nenkan chingin shoyo no jittai* (Actual conditions of new annual wages and bonuses). Tokyo: Romu Gyosei Kenkyusho.
Sabel, Charles F.
  1989. "Technology and the Determinacy of Indeterminacy." Mimeo, Political Science Department, MIT.
Sako, Mari.
  1988. "Neither Markets nor Hierarchies: A Comparative Study of Informal Networks in the Printed Circuit Board Industry." Paper presented at the first conference of the project "Comparing Capitalist Economies: Variations in the Governance of Sectors," Wingspread, WI, May.
Sato, Yoshinobu.
  1988. *Toyota gurupu no senryaku to jissho bunseki* (Strategy and empirical analysis of the Toyota group). Tokyo: Hakuto Shobo.
Sato, Yoshio, ed.
  1980. *Tei seichoki ni okeru gaichu shitauke kanri* (Subcontracting control in the slow-growth period). Tokyo: Chuo Keizaisha.
Sei, Shoichiro.
  1984. "Genchi seisan kigyo no jittai o miru" (Observation of the actual conditions of overseas manufacturing firms). *Kojo kanri* (Factory management) 30(7):17–57.
Shinohara, Miyohei.
  1961. *Nihon keizai no seicho to junkan* (Growth and cycles in the Japanese economy). Tokyo: Sobunsha.
  1968. "A Survey of the Japanese Literature on Small Industry." In Hoselitz, ed., 1968: 1–113.
Shirai, Taishiro.
  1983. "A Theory of Enterprise Unionism." In Shirai, ed., 1983:117–43.
  1988. *Gendai Nihon no romu kanri* (Labor management in contemporary Japan). Tokyo: Toyo Keizai Shinposha.
Shirai, Taishiro, ed.
  1983. *Contemporary Industrial Relations in Japan*. Madison, WI: University of Wisconsin Press.
Shoya, K.
  1979. "Niju kozo" (Dual structure). In Osaka Municipal University, Economic Research Institute, 1979.
Simon, Herbert A.
  1957. *Models of Man*. New York: Wiley.
Small and Medium Enterprise Agency (SMEA) (Chusho kigyo cho).
  1950. *Chusho kigyo no ichi to mondai ten* (Status and problems of small and medium enterprises). Tokyo: Nihon Keizai Shinbunsha.
  1959. *Chusho kigyo taisaku no genjo to mondaiten* (Present conditions and problems of small and medium enterprise policy). Tokyo: SMEA,Publishing Bureau.
  1963, 1966, 1975–76, 1979, 1983–84, 1985a. *Chusho kigyo hakusho* (Small and medium enterprise white paper). Tokyo: Ministry of Finance, Printing Bureau.
  1967. *Keiretsu shitauke kigyo chosa* (Survey of *keiretsu* subcontracting enterprises). Quoted in Kiyonari, 1970:171.
  1968. *Shitauke kigyo kozo chosa* (Survey of subcontracting enterprise structure). Quoted in Kiyonari, 1970:170; Central Bank for Commercial and Industrial Cooperatives, Survey Department, 1971:19; and Ikeda, 1975:81.

1975. *Kumiai no kyodoka, shisutemuka ni kansuru jittai chosa* (Survey of actual conditions concerning collaboration and systematization of cooperatives). Quoted in SMEA, 1976:303.

1982. *Chusho kigyo yoran* (An outline of small and medium enterprises). Tokyo: Ministry of Finance, Printing Bureau.

1983. *Outline of Small- and Medium-Scale Enterprise Policies of the Japanese Government.* Tokyo: SMEA, Ministry of International Trade and Industry.

1985b. *Small Business in Japan.* Tokyo: SMEA, Ministry of International Trade and Industry.

1986. *Seizo gyo bungyo kozo chosa* (Survey of the structural division of labor in manufacturing industries). Tokyo: SMEA, Ministry of International Trade and Industry.

Smitka, Michael J.
1989. "Competitive Ties: Subcontracting in the Japanese Automotive Industry" (compact version). Ph.D. dissertation, Yale University.

1991. *Competitive Ties: Subcontracting in the Japanese Automotive Industry.* New York: Columbia University Press.

Society for Promotion of the Machinery Industry, Economic Research Institute (Kikai shinko kyokai keizai kenkyusho).
1980. *Jidosha sangyo ni okeru kokusai bungyo no shinten to shitauke kozo* (Development of the international division of labor and subcontracting enterprises in the automotive industry). Tokyo: Kikai Shinko Kyokai.

1986. *Shitauke bungyo seisan shisutemu ni kansuru chosa kenkyu* (Survey and research on divisional production systems in subcontracting). Tokyo: Kikai Shinko Kyokai.

Suitsu, Yuzo.
1979. *Nihon chusho reisai kigyo ron* (On Japanese very small, small, and medium enterprises). Tokyo: Moriyama Shoten.

Sumiya, Mikio.
1966. *Nihon rodo undo shi* (A history of Japanese labor movements). Tokyo: Yushindo.

Tidd, Joseph.
1989. "Next Steps in Assembly Automation." Policy Forum Paper, International Motor Vehicle Program, MIT, May.

Tokyo City.
1937. *Tokyo shi shokojo chosasho* (An investigation of small factories in Tokyo City). Quoted in Fujita, Keizo, 1965:40.

Tokyo Metropolitan Government, Economic Bureau.
1958. *Jigyo kyodo kumiai jittai chosa shukei hokokusho* (Report of the data collection of common facility cooperatives). Quoted in Kato, 1960:280.

1974. *Shitauke kigyo keiretsu chosa hokokusho* (Report of subcontracting enterprise *keiretsu*). Tokyo: Tokyo Metropolitan Government.

Toshiba.
1963. *Tokyo Shibaura Denki kabushiki gaisha 85 nen shi* (A 85-year history of the Tokyo Shibaura Electric Company). Tokyo: Tokyo Shibaura Electric.

1977. *Toshiba 100 nen shi* (A 100-year history of Toshiba). Tokyo: Tokyo Shibaura Electric.

Totten, George O.
1967. "Collective Bargaining and Works Councils as Innovations in Industrial Relations in Japan." In Dore, ed., 1967:203–43.

Toyo Keizai Shinposha.
    1986a. *Kaisha shikiho* (Quarterly reports of firms). Vol. 1. Tokyo: Toyo Keizai Shin-
        posha.
    1986b. *Kaisha shikiho mijojogaisha-ban* (Quarterly reports of unquoted firms). Vol. 1.
        Tokyo: Toyo Keizai Shinposha.
Toyo Kogyo.
    1972. *Toyo Kogyo 50 nen shi* (A 50-year history of Toyo Kogyo). Hiroshima: Toyo
        Kogyo.
Toyota Motor Corporation.
    1958. *Toyota jidosha 20 nen shi* (A 20-year history of Toyota Motor). Quoted in
        Yamashita, 1980:148.
    1967. *Toyota jidosha 30 nen shi* (A 30-year history of Toyota Motor). Aichi: Toyota
        Motor Corporation.
    1978. *Toyota no ayumi* (The path of Toyota). Aichi: Toyota Motor Corporation.
    1987. *Sozo kagiri naku: Toyota jidosha 50 nen shi* (Unlimited creation: A 50-year
        history of Toyota Motor). Aichi: Toyota Motor Corporation.
Tsuru, Goro.
    1943. "Taryo seisan to kogu kanri" (Volume production and tooling management). In
        Heiki Koku Kogyo Shinbun Shuppanbu, 1943:183–209.
U.S. Congress, Joint Economic Committee, 91st Cong., 1st sess.
    1969. *The Analysis and Evaluation of Public Expenditure: The PPB System.* Vol. 1.
        Washington DC: U.S. Government Printing Office.
U.S. Department of Labor, Bureau of Labor Statistics.
    1989. "International Comparisons of Hourly Compensation Costs for Production
        Workers in Manufacturing, 1988." Report 766, March.
Walker, James P.
    1988. *A Disciplined Approach to Continuous Improvement.* Warren, OH: Packard
        Electric.
Wall Street Journal, The.
    1986. July 1.
Ward's Automotive Yearbook.
    1989.
White, Michael, & Trevor, Malcolm.
    1983. *Under Japanese Management: The Experience of British Workers.* London:
        Heinemann.
Wilkinson, Frank, ed.
    1981. *The Dynamics of Labour Market Segmentation.* London: Academic Press.
Williamson, Oliver E.
    1975. *Markets and Hierarchies: Analysis and Antitrust Implications.* New York: Free
        Press.
    1985. *The Economic Institutions of Capitalism.* New York: Free Press.
Womack, James P., Jones, Daniel T., & Roos, Daniel.
    1990. *The Machine That Changed the World.* New York: Rawson Associates.
Yamada, Fumio.
    1943. *Chusho kogyo keizai ron* (On the economy of small- and medium-sized man-
        ufacturing industries). Tokyo: Yuhikaku.
Yamanaka, Tokutaro, ed.
    1950. *Chusho kogyo to keizai hendo* (Small and medium industries and economic
        change). Tokyo: Kunimoto Shobo.

Yamashita, T.
  1980.   "Toyota jidosha kogyo ni okeru koyo kanri no tenkai" (Development of em-
          ployment management at Toyota Motor Corporation). In Japan University of
          Social Welfare, 1980: 146–69.
Yawata Steel.
  1924–29. *Seitetsujo kojo rodo tokei* (Steel mill labor statistics). Quoted in Hyodo,
          1971:431.
Zysman, John, & Tyson, Laura, eds.
  1983.   *American Industry in International Competition: Government Politics and Cor-
          porate Strategies.* Ithaca, NY: Cornell University Press.

Index